What Readers Said About *Agile Web Development with Rails 7*

The best book to get started in the Rails world. A comprehensive, coherent, and concise overview of the Ruby on Rails framework. It treats learning in a gradual way, creating an application from scratch using the latest technologies.

➤ **Luis Miguel Cabezas Granado**
    Ruby on Rails and PHP Developer at Hunta de Extremadura (Spain) and PHP Book Writer at Anaya Multimedia

I liked how the book guided me through each step of the tasks. This book gives a thorough introduction to Rails, and I'd suggest it to anyone who wants to start development with Rails.

➤ **Gábor László Hajba**
    Software Developer, EBCONT Enterprise Technologies

The book was really pleasant to read; I liked how it creates a foundational understanding of Rails with a realistic scenario and then builds upon it for the more advanced topics.

➤ **Alessandro Bahgat**
    Software Engineer, Google

Agile Web Development with Rails 8

Sam Ruby

The Pragmatic Bookshelf

Dallas, Texas

See our complete catalog of hands-on, practical,
and Pragmatic content for software developers:
https://pragprog.com

Sales, volume licensing, and support:
support@pragprog.com

Derivative works, AI training and testing,
international translations, and other rights:
rights@pragprog.com

The team that produced this book includes:

Publisher: Dave Thomas
COO: Janet Furlow
Executive Editor: Susannah Davidson
Series Editor: Noel Rappin
Development Editor: Adaobi Obi Tulton
Copy Editor: Corina Lebegioara
Indexing: Potomac Indexing, LLC
Layout: Gilson Graphics

Copyright © 2025 The Pragmatic Programmers, LLC.

All rights reserved. No part of this publication may be reproduced by any means, nor may any derivative works be made from this publication, nor may this content be used to train or test an artificial intelligence system, without the prior consent of the publisher.

When we are aware that a term used in this book is claimed as a trademark, the designation is printed with an initial capital letter or in all capitals.

The Pragmatic Starter Kit, The Pragmatic Programmer, Pragmatic Programming, Pragmatic Bookshelf, PragProg, and the linking *g* device are trademarks of The Pragmatic Programmers, LLC.

Every precaution was taken in the preparation of this book. However, the publisher assumes no responsibility for errors or omissions or for damages that may result from the use of information (including program listings) contained herein.

ISBN-13: 979-8-88865-134-6
Book version: P1.0—June 2025

Contents

Foreword to the Rails 8 Edition xi

Preface to the Rails 8 Edition xiii

Acknowledgments xv

Introduction xvii

Part I — Getting Started

1. **Installing Rails** 3
   Installing on Windows   4
   Installing on macOS   7
   Installing on Linux   9
   Choosing a Rails Version   11
   Setting Up Your Development Environment   12
   Rails and Databases   15

2. **Instant Gratification** 17
   Creating a New Application   17
   Hello, Rails!   20
   Linking Pages Together   26
   When Things Go Wrong   28

3. **The Architecture of Rails Applications** 33
   Models, Views, and Controllers   33
   Rails Model Support   36
   Action Pack: The View and Controller   39

4. **Introduction to Ruby** 41
   Ruby Is an Object-Oriented Language   41
   Data Types   43
   Logic   47
   Organizing Structures   50
   Marshaling Objects   53
   Pulling It All Together   53
   Ruby Idioms   54

Part II — Building an Application

5. **The Depot Application** 59
   Incremental Development   59
   What Depot Does   60
   Let's Code   64

6. **Task A: Creating the Application** 65
   Iteration A1: Creating the Product Maintenance Application   65
   Iteration A2: Making Prettier Listings   74
   Iteration A3: Making the Page Update in Real Time   78

7. **Task B: Validation and Unit Testing** 85
   Iteration B1: Validating!   85
   Iteration B2: Unit Testing of Models   89

8. **Task C: Catalog Display** 101
   Iteration C1: Creating the Catalog Listing   101
   Iteration C2: Adding a Page Layout   105
   Iteration C3: Using a Helper to Format the Price   107
   Iteration C4: Functional Testing of Controllers   108
   Iteration C5: Caching of Partial Results   110

9.	**Task D: Cart Creation**	**115**
	Iteration D1: Finding a Cart	115
	Iteration D2: Connecting Products to Carts	116
	Iteration D3: Adding a Button	119
10.	**Task E: A Smarter Cart**	**127**
	Iteration E1: Creating a Smarter Cart	127
	Iteration E2: Handling Errors	132
	Iteration E3: Finishing the Cart	136
11.	**Task F: Hotwiring the Storefront**	**143**
	Iteration F1: Moving the Cart	144
	Iteration F2: Creating a Hotwired Cart	150
	Iteration F3: Highlighting Changes	155
	Iteration F4: Broadcasting Updates with Action Cable	158
12.	**Task G: Check Out!**	**165**
	Iteration G1: Capturing an Order	165
	Iteration G2: Adding Fields Dynamically to a Form	178
	Iteration G3: Testing Our JavaScript Functionality	184
13.	**Task H: Sending Emails and Processing Payments Efficiently**	**189**
	Iteration H1: Sending Confirmation Emails	189
	Iteration H2: Connecting to a Slow Payment Processor with Active Job	196
14.	**Task I: Logging In**	**207**
	Iteration I1: Authenticating Users	207
	Iteration I2: Administration pages	215
	Iteration I3: Permitting Access	217
	Iteration I4: Adding a Sidebar, More Administration	218
15.	**Task J: Internationalization**	**225**
	Iteration J1: Selecting the Locale	226
	Iteration J2: Translating the Storefront	230

		Iteration J3: Translating Checkout	237
		Iteration J4: Adding a Locale Switcher	244
16.		**Task K: Receive Emails and Respond with Rich Text**	247
		Iteration K1: Receiving Support Emails with Action Mailbox	247
		Iteration K2: Storing Support Requests from Our Mailbox	253
		Iteration K3: Responding with Rich Text	259
17.		**Task L: Deployment and Production**	269
		Iteration L1: Deploying Locally	269
		Iteration L2: Deployment to the Cloud	278
		Iteration L3: Moving to Production	288
18.		**Depot Retrospective**	295
		Rails Concepts	295
		Documenting What We've Done	298

Part III — Rails in Depth

19.	**Finding Your Way Around Rails**	303
	Where Things Go	303
	Naming Conventions	311
20.	**Active Record**	315
	Defining Your Data	315
	Locating and Traversing Records	320
	Creating, Reading, Updating, and Deleting (CRUD)	324
	Participating in the Monitoring Process	339
	Transactions	344
21.	**Action Dispatch and Action Controller**	349
	Dispatching Requests to Controllers	350
	Processing of Requests	360
	Objects and Operations That Span Requests	371

22. Action View **381**
    Using Templates   381
    Generating Forms   383
    Processing Forms   386
    Uploading Files to Rails Applications   387
    Using Helpers   391
    Reducing Maintenance with Layouts and Partials   398

23. Migrations **407**
    Creating and Running Migrations   407
    Anatomy of a Migration   410
    Managing Tables   414
    Advanced Migrations   419
    When Migrations Go Bad   420
    Schema Manipulation Outside Migrations   421

24. Customizing and Extending Rails **423**
    Creating a Reusable Web Component   423
    Testing with RSpec   425
    Creating HTML Templates with Slim   430
    Customizing Rails in Other Ways   433
    Where to Go from Here   433

Bibliography **437**
Index **439**

Foreword to the Rails 8 Edition

I've been working on Rails for over twenty years now, and incredibly, this book has been around for almost as long, helping programmers get quickly up to speed on the framework. That kind of dedication doesn't come around by accident, but from a consistent commitment to teaching programmers how to write beautiful code for the web. That's what Rails is: a love letter to the web written in Ruby. And this book is here to help you become a coauthor.

In the past two decades, a lot has changed about how we build for the web. When Rails was first created, there were no web sockets, the use of JavaScript was modest (or even optional!), and cloud computing had barely gotten started. But as much as those factors have changed, there are also a lot that haven't. If you wrote a Rails application ten or even fifteen years ago, you'll instantly recognize the shape of the new app skeleton that Rails 8 delivers today. You'll be able to draw on experience working with Active Record and Action Controller because, while both have gotten better, they're still based on the same fundamentally sound principles.

That's the long-term magic of Ruby on Rails. The ability to draw a yield from investments made in mastering the basics for years if not decades to come. Making that first deposit towards those investments is what this book is all about. To put a stop to, or at least provide an alternative to, the constant churning and thrashing that has beset the world of web development.

This shows that the one-developer framework isn't just a dream, but a reality. Rails really does compress the complexity of modern web development to a point where it's feasible for an individual to create something amazing by themselves. Because that's how most novel ideas start: with a single individual taking it as far as they can before needing others to help go further. And with Rails, you can take it very far indeed.

Think of all the incredible applications that run the Internet with Rails as their backbone, like Shopify, GitHub, Procore, Cookpad, Intercom, Fleetio, Instacart, Gusto, Zendesk, Coinbase, and many, many more. My own life's work, Basecamp, the original Rails application, is still going strong, as is HEY, my email service. And all of it is built on Rails! That's all the evidence you'd ever need that Rails can take you from HELLO WORLD to IPO, as we say on the homepage.

That's an ambitious mission because Rails is an ambitious framework. We're tackling the entire web problem—not just a database mapper, a URL router, or a templating language—all of it, all at once, and so much more. Rails is the original full-stack framework, and as the web has evolved in the two decades since its release, we continued to keep up with the new problems and solutions that have arisen.

Many alternatives to Rails have come and gone over the years. Many more will. But Ruby on Rails remains. So you've made the right decision buying this book and inviting Sam and Dave to help you learn this incredible framework. I hope you have as much fun as I did discovering Ruby and riding Rails!

David Heinemeier Hansson
Creator of Ruby on Rails
david@hey.com
Copenhagen, Denmark

Preface to the Rails 8 Edition

Rails 7.2 was released in August of 2024. Rails 8.0 rc1 was released in October. As such, there are few changes to the core in this edition. The biggest focus of this release is to make your application easier to deploy without requiring a full staff of DevOps engineers.

Task L: Deployment and Production has been rewritten to reflect this. The introduction to Dockerfiles is still there, but the story continues on to show how to deploy your application to a cloud provider with a single command. And it continues further to show how to back up your data and send your logs to a service where they can be searched.

The biggest non-deployment related change is the introduction of a basic authentication generator.[1] This replaces much of the content of *Task I: Logging In*, with something that does much more with much less code. The code generated by this generator makes use of Active Job and Active Mailer, further demonstrating how these components work together.

Minor changes include text_area being renamed to textarea [2] and Parameters#expect replaces most usages of Parameters#require.[3] and the upgrade to Tailwind CSS 4.0.[4]

I also elected to introduce some concepts earlier. Previous editions started with a basic web application and then added features like Active Job, Active Storage, and Turbo Streams. A perennial theme of Rails is compressing complexity, and given that these features can now be demonstrated with very few lines of code and/or very few commands, it's possible to introduce basic usage of these from the very beginning. This also means that if you're in a hurry to explore Kamal, you can skip right to *Task L: Deployment and Production* immediately after completing *Task A: Creating the Application*.

---

1. https://github.com/rails/rails/issues/50446
2. https://github.com/rails/rails/commit/f9c51ec385a7b75e212954cd4b22c2da7c1d32f4
3. https://github.com/rails/rails/pull/51674/
4. https://tailwindcss.com/docs/upgrade-guide

Acknowledgments

Rails is constantly evolving, and as it has, so has this book. Parts of the Depot application were rewritten several times, and all of the text and code were updated. The avoidance of features as they become deprecated has repeatedly changed the structure of the book, as what was once hot became just lukewarm.

So, this book would not exist without a massive amount of assistance from the Ruby and Rails communities. And of course, none of this would exist without the developers contributing to Ruby on Rails every day. In particular, the Rails core team has been incredibly helpful, answering questions, checking out code fragments, and fixing bugs—even to the point where part of the release process includes verifying that new releases of Rails don't break the examples provided in this book.

Sam Ruby

Introduction

Ruby on Rails is a framework that makes it easier to develop, deploy, and maintain web applications. During the twenty-plus years since its initial release, Rails went from being an unknown toy to a worldwide phenomenon. More importantly, it has become the framework of choice for the implementation of a wide range of applications.

Why is that?

Rails Simply Feels Right

A large number of developers were frustrated with the technologies they were using to create web applications. It didn't seem to matter whether they used Java, PHP, or .NET—there was a growing sense that their jobs were just too damn hard. And then, suddenly, along came Rails, and Rails was easier.

But easy on its own doesn't cut it. We're talking about professional developers writing real-world websites. They wanted to feel that the applications they were developing would stand the test of time—that they were designed and implemented using modern, professional techniques. So, these developers dug into Rails and discovered it wasn't just a tool for hacking out sites.

For example, *all* Rails applications are implemented using the model-view-controller (MVC) architecture. MVC isn't a new concept for web development—the earliest Java-based web frameworks (like Struts) base their design on it. But Rails takes MVC further: when you develop in Rails, you start with a working application, each piece of code has its place, and all the pieces of your application interact in a standard way.

Professional programmers write tests. And again, Rails delivers. All Rails applications have testing support baked right in. As you add functionality to the code, Rails automatically creates test stubs for that functionality. The framework makes it easy to test applications, and, as a result, Rails applications tend to get tested.

Rails applications are written in Ruby, a modern, object-oriented language. Ruby is concise without being unintelligibly terse. You can express ideas naturally and cleanly in Ruby code. This leads to programs that are easy to write and (just as important) easy to read months later.

Rails takes Ruby to the limit, extending it in novel ways that make our programming lives easier. Using Rails makes our programs shorter and more readable. It also allows us to perform tasks that would normally be done in external configuration files inside the codebase instead. This makes it far easier to see what's happening. The following code defines the model class for a project. Don't worry about the details for now. Instead, think about how much information is being expressed in a few lines of code:

```ruby
class Project < ApplicationRecord
  belongs_to :portfolio
  has_one    :project_manager
  has_many   :milestones
  has_many   :deliverables, through: milestones

  validates :name, :description, presence: true
  validates :non_disclosure_agreement, acceptance: true
  validates :short_name, uniqueness: true
end
```

A major philosophical underpinning of Rails that keeps code short and readable is the DRY principle, which stands for Don't Repeat Yourself (see *The Pragmatic Programmer, 20th Anniversary Edition [TH19]*). Every piece of knowledge in a system should be expressed in one place. Rails uses the power of Ruby to bring that to life. You'll find little duplication in a Rails application; you say what you need to say in one place—a place often suggested by the conventions of the MVC architecture—and then move on. For programmers used to other web frameworks, where a simple change to the database schema could involve a dozen or more code changes, this was a revelation—and it still is.

From that principle, Rails is founded on the Rails Doctrine,[1] which is a set of nine pillars that explain why Rails works the way it does and how you can be most successful in using it. Not every pillar is relevant when just starting out with Rails, but one pillar in particular is most important: convention over configuration.

Convention over configuration means that Rails has sensible defaults for just about every aspect of knitting together your application. Follow the conventions, and you can write a Rails application using less code than a typical

---

1. http://rubyonrails.org/doctrine

JavaScript application uses in JSON configuration. If you need to override the conventions, Rails makes that easy, too.

Developers coming to Rails find something else too. Rails doesn't merely play catch-up with the de facto web standards: it helps define them. And Rails makes it easy for developers to integrate features such as user authentication, modern JavaScript frameworks, RESTful interfaces, and WebSockets into their code because support is built in. (And if you're not familiar with any of these terms, never fear—you'll learn what they mean as you proceed through the book.)

Rails was extracted from a real-world, commercial application. It turns out that the best way to create a framework is to find the central themes in a specific application and then package them in a generic foundation of code. When you're developing your Rails application, you're starting with half of a really good application already in place.

But there's something else to Rails—something that's hard to describe. Somehow, it feels right. Of course, you'll have to take our word for that until you write some Rails applications for yourself (which should be in the next forty-five minutes or so...). That's what this book is all about.

Rails Is Agile

The title of this book is *Agile Web Development with Rails 8*. You may be surprised to discover that we don't have explicit sections on applying agile practices *X*, *Y*, and *Z* to Rails coding. In fact, you won't find mention of many agile practices, such as Scrum or Extreme Programming, at all.

Over the years since Rails was introduced, the term *agile* has gone from being relatively unknown to being overhyped, to being treated as a formal set of practices, to receiving a well-deserved amount of pushback against formal practices that were never meant to be treated as gospel, to a return back to the original principles.

But it's more than that. The reason is both simple and subtle. Agility is part of the fabric of Rails.

Let's look at the values expressed in the Agile Manifesto (Dave Thomas was one of the seventeen authors of this document) as a set of four preferences:[2]

- Individuals and interactions over processes and tools
- Working software over comprehensive documentation

---

2. http://agilemanifesto.org/

- Customer collaboration over contract negotiation
- Responding to change over following a plan

Rails is all about individuals and interactions. It involves no heavy toolsets, no complex configurations, and no elaborate processes, just small groups of developers, their favorite editors, and chunks of Ruby code. This leads to transparency; what the developers do is reflected immediately in what the customer sees. It's an intrinsically interactive process.

The Rails development process isn't driven by documents. You won't find 500-page specifications at the heart of a Rails project. Instead, you'll find a group of users and developers jointly exploring their needs and the possible ways of answering those needs. You'll find solutions that change as both the developers and the users become more experienced with the problems they're trying to solve. You'll find a framework that delivers working software early in the development cycle. This software might be rough around the edges, but it lets the users start to get a glimpse of what you'll be delivering.

In this way, Rails encourages customer collaboration. When customers see how quickly a Rails project can respond to change, they start to trust that the team can deliver what's required, not just what's been requested. Confrontations are replaced by "What if?" sessions.

The agile way of working that Rails encourages is tied to the idea of being able to respond to change. The strong, almost obsessive, way that Rails honors the DRY principle means that changes to Rails applications impact a lot less code than the same changes would in other frameworks. And since Rails applications are written in Ruby, where concepts can be expressed accurately and concisely, changes tend to be localized and easy to write. The deep emphasis on both unit and system testing, along with support for test fixtures and stubs during testing, gives developers the safety net they need when making those changes. With a good set of tests in place, changes are less nerve-racking.

Rather than constantly trying to link Rails processes to agile principles, we've decided to let the framework speak for itself. As you read through the tutorial chapters, try to imagine yourself developing web applications this way, working alongside your customers and jointly determining priorities and solutions to problems. Then, as you read the more advanced concepts that follow in Part III, see how the underlying structure of Rails can enable you to meet your customers' needs faster and with less ceremony.

One last point about agility and Rails—although it's probably unprofessional to mention this—think how much fun the coding will be!

Who This Book Is For

This book is for programmers looking to build and deploy web-based applications. This includes application programmers who are new to Rails (and perhaps even new to Ruby) as well as those who are familiar with the basics but want a more in-depth understanding of Rails.

We presume some familiarity with HTML, Cascading Style Sheets (CSS), and JavaScript—in other words, the ability to view source on web pages. You needn't be an expert on these subjects; the most you'll be expected to do is copy and paste material from the book, all of which can be downloaded.

The focus of this book is on the features and choices made by the Rails core team. More specifically, this book is for *users* of the Rails framework—people who tend to be more concerned about what Rails does, as opposed to how it does it or how to change Rails to suit their needs. Examples of topics not covered in this book include the following:

- Turbo Drive[3] is a way to load pages more quickly by just loading markup. If you want to know more about how Rails makes your pages load faster, follow that link. But should you instead be content with the knowledge that Rails makes pages load fast and not need to know more, that's OK too.

- Propshaft[4] replaces Sprockets[5] as the asset pipeline for Rails. It is responsible for adding hashes to the end of asset URLs. If you're interested in how Rails makes sure that your assets are always up-to-date, you can follow that link. But if you're happy with the knowledge that Rails makes sure your assets are always up-to-date and don't need to know more, that's OK too.

How to Read This Book

The first part of this book makes sure you're ready. By the time you're done with it, you'll have been introduced to Ruby (the language), you'll have been exposed to an overview of Rails, you'll have Ruby and Rails installed, and you'll have verified the installation with a simple example.

The next part takes you through the concepts behind Rails via an extended example: we build a simple online store. It doesn't take you one by one through each component of Rails (such as "here's a chapter on models, here's a chapter on views," and so forth). These components are designed to work

---

3. https://turbo.hotwired.dev/handbook/drive
4. hhttps://github.com/rails/propshaft
5. https://github.com/rails/sprockets

together, and each chapter in this section tackles a specific set of related tasks that involve a number of these components working together.

Most folks seem to enjoy building the application along with the book. If you don't want to do all that typing, you can cheat and download the source code (a compressed tar archive[6] or a zip file).[7]

Be careful if you ever choose to copy files directly from the download into your application: if the timestamps on the files are old, the server won't know that it needs to pick up these changes. You can update the timestamps using the touch command on either MacOS or Linux, or you can edit the file and save it. Alternatively, you can restart your Rails server.

Part III, Rails in Depth, on page 301, surveys the entire Rails ecosystem. This starts with the functions and facilities of Rails that you'll now be familiar with. It then covers a number of key dependencies that the Rails framework makes use of that contribute directly to the overall functionality that the Rails framework delivers. Finally, we survey a number of popular plugins that augment the Rails framework and make Rails an open ecosystem rather than merely a framework.

Along the way, you'll see various conventions we've adopted:

Live code
> Most of the code snippets we show come from full-length, running examples that you can download.
>
> To help you find your way, if a code listing can be found in the download, you'll see a bar before the snippet (like the one here):
>
> rails80/demo1/app/controllers/say_controller.rb
> ```
> class SayController < ApplicationController
>   def hello
>   end
>
>   def goodbye
>   end
> end
> ```
>
> The bar contains the path to the code within the download. If you're reading the ebook version of this book and your ebook viewer supports hyperlinks, you can click the bar and the code should appear in a browser window. Some browsers may mistakenly try to interpret some of

---

6. https://media.pragprog.com/titles/rails8/code/rails8-code.tgz
7. https://media.pragprog.com/titles/rails8/code/rails8-code.zip

the HTML templates as HTML. If this happens, view the source of the page to see the real source code.

And in some cases involving the modification of an existing file where the lines to be changed may not be immediately obvious, you'll also see some helpful little triangles to the left of the lines that you'll need to change. Two such lines are indicated in the previous code.

David says
> Every now and then you'll come across a "David says" sidebar. Here's where David Heinemeier Hansson gives you the real scoop on some particular aspects of Rails—rationales, tricks, recommendations, and more. Because he's the fellow who invented Rails, these are the sections to read if you want to become a Rails pro.

Joe asks
> Joe, the mythical developer, sometimes pops up to ask questions about stuff we talk about in the text. We answer these questions as we go along.

This book isn't meant to be a reference manual for Rails. Our experience is that reference manuals aren't the way most people learn. Instead, we show most of the modules and many of their methods, either by example or narratively in the text, in the context of how these components are used and how they fit together.

Nor do we have hundreds of pages of API listings. There's a good reason for this: you get that documentation whenever you install Rails, and it's guaranteed to be more up-to-date than the material in this book. If you install Rails using RubyGems (which we recommend), start the gem documentation server (using the gem server command), and you can access all the Rails APIs by pointing your browser at http://localhost:8808.

In addition, you'll see that Rails helps you by producing responses that clearly identify any error found as well as traces that tell you not only the point at which the error was found but also how you got there. You'll see an example on page 133. If you need additional information, peek ahead to Iteration E2: Handling Errors, on page 132, to see how to insert logging statements.

If you get really stuck, plenty of online resources can help. In addition to the code listings mentioned, you can find more resources on the Pragmatic Bookshelf site page for this book, including links to the book forum and errata.[8] The resources listed on these pages are shared resources. Feel free to post not only questions and problems to the forum but also any suggestions and answers you may have to questions that others have posted.

Let's get started! The first steps are to install Ruby and Rails and verify the installation with a simple demonstration.

---

8. https://pragprog.com/titles/rails8/agile-web-development-with-rails-8/

Part I

Getting Started

In this chapter, you'll see:
- Installing Ruby, RubyGems, SQLite 3, and Rails
- Development environments and tools

CHAPTER 1

Installing Rails

In Part I of this book, we'll introduce you to both the Ruby language and the Rails framework. But we can't get anywhere until you've installed both and verified that they're operating correctly.

To get Rails running on your system, you'll need the following:

- A Ruby interpreter. Rails is written in Ruby, and you'll be writing your applications in Ruby too. Rails 8.0 will run on Ruby versions 3.2, 3.3, and 3.4. It won't work on prior versions of Ruby.

- Ruby on Rails. This book was written using Rails version 8.0 (specifically, Rails 8.0.2).

- Some libraries (depending on the operating system).

- A database. We're using SQLite 3[1] for development. We'll also describe how to deploy with PostgreSQL,[2] but you won't need to install this on your machine.

- Docker. You'll need it when you reach the deployment stage. It can also be used to isolate your development environment from your actual computer.

For a development machine, that's about all you'll need (apart from an editor, and we'll talk about editors separately).

So, how do you get all this installed? It depends on your choice of development environment. We'll go over three common choices: Windows, macOS, and Ubuntu Linux.

---

1. https://www.sqlite.org/index.html
2. https://www.postgresql.org/

But before you dive in, recognize that, for best results, these instructions are meant for a fairly fresh, up-to-date, and clean machine. If this doesn't match your situation, consider doing your development in a Docker container.[3] If you choose to go this way, you can skip the rest of this chapter and go to Chapter 2, Instant Gratification, on page 17.

Installing on Windows

> **Please Use WSL2**
>
> We recommend using WSL2 for Rails development on Windows. This will give you a Linux environment that's much more compatible with Rails development.
>
> Most Rails applications are developed on MacOS machines and deployed to Linux machines. This puts Windows developers at a disadvantage, as much of the helpful advice you can find online won't be geared toward you. Fortunately, Microsoft provides three tools that will provide you with an absolutely first-class developer environment:
>
> - Windows Subsystem for Linux (WSL)[a]
> - Windows Terminal[b]
> - Visual Studio Code[c]
>
> With WSL2, select the latest Ubuntu version and proceed with the instructions in Installing on Linux, on page 9.
>
> ---
>
> a. https://docs.microsoft.com/en-us/windows/wsl/install
> b. https://www.microsoft.com/en-us/p/windows-terminal/9n0dx20hk701
> c. https://code.visualstudio.com/

The following instructions are for non-WSL2 Windows installations.

First, you need to install Ruby. We recommend using the RubyInstaller for Windows package.[4] At the time of this writing, the latest version of Ruby available via RubyInstaller is Ruby 3.4.3. If you use RubyInstaller, be sure to pick a version that includes Devkit. If you use a different installer, make sure you install MSYS2 along with Ruby.

At this point, Windows Defender may intervene as it doesn't recognize the RubyInstaller package. If this happens, click the downloads folder icon to see a list of downloads. Find the download, and double-click it. You may see a screen that says, "Windows protected your PC." If so, click "More info" and then click "Run anyway."

---

3. https://guides.rubyonrails.org/getting_started_with_devcontainer.html
4. http://rubyinstaller.org/downloads

Once you get past Windows Defender, installation is a snap. Choose the "Install for me only" option and then select "I accept the License" (after reading it carefully, of course) and then click Next. Ensure "Add Ruby executables to your PATH" is selected, and click Install. See the following screenshot.

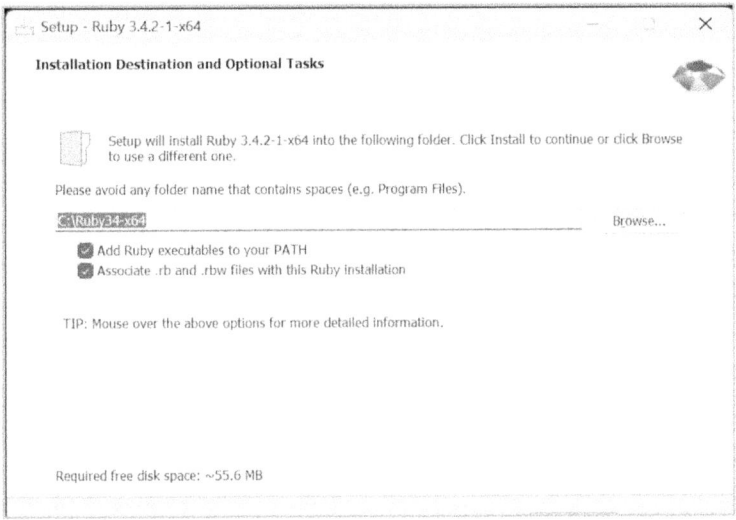

Next, you'll need to select the components to be installed. Ensure that the MSYS2 development toolchain is selected. Click Next. See the following screenshot:

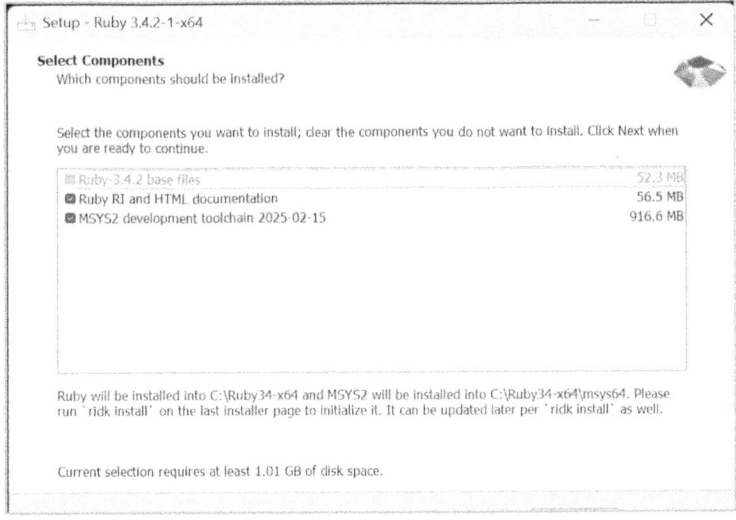

Click Next to begin the installation. When you see the following screen, you'll be done with the first part of the installation. Click Finish to proceed to the next and final part.

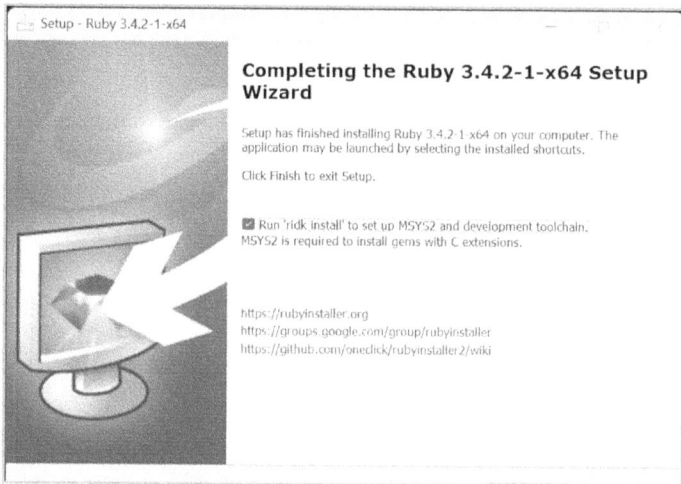

The next screen installs the development toolchains. Press Enter. This will take a while and ultimately prompt you again for which tools to install. The second time you're prompted, again press Enter, and the window will be dismissed.

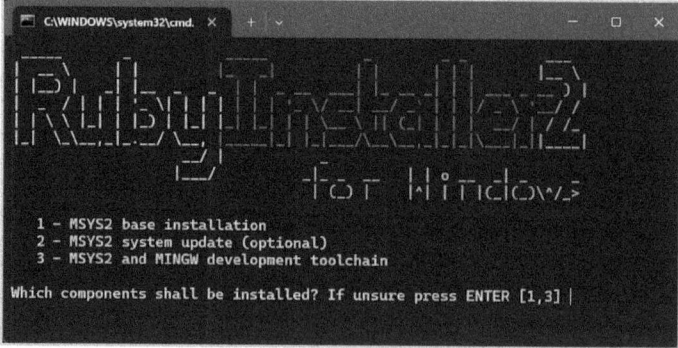

From the Windows start screen, you'll launch your preferred terminal: either the Command Prompt or PowerShell. You can also use the Windows Terminal.

From there, you can verify that Ruby was installed correctly by entering the command ruby -v as follows:

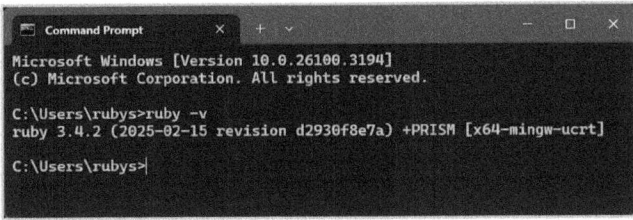

Next, configure Git, adjusting the user.name and user.email as appropriate:

```
> git config --global user.name "John Doe"
> git config --global user.email johndoe@example.com
```

With this in place, proceed to install Rails itself with the following command:

```
> gem install rails -v 8.0.2 --no-document
```

This will take a while. Once it completes, skip to Choosing a Rails Version, on page 11, to ensure that the version of Rails you've installed matches the version described in this edition. See you there.

Installing on macOS

Since macOS Sequoia ships with Ruby 2.6.10, you'll need to download a newer version of Ruby that works with Rails 8. The easiest way to do this is to use Homebrew.[5]

Before you start, go to your Utilities folder and drag the Terminal application onto your dock. You'll be using this during the installation and then frequently as a Rails developer. Open the terminal and run the following command:

```
$ /bin/bash -c "$(curl -fsSL \
    https://raw.githubusercontent.com/Homebrew/install/HEAD/install.sh)"
```

You'll be asked for your password and then to press Enter. Once the installation completes, it will output some next steps for you to take. At the present time, those steps are as follows:

```
$ echo >> ~/.zprofile
$ echo 'eval "$(/opt/homebrew/bin/brew shellenv)"' >> ~/.zprofile
$ eval "$(/opt/homebrew/bin/brew shellenv)"
```

Next, you have a choice. You can let Homebrew install the latest version of Ruby (currently Ruby 3.4.3). Or, you can install mise-en-place,[6] and install the

---

5. https://brew.sh/
6. https://mise.jdx.dev/

Ruby version of your choice, which can be important if you're working with a team that has standardized on a particular version of Ruby, or if you're working on multiple projects that require different versions of Ruby.

If you're not sure, you can start with Homebrew and then switch to mise later if you need to. To install Ruby with Homebrew, run the following command:

```
$ brew install ruby
```

Next, you'll need to follow the post-installation instructions provided, which involve adding lines to your ~/.zshrc file. (If the file doesn't exist, create it using touch ~/.zshrc.)

```
export PATH="/opt/homebrew/lib/ruby/gems/3.4.0/bin:$PATH"
export PATH="/opt/homebrew/opt/ruby/bin:$PATH"
export LDFLAGS="-L/opt/homebrew/opt/ruby/lib"
export CPPFLAGS="-I/opt/homebrew/opt/ruby/include"
```

Alternatively, you can install mise and use it to install Ruby 3.4.3.

```
$ brew install mise
$ echo 'eval "$(mise activate zsh)"' >> ~/.zshrc
$ eval "$(mise activate zsh)"
```

After that, you can install Ruby:

```
$ mise use -g ruby@3.4.3
```

If you're wanting to use different versions of Ruby for different projects, you can use the mise trust[7] command to trust the .ruby-version file in the root of each project.

These are the two most popular routes for Mac developers. rbenv,[8] RVM,[9] asdf,[10] and chruby[11] are four other alternatives.

Whichever path you take, run the following command to see which version of Ruby you're working with:

```
$ ruby -v
```

You should see the following type of result:

```
ruby 3.4.3 (2025-02-15 revision d2930f8e7a) +PRISM [arm64-darwin24]
```

---

7. https://mise.jdx.dev/cli/trust.html
8. https://github.com/rbenv/rbenv#readme
9. https://rvm.io/rvm/install
10. https://asdf-vm.com/
11. https://github.com/postmodern/chruby#readme

Next, run this command to update Rails to the version used by this book:

```
$ gem install rails -v 8.0.2 --no-document
```

OK, you OS X users are done. You can skip forward to join the Windows users in Choosing a Rails Version, on page 11. See you there.

Installing on Linux

Linux has many different distributions, each having its own method of installing software, along with various idiosyncrasies around how it behaves. It would be too difficult to cover them all, so in this section, we'll outline how to get a Rails environment running on Ubuntu Linux. Most of the software we'll install would be needed on any Linux distribution, so if you aren't using Ubuntu, hopefully, this will help you know what you need to set up.

With that disclaimer out of the way, our setup will require a few different steps. First, we'll install some system software that the Ruby and Rails development tools require before finally installing Ruby and Rails.

Installing System Software

The commands that follow assume you're logged in as a user who can execute sudo. Also, note that in this case, you may have some software installed already. If you experience problems, you might want to update that software to the latest versions.

Many Ruby libraries are actually wrappers for C libraries, and when you install them, your system will try to build those libraries or build native connectors. This is the main reason we need certain software installed before we get to Ruby. First, refresh the list of packages available for your operating system:

```
$ sudo apt-get update
```

That will produce a large amount of output. Once that's done, we'll install several different libraries and tools. This is what it will look like on Ubuntu and most Debian-based Linuxes:

```
$ sudo apt-get install -y \
    build-essential \
    git \
    libsqlite3-dev \
    libyaml-dev \
    ruby-bundler \
    ruby-dev \
    tzdata
```

For AlmaLinux and most RedHat-based Linuxes, the following will get you started:

```
$ sudo dnf module -y enable ruby:3.3
$ sudo dnf --enablerepo=crb install -y \
    gcc \
    git \
    libyaml-devel \
    ruby-devel \
    sqlite-devel \
    which
```

As a tip here, to avoid the need for sudo after this point, add the following to your .bashrc:

```
export GEM_HOME=$HOME/.gem
```

Now, we can install Ruby and Rails!

Installing Ruby and Rails

At this point, your system will have Ruby installed, though it may not be the version you need to run Rails. You need Ruby 3.2 or higher. The 3.2.3 version that comes with Ubuntu 24.04 will do just fine.

If you want a different version of Ruby and are concerned about there being unintended consequences to upgrading your system's Ruby, you can use mise-en-place[12] to install Ruby in parallel to your system Ruby. This also allows you to use many different versions of Ruby on the same computer without disrupting the version of Ruby your system may depend on. mise is widely used for exactly this purpose. First, install it like so:

```
$ curl https://mise.run | sh
$ echo 'eval "$(~/.local/bin/mise activate bash)"' >> ~/.bashrc
$ eval "$(~/.local/bin/mise activate bash)"
```

If you're using another shell, consult the mise website for instructions. Next, we'll install Ruby 3.4.3, the latest version of Ruby 3.4 at the time of this writing:

```
$ mise use -g ruby@3.4.3
```

With this done, you can try running ruby -v on the command line. You should see 3.4.3 in the output.

---

12. https://mise.jdx.dev/

Next, we'll install Rails itself. Rails is a RubyGem, and Ruby comes with the command gem that installs RubyGems. We'll use that to install Rails:

`$ gem install rails -v 8.0.2 --no-document`

When that completes, you can verify it worked by running rails --version. You should see 8.0.2 in the output.

This completes the setup of Ruby and Rails. The rest of this chapter will outline other software you might need to do development.

Choosing a Rails Version

The previous instructions helped you install the version of Rails used by the examples in this book. But, occasionally, you might not want to run that version. For example, a newer version with some fixes or new features might become available. Or, perhaps, you're developing on one machine but intending to deploy on another machine that contains a version of Rails that you don't have any control over.

If either of these situations applies to you, you need to be aware of a few things. For starters, you can use the gem command to find all the versions of Rails you have installed:

`$ gem list --local rails`

You can also verify which version of Rails you're running as the default by using the rails --version command. It should return 8.0.2.

If it doesn't, start by inserting the version of Rails surrounded by underscores before the first parameter of any rails command. Here's an example:

`$ rails _8.0.2_ --version`

What this will do is generate a file named Gemfile in the current directory with the following contents:

`gem "rails", "~> 8.0.2"`

That strange syntax is called a *twiddle-wakka*,[13] or (more formally) the pessimistic version operator, and it means that you're asking for the latest version of Rails that's compatible with 8.0.2.

To upgrade, simply update the version number in the Gemfile that's in the root directory of your application and run bundle install. You can also pin to a specific version of Rails by replacing the twiddle-wakka with an equals sign.

---

13. https://guides.rubygems.org/patterns/#semantic-versioning

Setting Up Your Development Environment

The day-to-day business of writing Rails programs is pretty straightforward. Everyone works differently; here's how we work.

The Command Line

We do a lot of work at the command line. Although an increasing number of GUI tools help generate and manage a Rails application, we find the command line is still the most powerful place to be. It's worth spending a little while getting familiar with the command line on your operating system. Find out how to use it to edit commands that you're typing, how to search for and edit previous commands, and how to complete the names of files and commands as you type.

The so-called tab completion is standard on Unix shells such as bash and zsh. It allows you to type the first few characters of a filename, hit Tab, and have the shell look for and complete the name based on matching files.

Version Control

We keep all our work in a version control system (currently Git). We make a point of checking a new Rails project into Git when we create it and committing changes once we've passed the tests. We normally commit to the repository many times an hour.

If you're not familiar with Git, don't worry, because this book will introduce you to the few commands that you'll need to follow along with the application being developed. If you ever need it, extensive documentation is available online.[14]

If you're working on a Rails project with other people, make use of the continuous integration (CI) system that's included with Rails 8. When anyone checks in changes, the CI system will check out a fresh copy of the application and run all the tests. It's a common way to ensure that accidental breakages get immediate attention. You can also set up your CI system so that your customers can use it to play with the bleeding-edge version of your application. This kind of transparency is a great way to ensure that your project isn't going off track.

---

14. https://git-scm.com/book/en/v2

Editors

We write our Rails programs using a programmer's editor. We've found over the years that different editors work best with different languages and environments. For example, Dave originally wrote this chapter using Emacs because he thinks that its Filladapt mode is unsurpassed when it comes to neatly formatting XML as he types. Sam updates the chapter using Vim. But many think that neither Emacs nor Vim is ideal for Rails development. Although the choice of editor is a personal one, here are some suggestions for features to look for in a Rails editor:

- You'll want support for syntax highlighting of Ruby and HTML—ideally, support for .erb files (a Rails file format that embeds Ruby snippets within HTML).

- Support for automatic indentation and reindentation of Ruby source. This is more than an aesthetic feature: having an editor indent your program as you type is the best way to spot bad nesting in your code. Being able to reindent is important when you refactor your code and move stuff.

- Support for insertion of common Ruby and Rails constructs. You'll be writing lots of short methods, and if the IDE creates method skeletons with a keystroke or two, you can concentrate on the interesting stuff inside.

- Good file navigation. As you'll see, Rails applications are spread across many files; for example, a newly created Rails application enters the world containing 77 files spread across 45 directories. That's before you've written a thing.

  You need an environment that helps you navigate quickly among these. You'll add a line to a controller to load a value, switch to the view to add a line to display it, and then switch to the test to verify you did it all right. Something like Notepad, where you traverse a File Open dialog box to select each file to edit, won't cut it. We prefer a combination of a tree view of files in a sidebar, a small set of keystrokes that help us find a file (or files) in a directory tree by name, and some built-in smarts that know how to navigate (say) between a controller action and the corresponding view.

- Name completion. Names in Rails tend to be long. A nice editor will let you type the first few characters and then suggest possible completions to you at the touch of a key.

We hesitate to recommend specific editors because we've used only a few in earnest, and we'll undoubtedly leave someone's favorite editor off the list.

> **Where's My IDE?**
>
> If you're coming to Ruby and Rails from languages such as C# and Java, you may be wondering about IDEs. After all, we all know that it's impossible to code modern applications without at least 100 MB of IDE supporting our every keystroke. For you enlightened ones, here's the point in the book where we recommend you sit down—ideally propped up on each side by a pile of framework references and 1,000-page Made Easy books.
>
> It may surprise you to know that most Rails developers don't use fully-fledged IDEs for Ruby or Rails (although some of the environments come close). Indeed, many Rails developers use plain old editors. And it turns out that this isn't as much of a problem as you might think. With other, less expressive languages, programmers rely on IDEs to do much of the grunt work for them because IDEs do code generation, assist with navigation, and compile incrementally to give early warning of errors.
>
> With Ruby, however, much of this support isn't necessary. Editors such as Zed, Neovim, and RubyMine give you 90 percent of what you'd get from an IDE but are far lighter weight.

Nevertheless, to help you get started with something other than Notepad, here are some suggestions:

- Visual Studio Code is a free editor built on open source that runs everywhere.[15] It's a good choice for Windows, macOS, and Linux. It has a large number of extensions available, including a Ruby extension that provides syntax highlighting, code completion, and debugging support. It's the most popular choice among Rails developers at the time of this writing.

- rails.vim is a Vim/NeoVim plugin for editing Ruby on Rails applications.[16]

- RubyMine is a commercial IDE for Ruby and is available for free to qualified educational and open-source projects.[17] It runs on Windows, macOS, and Linux.

- Zed is a next-generation code editor designed for high-performance collaboration with humans and AI. It is not yet available for Windows, but it is for macOS and Linux.[18]

Ask experienced developers who use your kind of operating system which editor they use. Spend a week or so trying alternatives before settling in.

---

15. https://code.visualstudio.com/
16. https://github.com/tpope/vim-rails
17. http://www.jetbrains.com/ruby/features/index.html
18. https://zed.dev/

The Desktop

We're not going to tell you how to organize your desktop while working with Rails, but we'll describe what we do.

Most of the time, we're writing code, running tests, and poking at an application in a browser. So, our main development desktop has an editor window and a browser window that are permanently open. We also want to keep an eye on the logging that's generated by the application, so we keep a terminal window open. In it, we use tail -f to scroll the contents of the log file as it's updated. We normally run this window with a small font, so it takes up less space. If we see something interesting flash by, we increase the font size to investigate.

Alternatively, you can use less +F to scroll through messages. This has the advantage of being able to exit the follow mode by pressing Ctrl-C, at which point you can do searches by typing / followed by the string you want to search for.

Windows developers should take a look at the Windows Terminal.[19]

We also need access to the Rails API documentation, which we view in a browser. In the Introduction, we talked about using the gem server command to run a local web server containing the Rails documentation. This is convenient, but it unfortunately splits the Rails documentation across a number of separate documentation trees. If you're online, you can see a consolidated view of all the Rails documentation in one place.[20]

Rails and Databases

The examples in this book were written using SQLite 3 (version 3.43.2 or thereabouts). If you want to follow along with our code, it's probably simplest if you use SQLite 3 as well. If you decide to use something else, it won't be a major problem. You may have to make minor adjustments to any explicit SQL in our code, but Rails pretty much eliminates database-specific SQL from applications.

If you want to connect to a database other than SQLite 3, Rails also works with MySQL, trilogy, PostgreSQL, Oracle, SQLServer, JDBC My SQL, JDBC Sqlite3, JDBC PostgreSQL, and just plain JDBC. For all but SQLite 3, you'll need to install a database driver—a library that Rails can use to connect to and use with your database engine. This section contains links to instructions on how to get that done.

---

19. https://www.microsoft.com/en-us/p/windows-terminal/9n0dx20hk701
20. http://api.rubyonrails.org/

The database drivers are all written in C and are primarily distributed in source form. If you don't want to bother building a driver from source, take a careful look at the driver's website. Many times, you'll find that the author also distributes binary versions.

If you can't find a binary version, or if you'd rather build from source anyway, you need a development environment on your machine to build the library. For Windows, you need a copy of Visual C++. For Linux, you need gcc and friends (but these will likely already be installed).

On OS X, you need to install the developer tools, which come with the operating system but aren't installed by default. You also need to install your database driver into the correct version of Ruby. If you installed your own copy of Ruby, bypassing the built-in one, it's important to have this version of Ruby first in your path when building and installing the database driver. You can use the which ruby command to make sure you're *not* running Ruby from /usr/bin.

The following are the available database adapters and the links to their respective home pages:

Firebird	https://rubygems.org/gems/fireruby
JDBC	https://rubygems.org/search?query=jdbc
MySQL	https://rubygems.org/gems/mysql2
Oracle Database	https://rubygems.org/gems/activerecord-oracle_enhanced-adapter
Postgres	https://rubygems.org/gems/pg
SQL Server	https://github.com/rails-sqlserver
SQLite	https://github.com/luislavena/sqlite3-ruby
Trilogy	https://rubygems.org/gems/trilogy

What We Just Did

In this chapter, we installed everything you need to get you up and running:

- We installed (or upgraded) the Ruby language.
- We installed (or upgraded) the Rails framework.
- We selected an editor.
- We installed (or upgraded) the SQLite 3 database.

Now that we have Rails installed, let's use it. It's time to move on to the next chapter, where you'll create your first application.

In this chapter, you'll see:
- Creating a new application
- Starting the server
- Accessing the server from a browser
- Producing dynamic content
- Adding hypertext links
- Passing data from the controller to the view
- Basic error recovery and debugging

CHAPTER 2

Instant Gratification

Let's write a simple application to verify that we have Rails snugly installed on our machines. Along the way, you'll get a peek at the way Rails applications work.

Creating a New Application

When you install the Rails framework, you also get a new command-line tool, rails, that's used to construct each new Rails application you write.

Why do we need a tool to do this? Why can't we just hack away in our favorite editor and create the source for our application from scratch? Well, we could just hack. After all, a Rails application is just Ruby source code. But Rails also does a lot of magic behind the curtain to get our applications to work with a minimum of explicit configuration. To get this magic to work, Rails needs to find all the various components of your application. As you'll see later (in Where Things Go, on page 303), this means we need to create a specific directory structure, slotting the code we write into the appropriate places. The rails command creates this directory structure for us and populates it with some standard Rails code.

To create your first Rails application, pop open a shell window and navigate to a place in your filesystem where you want to create your application's directory structure. In our example, we'll be creating our projects in a directory called work. In that directory, use the rails command to create an application called demo. Be slightly careful here—if you have an existing directory called demo, you'll be asked if you want to overwrite any existing files. (Note that if you want to specify which Rails version to use, as described in Choosing a Rails Version, on page 11, now is the time to do so.)

```
rubys> cd work
work> rails new demo
      create
      create   README.md
      create   Rakefile
      create   .ruby-version
         :        :       :
      remove   config/initializers/cors.rb
      remove   config/initializers/new_framework_defaults_8_0.rb
         run   bundle install --quiet
         run   bundle lock --add-platform=x86_64-linux
         :        :       :
      create   db/cable_schema.rb
       force   config/cable.yml
work>
```

The command has created a directory named demo. Pop down into that directory and list its contents (using ls on a Unix box or using dir on Windows). You should see a bunch of files and subdirectories:

```
work> cd demo
demo> ls -p
Dockerfile       Rakefile      config.ru    public/     tmp/
Gemfile          app/          db/          script/     vendor/
Gemfile.lock     bin/          lib/         storage/
README.md        config/       log/         test/
```

All these directories (and the files they contain) can be intimidating to start with, but you can ignore most of them for now. In this chapter, we'll only use two of them directly: the bin directory, where we'll find the Rails executables, and the app directory, where we'll write our application.

Examine your installation using the following command:

```
demo> bin/rails about
```

Windows Powershell and Command Prompt users need to prefix the command with ruby and use a backslash:

```
demo> ruby bin\rails about
```

If you get a Rails version other than 8.0.2, reread Choosing a Rails Version, on page 11.

This command also detects common installation errors. For example, if it can't find a JavaScript runtime, it provides you with a link to available runtimes.

As you can see from the bin/ prefix, this is running the rails command from the bin directory. This command is a wrapper, or *binstub*, for the Rails executable. This ensures that you're running with the correct version of every dependency.

If that doesn't work, use bundle exec[1] to run rails commands:

demo> `bundle exec rails about`

Once you get bin/rails about working, you have everything you need to start a stand-alone web server that can run our newly created Rails application. So without further ado, let's start our demo application:

demo> `bin/dev`
```
=> Booting Puma
=> Rails 8.0.2 application starting in development
=> Run `bin/rails server --help` for more startup options
Puma starting in single mode...
* Puma version: 6.5.0 ("Sky's Version")
* Ruby version: ruby 3.4.3 (2024-12-25 revision 48d4efcb85) +YJIT +PRISM
*  Min threads: 3
*  Max threads: 3
*  Environment: development
*          PID: 43617
* Listening on http://127.0.0.1:3000
* Listening on http://[::1]:3000
Use Ctrl-C to stop
```

Note, if you're using a virtual machine, you need to run Rails like so:

demo> `bin/rails server -b 0.0.0.0`

As the third line from the bottom of the startup tracing indicates, we started a web server on port 3000. The 127.0.0.1 part of the address means the Puma web server will only accept requests that originate from your machine. We can access the application by pointing a browser at the URL http://localhost:3000. The result is shown in the following screenshot.

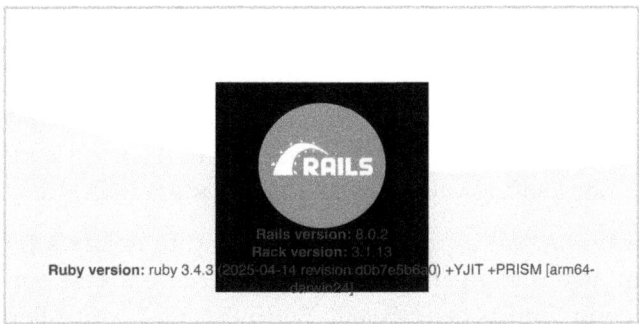

If you look at the window where you started the server, you can see tracing showing that you started the application. We're going to leave the server running in this console window. Later, as we write application code and run

---

1. http://gembundler.com/v1.3/bundle_exec.html

it via our browser, we'll be able to use this console window to trace the incoming requests. When the time comes to shut down your application, you can press Ctrl-C in this window to stop the server. (Don't do that yet—we'll be using this particular application in a minute.)

If you want to enable this server to be accessed by other machines on your network, either you'll need to list each server you want to have access separately or you can enable everybody to access your development server by adding the following to config/environments/development.rb inside the Rails.application.configure do block:

```
config.hosts.clear
```

You'll also need to specify 0.0.0.0 as the host to bind to the following code:

```
demo> bin/rails server -b 0.0.0.0
```

At this point, we have a new application running, but it has none of our code in it. Let's rectify this situation.

Hello, Rails!

We can't help it—we just have to write a Hello, World! program to try a new system. Let's start by creating a simple application that sends our cheery greeting to a browser. After we get that working, we'll embellish it with the current time and links.

As you'll explore further in Chapter 3, The Architecture of Rails Applications, on page 33, Rails is a model-view-controller (MVC) framework. Rails accepts incoming requests from a browser, decodes the request to find a controller, and calls an action method in that controller. The controller then invokes a particular view to display the results to the user. The good news is that Rails takes care of most of the internal plumbing that links all these actions. To write our Hello, World! application, we need code for a controller and a view, and we need a route to connect the two. We don't need code for a model, because we're not dealing with any data. Let's start with the controller.

In the same way that we used the rails command to create a new Rails application, we can also use a generator script to create a new controller for our project. This command is rails generate. So to create a controller called say, we make sure we are in the demo directory and run the command, passing in the name of the controller we want to create and the names of the actions we intend for this controller to support:

```
demo> bin/rails generate controller Say hello goodbye
      create  app/controllers/say_controller.rb
```

```
    route    get 'say/hello'
             get 'say/goodbye'
    invoke   erb
    create     app/views/say
    create     app/views/say/hello.html.erb
    create     app/views/say/goodbye.html.erb
    invoke   test_unit
    create     test/controllers/say_controller_test.rb
    invoke   helper
    create     app/helpers/say_helper.rb
    invoke     test_unit
```

The rails generate command logs the files and directories it examines, noting when it adds new Ruby scripts or directories to our application. For now, we're interested in one of these scripts and (in a minute) the .html.erb files.

The first source file we'll be looking at is the controller. You can find it in the app/controllers/say_controller.rb file.

Let's take a look at it:

rails80/demo1/app/controllers/say_controller.rb
```ruby
class SayController < ApplicationController
  def hello
  end

  def goodbye
  end
end
```

Pretty minimal, eh? SayController is a class that inherits from ApplicationController, so it automatically gets all the default controller behavior. What does this code have to do? For now, it does nothing—we simply have empty action methods named hello() and goodbye(). To understand why these methods are named this way, you need to look at the way Rails handles requests.

Rails and Request URLs

Like any other web application, a Rails application appears to its users to be associated with a URL. When you point your browser at that URL, you're talking to the application code, which generates a response to you.

Let's try it now. Navigate to the URL http://localhost:3000/say/hello in a browser. You'll see something that looks like the following screenshot.

Say#hello

Find me in app/views/say/hello.html.erb

Our First Action

At this point, we can see not only that we've connected the URL to our controller but also that Rails is pointing the way to our next step—namely, to tell Rails what to display. That's where views come in. Remember when we ran the script to create the new controller? That command added several files and a new directory to our application. That directory contains the template files for the controller's views. In our case, we created a controller named say, so the views will be in the app/views/say directory.

By default, Rails looks for templates in a file with the same name as the action it's handling. In our case, that means we need to edit a file called hello.html.erb in the app/views/say directory. (Why .html.erb? We'll explain in a minute.) For now, let's put some basic HTML in there:

```
rails80/demo1/app/views/say/hello.html.erb
<h1>Hello from Rails!</h1>
```

Save the hello.html.erb file, and refresh your browser window. You should see it display our friendly greeting, as in the following screenshot.

Hello from Rails!

In total, we've looked at two files in our Rails application tree. We looked at the controller, and we modified a template to display a page in the browser. These files live in standard locations in the Rails hierarchy: controllers go into app/controllers, and views go into subdirectories of app/views. You can see this structure in the following diagram.

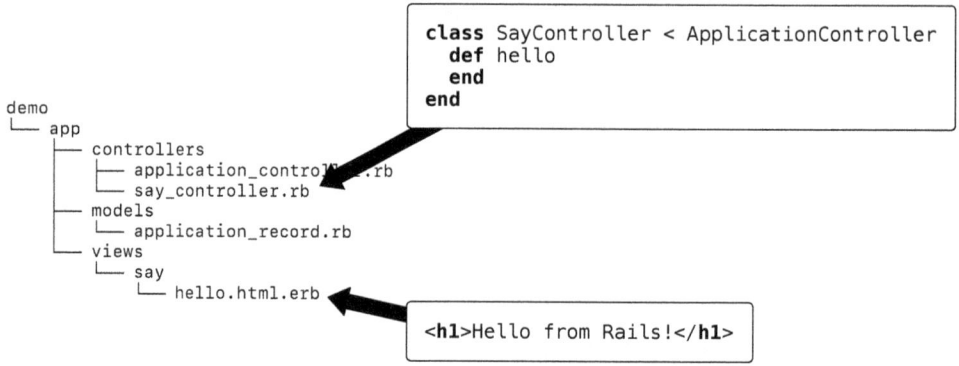

Making It Dynamic

So far, our Rails application is boring—it just displays a static page. To make it more dynamic, let's have it show the current time each time it displays the page.

To do this, we need to change the template file in the view—it now needs to include the time as a string. That raises two questions. First, how do we add dynamic content to a template? Second, where do we get the time from?

Dynamic Content

You can create dynamic templates in Rails in many ways. The most common way, which we'll use here, is to embed Ruby code in the template. That's why the template file is named hello.html.erb; the .html.erb suffix tells Rails to expand the content in the file using a system called ERB.

ERB is a filter, installed as part of the Rails installation, that takes an .erb file and outputs a transformed version. The output file is often HTML in Rails, but it can be anything. Normal content is passed through without being changed. However, content between <%= and %> is interpreted as Ruby code and executed. The result of that execution is converted into a string, and that value is substituted in the file in place of the <%=…%> sequence. For example, change hello.html.erb to display the current time:

rails80/demo2/app/views/say/hello.html.erb
```
<h1>Hello from Rails!</h1>
<p>
   It is now <%= Time.now %>
</p>
```

When we refresh our browser window, we see the time displayed using Ruby's standard format, as shown in the following screenshot.

Hello from Rails!

It is now 2025-04-20 20:32:23 -0400

Notice that the time displayed updates each time the browser window is refreshed. It looks as if we're really generating dynamic content.

> **Making Development Easier**
>
> You might have noticed something about the development we've been doing so far. As we've been adding code to our application, we haven't had to restart the running application. It's been happily chugging away in the background. And yet each change we make is available whenever we access the application through a browser. What gives?
>
> It turns out that the Rails dispatcher is pretty clever. In development mode (as opposed to testing or production), it automatically reloads changed application source files when a new request comes along. That way, when we edit our application, the dispatcher makes sure it's running the most recent changes. Any delays will be small and generally unnoticeable since we're usually dealing with only one user at a time in development.
>
> In testing and production, this feature is disabled because files won't be changing, and by not watching for file system changes, Rails can run a little faster. But in development, it's a real time-saver.

Adding the Time

Our original problem was to display the time to users of our application. We now know how to make our application display dynamic data. The second issue we have to address is working out where to get the time from.

We've shown that the approach of embedding a call to Ruby's Time.now() method in our hello.html.erb template works. Each time they access this page, users will see the current time substituted into the body of the response. And for our trivial application, that might be good enough. In general, though, we probably want to do something slightly different. We'll move the determination of the time to be displayed into the controller and leave the view with the job of displaying it. We'll change our action method in the controller to set the time value into an instance variable called @time:

```ruby
rails80/demo3/app/controllers/say_controller.rb
class SayController < ApplicationController
  def hello
➤   @time = Time.now
  end

  def goodbye
  end
end
```

In the .html.erb template, we'll use this instance variable to substitute the time into the output:

rails80/demo3/app/views/say/hello.html.erb
```
<h1>Hello from Rails!</h1>
<p>
  It is now <%= @time %>
</p>
```

When we refresh our browser window, we again see the current time, showing that the communication between the controller and the view was successful.

Why did we go to the extra trouble of setting the time to be displayed in the controller and then using it in the view? Good question. In this application, it doesn't make much difference, but by putting the logic in the controller instead, we buy ourselves some benefits. For example, we may want to extend our application in the future to support users in many countries. In that case, we'd want to localize the display of the time, choosing a time appropriate to the user's time zone. That would require a fair amount of application-level code, and it would probably not be appropriate to embed it at the view level. By setting the time to display in the controller, we make our application more flexible: we can change the time zone in the controller without having to update any view using that time object. The time is *data*, and it should be supplied to the view by the controller. We'll see a lot more of this when we introduce models into the equation.

The Story So Far

Let's briefly review how our current application works.

1. The user navigates to our application. In our case, we do that using a local URL such as http://localhost:3000/say/hello.

2. Rails then matches the route pattern, which it previously split into two parts and analyzed. The say part is taken to be the name of a controller, so Rails creates a new instance of the Ruby SayController class (which it finds in app/controllers/say_controller.rb).

3. The next part of the pattern, hello, identifies an action. Rails invokes a method of that name in the controller. This action method creates a new Time object holding the current time and tucks it away in the @time instance variable.

4. Rails looks for a template to display the result. It searches the app/views directory for a subdirectory with the same name as the controller (say) and in that subdirectory for a file named after the action (hello.html.erb).

5. Rails processes this file through the ERB templating system, executing any embedded Ruby and substituting in values set up by the controller.

6. The result is returned to the browser, and Rails finishes processing this request.

This isn't the whole story. Rails gives you lots of opportunities to override this basic workflow (and we'll be taking advantage of them shortly). As it stands, our story illustrates convention over configuration, one of the fundamental parts of the philosophy of Rails. Rails applications are typically written using little or no external configuration. That's because Rails provides convenient defaults, and because you apply certain conventions to how a URL is constructed, which file a controller definition is placed in, or which class name and method names are used. Things knit themselves together in a natural way.

Linking Pages Together

It's a rare web application that has just one page. Let's see how we can add another stunning example of web design to our Hello, World! application.

Normally, each page in our application will correspond to a separate view. While we'll also use a new action method to handle the new page, we'll use the same controller for both actions. This needn't be the case, but we have no compelling reason to use a new controller right now.

We already defined a goodbye action for this controller, so all that remains is to update the scaffolding that was generated in the app/views/say directory. This time the file we'll be updating is called goodbye.html.erb because by default templates are named after their associated actions:

```
rails80/demo4/app/views/say/goodbye.html.erb
<h1>Goodbye!</h1>
<p>
  It was nice having you here.
</p>
```

Fire up your trusty browser again, but this time point to our new view using the URL http://localhost:3000/say/goodbye. You should see something like the following screenshot.

Goodbye!

It was nice having you here.

Now we need to link the two screens. We'll put a link on the hello screen that takes us to the goodbye screen, and vice versa. In a real application, we might want to make these proper buttons, but for now we'll use hyperlinks.

We already know that Rails uses a convention to parse the URL into a target controller and an action within that controller. So a simple approach would be to adopt this URL convention for our links.

The hello.html.erb file would contain the following:

```
...
<p>
  Say <a href="/say/goodbye">Goodbye</a>!
</p>
...
```

And the goodbye.html.erb file would point the other way:

```
...
<p>
  Say <a href="/say/hello">Hello</a>!
</p>
...
```

This approach would certainly work, but it's a bit fragile. If we were to move our application to a different place on the web server, the URLs would no longer be valid. It also encodes assumptions about the Rails URL format into our code; it's possible a future version of Rails could change that format.

Fortunately, these aren't risks we have to take. Rails comes with a bunch of *helper methods* that can be used in view templates. Here, we'll use the link_to() helper method, which creates a hyperlink to an action. (The link_to() method can do a lot more than this, but let's take it gently for now.) Using link_to(), hello.html.erb becomes the following:

rails80/demo5/app/views/say/hello.html.erb
```
<h1>Hello from Rails!</h1>
<p>
  It is now <%= @time %>
</p>
➤ <p>
➤   Time to say
➤   <%= link_to "Goodbye", say_goodbye_path %>!
➤ </p>
```

A link_to() call is within an ERB <%=...%> sequence. This creates a link to a URL that will invoke the goodbye() action. The first parameter in the call to link_to() is the text to be displayed in the hyperlink, and the next parameter tells Rails to generate the link to the goodbye() action.

Let's stop for a minute to consider how we generated the link. We wrote this:

```
link_to "Goodbye", say_goodbye_path
```

First, link_to() is a method call. (In Rails, we call methods that make it easier to write templates *helpers*.) If you come from a language such as Java, you might be surprised that Ruby doesn't insist on parentheses around method parameters. You can always add them if you like.

say_goodbye_path is a precomputed value that Rails makes available to application views. It evaluates to the /say/goodbye path. Over time, you'll see that Rails provides the ability to name all the routes that you use in your application.

Let's get back to the application. If we point our browser at our hello page, it now contains the link to the goodbye page, as shown in the following screenshot.

> # Hello from Rails!
>
> It is now 2025-04-20 20:32:26 -0400
>
> Time to say Goodbye!

We can make the corresponding change in goodbye.html.erb, linking it back to the initial hello page:

```
rails80/demo5/app/views/say/goodbye.html.erb
<h1>Goodbye!</h1>
<p>
  It was nice having you here.
</p>
➤ <p>
➤   Say <%= link_to "Hello", say_hello_path %> again.
➤ </p>
```

So far, we've just done things that should work, and—unsurprisingly—they've worked. But the true test of the developer friendliness of a framework is how it responds when things go wrong. As we've not invested much time into this code yet, now is a perfect time to try to break things.

When Things Go Wrong

Let's start by introducing a typo in the source code—one that perhaps is introduced by a misfiring autocorrect function in your favorite editor:

```
rails80/demo5/app/controllers/say_controller.rb
class SayController < ApplicationController
  def hello
    @time = Time.know
  end

  def goodbye
  end
end
```

Refresh the following page in your browser: http://localhost:3000/say/hello. You should see something like the following screenshot.

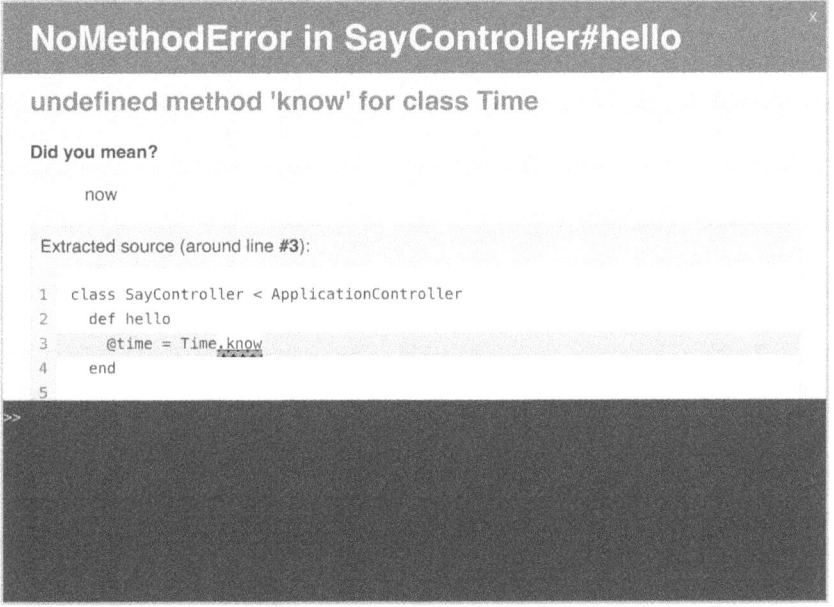

What you see is that Ruby tells you about the error ("undefined method 'know'"), and Rails shows you the extracted source where the code can be found (Rails.root), the stack traceback, and request parameters (at the moment, None). It also provides the ability to toggle the display of session and environment dumps.

You'll even see a suggestion: "Did you mean? now." What a nice touch.

At the bottom of the window you see an area consisting of black text on a white background, looking much like a command-line prompt. This is the Rails *web console*. You can use it to try out suggestions and evaluate expressions. Let's try it out, as shown in the following screenshot.

```
Loading development environment (Rails 8.0.2)
work(dev)> Time.now
=> 2025-04-20 13:53:11.882487 -0400
work(dev)>
```

All in all, helpful stuff.

Note that for security reasons, the web console is configured to only be shown when accessed from the same machine that the web server is running on. If you're running on a different machine, you'll need to adjust the configuration to see this. For example, to enable the web console to be seen by all, add the following to config/environments/development.rb and restart your server:

```
config.web_console.whitelisted_ips = %w( 0.0.0.0/0 ::/0 )
```

At this point, we have only broken the code. Now, let's break the other thing we have used so far: the URL. Visit the following page in your browser: http://localhost:3000/say/hullo. You should see something like the following screenshot.

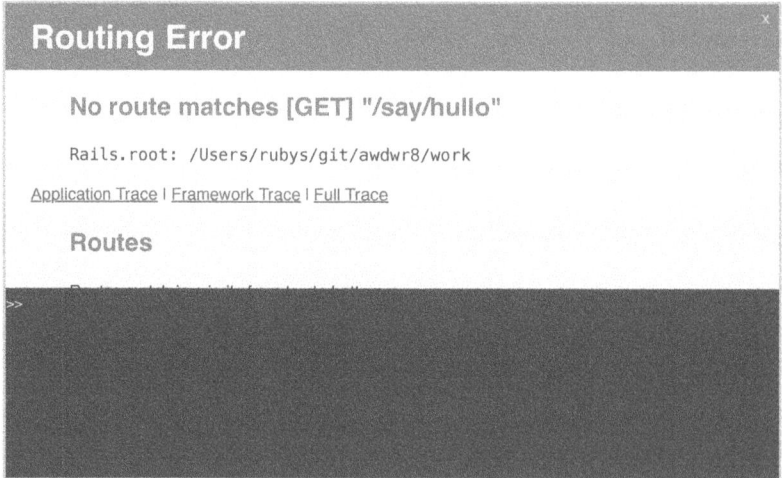

This is similar to what we saw before, but in place of source code we see a list of possible routes, how they can be accessed, and the controller action they're associated with. We'll explain this later in detail, but for now look at the Path Match input field. If you enter a partial URL in there, you can see a list of routes that match. That's not needed right now, as we have only two routes, but can be helpful later when we have many.

At this point, we've completed our toy application and in the process verified that our installation of Rails is functioning properly and provides helpful information when things go wrong. After a brief recap, it's now time to move on to building a real application.

What We Just Did

We constructed a toy application that showed you the following:

- How to create a new Rails application and how to create a new controller in that application
- How to create dynamic content in the controller and display it via the view template

- How to link pages together
- How to debug problems in the code or the URL

This is a great foundation, and it didn't take much time or effort. This experience will continue as we move on to the next chapter and build a much bigger application.

Playtime

Here's some stuff to try on your own:

- Experiment with the following expressions:
  - Addition: `<%= 1+2 %>`
  - Concatenation: `<%= "cow" + "boy" %>`
  - Time in one hour: `<%= 1.hour.from_now.localtime %>`
- A call to the following Ruby method returns a list of all the files in the current directory:

  ```
  @files = Dir.glob('*')
  ```

  Use it to set an instance variable in a controller action, and then write the corresponding template that displays the filenames in a list on the browser.

  Hint—you can iterate over a collection using something like this:

  ```
  <% @files.each do |file| %>
    file name is: <%= file %>
  <% end %>
  ```

  Note that the first and last lines of this loop use `<%` *without* an equal sign. This causes the code embedded in these markers to be executed *without* inserting the results returned into the output.

  You might want to use a `<ul>` for the list.

Cleaning Up

Maybe you've been following along and writing the code in this chapter. If so, chances are that the application is still running on your computer. When we start coding our next application in Chapter 6, Task A: Creating the Application, on page 65, we'll get a conflict the first time we run it because it'll also try to use the computer's port 3000 to talk with the browser. Now is a good time to stop the current application by pressing Ctrl-C in the window you used to start it. Microsoft Windows users may need to press Ctrl-Pause/Break instead.

Now let's move on to an overview of Rails.

In this chapter, you'll see:
- Models
- Views
- Controllers

CHAPTER 3

The Architecture of Rails Applications

One of the interesting features of Rails is it imposes some fairly serious constraints on how you structure your web applications. Surprisingly, these constraints make it easier to create applications—a lot easier. Let's see why.

Models, Views, and Controllers

Back in 1979, Trygve Reenskaug came up with a new architecture for developing interactive applications. In his design, applications were broken into three types of components: models, views, and controllers.

The *model* is responsible for maintaining the state of the application. Sometimes this state is transient, lasting for just a couple of interactions with the user. Sometimes the state is permanent and is stored outside the application, often in a database.

A model is more than data; it enforces all the business rules that apply to that data. For example, if a discount shouldn't be applied to orders of less than $20, the model enforces the constraint. This makes sense; by putting the implementation of these business rules in the model, we make sure that nothing else in the application can make our data invalid. The model acts as both a gatekeeper and a data store.

The *view* is responsible for generating a user interface, normally based on data in the model. For example, an online store has a list of products to be displayed on a catalog screen. This list is accessible via the model, but it's a view that formats the list for the end user. Although the view might present the user with various ways of inputting data, the view itself never handles incoming data. The view's work is done once the data is displayed. There may well be many views that access the same model data, often for different purposes. The online store has a view that displays product information on a catalog page and another set of views used by administrators to add and edit products.

Controllers orchestrate the application. Controllers receive events from the outside world (normally, user input), interact with the model, and display an appropriate view to the user.

This triumvirate—the model, view, and controller—together form an architecture known as MVC. To learn how the three concepts fit together, see the following figure.

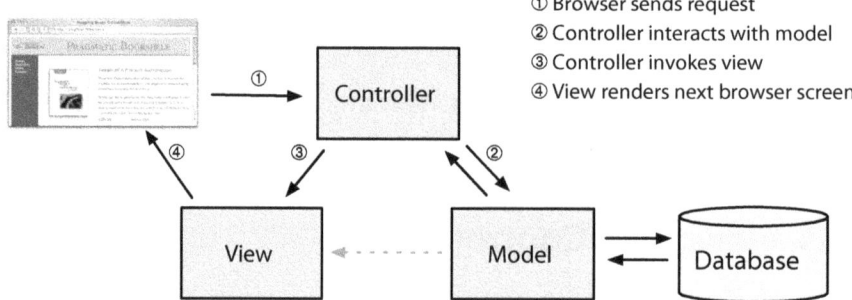

The MVC architecture was originally intended for conventional GUI applications, where developers found that the separation of concerns led to far less coupling, which in turn made the code easier to write and maintain. Each concept or action was expressed in a single, well-known place. Using MVC was like constructing a skyscraper with the girders already in place—it was a lot easier to hang the rest of the pieces with a structure already there. During the development of our application, we'll make heavy use of Rails' ability to generate *scaffolding* for our application.

Ruby on Rails is an MVC framework too. Rails enforces a structure for your application: you develop models, views, and controllers as separate chunks of functionality, and it knits them together as your program executes. One of the joys of Rails is that this knitting process is based on the use of intelligent defaults so that you typically don't need to write any external configuration metadata to make it all work. This is an example of the Rails philosophy of favoring convention over configuration.

In a Rails application, an incoming request is first sent to a router, which works out where in the application the request should be sent and how the request should be parsed. Ultimately, this phase identifies a particular method (called an *action* in Rails parlance) somewhere in the controller code. The action might look at data in the request, it might interact with the model, and it might cause other actions to be invoked. Eventually the action prepares information for the view, which renders something to the user.

Rails handles an incoming request as shown in the following figure. In this example, the application has previously displayed a product catalog page, and the user has just clicked the Add to Cart button next to one of the products. This button posts to http://localhost:3000/line_items?product_id=2, where line_items is a resource in the application and 2 is the internal ID for the selected product.

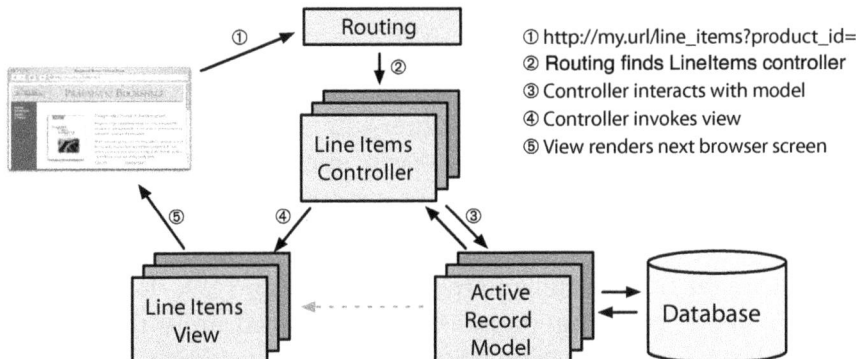

① http://my.url/line_items?product_id=2
② Routing finds LineItems controller
③ Controller interacts with model
④ Controller invokes view
⑤ View renders next browser screen

The routing component receives the incoming request and immediately picks it apart. The request contains a path (/line_items?product_id=2) and a method (this button does a POST operation; other common methods are GET, PUT, PATCH, and DELETE). In this simple case, Rails takes the first part of the path, line_items, as the name of the controller and the product_id as the ID of a product. By convention, POST methods are associated with create() actions. As a result of all this analysis, the router knows it has to invoke the create() method in the LineItems Controller controller class (we'll talk about naming conventions in Naming Conventions, on page 311).

The create() method handles user requests. In this case, it finds the current user's shopping cart (which is an object managed by the model). It also asks the model to find the information for product 2. It then tells the shopping cart to add that product to itself. (See how the model is being used to keep track of all the business data? The controller tells it *what* to do, and the model knows *how* to do it.)

Now that the cart includes the new product, we can show it to the user. The controller invokes the view code, but before it does, it arranges things so that the view has access to the cart object from the model. In Rails, this invocation is often implicit; again, conventions help link a particular view with a given action.

That's all there is to an MVC web application. By following a set of conventions and partitioning your functionality appropriately, you'll discover that your code becomes easier to work with and your application becomes easier to extend and maintain. That seems like a good trade.

If MVC is simply a question of partitioning your code a particular way, you might be wondering why you need a framework such as Ruby on Rails. The answer is straightforward: Rails handles all of the low-level housekeeping for you—all those messy details that take so long to handle by yourself—and lets you concentrate on your application's core functionality. Let's see how.

Rails Model Support

In general, we want our web applications to keep their information in a relational database. Order-entry systems will store orders, line items, and customer details in database tables. Even applications that normally use unstructured text, such as weblogs and news sites, often use databases as their back-end data store.

Although it might not be immediately apparent from the database queries you've seen so far, relational databases are designed around mathematical set theory. This is good from a conceptual point of view, but it makes it difficult to combine relational databases with object-oriented (OO) programming languages. Objects are all about data and operations, and databases are all about sets of values. Operations that are easy to express in relational terms are sometimes difficult to code in an OO system. The reverse is also true.

Over time, folks have worked out ways of reconciling the relational and OO views of their corporate data. Let's look at the way that Rails chooses to map relational data onto objects.

Object-Relational Mapping

Object-relational mapping (ORM) libraries map database tables to classes. If a database has a table called orders, our program will have a class named Order. Rows in this table correspond to objects of the class—a particular order is represented as an object of the Order class. Within that object, attributes are used to get and set the individual columns. Our Order object has methods to get and set the amount, the sales tax, and so on.

In addition, the Rails classes that wrap our database tables provide a set of class-level methods that perform table-level operations. For example, we might need to find the order with a particular ID. This is implemented as a class method that returns the corresponding Order object. In Ruby code, that might look like this:

```
order = Order.find(1)
puts "Customer #{order.customer_id}, amount=$#{order.amount}"
```

Sometimes these class-level methods return collections of objects:

```
Order.where(name: 'dave').each do |order|
  puts order.amount
end
```

Finally, the objects corresponding to individual rows in a table have methods that operate on that row. Probably the most widely used is save(), the operation that saves the row to the database:

```
Order.where(name: 'dave').each do |order|
  order.pay_type = "Purchase order"
  order.save
end
```

So an ORM layer maps tables to classes, rows to objects, and columns to attributes of those objects. Class methods are used to perform table-level operations, and instance methods perform operations on the individual rows.

In a typical ORM library, you supply configuration data to specify the mappings between entities in the database and entities in the program. Programmers using these ORM tools often find themselves creating and maintaining a boatload of XML configuration files.

Active Record

Active Record is the ORM layer supplied with Rails. It closely follows the standard ORM model: tables map to classes, rows to objects, and columns to object attributes. It differs from most other ORM libraries in the way it's configured. By relying on convention and starting with sensible defaults, Active Record minimizes the amount of configuration that developers perform.

To show this, here's a program that uses Active Record to wrap our orders table:

```
require 'active_record'

ActiveRecord::Base.establish_connection({
  adapter: 'sqlite3',
  database: 'storage/development.sqlite3'
})

class Order < ActiveRecord::Base
end

order = Order.find(1)
order.pay_type = "Purchase order"
order.save
```

This code uses the new Order class to fetch the order with an id of 1 and modify the pay_type. Active Record relieves us of the hassles of dealing with the underlying database, leaving us free to work on business logic.

But Active Record does more than that. As you'll see when we develop our shopping cart application, starting in Chapter 5, The Depot Application, on page 59, Active Record integrates seamlessly with the rest of the Rails framework. If a web form sends the application data related to a business object, Active Record can extract it into our model. Active Record supports sophisticated validation of model data, and if the form data fails validations, the Rails views can extract and format errors.

Active Record is the solid model foundation of the Rails MVC architecture.

Active Storage

Active Storage is a library that makes it easy to upload files to cloud storage services like Amazon S3, Google Cloud Storage, and Microsoft Azure Storage. It also provides a disk service for development and testing.

While Active Record is great for storing data in a database, Active Storage is great for storing files. Active Storage is designed to work with Active Record models, so you can associate files with records in your database. For example, you can attach an image to a product record in your database.

```
class Product < ApplicationRecord
  has_one_attached :image
end
```

Once defined this way, you can access images attached to a product class even though the image data is stored in a separate table. Active Storage takes care of the details of storing and retrieving the file:

```
product = Product.first
product.image.attach(io: File.open('/path/to/image.jpg'), filename: 'image.jpg')
puts product.image.filename
puts product.image.byte_size
puts product.image.url
puts product.image.content_type
contents = product.image.download
```

Active Storage also provides methods for resizing images, attaching metadata, and generating URLs for the files. Sample usage:

```
puts product.image.url
puts product.image.content_type
```

As you can see, Active Storage complements Active Record.

Action Pack: The View and Controller

When you think about it, the view and controller parts of MVC are pretty intimate. The controller supplies data to the view, and the controller receives events from the pages generated by the views. Because of these interactions, support for views and controllers in Rails is bundled into a single component, Action Pack.

Don't be fooled into thinking that your application's view code and controller code will be jumbled up because Action Pack is a single component. Quite the contrary—Rails gives you the separation you need to write web applications with clearly demarcated code for control and presentation logic.

View Support

In Rails, the view is responsible for creating all or part of a response to be displayed in a browser, to be processed by an application, or to be sent as an email. At its simplest, a view is a chunk of HTML code that displays some fixed text. More typically, you'll want to include dynamic content created by the action method in the controller.

In Rails, dynamic content is generated by templates, which come in three flavors. The most common templating scheme, called Embedded Ruby (ERB), embeds snippets of Ruby code within a view document, in many ways similar to the way it's done in other web frameworks, such as PHP or JavaServer Pages (JSP). Although this approach is flexible, some are concerned that it violates the spirit of MVC. By embedding code in the view, we risk adding logic that should be in the model or the controller. As with everything, while judicious use in moderation is healthy, overuse can become a problem. Maintaining a clean separation of concerns is part of the developer's job.

You can also use ERB to construct HTML fragments on the server that can then be used by the browser to perform partial page updates. This is great for creating dynamic Hotwire interfaces. We talk about these starting in Iteration F2: Creating a Hotwired Cart, on page 150.

Rails also provides libraries to construct XML or JSON documents using Ruby code. The structure of the generated XML or JSON automatically follows the structure of the code.

And the Controller!

The Rails controller is the logical center of your application. It coordinates the interaction among the user, the views, and the model. However, Rails handles most of this interaction behind the scenes; the code you write concentrates on application-level functionality. This makes Rails controller code remarkably easy to develop and maintain.

The controller is also home to a number of important ancillary services:

- It's responsible for routing external requests to internal actions. It handles people-friendly URLs extremely well.
- It manages caching, which can give applications orders-of-magnitude performance boosts.
- It manages helper modules, which extend the capabilities of the view templates without bulking up their code.
- It manages sessions, giving users the impression of ongoing interaction with our applications.

We've already seen and modified a controller in Hello, Rails!, on page 20, and we'll be seeing and modifying a number of controllers in the development of a sample application, starting with the products controller in Iteration C1: Creating the Catalog Listing, on page 101.

There's a lot to Rails. But before going any further, let's have a brief refresher—and for some of you, a brief introduction—to the Ruby language.

In this chapter, you'll see:
- Objects: names and methods
- Data: strings, arrays, hashes, and regular expressions
- Control: if, while, blocks, iterators, and exceptions
- Building blocks: classes and modules
- YAML and marshaling
- Common idioms that you'll see used in this book

CHAPTER 4

Introduction to Ruby

Many people who are new to Rails are also new to Ruby. If you're familiar with a language such as Java, JavaScript, PHP, Perl, or Python, you'll find Ruby pretty easy to pick up.

This chapter isn't a complete introduction to Ruby. It doesn't cover topics such as precedence rules (as in most other programming languages, 1+2*3==7 in Ruby). It's only meant to explain enough Ruby that the examples in the book make sense.

This chapter draws heavily from material in *Programming Ruby 3.3 [Tho24]*. If you think you need more background on the Ruby language (and at the risk of being grossly self-serving), we'd like to suggest that the best way to learn Ruby and the best reference for Ruby's classes, modules, and libraries is *Programming Ruby 3.3 [Tho24]* (also known as the PickAxe book). Welcome to the Ruby community!

Ruby Is an Object-Oriented Language

Everything you manipulate in Ruby is an object, and the results of those manipulations are themselves objects.

When you write object-oriented code, you're normally looking to model concepts from the real world. Typically, during this modeling process you discover categories of things that need to be represented. In an online store, the concept of a line item could be such a category. In Ruby, you'd define a *class* to represent each of these categories. You then use this class as a kind of factory that generates *objects*—instances of that class. An object is a combination of state (for example, the quantity and the product ID) and methods that use that state (perhaps a method to calculate the line item's total cost). We'll show how to create classes in Classes, on page 50.

You create objects by calling a *constructor*, a special method associated with a class. The standard constructor is called new(). Given a class called LineItem, you could create line item objects as follows:

```
line_item_one = LineItem.new
line_item_one.quantity = 1
line_item_one.sku      = "AUTO_B_00"
```

You invoke methods by sending a message to an object. The message contains the method's name along with any parameters the method may need. When an object receives a message, it looks into its own class for a corresponding method. Let's look at some method calls:

```
"dave".length
line_item_one.quantity()
cart.add_line_item(next_purchase)
submit_tag "Add to Cart"
```

Parentheses are generally optional in method calls. In Rails applications, you'll find that most method calls involved in larger expressions have parentheses, while those that look more like commands or declarations tend not to have them.

Methods have names, as do many other constructs in Ruby. Names in Ruby have special rules—rules that you may not have seen if you come to Ruby from another language.

Ruby Names

Local variables, method parameters, and method names should all start with a lowercase letter or with an underscore: order, line_item, and xr2000 are all valid. Instance variables begin with an at (@) sign—for example, @quantity and @product_id. The Ruby convention is to use underscores to separate words in a multiword method or variable name (so line_item is preferable to lineItem).

Class names, module names, and constants must start with an uppercase letter. By convention they use capitalization, rather than underscores, to distinguish the start of words within the name. Class names look like Object, PurchaseOrder, and LineItem.

Rails uses *symbols* to identify things. In particular, it uses them as keys when naming method parameters and looking things up in hashes. Here's an example:

```
redirect_to :action => "edit", :id => params[:id]
```

As you can see, a symbol looks like a variable name, but it's prefixed with a colon. Examples of symbols include :action, :line_items, and :id. You can think of symbols as string literals magically made into constants. Alternatively, you can consider the colon to mean *thing named*, so :id is the thing named id.

Now that we've used a few methods, let's move on to how they're defined.

Methods

Let's write a method that returns a cheery, personalized greeting. We'll invoke that method a couple of times:

```
def say_goodnight(name)
  result = "Good night, " + name
  return result
end

# Time for bed...
puts say_goodnight("Mary-Ellen") # => "Goodnight, Mary-Ellen"
puts say_goodnight("John-Boy")   # => "Goodnight, John-Boy"
```

Having defined the method, we call it twice. In both cases, we pass the result to the puts() method, which outputs to the console its argument followed by a newline (moving on to the next line of output).

You don't need a semicolon at the end of a statement as long as you put each statement on a separate line. Ruby comments start with a # character and run to the end of the line. Indentation isn't significant. (But two-character indentation is the de facto Ruby standard.)

Ruby doesn't use braces to delimit the bodies of compound statements and definitions (such as methods and classes). Instead, you simply finish the body with the end keyword. The return keyword is optional, and if it's not present, the results of the last expression evaluated are returned.

Data Types

While everything in Ruby is an object, some of the data types in Ruby have special syntax support, in particular for defining literal values. In the preceding examples, we used some simple strings and even string concatenation.

Strings

The previous example also showed some Ruby string objects. One way to create a string object is to use *string literals*, which are sequences of characters between single or double quotation marks. The difference between the two forms is the amount of processing Ruby does on the string while constructing the literal. In the single-quoted case, Ruby does very little. With only a few exceptions, what you type into the single-quoted string literal becomes the string's value.

With double-quotes, Ruby does more work. It looks for *substitutions*—sequences that start with a backslash character—and replaces them with a binary value. The most common of these is \n, which is replaced with a newline character. When you write a string containing a newline to the console, the \n forces a line break.

Then, Ruby performs *expression interpolation* in double-quoted strings. In the string, the sequence #{expression} is replaced by the value of expression. We could use this to rewrite our previous method:

```
def say_goodnight(name)
  "Good night, #{name.capitalize}"
end
puts say_goodnight("pa")
```

When Ruby constructs this string object, it looks at the current value of name and substitutes it into the string. Arbitrarily complex expressions are allowed in the #{...} construct. Here we invoked the capitalize() method, defined for all strings, to output our parameter with a leading uppercase letter.

Strings are a fairly primitive data type that contain an ordered collection of bytes or characters. Ruby also provides means for defining collections of arbitrary objects via *arrays* and *hashes*.

Arrays and Hashes

Ruby's arrays and hashes are indexed collections. Both store collections of objects, accessible using a key. With arrays, the key is an integer, whereas hashes support any object as a key. Both arrays and hashes grow as needed to hold new elements. It's more efficient to access array elements, but hashes provide more flexibility. Any particular array or hash can hold objects of differing types; you can have an array containing an integer, a string, and a floating-point number, for example.

You can create and initialize a new array object by using an *array literal*—a set of elements between square brackets. Given an array object, you can access individual elements by supplying an index between square brackets, as the next example shows. Ruby array indices start at zero:

```
a = [ 1, "cat", 3.14 ]   # array with three elements
a[0]                     # access the first element (1)
a[2] = nil               # set the third element
                         # array now [ 1, "cat", nil ]
```

You may have noticed that we used the special value nil in this example. In many languages, the concept of *nil* (or *null*) means *no object*. In Ruby, that's not the case; nil is an object, like any other, that happens to represent nothing.

The <<() method is often used with arrays. It appends a single value to its receiver:

```ruby
ages = []
for person in @people
  ages << person.age
end
```

Ruby has a shortcut for creating an array of words:

```ruby
a = [ 'ant', 'bee', 'cat', 'dog', 'elk' ]
# this is the same:
a = %w[ ant bee cat dog elk ]
```

Ruby hashes are similar to arrays. A hash literal uses braces rather than square brackets. The literal must supply two objects for every entry: one for the key, the other for the value. For example, you may want to map musical instruments to their orchestral sections:

```ruby
inst_section = {
  :cello    => "string",
  :clarinet => "woodwind",
  :drum     => "percussion",
  :oboe     => "woodwind",
  :trumpet  => "brass",
  :violin   => "string"
}
```

The thing to the left of the => is the key, and that on the right is the corresponding value. Keys in a particular hash must be unique; if you have two entries for :drum, the last one will *win*. The keys and values in a hash can be arbitrary objects: you can have hashes in which the values are arrays, other hashes, and so on. In Rails, hashes typically use symbols as keys. Many Rails hashes have been subtly modified so you can use either a string or a symbol interchangeably as a key when inserting and looking up values.

The use of symbols as hash keys is so commonplace that Ruby has a special syntax for it, saving both keystrokes and eyestrain:

```ruby
inst_section = {
  cello:    "string",
  clarinet: "woodwind",
  drum:     "percussion",
  oboe:     "woodwind",
  trumpet:  "brass",
  violin:   "string"
}
```

Doesn't that look much better?

Feel free to use whichever syntax you like. You can even intermix usages in a single expression. Obviously, you'll need to use the arrow syntax whenever the key is *not* a symbol. One other thing to watch out for—if the *value* is a symbol, you'll need to have at least one space between the colons or else you'll get a syntax error:

```
inst_section = {
  cello:    :string,
  clarinet: :woodwind,
  drum:     :percussion,
  oboe:     :woodwind,
  trumpet:  :brass,
  violin:   :string
}
```

Hashes are indexed using the same square bracket notation as arrays:

```
inst_section[:oboe]     #=> :woodwind
inst_section[:cello]    #=> :string
inst_section[:bassoon]  #=> nil
```

As the preceding example shows, a hash returns nil when indexed by a key it doesn't contain. Normally this is convenient because nil means false when used in conditional expressions.

You can pass hashes as parameters on method calls. Ruby allows you to omit the braces but only if the hash is the last parameter of the call. Rails makes extensive use of this feature. The following code fragment shows a two-element hash being passed to the redirect_to() method. Note that this is the same syntax that Ruby uses for keyword arguments:

```
redirect_to action: "show", id: product.id
```

One more data type is worth mentioning: the regular expression.

Regular Expressions

A regular expression lets you specify a *pattern* of characters to be matched in a string. In Ruby, you typically create a regular expression by writing /pattern/ or %r{pattern}.

For example, we can use the regular expression /Perl|Python/ to write a pattern that matches a string containing the text *Perl* or the text *Python*.

The forward slashes delimit the pattern, which consists of the two things that we're matching, separated by a vertical bar (|). The bar character means either the thing on the left or the thing on the right—in this case, either *Perl* or *Python*. You can use parentheses within patterns, just as you can in arithmetic expressions, so we could also write this pattern as /P(erl|ython)/. Programs typically use the =~ match operator to test strings against regular expressions:

```
if line =~ /P(erl|ython)/
  puts "There seems to be another scripting language here"
end
```

You can specify *repetition* within patterns. /ab+c/ matches a string containing an *a* followed by one or more *b*s, followed by a *c*. Change the plus to an asterisk, and /ab*c/ creates a regular expression that matches one *a*, zero or more *b*s, and one *c*.

Backward slashes start special sequences; most notably, \d matches any digit, \s matches any whitespace character, and \w matches any alphanumeric (*word*) character, \A matches the start of the string and \z matches the end of the string. A backslash before a wildcard character, for example \., causes the character to be matched as is.

Ruby's regular expressions are a deep and complex subject; this section barely skims the surface. See the PickAxe book for a full discussion.

This book will make only light use of regular expressions.

With that brief introduction to data, let's move on to logic.

Logic

Method calls are statements. Ruby also provides a number of ways to make decisions that affect the repetition and order in which methods are invoked.

Control Structures

Ruby has all the usual control structures, such as if statements and while loops. Java, C, and Perl programmers may well get caught by the lack of braces around the bodies of these statements. Instead, Ruby uses the end keyword to signify the end of a body:

```
if count > 10
  puts "Try again"
elsif tries == 3
  puts "You lose"
else
  puts "Enter a number"
end
```

Similarly, while statements are terminated with end:

```
while weight < 100 and num_pallets <= 30
  pallet = next_pallet()
  weight += pallet.weight
  num_pallets += 1
end
```

Ruby also contains variants of these statements. unless is like if, except that it checks for the condition to *not* be true. Similarly, until is like while, except that the loop continues until the condition evaluates to be true.

Ruby *statement modifiers* are a useful shortcut if the body of an if, unless, while, or until statement is a single expression. Simply write the expression, followed by the modifier keyword and the condition:

```
puts "Danger, Will Robinson" if radiation > 3000
distance = distance * 1.2 while distance < 100
```

Although if statements are fairly common in Ruby applications, newcomers to the Ruby language are often surprised to find that looping constructs are rarely used. *Blocks* and *iterators* often take their place.

Blocks and Iterators

Code blocks are chunks of code between braces or between do...end. A common convention is that people use braces for single-line blocks and do/end for multiline blocks:

```
{ puts "Hello" }        # this is a block
do                      ###
  club.enroll(person)   # and so is this
  person.socialize      #
end                     ###
```

To pass a block to a method, place the block after the parameters (if any) to the method. In other words, put the start of the block at the end of the source line containing the method call. For example, in the following code, the block containing puts "Hi" is associated with the call to the greet() method:

```
greet { puts "Hi" }
```

If a method call has parameters, they appear before the block:

```
verbose_greet("Dave", "loyal customer")  { puts "Hi" }
```

A method can invoke an associated block one or more times by using the Ruby yield statement. You can think of yield as being something like a method call that calls out to the block associated with the method containing the yield.

You can pass values to the block by giving parameters to yield. Within the block, you list the names of the arguments to receive these parameters between vertical bars (|).

Code blocks appear throughout Ruby applications. Often they're used in conjunction with iterators—methods that return successive elements from some kind of collection, such as an array:

```ruby
animals = %w[ ant bee cat dog elk ]    # create an array
animals.each {|animal| puts animal }   # iterate over the contents
```

Each integer N implements a times() method, which invokes an associated block N times:

```ruby
3.times { print "Ho! " }    #=>  Ho! Ho! Ho!
```

The & prefix operator allows a method to capture a passed block as a named parameter:

```ruby
def wrap &b
  print "Santa says: "
  3.times(&b)
  print "\n"
end
wrap { print "Ho! " }
```

Within a block, or a method, control is sequential except when an exception occurs.

Exceptions

Exceptions are objects of the Exception class or its subclasses. The raise method causes an exception to be raised. This interrupts the normal flow through the code. Instead, Ruby searches back through the call stack for code that says it can handle this exception.

Both methods and blocks of code wrapped between begin and end keywords intercept certain classes of exceptions using rescue clauses:

```ruby
begin
  content = load_blog_data(file_name)
rescue BlogDataNotFound
  STDERR.puts "File #{file_name} not found"
rescue BlogDataFormatError
  STDERR.puts "Invalid blog data in #{file_name}"
rescue Exception => exc
  STDERR.puts "General error loading #{file_name}: #{exc.message}"
end
```

rescue clauses can be directly placed on the outermost level of a method definition without needing to enclose the contents in a begin/end block.

That concludes our brief introduction to control flow. At this point you have the basic building blocks for creating larger structures.

Organizing Structures

Ruby has two basic concepts for organizing methods: classes and modules. We cover each in turn.

Classes

Here's a Ruby class definition:

```
class Order < ApplicationRecord
    has_many :line_items
    def self.find_all_unpaid
      self.where("paid = 0")
    end
    def total
      sum = 0
      line_items.each {|li| sum += li.total}
      sum
    end
end
```

Class definitions start with the class keyword and are followed by the class name (which must start with an uppercase letter). This Order class is defined to be a subclass of the ApplicationRecord class.

Rails makes heavy use of class-level declarations. Here, has_many is a method that's defined by Active Record. It's called as the Order class is being defined. Normally these kinds of methods make assertions about the class, so in this book we call them *declarations.*

Within a class body, you can define class methods and instance methods. Prefixing a method name with self. (as we do on line 3) makes it a class method; it can be called on the class generally. In this case, we can make the following call anywhere in our application:

```
to_collect = Order.find_all_unpaid
```

Objects of a class hold their state in *instance variables*. These variables, whose names all start with @, are available to all the instance methods of a class. Each object gets its own set of instance variables.

Instance variables aren't directly accessible outside the class. To make them available, write methods that return their values:

```ruby
class Greeter
  def initialize(name)
    @name = name
  end

  def name
    @name
  end

  def name=(new_name)
    @name = new_name
  end
end
g = Greeter.new("Barney")
g.name      # => Barney
g.name = "Betty"
g.name      # => Betty
```

Ruby provides convenience methods that write these accessor methods for you (which is great news for folks tired of writing all those getters and setters):

```ruby
class Greeter
  attr_accessor  :name      # create reader and writer methods
  attr_reader    :greeting  # create reader only
  attr_writer    :age       # create writer only
end
```

A class's instance methods are public by default; anyone can call them. You'll probably want to override this for methods that are intended to be used only by other instance methods:

```ruby
class MyClass
  def m1      # this method is public
  end
  protected
  def m2      # this method is protected
  end
  private
  def m3      # this method is private
  end
end
```

The private directive is the strictest; private methods can be called only from within the same instance. Protected methods can be called both in the same instance and by other instances of the same class and its subclasses.

Classes aren't the only organizing structure in Ruby. The other organizing structure is a *module*.

Modules

Modules are similar to classes in that they hold a collection of methods, constants, and other module and class definitions. Unlike with classes, you can't create objects based on modules.

Modules serve two purposes. First, they act as a namespace, letting you define methods whose names won't clash with those defined elsewhere. Second, they allow you to share functionality among classes. If a class *mixes in* a module, that module's methods become available as if they'd been defined in the class. Multiple classes can mix in the same module, sharing the module's functionality without using inheritance. You can also mix in multiple modules into a single class.

Helper methods are an example of where Rails uses modules. Rails automatically mixes these helper modules into the appropriate view templates. For example, if you wanted to write a helper method that's callable from views invoked by the store controller, you could define the following module in the store_helper.rb file in the app/helpers directory:

```ruby
module StoreHelper
  def capitalize_words(string)
    string.split(" ").map {|word| word.capitalize}.join(" ")
  end
end
```

One module that's part of the standard library of Ruby deserves special mention, given its usage in Rails: YAML.

YAML

YAML[1] is a recursive acronym that stands for YAML Ain't Markup Language. In the context of Rails, YAML is used as a convenient way to define the configuration of things such as databases, test data, and translations. Here's an example:

```
development:
  adapter: sqlite3
  database: storage/development.sqlite3
  pool: 5
  timeout: 5000
```

In YAML, indentation is important, so this defines development as having a set of four key-value pairs, separated by colons. While YAML is one way to represent data, particularly when interacting with humans, Ruby provides a more general way for representing data for use by applications.

---

1. http://www.yaml.org/

Marshaling Objects

Ruby can take an object and convert it into a stream of bytes that can be stored outside the application. This process is called *marshaling*. This saved object can later be read by another instance of the application (or by a totally separate application), and a copy of the originally saved object can be reconstituted.

Two potential issues arise when you use marshaling. First, some objects can't be dumped. If the objects to be dumped include bindings, procedure or method objects, instances of the IO class, or singleton objects—or if you try to dump anonymous classes or modules—a TypeError will be raised.

Second, when you load a marshaled object, Ruby needs to know the definition of the class of that object (and of all the objects it contains).

Rails uses marshaling to store session data. If you rely on Rails to dynamically load classes, it's possible that a particular class may not have been defined at the point it reconstitutes session data. For that reason, use the model declaration in your controller to list all models that are marshaled. This preemptively loads the necessary classes to make marshaling work.

Now that you have the Ruby basics down, let's give what we learned a whirl with a slightly larger, annotated example that pulls together a number of concepts. We'll follow that with a walk-through of special features that will help you with your Rails coding.

Pulling It All Together

Let's look at an example of how Rails applies a number of Ruby features together to make the code you need to maintain more declarative. You'll see this example again in Generating the Scaffold, on page 66. For now, we'll focus on the Ruby-language aspects of the example:

```ruby
class CreateProducts < ActiveRecord::Migration[8.0]
  def change
    create_table :products do |t|
      t.string :title
      t.text :description
      t.decimal :price, precision: 8, scale: 2

      t.timestamps
    end
  end
end
```

Even if you didn't know any Ruby, you'd probably be able to decipher that this code creates a table named products. The fields defined when this table is created include title, description, and price, as well as a few timestamps. We'll describe these in Chapter 23, Migrations, on page 407.

Now let's look at the same example from a Ruby perspective. We define a class named CreateProducts, which inherits from the versioned[2] Migration class from the ActiveRecord module, specifying that compatibility with Rails 8 is desired. We define one method, named change(). This method calls the create_table() method (defined in ActiveRecord::Migration), passing it the name of the table in the form of a symbol.

The call to create_table() also passes a block that is to be evaluated before the table is created. This block, when called, is passed an object named t, which is used to accumulate a list of fields. Rails defines a number of methods on this object—methods named after common data types. These methods, when called, simply add a field definition to the ever-accumulating set of names.

The definition of decimal also accepts a number of optional parameters, expressed as a hash.

To someone new to Ruby, this is a lot of heavy machinery thrown at solving such a simple problem. To someone familiar with Ruby, none of this machinery is particularly heavy. In any case, Rails makes extensive use of the facilities provided by Ruby to make defining operations (for example, migration tasks) as simple and as declarative as possible. Even small features of the language, such as optional parentheses and braces, contribute to the overall readability and ease of authoring.

Finally, a number of small features—or, rather, idiomatic combinations of features—are often not immediately obvious to people new to the Ruby language. We close this chapter with them.

Ruby Idioms

A number of individual Ruby features can be combined in interesting ways. We use these common Ruby idioms in this book:

---

2. http://blog.bigbinary.com/2016/03/01/migrations-are-versioned-in-rails-5.html

Methods such as empty! and empty?

    Ruby method names can end with an exclamation mark (a *bang method*) or a question mark (a *predicate method*). Bang methods normally do something destructive to the receiver. Predicate methods return true or false, depending on some condition.

a || b

    The expression a || b evaluates a. If it isn't false or nil, then evaluation stops and the expression returns a. Otherwise, the statement returns b. This is a common way of returning a default value if the first value hasn't been set.

a ||= b

    The assignment statement supports a set of shortcuts: a op= b is the same as a = a op b. This works for most operators:

```
count += 1          # same as count = count + 1
price *= discount   #          price = price * discount
count ||= 0         #          count = count || 0
```

So, count ||= 0 gives count the value 0 if count is nil or false.

obj = self.new

    Sometimes a class method needs to create an instance of that class:

```
class Person < ApplicationRecord
  def self.for_dave
    Person.new(name: "Dave")
  end
end
```

This works fine, returning a new Person object. But later, someone might subclass our class:

```
class Employee < Person
  # ..
end

dave = Employee.for_dave   # returns a Person
```

The for_dave() method was hardwired to return a Person object, so that's what's returned by Employee.for_dave. Using self.new instead returns a new object of the receiver's class, Employee.

lambda
> The lambda operator converts a block into an object of type Proc. An alternative syntax, introduced in Ruby 1.9, is ->. As a matter of style, the Rails team prefers the latter syntax. You can see example usages of this operator in Scopes, on page 332.

require File.expand_path("../../config/environment", __FILE__)
> Ruby's require method loads an external source file into our application. This is used to include library code and classes that our application relies on. In normal use, Ruby finds these files by searching in a list of directories, the LOAD_PATH.
>
> Sometimes we need to be specific about which file to include. We can do that by giving require a full filesystem path. The problem is, we don't know what that path will be—our users could install our code anywhere.
>
> Wherever our application ends up getting installed, the relative path between the file doing the requiring and the target file will be the same. Knowing this, we can construct the absolute path to the target by using the File.expand_path() method, passing in the relative path to the target file, and passing the absolute path to the file doing the requiring (available in the special __FILE__ variable).

In addition, the web has many good resources that show Ruby idioms and Ruby gotchas. Here are a few of them:

- http://www.ruby-lang.org/en/documentation/ruby-from-other-languages/
- http://en.wikipedia.org/wiki/Ruby_programming_language
- https://www.zenspider.com/ruby/quickref.html

By this point, you have a firm foundation to build on. You've installed Rails, verified that you have things working with a simple application, read a brief description of what Rails is, and reviewed (or for some of you, learned for the first time) the basics of the Ruby language. Now it's time to put this knowledge in place to build a larger application.

Part II

Building an Application

In this chapter, you'll see:
- Incremental development
- Use cases, page flow, and data
- Priorities

CHAPTER 5

The Depot Application

We could mess around all day hacking together simple test applications, but that won't help us pay the bills. So let's sink our teeth into something meatier. Let's create a web-based shopping cart application called Depot.

Does the world need another shopping cart application? Nope, but that hasn't stopped hundreds of developers from writing one. Why should we be different?

More seriously, it turns out that our shopping cart will illustrate many of the features of Rails development. You'll see how to create maintenance pages, link database tables, handle sessions, create forms, and wrangle modern JavaScript. Over the next twelve chapters, we'll also touch on peripheral topics such as unit and system testing, security, and page layout.

Incremental Development

We'll be developing this application incrementally. We won't attempt to specify everything before we start coding. Instead, we'll work out enough of a specification to let us start and then immediately create some functionality. We'll try ideas, gather feedback, and continue with another cycle of mini design and development.

This style of coding isn't always applicable. It requires close cooperation with the application's users because we want to gather feedback as we go along. We might make mistakes, or the client might ask for one thing at first and later want something different. It doesn't matter what the reason is. The earlier we discover we've made a mistake, the less expensive it'll be to fix that mistake. All in all, with this style of development, there's a lot of change as we go along.

Because of this, we need to use a toolset that doesn't penalize us for changing our minds. If we decide we need to add a new column to a database table or change the navigation among pages, we need to be able to get in there and do it without a bunch of coding or configuration hassle. As you'll see, Ruby on Rails shines when it comes to dealing with change. It's an ideal agile programming environment.

Along the way, we'll be building and maintaining a corpus of tests. These tests will ensure that the application is always doing what we intend to do. Not only does Rails enable the creation of such tests but it even provides you with an initial set of tests each time you define a new controller.

On with the application.

What Depot Does

Let's start by jotting down an outline specification for the Depot application. We'll look at the high-level use cases and sketch out the flow through the web pages. We'll also try working out what data the application needs (acknowledging that our initial guesses will likely be wrong).

Use Cases

A *use case* is simply a statement about how some entity uses a system. Consultants invent these kinds of phrases to label things we've known all along. (It's a perversion of business life that fancy words always cost more than plain ones, even though the plain ones are more valuable.)

Depot's use cases are simple (some would say tragically so). We start off by identifying two different roles or actors: the *buyer* and the *seller*.

The buyer uses Depot to browse the products we have to sell, select some to purchase, and supply the information needed to create an order.

The seller uses Depot to maintain a list of products to sell, to determine the orders that are awaiting shipment, and to mark orders as shipped. (The seller also uses Depot to make scads of money and retire to a tropical island, but that's the subject of another book.)

For now, that's all the detail we need. We *could* go into excruciating detail about what it means to maintain products and what constitutes an order ready to ship, but why bother? If some details aren't obvious, we'll discover them soon enough as we reveal successive iterations of our work to the customer.

Speaking of getting feedback, let's get some right now. Let's make sure our initial (admittedly sketchy) use cases are on the mark by asking our users. Assuming the use cases pass muster, let's work out how the application will work from the perspectives of its various users.

Page Flow

We always like to have an idea of the main pages in our applications and to understand roughly how users navigate among them. This early in the development, these page flows are likely to be incomplete, but they still help us focus on what needs doing and know how actions are sequenced.

Some folks like to use Photoshop, Word, or (shudder) HTML to mock up web application page flows. We like using a pencil and paper. It's quicker, and the customer gets to play too, grabbing the pencil and scribbling alterations right on the paper.

The first sketch of the buyer flow is shown in the following figure.

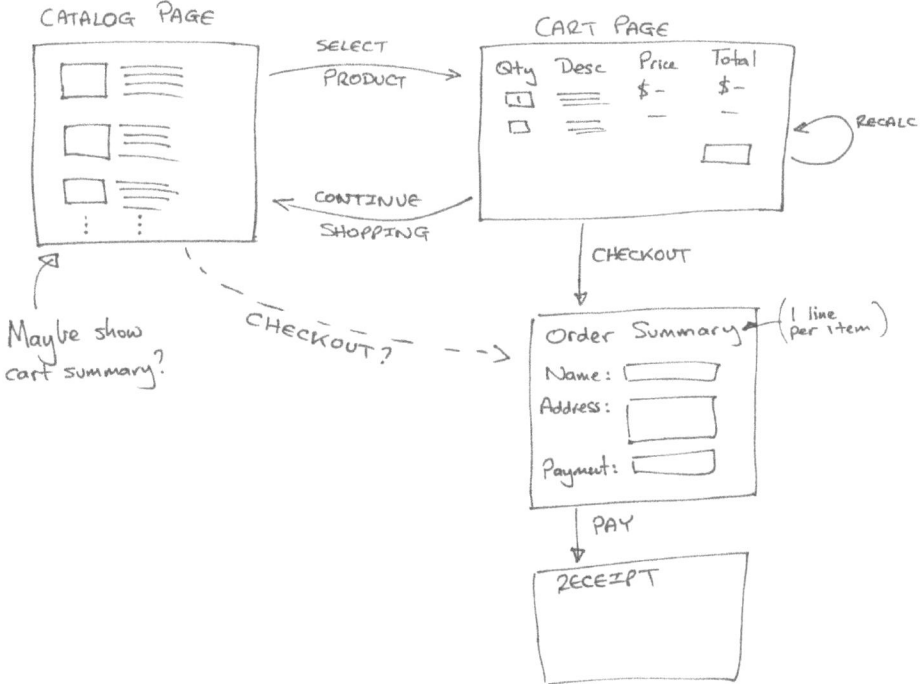

It's pretty traditional. The buyer sees a catalog page, from which he selects one product at a time. Each product selected gets added to the cart, and the cart is displayed after each selection. The buyer can continue shopping using the catalog pages or check out and buy the contents of the cart. During checkout, we capture contact and payment details and then display a receipt page. We don't yet know how we're going to handle payment, so those details are fairly vague in the flow.

The seller flow, shown in the following figure, is also fairly basic. After logging in, the seller sees a menu letting her create or view a product or ship existing orders. When viewing a product, the seller can optionally edit the product information or delete the product entirely.

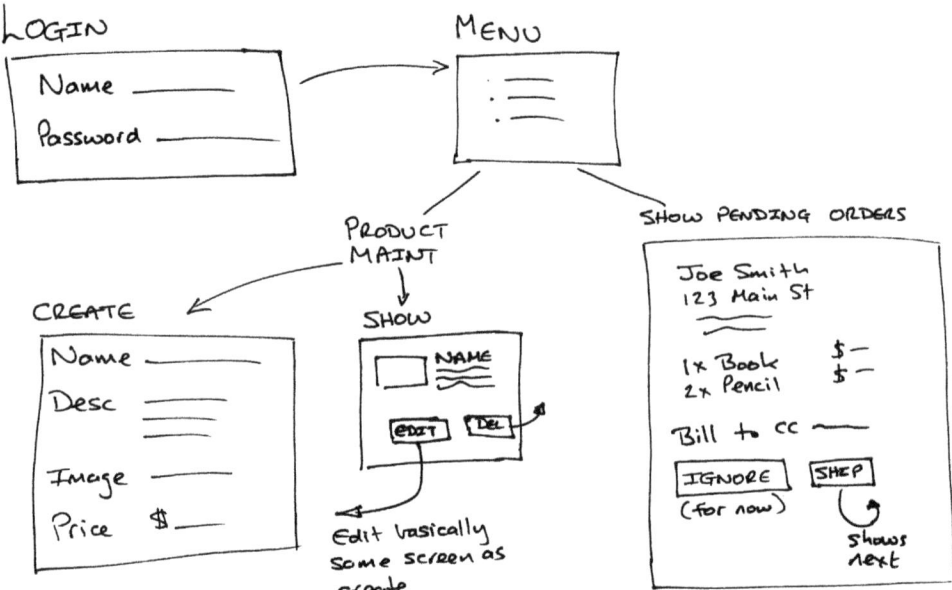

The shipping option is simplistic. It displays each order that hasn't yet been shipped, one order per page. The seller can choose to skip to the next or can ship the order, using the information from the page as appropriate.

The shipping function is clearly not going to survive long in the real world, but shipping is also one of those areas where reality is often stranger than you might think. Overspecify it up front, and we're likely to get it wrong. For now, let's leave it as it is, confident that we can change it as the user gains experience using our application.

Data

Finally, we need to think about the data we're going to be working with.

Notice that we're not using words such as *schema* or *classes* here. We're also not talking about databases, tables, keys, and the like. We're talking about data. At this stage in the development, we don't know if we'll even be using a database.

Based on the use cases and the flows, it seems likely that we'll be working with the data shown in the figure on page 63. Again, using pencil and paper seems a whole lot easier than some fancy tool, but use whatever works for you.

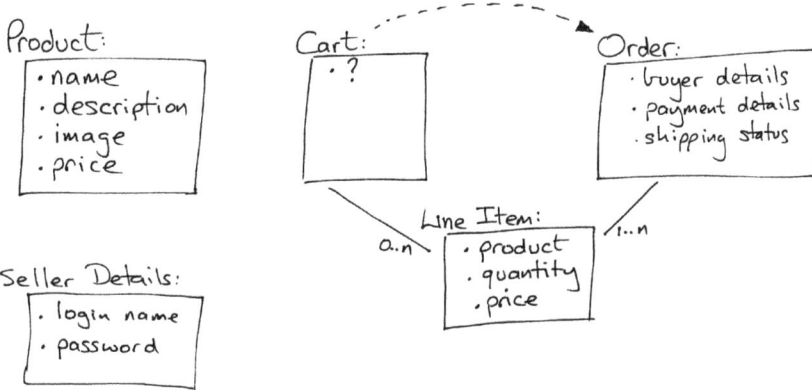

Working on the data diagram raised a couple of questions. As the user buys items, we'll need somewhere to keep the list of products they bought, so we added a cart. But apart from its use as a transient place to keep this product list, the cart seems to be something of a ghost—we couldn't find anything meaningful to store in it. To reflect this uncertainty, we put a question mark inside the cart's box in the diagram. We're assuming this uncertainty will get resolved as we implement Depot.

Coming up with the high-level data also raised the question of what information should go into an order. Again, we chose to leave this fairly open for now. We'll refine this further as we start showing our early iterations to the customer.

> **General Recovery Advice**
>
> Everything in this book has been tested. If you follow along with this scenario precisely, using the recommended version of Rails and SQLite 3 on Linux, MacOS, or Windows, everything should work as described. However, deviations from this path can occur. Typos happen to the best of us, and not only are side explorations possible, but they're positively encouraged. Be aware that this might lead you to strange places. Don't be afraid: specific recovery actions for common problems appear in the specific sections where such problems often occur. A few additional general suggestions are included here.
>
> You should only ever need to restart the server in the few places where doing so is noted in the book. But if you ever get truly stumped, restarting the server might be worth trying.
>
> A "magic" command worth knowing, explained in detail in Part III, is `bin/rails db:migrate:redo`. It'll undo and reapply the last migration.
>
> If your server won't accept some input on a form, refresh the form on your browser and resubmit it.

Finally, you might have noticed that we've duplicated the product's price in the line item data. Here we're breaking the "initially, keep it simple" rule slightly, but it's a transgression based on experience. If the price of a product changes, that price change shouldn't be reflected in the line item price of currently open orders, so each line item needs to reflect the price of the product at the time the order was made.

Again, at this point we'll double-check with the customer that we're still on the right track. (The customer was most likely sitting in the room with us while we drew these three diagrams.)

Let's Code

So after sitting down with the customer and doing some preliminary analysis, we're ready to start using a computer for development! We'll be working from our original three diagrams, but the chances are pretty good that we'll be throwing them away fairly quickly—they'll become outdated as we gather feedback. Interestingly, that's why we didn't spend too long on them; it's easier to throw something away if you didn't spend a long time creating it.

In the chapters that follow, we'll start developing the application based on our current understanding. However, before we turn that page, we have to answer one more question: what should we do first?

We like to work with the customer so we can jointly agree on priorities. In this case, we'd point out to her that it's hard to develop anything else until we have some basic products defined in the system, so we suggest spending a couple of hours getting the initial version of the product maintenance functionality up and running. And, of course, the client would agree.

In this chapter, you'll see:
- Creating a new application
- Installing Active Storage
- Configuring the database
- Adding seed data
- Creating models and controllers
- Updating a view
- Running tests
- Making pages update automatically

CHAPTER 6

Task A: Creating the Application

Our first development task is to create the web interface that lets us maintain our product information—create new products, edit existing products, delete unwanted ones, and so on. We'll develop this application in small iterations, where "small" means measured in minutes. Typically, our iterations involve multiple steps, as in iteration C, which has steps C1, C2, C3, and so on. In this case, the iteration has two steps.

Let's get started.

Iteration A1: Creating the Product Maintenance Application

At the heart of the Depot application is a database. Getting this installed and configured and tested before proceeding will prevent a lot of headaches. If you're not certain about what you want, take the defaults, and it will go easily. If you know what you want, Rails makes it easy for you to describe your configuration.

For this project, let's make use of the Tailwind CSS[1] framework, which enables you to make pretty websites without authoring any CSS. We'll do so by specifying an additional option when we create our application, and as you'll shortly see it will also affect how we start our server during development.

Creating a Rails Application

In Creating a New Application, on page 17, you saw how to create a new Rails application. We'll do the same thing here. Go to a command prompt and type rails new followed by the name of our project, and then add the option to make

---

1. https://tailwindcss.com/

use of the Tailwind CSS framework. Here, our project is called depot, so make sure you're not inside an existing application directory, and type this:

```
work> rails new depot --css tailwind
```

We see a bunch of output scroll by. When it has finished, we find that a new directory, depot, has been created. That's where we'll be doing our work:

```
work> cd depot
depot> ls -p
Dockerfile      README.md    config/      log/       test/
Gemfile         Rakefile     config.ru    public/    tmp/
Gemfile.lock    app/         db/          script/    vendor/
Procfile.dev    bin/         lib/         storage/
```

Of course, Windows users need to use dir /w instead of ls -p.

Creating the Database

For this application, we'll use the open source SQLite database (which you'll need if you're following along with the code). We're using SQLite version 3 here.

SQLite 3 is the default database for Rails development and was installed along with Rails in Chapter 1, Installing Rails, on page 3. With SQLite 3, no steps are required to create a database, and we have no special user accounts or passwords to deal with. So now you get to experience one of the benefits of going with the flow (or, convention over configuration, as the Rails folks say…ad nauseam).

If it's important to you to use a database server other than SQLite 3, the commands to create the database and grant permissions will be different. You can find some helpful hints in the database configuration section of Configuring Rails Applications in the Ruby on Rails Guides.[2]

Generating the Scaffold

Back in our initial guess at application data on page 63, we sketched out the basic content of the products table. Now let's turn that into reality. We need to create a database table and a Rails *model* that lets our application use that table, a number of *views* to make up the user interface, and a *controller* to orchestrate the application.

So let's create the model, views, controller, and migration for our products table. With Rails, you can do all that with one command by asking Rails to generate a *scaffold* for a given model. Note that on the command line that follows, we

---

2. http://guides.rubyonrails.org/configuring.html#configuring-a-database

use the singular form, Product. In Rails, a model is automatically mapped to a database table whose name is the plural form of the model's class. In our case, we ask for a model called Product, so Rails associates it with the table called products. (And how will it find that table? The development entry in config/database.yml tells Rails where to look for it. For SQLite 3 users, this'll be a file in the storage directory.)

Note that the command is too wide to fit comfortably on the page. To enter a command on multiple lines, put a backslash as the last character on all but the last line, and you'll be prompted for more input. Windows users need to substitute a caret (^) for the backslash at the end of the first line and a backslash for the forward slash in bin/rails:

```
depot> bin/rails generate scaffold Product \
         title:string description:text image:attachment price:decimal
    invoke  active_record
    create    db/migrate/20250420000001_create_products.rb
    create    app/models/product.rb
    invoke    test_unit
    create      test/models/product_test.rb
    create      test/fixtures/products.yml
    invoke  resource_route
     route    resources :products
    invoke  scaffold_controller
    create    app/controllers/products_controller.rb
    invoke    tailwindcss
    create      app/views/products
    create      app/views/products/index.html.erb
    create      app/views/products/edit.html.erb
    create      app/views/products/show.html.erb
    create      app/views/products/new.html.erb
    create      app/views/products/_form.html.erb
    create      app/views/products/_product.html.erb
    invoke    resource_route
    invoke    test_unit
    create      test/controllers/products_controller_test.rb
    create      test/system/products_test.rb
    invoke    helper
    create      app/helpers/products_helper.rb
    invoke      test_unit
    invoke    jbuilder
    create      app/views/products/index.json.jbuilder
    create      app/views/products/show.json.jbuilder
    create      app/views/products/_product.json.jbuilder
```

The generator creates a bunch of files. The one we're interested in first is the *migration* one, namely, 20250420000001_create_products.rb.

A migration represents a change we either want to make to a database as a whole or to the data contained within the database, and it's expressed in a source file in database-independent terms. These changes can update both the database schema and the data in the database tables. We apply these migrations to update our database, and we can unapply them to roll our database back. We have a whole section on migrations starting in Chapter 23, Migrations, on page 407. For now, we'll just use them without too much more comment.

The migration has a UTC-based timestamp prefix (20250420000001), a name (create_products), and a file extension (.rb, because it's Ruby code).

The timestamp prefix that you see will be different. In fact, the timestamps used in this book are clearly fictitious. Typically, your timestamps won't be consecutive; instead, they'll reflect the time the migration was created.

Applying the Migration

Although we've already told Rails about the basic data types of each property, let's refine the definition of the price to have eight digits of significance and two digits after the decimal point:

```
rails80/depot_a/db/migrate/20250420000001_create_products.rb
class CreateProducts < ActiveRecord::Migration[8.0]
  def change
    create_table :products do |t|
      t.string :title
      t.text :description
      t.decimal :price, precision: 8, scale: 2

      t.timestamps
    end
  end
end
```

Since we've defined an attachment, we need to install the tables that Active Storage uses to track the attachments. This only needs to be done once per database. We do this by running the following command:

```
depot> bin/rails active_storage:install
Copied migration 20250420000002_create_active_storage_tables.active_storage.rb
  from active_storage_attachments
```

Now that we're done with our changes, we need to get Rails to apply this migration to our development database. We do this by using the bin/rails db:migrate command:

```
depot> bin/rails db:migrate
== 20250420000001 CreateProducts: migrating ===================================
-- create_table(:products)
   -> 0.0025s
== 20250420000001 CreateProducts: migrated (0.0025s) ==========================

== 20250420000002 CreateActiveStorageTables: migrating ========================
-- create_table(:active_storage_blobs, {:id=>:primary_key})
   -> 0.0065s
-- create_table(:active_storage_attachments, {:id=>:primary_key})
   -> 0.0270s
-- create_table(:active_storage_variant_records, {:id=>:primary_key})
   -> 0.0113s
== 20250420000002 CreateActiveStorageTables: migrated (0.0451s) ===============
```

And that's it. Rails looks for all the migrations not yet applied to the database and applies them. In our case, the products table is added to the database defined by the development section of the database.yml file, and three tables are created for Active Storage to use.

OK, all the groundwork has been done. We set up our Depot application as a Rails project. We created the development database and configured our application to be able to connect to it. We created a products controller and a Product model and used a migration to create the corresponding products table. And a number of views have been created for us. It's time to see all this in action.

Seeing the List of Products

With four commands, we've created an application and a database (or a table inside an existing database if you chose something else besides SQLite 3) and installed Active Storage. Before we worry too much about what happened behind the scenes here, let's try our shiny new application.

We mentioned previously that using a CSS processor will affect how we start our server during development. This is because things like CSS processors and JavaScript bundlers require a build step. Rather than requiring you to start multiple processes, Rails provides bin/dev, which is a small script that will start everything:

```
depot> bin/dev
Installing foreman...
Fetching foreman-0.88.1.gem
Successfully installed foreman-0.88.1
Parsing documentation for foreman-0.88.1
Installing ri documentation for foreman-0.88.1
Done installing documentation for foreman after 0 seconds
1 gem installed
08:43:51 web.1    | started with pid 31227
```

```
08:43:51 css.1  | started with pid 31228
08:43:52 web.1  | => Booting Puma
08:43:52 web.1  | => Rails 8.0.2 application starting in development
08:43:52 web.1  | => Run `bin/rails server --help` for more startup options
08:43:52 web.1  | Puma starting in single mode...
08:43:52 web.1  | * Puma version: 6.5.0 ("Sky's Version")
08:43:52 web.1  | * Ruby version: ruby 3.4.3 (2024-12-25 revision 48d4efcb85)
08:43:52 web.1  | *  Min threads: 3
08:43:52 web.1  | *  Max threads: 3
08:43:52 web.1  | *  Environment: development
08:43:52 web.1  | *          PID: 31227
08:43:52 web.1  | * Listening on http://127.0.0.1:3000
08:43:52 web.1  | * Listening on http://[::1]:3000
08:43:52 web.1  | Use Ctrl-C to stop
08:43:52 css.1  |
08:43:52 css.1  | Rebuilding...
08:43:53 css.1  |
08:43:53 css.1  | Done in 228ms.
```

Note that in some environments, you may need sudo to install foreman. If so, run sudo gem install foreman and rerun the bin/dev command. Windows Powershell and Command Prompt users will need to run the command ruby bin\dev.

If you examine that output, in addtion to the lines containing web.1 that show the Rails server starting, you see lines containing css.1 that show the CSS rebuilding. This is all controlled by a file named Procfile.dev:

rails80/depot_a/Procfile.dev
```
web: bin/rails server
css: bin/rails tailwindcss:watch
```

Feel free to modify this file to suit your needs. For example, if you're using a virtual machine, you might need to add -b 0.0.0.0 to the rails server line to accept connections from your host.

As with our demo application on page 17, this command starts a web server on our local host, port 3000. If you get an error saying Address already in use when you try to run the server, that means you already have a Rails server running on your machine. If you've been following along with the examples in the book, that might well be the Hello, World! application from Chapter 4. Find its console and kill the server using Ctrl-C . If you're running on Windows, you might see the prompt Terminate batch job (Y/N)?. If so, respond with y.

Let's connect to our application. Remember, the URL we give to our browser is http://localhost:3000/products, which has both the port number (3000) and the name of the controller in lowercase (products). The application looks like the screenshot shown on page 71.

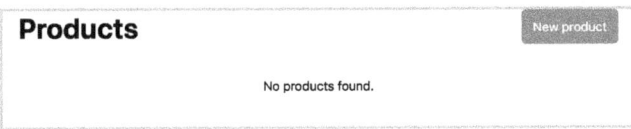

That's pretty boring. It's showing us an empty list of products. Let's add some. Click the New Product link. A form should appear, as shown in the following screenshot.

These forms are simply HTML templates, like the ones you created in Hello, Rails!, on page 20. In fact, we can modify them. Let's change the number of rows in the Description field and limit the acceptable files to select for upload to images:

```erb
rails80/depot_a/app/views/products/_form.html.erb
<%= form_with(model: product, class: "contents") do |form| %>
  <% if product.errors.any? %>
    <div id="error_explanation"
      class="bg-red-50 text-red-500 px-3 py-2 font-medium rounded-md mt-3">
      <h2><%= pluralize(product.errors.count, "error") %>
      prohibited this product from being saved:</h2>

      <ul class="list-disc ml-6">
        <% product.errors.each do |error| %>
          <li><%= error.full_message %></li>
        <% end %>
      </ul>
    </div>
  <% end %>

  <div class="my-5">
    <%= form.label :title %>
    <%= form.text_field :title, class:
      ["block shadow-sm rounded-md border px-3 py-2 mt-2 w-full",
      {"border-gray-400 focus:outline-blue-600": product.errors[:title].none?",
      "border-red-400 focus:outline-red-600": product.errors[:title].any?}] %>
  </div>
```

```erb
    <div class="my-5">
      <%= form.label :description %>
      <%= form.textarea :description, rows: 10, class:
        ["block shadow-sm rounded-md border px-3 py-2 mt-2 w-full",
        {"border-gray-400 focus:outline-blue-600":
          product.errors[:description].none?",
        "border-red-400 focus:outline-red-600":
          product.errors[:description].any?}] %>
    </div>

    <div class="my-5">
      <%= form.label :image %>
      <%= form.file_field :image, accept: "image/*", class:
        ["block shadow-sm rounded-md border px-3 py-2 mt-2 w-full",
        {"border-gray-400 focus:outline-blue-600": product.errors[:image].none?",
        "border-red-400 focus:outline-red-600": product.errors[:image].any?}] %>
    </div>

    <div class="my-5">
      <%= form.label :price %>
      <%= form.text_field :price, class:
        ["block shadow-sm rounded-md border px-3 py-2 mt-2 w-full",
        {"border-gray-400 focus:outline-blue-600": product.errors[:price].none?",
        "border-red-400 focus:outline-red-600": product.errors[:price].any?}] %>
    </div>

    <div class="inline">
      <%= form.submit class: "w-full sm:w-auto rounded-md px-3.5 py-2.5
        bg-blue-600 hover:bg-blue-500 text-white inline-block
        font-medium cursor-pointer" %>
    </div>
<% end %>
```

We'll explore this more in Chapter 8, Task C: Catalog Display, on page 101. But for now, we've adjusted two fields to taste, so let's fill them in, as shown in screenshot on page 73. (Note the use of HTML tags in the description—this is intentional and will make more sense later.)

Now we need some files to upload. Create a directory named db/images in your application, and download the images there.[3]

Fill in the fields, select a file, and click the Create button, and you should see that the new product was successfully created. If you now click the Back link, you should see the new product in the list, as shown in the screenshot on page 73.

Perhaps it isn't the prettiest interface, but it works, and we can show it to our client for approval. She can play with the other links (showing details,

---

3. https://media.pragprog.com/titles/rails8/code/rails80/depot_a/db/images/

New product

Title

Programming Ruby 3.3 (5th Edition)

Description

```
<p>
<em>The Pragmatic Programmers' Guide</em>
Ruby is one of the most important programming languages in use for web
development. It powers the Rails framework, which is the backing of some of the most
important sites on the web. The Pickaxe Book, named for the tool on the cover, is the
definitive reference on Ruby, a highly-regarded, fully object-oriented programming
language. This updated edition is a comprehensive reference on the language itself,
with a tutorial on the most important features of Ruby—including pattern matching and
Ractors—and describes the language through Ruby 3.3.
</p>
```

Image

Choose File ruby5.jpg

Price

33.95

[Create Product]   Back to products

Products   [New product]

Title:

Programming Ruby 3.3 (5th Edition)

Description:

<p> <em>The Pragmatic Programmers' Guide</em> Ruby is one of the most important programming languages in use for web development. It powers the Rails framework, which is the backing of some of the most important sites on the web. The Pickaxe Book, named for the tool on the cover, is the definitive reference on Ruby, a highly-regarded, fully object-oriented programming language. This updated edition is a comprehensive reference on the language itself, with a tutorial on the most important features of Ruby—including pattern matching and Ractors—and describes the language through Ruby 3.3. </p>

Show   Edit   [Destroy]

Image:

ruby5.jpg

Price:

33.95

editing existing products, and so on). We explain to her that this is only a first step—we know it's rough, but we wanted to get her feedback early. (And five commands probably count as early in anyone's book.)

Note that if you've used a database other than SQLite 3, this step may have failed. Check your config/database.yml file.

Iteration A2: Making Prettier Listings

Our customer has one more request. (Customers always seem to have one more request, don't they?) The listing of all the products is ugly. Can we pretty it up a bit? And while we're in there, can we also display the product image instead of just the image file name?

We're faced with a dilemma here. As developers, we're trained to respond to these kinds of requests with a sharp intake of breath, a knowing shake of the head, and a murmured, "You want what?" At the same time, we also like to show off a bit. In the end, the fact that it's fun to make these kinds of changes using Rails wins out, and we fire up our trusty editor.

Before we get too far, though, it would be nice if we had a consistent set of test data to work with. We *could* use our scaffold-generated interface and type data in from the browser. However, if we did this, future developers working on our codebase would have to do the same. And if we were working as part of a team on this project, each member of the team would have to enter his or her own data. It would be nice if we could load the data into our table in a more controlled way. It turns out that we can. Rails has the ability to import seed data.

To start, we modify the file in the db directory named seeds.rb.

In this file, we add the code to populate the products table. This uses the create!() method of the Product model. The following is an extract from that file. Rather than type the file by hand, you might want to download the file from the sample code available online.[4]

Be warned: this seeds.rb script removes existing data from the products table before loading the new data. You might not want to run it if you've just spent several hours typing your own data into your application!

rails80/depot_a/db/seeds.rb
```
Product.delete_all
# . . .
product = Product.create(title: 'Rails Scales!',
```

---

4. https://media.pragprog.com/titles/rails8/code/rails80/depot_a/db/seeds.rb

```
    description:
      %(<p>
        <em>Practical Techniques for Performance and Growth</em>
        Rails doesn't scale. So say the naysayers. They're wrong. Ruby on Rails
        runs some of the biggest sites in the world, impacting the lives of
        millions of users while efficiently crunching petabytes of data. This
        book reveals how they do it, and how you can apply the same techniques
        to your applications. Optimize everything necessary to make an
        application function at scale: monitoring, product design, Ruby code,
        software architecture, database access, caching, and more. Even if your
        app may never have millions of users, you reduce the costs of hosting
        and maintaining it.
      </p>),
    price: 30.95)
    product.image.attach(io: File.open(
      Rails.root.join('db', 'images', 'cprpo.jpg')),
        filename: 'cprpo.jpg')
    product.save!
# . . .
```

This code starts by deleting all the existing products from the database. It then creates a new set of products, attaches an image to each one, and saves the record. The save!() method is used to save the record to the database. If there's an error, it'll raise an exception.

Note that this code uses %(...). This is an alternative syntax for double-quoted string literals, convenient for use with long strings.

To populate your products table with test data, run the following command:

depot> **bin/rails db:seed**

Now let's get the product listing tidied up. Normally this would require multiple steps: creating a CSS style sheet, linking that style sheet to your HTML, defining a set of style rules within the new style sheet, connecting these rules to the page by defining an HTML class attribute on the page, and changing the HTML to make styling the page easier.

Fortunately, we installed Tailwind CSS support, which is ideal for rapid development. Instead of spending time managing global CSS classes and trying to understand and debug the scope of your changes, you safely style your HTML page through an extensive set of predefined CSS utility classes.

With Tailwind doing the heavy lifting for us, we'll use a table-based template, editing the index.html.erb file in app/views/products and replacing the scaffold-generated view:

rails80/depot_a/app/views/products/index.html.erb
```erb
<div class="w-full">
  <% if notice.present? %>
    <p class="py-2 px-3 bg-green-50 mb-5 text-green-500 font-medium
              rounded-lg inline-block" id="notice">
      <%= notice %>
    </p>
  <% end %>

  <div class="flex justify-between items-center pb-8">
    <h1 class="mx-auto font-bold text-4xl">Products</h1>
  </div>

  <table id="products" class="mx-auto">
    <tfoot>
      <tr>
        <td colspan="3">
          <div class="mt-8">
            <%= link_to 'New product',
                    new_product_path,
                    class: "inline rounded-lg py-3 px-5 bg-green-600
                            text-white block font-medium" %>
          </div>
        </td>
      </tr>
    </tfoot>

    <tbody>
      <% @products.each do |product| %>
        <tr class="<%= cycle('bg-green-50', 'bg-white') %>">

          <td class="px-2 py-3">
            <%= image_tag(product.image, class: 'w-40') %>
          </td>

          <td>
            <h1 class="text-xl font-bold"><%= product.title %></h1>
            <p class="my-3">
              <%= truncate(strip_tags(product.description),
                      length: 80) %>
            </p>
            <p>
              <%= number_to_currency(product.price) %>
            </p>
          </td>

          <td class="px-3">
            <ul>
              <li>
                <%= link_to 'Show',
                        product,
                        class: 'hover:underline' %>
              </li>
```

```erb
          <li>
            <%= link_to 'Edit',
                        edit_product_path(product),
                        class: 'hover:underline' %>
          </li>
          <li>
            <%= button_to 'Destroy',
                          product,
                          method: :delete,
                          class: 'hover:underline',
                          data: { turbo_confirm: "Are you sure?" } %>
          </li>
        </ul>
      </td>
    </tr>
  <% end %>
  </tbody>
</table>
</div>
```

This template uses a number of built-in Rails features:

- The rows in the listing have alternating background colors. The Rails helper method called cycle() does this by setting the CSS class of each row to either bg-green-50 or bg-white, automatically toggling between the two style names on successive lines.

- The truncate() helper is used to display the first eighty characters of the description. But before we call truncate(), we call strip_tags() to remove the HTML tags from the description.

- The number_to_currency() helper is used to format the price. We'll explore this more in Iteration C3: Using a Helper to Format the Price, on page 107.

- The image_tag() helper is used to display the image. We provide product.image.url as the link to the image file, as described in Active Storage, on page 38.

- Look at the link_to 'Destroy' line. See how it has the parameter data: { turbo_confirm: 'Are you sure?' }. If you click this link, Rails arranges for your browser to pop up a dialog box asking for confirmation before following the link and deleting the product. (Also, see the sidebar on page 81 for an inside scoop on this action.)

As far as styling goes:

- We left the notice alone.

- We added mx-auto to the h1 and table to center them horizontally on the page. This corresponds to setting the CSS margin to auto, where x is the horizontal axis and y would be the vertical axis.

- We added classes like px-2 and py-3 to add vertical and horizontal padding.

- Most of the rest of the changes are self-explanatory, with names like text-xl, bg-green-600, and hover:underline.

We loaded some test data into the database, and we rewrote the index.html.erb file that displays the listing of products. Before we proceed, there is a small bit of administrivia we need to attend to. Much like how we installed active storage tables earlier, we need to connect Active Storage to our views. We do this by adding the following line to the app/controller/application_controller.rb file:

```
rails80/depot_a/app/controllers/application_controller.rb
class ApplicationController < ActionController::Base
  # Only allow modern browsers supporting webp images, web push, badges,
  # import maps, CSS nesting, and CSS :has.
  allow_browser versions: :modern

  include ActiveStorage::SetCurrent
end
```

Like before, this only needs to be done once, and only if we're storing files on disk. If you're using a cloud storage provider, you can skip this step.

Unrelated to this change, this file also contains a line that blocks browsers that don't support modern standards.[5] Feel free to remove or modify this line at this time.

Now let's bring up a browser and point to http://localhost:3000/products. The resulting product listing might look something like the screenshot shown on page 79.

So we proudly show our customer her new product listing. She is pleased but notices that when she makes changes they aren't reflected on the screen until she refreshes the page. She asks if there's a way to make the changes appear automatically. We tell her that there is, and we do that next.

Iteration A3: Making the Page Update in Real Time

Real-time updates require WebSockets, JavaScript, and a bit of server code to make it all work. Fortunately, Rails has a feature called Hotwire that makes this easy.

---

5. https://api.rubyonrails.org/v7.2.1.2/classes/ActionController/AllowBrowser/ClassMethods.html#method-i-allow_browser

Iteration A3: Making the Page Update in Real Time • 79

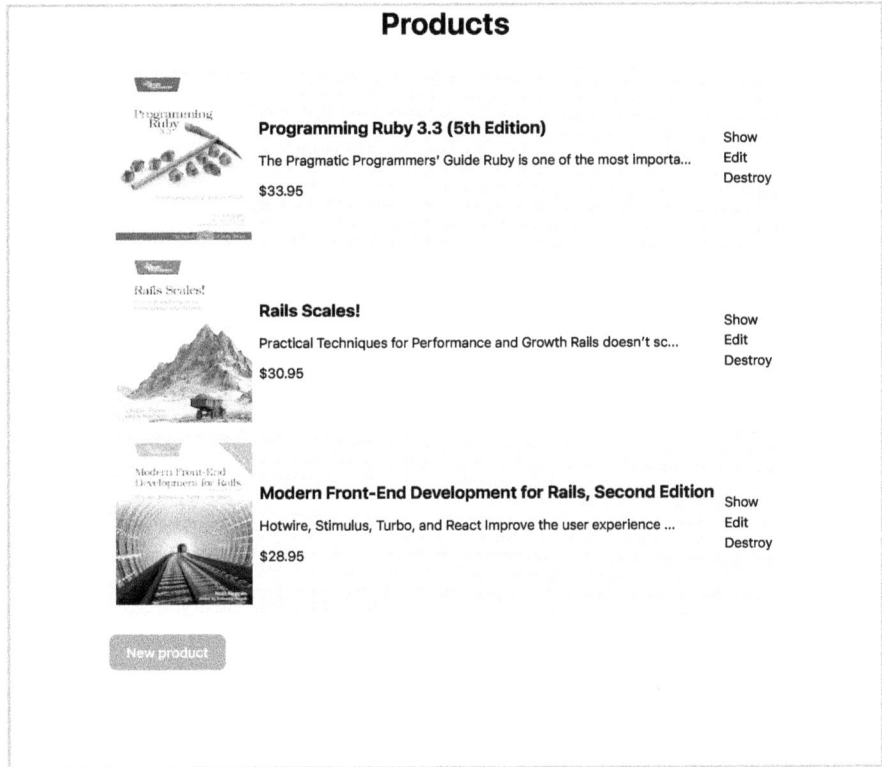

First, we add the following line to the app/models/product.rb file:

```
rails80/depot_a/app/models/product.rb
class Product < ApplicationRecord
  has_one_attached :image
➤ after_commit -> { broadcast_refresh_later_to "products" }
end
```

This line tells Rails to broadcast changes to the product model to any clients that are listening. We also need to add the following lines to the top of the app/views/products/index.html.erb file:

```
rails80/depot_a/app/views/products/index.html.erb
➤ <%= turbo_stream_from "products" %>
➤ <%= turbo_refreshes_with method: :morph, scroll: :preserve %>
```

The first line tells the browser to listen for changes to the product model and update the page when they occur. The second line tells the browser to apply the changes directly to the page without refreshing it and to preserve the scroll position.

This is some pretty advanced stuff, and there is a lot more to the story.

- after_commit() is an Active Record callback that's called after a record is saved to the database. We cover Active Record hooks in more detail starting with Chapter 7, Task B: Validation and Unit Testing, on page 85.

- Methods with names that end with _later are Active Job methods. Active Job is a framework for declaring jobs and making them run on a variety of queuing backends. We cover Active Job in more detail starting with Iteration H1: Sending Confirmation Emails, on page 189.

- Methods with names that start with turbo_ are part of the Turbo framework. Turbo is a set of tools that make it easy to build modern, reactive web applications. We cover Turbo in more detail starting with Iteration F2: Creating a Hotwired Cart, on page 150.

Now, when you make changes to the product listing, they should appear automatically on the page. With that, we've completed the styling of the product listing. Now it's time to create the storefront.

What We Just Did

In this chapter, we laid the groundwork for our store application:

- We created a development database.
- We installed Active Storage to handle file uploads.
- We used a migration to create and modify the schema in our development database.
- We created the products table and used the scaffold generator to write an application to maintain it.
- We updated a controller-specific view to show a list of products.
- We made the product listing update in real time.

What we've done didn't require much effort, and it got us up and running quickly. Databases are vital to this application but need not be scary. In fact, in many cases we can defer the selection of the database and get started using the default that Rails provides.

Getting the model right is more important at this stage. As you'll see, selection of data types doesn't always fully capture the *essence* of all the properties of the model, even in this small application, so that's what we'll tackle next.

> **What's with method: :delete?**
>
> You may have noticed that the Destroy link includes the method: :delete parameter. This parameter determines which method is called in the ProductsController class and also affects which HTTP method is used.
>
> Browsers use HTTP to talk with servers. HTTP defines a set of verbs that browsers can employ and defines when each can be used. A regular hyperlink, for example, uses an HTTP GET request. A GET request is defined by HTTP as a means of retrieving data and therefore isn't supposed to have any side effects. Using the method parameter in this way indicates that an HTTP DELETE method should be used for this hyperlink. Rails uses this information to determine which action in the controller to route this request to.
>
> Note that when used within a browser, Rails substitutes the HTTP POST method for PUT, PATCH, and DELETE methods and in the process tacks on an additional parameter so that the router can determine the original intent. Either way, the request isn't cached or triggered by web crawlers.

Playtime

Here's some stuff to try on your own:

- We created tables in our database using a migration. Try examining the tables directly by running bin/rails dbconsole. This will put you directly into the SQLite database that the app uses. Type .help and hit `Return` to see the commands you can run to examine the database. If you know SQL, you can execute SQL in here as well.

- If you're feeling frisky, you can experiment with rolling back the migration. Type the following:

    depot> **bin/rails db:rollback**

    Your schema will be transported back in time, and the products table will be gone. Calling bin/rails db:migrate again will re-create it. You'll also want to reload the seed data. More information can be found in Chapter 23, Migrations, on page 407.

- We made the product listing update in real time as the database changes. Hotwire Spark[6] updates views in real time as the application changes. Try running this:

    depot> **bundle add hotwire-spark --group development**

---

6. https://dev.37signals.com/announcing-hotwire-spark-live-reloading-for-rails/

Then restart your server and make a change to a controller or view. You should see the change reflected in your browser without needing to refresh the page.

- We mentioned version control in Version Control, on page 12, and now would be a great point at which to save your work. Should you happen to choose Git (highly recommended, by the way), you need to do a tiny bit of configuration first; all you need to do is provide your name and email address:

```
depot> git config --global --add user.name "Sam Ruby"
depot> git config --global --add user.email rubys@intertwingly.net
```

You can verify the configuration with the following command:

```
depot> git config --global --list
```

Rails also provides a file named .gitignore, which tells Git which files are not to be version-controlled:

rails80/depot_a/.gitignore
```
# Ignore bundler config.
/.bundle

# Ignore all environment files.
/.env*

# Ignore all logfiles and tempfiles.
/log/*
/tmp/*
!/log/.keep
!/tmp/.keep

# Ignore pidfiles, but keep the directory.
/tmp/pids/*
!/tmp/pids/
!/tmp/pids/.keep

# Ignore storage (uploaded files in development and any SQLite databases).
/storage/*
!/storage/.keep
/tmp/storage/*
!/tmp/storage/
!/tmp/storage/.keep

/public/assets

# Ignore master key for decrypting credentials and more.
/config/master.key

/app/assets/builds/*
!/app/assets/builds/.keep
```

Note that because this filename begins with a dot, Unix-based operating systems won't show it by default in directory listings. Use ls -a to see it.

At this point, you're fully configured. The only tasks that remain are to add all the files and commit them with a commit message (note that Rails has initialized our repository with git init already):

depot> **git add .**
depot> **git commit -m** *"Depot Scaffold"*

Being fully configured may not seem very exciting, but it does mean you're free to experiment. If you overwrite or delete a file that you didn't mean to, you can always get back to this point by issuing a single command:

depot> **git checkout .**

In this chapter, you'll see:
- Performing validation and error reporting
- Unit testing

CHAPTER 7

Task B: Validation and Unit Testing

At this point, we have an initial model for a product as well as a complete maintenance application for this data provided for us by Rails scaffolding. In this chapter, we're going to focus on making the model more bulletproof—as in, making sure that errors in the data provided never get committed to the database—before we proceed to other aspects of the Depot application in subsequent chapters.

Iteration B1: Validating!

While playing with the results of iteration A1, our client noticed something. If she entered an invalid price or forgot to set up a product description, the application happily accepted the form and added a line to the database. A missing description is embarrassing, and a price of $0.00 costs her actual money, so she asked that we add validation to the application. No product should be allowed in the database if it has an empty title or description field, an invalid URL for the image, or an invalid price.

So where do we put the validation? The model layer is the gatekeeper between the world of code and the database. Nothing to do with our application comes out of the database or gets stored into the database that doesn't first go through the model. This makes models an ideal place to put validations; it doesn't matter whether the data comes from a form or from some programmatic manipulation in our application. If a model checks it before writing to the database, the database will be protected from bad data.

Let's look at the source code of the model class (in app/models/product.rb):

```
class Product < ApplicationRecord
  has_one_attached :image
  after_commit -> { broadcast_refresh_later_to "products" }
end
```

Adding our validation should be fairly clean. Let's start by validating that the text fields all contain something before a row is written to the database. We do this by adding some code to the existing model:

```
validates :title, :description, :image, presence: true
```

The validates() method is the standard Rails validator. It checks one or more model fields against one or more conditions.

presence: true tells the validator to check that each of the named fields is present and that its contents aren't empty. The following screenshot shows what happens if we try to submit a new product with none of the fields filled in. Try it by visiting http://localhost:3000/products/new and submitting the form without entering any data. You'll see the errors summarized in a nice list at the top of the form. That's not bad for one line of code. You might also have noticed that after editing and saving the product.rb file, you didn't have to restart the application to test your changes. The same reloading that caused Rails to notice the earlier change to our schema also means it'll always use the latest version of our code.

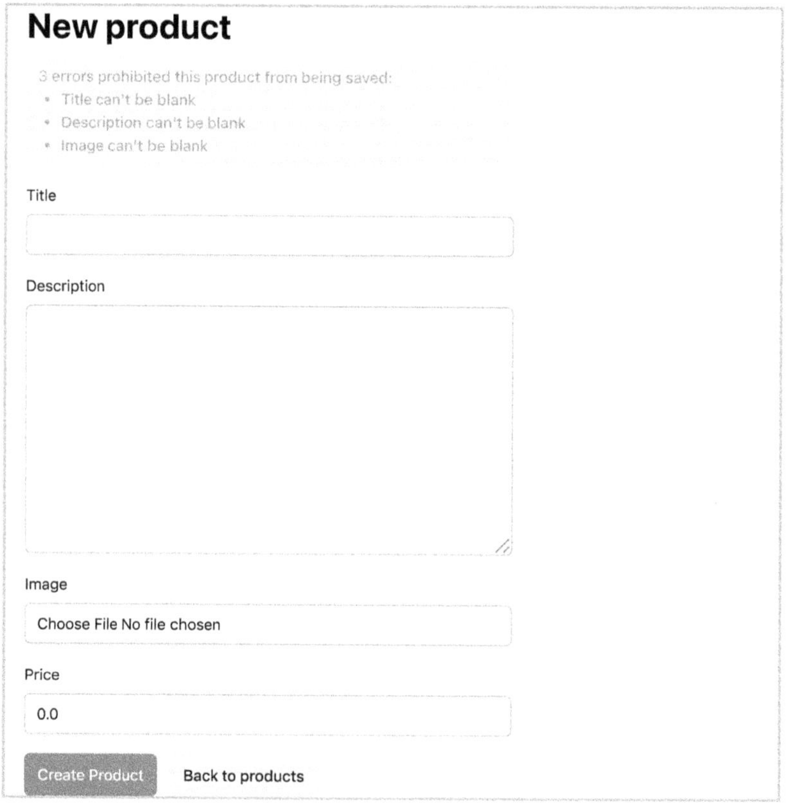

New product

3 errors prohibited this product from being saved:
- Title can't be blank
- Description can't be blank
- Image can't be blank

Title

Description

Image

Choose File No file chosen

Price

0.0

Create Product   Back to products

We'd also like to validate that the price is a valid, positive number. We'll use the delightfully named numericality() option to verify that the price is a valid number. We also pass the rather verbosely named :greater_than_or_equal_to option a value of 0.01:

```
validates :price, numericality: { greater_than_or_equal_to: 0.01 }
```

Now, if we add a product with an invalid price, the appropriate message will appear, as shown in the following screenshot.

Why test against one cent rather than zero? Well, it's possible to enter a number such as 0.001 into this field. Because the database stores just two digits after the decimal point, this would end up being zero in the database, even though it would pass the validation if we compared against zero. Checking that the number is at least one cent ensures that only correct values end up being stored.

We have two more items to validate. First, we want to make sure that each product has a unique title. One more line in the Product model will do this. The uniqueness validation will perform a check to ensure that no other row in the products table has the same title as the row we're about to save:

```
validates :title, uniqueness: true
```

Lastly, we need to validate that the image uploaded is of a supported type. We'll do this by calling validate() with the value :acceptable_image and by defining a corresponding acceptable_image method, which matches image.content_type against a list of supported types:

```ruby
validate :acceptable_image

def acceptable_image
  return unless image.attached?

  acceptable_types = [ "image/gif", "image/jpeg", "image/png" ]
  unless acceptable_types.include?(image.content_type)
    errors.add(:image, "must be a GIF, JPG or PNG image")
  end
end
```

Note that we previously specified the set of acceptable content types in the product form, but it's possible for that to be bypassed. This validation ensures that only the specified types are accepted.

So in a couple of minutes we've added validations that check the following:

- The title, description, and image URL fields aren't empty.
- The price is a valid number not less than $0.01.
- The title is unique among all products.
- The image is of the right content type.

Your updated Product model should look like this:

rails80/depot_b/app/models/product.rb
```ruby
class Product < ApplicationRecord
  has_one_attached :image
➤ after_commit -> { broadcast_refresh_later_to "products" }
  validates :title, :description, :image, presence: true
  validates :title, uniqueness: true
  validate :acceptable_image

  def acceptable_image
    return unless image.attached?

    acceptable_types = [ "image/gif", "image/jpeg", "image/png" ]
    unless acceptable_types.include?(image.content_type)
      errors.add(:image, "must be a GIF, JPG or PNG image")
    end
  end
  validates :price, numericality: { greater_than_or_equal_to: 0.01 }
end
```

Nearing the end of this cycle, we ask our customer to play with the application, and she's a lot happier. It took only a few minutes, but the simple act of adding validation has made the product maintenance pages seem a lot more solid.

Iteration B2: Unit Testing of Models

One of the joys of the Rails framework is that it has support for testing baked right in from the start of every project. As you've seen, from the moment you create a new application using the rails command, Rails starts generating a test infrastructure for you. Let's take a peek inside the models subdirectory to see what's already there:

depot> `ls test/models`
product_test.rb

product_test.rb is the file that Rails created to hold the unit tests for the model we created earlier with the generate script. This is a good start, but Rails can help us only so much. Let's see what kind of test goodies Rails generated inside test/models/product_test.rb when we generated that model:

rails80/depot_a/test/models/product_test.rb
```
require "test_helper"

class ProductTest < ActiveSupport::TestCase
  # test "the truth" do
  #   assert true
  # end
end
```

The generated ProductTest is a subclass of ActiveSupport::TestCase.[1] The fact that ActiveSupport::TestCase is a subclass of the MiniTest::Test class tells us that Rails generates tests based on the MiniTest[2] framework that comes preinstalled with Ruby. This is good news, because it means if we've already been testing our Ruby programs with MiniTest tests (and why wouldn't we be?), we can build on that knowledge to test Rails applications. If you're new to MiniTest, don't worry. We'll take it slow.

Inside this test case, Rails generated a single commented-out test called "the truth". The test...do syntax may seem surprising at first, but here ActiveSupport::TestCase is combining a class method, optional parentheses, and a block to make defining a test method the tiniest bit simpler for you. Sometimes it's the little things that make all the difference.

The assert line in this method is a test. It isn't much of one, though—all it does is test that true is true. Clearly, this is a placeholder, one that's intended to be replaced by your actual tests.

---

1. http://api.rubyonrails.org/classes/ActiveSupport/TestCase.html
2. http://docs.seattlerb.org/minitest/

A Real Unit Test

Let's get on to the business of testing validation. First, if we create a product with no attributes set, we'll expect it to be invalid and for an error to be associated with each field. We can use the model's errors() and invalid?() methods to see if it validates, and we can use the any?() method of the error list to see if an error is associated with a particular attribute.

Now that we know *what* to test, we need to know *how* to tell the test framework whether our code passes or fails. We do that using *assertions*. An assertion is a method call that tells the framework what we expect to be true. The simplest assertion is the assert() method, which expects its argument to be true. If it is, nothing special happens. However, if the argument to assert() is false, the assertion fails. The framework will output a message and will stop executing the test method containing the failure. In our case, we expect that an empty Product model won't pass validation, so we can express that expectation by asserting that it isn't valid:

```
assert product.invalid?
```

Replace the test the truth with the following code:

rails80/depot_b/test/models/product_test.rb
```
test "product attributes must not be empty" do
  product = Product.new
  assert product.invalid?
  assert product.errors[:title].any?
  assert product.errors[:description].any?
  assert product.errors[:price].any?
  assert product.errors[:image].any?
end
```

We can rerun just the unit tests by issuing the rails test:models command. When we do so, we now see the test execute successfully:

```
depot> bin/rails test:models
Rebuilding...

Done in 225ms.
Running 1 tests in a single process (parallelization threshold is 50)
Run options: --seed 44564

# Running:

.

Finished in 0.055882s, 17.8948 runs/s, 89.4742 assertions/s.
1 runs, 5 assertions, 0 failures, 0 errors, 0 skips
```

Sure enough, the validation kicked in, and all our assertions passed.

Clearly, at this point we can dig deeper and exercise individual validations. Let's look at three of the many possible tests.

First, we'll check that the validation of the price works the way we expect:

```ruby
rails80/depot_c/test/models/product_test.rb
test "product price must be positive" do
  product = Product.new(title:       "My Book Title",
                        description: "yyy")
  product.image.attach(io: File.open("test/fixtures/files/lorem.jpg"),
                       filename: "lorem.jpg", content_type: "image/jpeg")
  product.price = -1
  assert product.invalid?
  assert_equal [ "must be greater than or equal to 0.01" ],
    product.errors[:price]

  product.price = 0
  assert product.invalid?
  assert_equal [ "must be greater than or equal to 0.01" ],
    product.errors[:price]

  product.price = 1
  assert product.valid?
end
```

In this code, we create a new product and then try setting its price to -1, 0, and +1, validating the product each time. If our model is working, the first two should be invalid, and we verify that the error message associated with the price attribute is what we expect.

The last price is acceptable, so we assert that the model is now valid. (Some folks would put these three tests into three separate test methods—that's perfectly reasonable.)

Next, we test that we're validating that the image URL ends with one of .gif, .jpg, or .png:

```ruby
rails80/depot_c/test/models/product_test.rb
def new_product(filename, content_type)
  Product.new(
    title:       "My Book Title",
    description: "yyy",
    price:       1
  ).tap do |product|
    product.image.attach(
      io: File.open("db/images/#{filename}"), filename:, content_type:)
  end
end

test "image url" do
  product = new_product("lorem.jpg", "image/jpeg")
```

```
    assert product.valid?, "image/jpeg must be valid"
    product = new_product("logo.svg", "image/svg+xml")
    assert_not product.valid?, "image/svg+xml must be invalid"
end
```

You'll notice that we also added an extra parameter to our assert method calls. All of the testing assertions accept an optional trailing parameter containing a string. This will be written along with the error message if the assertion fails and can be useful for diagnosing what went wrong.

Finally, our model contains a validation that checks that all the product titles in the database are unique. To test this one, we need to store product data in the database.

One way to do this would be to have a test create a product, save it, then create another product with the same title and try to save it too. This would clearly work. But a much simpler way is to use Rails fixtures.

Test Fixtures

In the world of testing, a *fixture* is an environment in which you can run a test. If you're testing a circuit board, for example, you might mount it in a test fixture that provides it with the power and inputs needed to drive the function to be tested.

In the world of Rails, a test fixture is a specification of the initial contents of a model (or models) under test. If, for example, we want to ensure that our products table starts off with known data at the start of every unit test, we can specify those contents in a fixture, and Rails takes care of the rest.

You specify fixture data in files in the test/fixtures directory. These files contain test data in YAML format. Each fixture file contains the data for a single model. The name of the fixture file is significant: the base name of the file must match the name of a database table. Because we need some data for a Product model, which is stored in the products table, we'll add it to the file called products.yml.

Rails already created this fixture file when we first created the model:

```
rails80/depot_a/test/fixtures/products.yml
# Read about fixtures at
# https://api.rubyonrails.org/classes/ActiveRecord/FixtureSet.html

one:
  title: MyString
  description: MyText
  price: 9.99
```

```
two:
  title: MyString
  description: MyText
  price: 9.99
```

The fixture file contains an entry for each row that we want to insert into the database. Each row is given a name. In the case of the Rails-generated fixture, the rows are named one and two. This name has no significance as far as the database is concerned—it isn't inserted into the row data. Instead, as you'll see shortly, the name gives us a convenient way to reference test data inside our test code. They also are the names used in the generated integration tests, so for now, we'll leave them alone.

> **David says:**
> ### Picking Good Fixture Names
>
> As with the names of variables in general, you want to keep the names of fixtures as self-explanatory as possible. This increases the readability of the tests when you're asserting that product(:valid_order_for_fred) is indeed Fred's valid order. It also makes it a lot easier to remember which fixture you're supposed to test against, without having to look up p1 or order4. The more fixtures you get, the more important it is to pick good fixture names. So starting early keeps you happy later.
>
> But what do we do with fixtures that can't easily get a self-explanatory name like valid_order_for_fred? Pick natural names that you have an easier time associating to a role. For example, instead of using order1, use christmas_order. Instead of customer1, use fred. Once you get into the habit of natural names, you'll soon be weaving a nice little story about how fred is paying for his christmas_order with his invalid_credit_card first, then paying with his valid_credit_card, and finally choosing to ship it all off to aunt_mary.
>
> Association-based stories are key to remembering large worlds of fixtures with ease.

Inside each entry you can see an indented list of name-value pairs. As in your config/database.yml, you must use spaces, not tabs, at the start of each of the data lines, and all the lines for a row must have the same indentation. Be careful as you make changes, because you need to make sure the names of the columns are correct in each entry; a mismatch with the database column names can cause a hard-to-track-down exception.

This data is used in tests. In fact, if you rerun bin/rails test now you'll see a number of errors, including the following error:

```
Error:
ProductsControllerTest#test_should_get_index:
ActionView::Template::Error: The asset "MyString" is not present in
the asset pipeline.
```

The reason for the failure is that we recently added an image_tag to the product index page and Rails can't find an image by the name MyString (remember that image_tag() is a Rails helper method that produces an HTML <img> element). Let's correct that error and, while we're here, add some more data to the fixture file with something we can use to test our Product model:

```
rails80/depot_c/test/fixtures/products.yml
# Read about fixtures at
# https://api.rubyonrails.org/classes/ActiveRecord/FixtureSet.html
one:
  title: MyString
  description: MyText
  price: 9.99

two:
  title: MyString
  description: MyText
  price: 9.99

➤ pragprog:
➤   title:       The Pragmatic Programmer
➤   description:
➤     Your Journey To Mastery, 20th Anniversary Edition (2nd Edition)
➤   price:       39.99
```

Note that the attached images aren't defined here. We'll need to add them. We start by defining "blobs" for the content of the images.

```
rails80/depot_c/test/fixtures/active_storage/blobs.yml
blob_one: <%= ActiveStorage::FixtureSet.blob filename: 'lorem.jpg' %>
blob_two: <%= ActiveStorage::FixtureSet.blob filename: 'rails.png' %>

blob_pragprog: <%= ActiveStorage::FixtureSet.blob filename: 'lorem.jpg' %>
```

Now we attach these blobs to the products in the fixture file.

```
rails80/depot_c/test/fixtures/active_storage/attachments.yml
one:
  name: image
  record: one (Product)
  blob: blob_one

two:
  name: image
  record: two (Product)
  blob: blob_two

➤ pragprog:
➤   name: image
➤   record: pragprog (Product)
➤   blob: blob_pragprog
```

Now that we have a fixture file, we want Rails to load the test data into the products table when we run the unit test. And, in fact, Rails is already doing this (convention over configuration for the win!), but you can control which fixtures to load by specifying the following line in test/models/product_test.rb:

```
class ProductTest < ActiveSupport::TestCase
  fixtures :products
  #...
end
```

The fixtures() directive loads the fixture data corresponding to the given model name into the corresponding database table before each test method in the test case is run. The name of the fixture file determines the table that's loaded, so using :products will cause the products.yml fixture file to be used.

Let's say that again another way. In the case of our ProductTest class, adding the fixtures directive means that the products table will be emptied out and then populated with the three rows defined in the fixture before each test method is run.

Note that most of the scaffolding that Rails generates doesn't contain calls to the fixtures method. That's because the default for tests is to load *all* fixtures before running the test. Because that default is generally the one you want, there usually isn't any need to change it. Once again, conventions are used to eliminate the need for unnecessary configuration.

So far, we've been doing all our work in the development database. Now that we're running tests, though, Rails needs to use a test database. If you look in the database.yml file in the config directory, you'll notice Rails actually created a configuration for three separate databases.

- storage/development.sqlite3 will be our development database. All of our programming work will be done here.
- storage/test.sqlite3 is a test database.
- storate/production.sqlite3 is the production database. Our application would use this when we put it online; but using sqlite3 in production isn't recommended, so when we get to deployment, we'll switch this to a more robust database.

Each test method gets a freshly initialized table in the test database, loaded from the fixtures we provide. This is automatically done by the bin/rails test command but can be done separately via bin/rails db:test:prepare.

Using Fixture Data

Now that you know how to get fixture data into the database, we need to find ways of using it in our tests.

Clearly, one way would be to use the finder methods in the model to read the data. However, Rails makes it easier than that. For each fixture it loads into a test, Rails defines a method with the same name as the fixture. You can use this method to access preloaded model objects containing the fixture data: simply pass it the name of the row as defined in the YAML fixture file, and it'll return a model object containing that row's data.

In the case of our product data, calling products(:pragprog) returns a Product model containing the data we defined in the fixture. Let's use that to test the validation of unique product titles:

rails80/depot_c/test/models/product_test.rb
```
test "product is not valid without a unique title" do
  product = Product.new(title:       products(:pragprog).title,
                        description: "yyy",
                        price:       1)
  product.image.attach(io: File.open("test/fixtures/files/lorem.jpg"),
                       filename: "lorem.jpg", content_type: "image/jpeg")

  assert product.invalid?
  assert_equal [ "has already been taken" ], product.errors[:title]
end
```

The test assumes that the database already includes a row for the Ruby book. It gets the title of that existing row using this:

```
products(:pragprog).title
```

It then creates a new Product model, setting its title to that existing title. It asserts that attempting to save this model fails and that the title attribute has the correct error associated with it.

If you want to avoid using a hardcoded string for the Active Record error, you can compare the response against its built-in error message table:

rails80/depot_c/test/models/product_test.rb
```
test "product is not valid without a unique title - i18n" do
  product = Product.new(title:       products(:pragprog).title,
                        description: "yyy",
                        price:       1)
  product.image.attach(io: File.open("test/fixtures/files/lorem.jpg"),
                       filename: "lorem.jpg", content_type: "image/jpeg")
```

```
    assert product.invalid?
    assert_equal [ I18n.translate("errors.messages.taken") ],
                 product.errors[:title]
end
```

We'll cover the I18n functions in Chapter 15, Task J: Internationalization, on page 225.

Before we move on, we once again try our tests:

```
$ bin/rails test
```

This time we see two remaining failures, both in test/controllers/products_controllertest.rb: one in should create product and the other in should update product. Clearly, something we did caused something to do with the creation and update of products to fail. Since we just added validations on how products are created or updated, it's likely this is the source of the problem, and our test is out-of-date.

The specifics of the problem might not be obvious from the test failure message, but the failure for should create product gives us a clue: "Product.count didn't change by 1." Since we just added validations, it seems likely that our attempts to create a product in the test are creating an invalid product, which we can't save to the database.

Let's verify this assumption by adding a call to puts() in the controller's create() method:

```
def create
  @product = Product.new(product_params)

  respond_to do |format|
    if @product.save
      format.html { redirect_to @product,
        notice: "Product was successfully created." }
      format.json { render :show, status: :created,
        location: @product }
    else
➤     puts @product.errors.full_messages
      format.html { render :new,
        status: :unprocessable_entity }
      format.json { render json: @product.errors,
        status: :unprocessable_entity }
    end
  end
end
```

If we rerun just the test for creating a new product, we'll see the problem:

```
> bin/rails test test/controllers/products_controller_test.rb:19
# Running:
```

```
Title has already been taken
F

Failure:
ProductsControllerTest#test_should_create_product [«path to test»]
"Product.count" didn't change by 1.
Expected: 3
  Actual: 2

bin/rails test test/controllers/products_controller_test.rb:18

Finished in 0.427810s, 2.3375 runs/s, 2.3375 assertions/s.
1 runs, 1 assertions, 1 failures, 0 errors, 0 skips
```

Our puts() is printing the validation error, which in this case is "Title has already been taken." In other words, we're trying to create a product whose title already exists. Instead, let's create a random book title and use that instead of the value coming out of the test fixture. First, we'll create a random title in the setup() block:

rails80/depot_b/test/controllers/products_controller_test.rb
```ruby
require "test_helper"

class ProductsControllerTest < ActionDispatch::IntegrationTest
  setup do
    @product = products(:one)
➤   @title = "The Great Book #{rand(1000)}"
  end
```

Next, we'll use that instead of the default @product.title the Rails generator put into the test. The actual change is highlighted (the use of @title), but the code had to be reformatted to fit the space, so this will look a bit different for you:

rails80/depot_b/test/controllers/products_controller_test.rb
```ruby
test "should create product" do
  assert_difference("Product.count") do
    post products_url, params: {
      product: {
        description: @product.description,
➤       image: file_fixture_upload("lorem.jpg", "image/jpeg"),
        price: @product.price,
➤       title: @title
      }
    }
  end

  assert_redirected_to product_url(Product.last)
end
```

rails80/depot_b/test/controllers/products_controller_test.rb
```
test "should update product" do
    patch product_url(@product), params: {
      product: {
        description: @product.description,
➤       image: file_fixture_upload("lorem.jpg", "image/jpeg"),
        price: @product.price,
➤       title: @title
      }
    }
    assert_redirected_to product_url(@product)
end
```

After making these changes, we rerun the tests, and they report that all is well.

Now we can feel confident that our validation code not only works but will continue to work. Our product now has a model, a set of views, a controller, and a set of unit tests. It'll serve as a good foundation on which to build the rest of the application.

One Final Change

We originally stored product images in the db/images directory, but now we have our test fixtures, let's create a new place to store them: text/fixtures/files. Move the images over, and update the paths in the new_product method in test/models/products.rb.

What We Just Did

In a few dozen lines of code, we augmented the generated code with validation:

- We ensured that required fields are present.
- We ensured that price fields are numeric and at least one cent.
- We ensured that titles are unique.
- We ensured that images have a supported content type.
- We updated the unit tests that Rails provided, both to conform to the constraints we've imposed on the model and to verify the new code we added.

We show this to our customer, and although she agrees that this is something an administrator could use, she says that it certainly isn't anything that she would feel comfortable turning loose on her customers. Clearly, in the next iteration we're going to have to focus a bit on the user interface.

Playtime

Here's some stuff to try on your own:

- If you're using Git, now is a good time to commit your work. You can first see which files we changed by using the git status command:

```
depot> git status
# On branch master
# Changes not staged for commit:
#   (use "git add <file>..." to update what will be committed)
#   (use "git checkout -- <file>..." to discard changes
#    in working directory)
#
# modified:   app/models/product.rb
# modified:   test/fixtures/products.yml
# modified:   test/controllers/products_controller_test.rb
# modified:   test/models/product_test.rb
# no changes added to commit (use "git add" and/or "git commit -a")
```

Since we modified only some existing files and didn't add any new ones, you can combine the git add and git commit commands and simply issue a single git commit command with the -a option:

```
depot> git commit -a -m 'Validation!'
```

With this done, you can play with abandon, secure in the knowledge that you can return to this state at any time by using a single git checkout . command.

- The :length validation option checks the length of a model attribute. Add validation to the Product model to check that the title is at least ten characters.

- Change the error message associated with one of your validations.

In this chapter, you'll see:
- Writing our own views
- Using layouts to decorate pages
- Integrating CSS
- Using helpers
- Writing functional tests

CHAPTER 8

Task C: Catalog Display

All in all, it's been a successful set of iterations. We gathered the initial requirements from our customer, documented a basic flow, worked out a first pass at the data we'll need, and put together the management page for the Depot application's products. It hasn't taken many lines of code, and we even have a small but growing test suite.

Thus emboldened, it's on to our next task. We chatted about priorities with our customer, and she said she'd like to start seeing what the application looks like from the buyer's point of view. Our next task is to create a catalog display.

This also makes a lot of sense from our point of view. Once we have the products safely tucked into the database, it should be fairly straightforward to display them. It also gives us a basis from which to develop the shopping cart portion of the code later.

We should also be able to draw on the work we just did in the product management task. The catalog display is really just a glorified product listing.

Finally, we'll also need to complement our unit tests for the model with some functional tests for the controller.

Iteration C1: Creating the Catalog Listing

We've already created the products controller, used by the seller to administer the Depot application. Now it's time to create a second controller, one that interacts with the paying customers. Let's call it Store:

```
depot> bin/rails generate controller Store index
    create  app/controllers/store_controller.rb
     route  get 'store/index'
    invoke  tailwindcss
    create    app/views/store
    create    app/views/store/index.html.erb
```

```
invoke  test_unit
create    test/controllers/store_controller_test.rb
invoke  helper
create    app/helpers/store_helper.rb
invoke  test_unit
```

As in the previous chapter, where we used the generate utility to create a controller and associated scaffolding to administer the products, here we've asked it to create a controller (the StoreController class in the store_controller.rb file) containing a single action method, index().

While everything is already set up for this action to be accessed via http://localhost:3000/store/index (feel free to try it!), we can do better. Let's simplify things and make this the root URL for the website. We do this by editing config/routes.rb:

rails80/depot_d/config/routes.rb
```
Rails.application.routes.draw do
➤  root "store#index", as: "store_index"
  resources :products
  # Define your application routes per the DSL in
  # https://guides.rubyonrails.org/routing.html

  # Reveal health status on /up that returns 200 if the app boots with no
  # exceptions, otherwise 500.
  # Can be used by load balancers and uptime monitors to verify that the
  # app is live.
  get "up" => "rails/health#show", as: :rails_health_check

  # Render dynamic PWA files from app/views/pwa/*
  # (remember to link manifest in application.html.erb)
  # get "manifest" => "rails/pwa#manifest", as: :pwa_manifest
  # get "service-worker" => "rails/pwa#service_worker", as: :pwa_service_worker

  # Defines the root path route ("/")
  # root "posts#index"
end
```

We've replaced the get 'store/index' line with a call to define a root path, and in the process we added an as: 'store_index' option. The latter tells Rails to create store_index_path and store_index_url accessor methods, enabling existing code—and tests!—to continue to work correctly. Let's try it. Point a browser at http://localhost:3000/, and up pops our web page. See the following screenshot.

> **Store#index**
> Find me in app/views/store/index.html.erb

It might not make us rich, but at least we know everything is wired together correctly. It even tells us where to find the template file that draws this page.

Let's start by displaying a list of all the products in our database. We know that eventually we'll have to be more sophisticated, breaking them into categories, but this'll get us going.

We need to get the list of products out of the database and make it available to the code in the view that'll display the table. This means we have to change the index() method in store_controller.rb. We want to program at a decent level of abstraction, so let's assume we can ask the model for a list of the products:

rails80/depot_d/app/controllers/store_controller.rb
```ruby
class StoreController < ApplicationController
  def index
    @products = Product.order(:title)
  end
end
```

We asked our customer if she had a preference regarding the order things should be listed in, and we jointly decided to see what happens if we display the products in alphabetical order. We do this by adding an order(:title) call to the Product model.

Now we need to write our view template. To do this, edit the index.html.erb file in app/views/store. (Remember that the path name to the view is built from the name of the controller [store] and the name of the action [index]. The .html.erb part signifies an ERB template that produces an HTML result.)

rails80/depot_d/app/views/store/index.html.erb
```erb
<div class="w-full">
<% if notice.present? %>
  <p class="py-2 px-3 bg-green-50 mb--5 text-green-500 font-medium rounded-lg
            inline-block" id="notice">
    <%= notice %>
  </p>
<% end %>
<h1 class="font-bold text-xl mb-6 pb--2 border-b-2">
  Your Pragmatic Catalog
</h1>
<ul>
  <% @products.each do |product| %>
    <li class='flex mb-6'>
      <%= image_tag(product.image,
          class: 'object-contain w-40 h-48 shadow mr-6') %>
      <div>
        <h2 class="font-bold text-lg mb-3"><%= product.title %></h2>
        <p>
          <%= sanitize(product.description) %>
        </p>
```

```
        <div class="mt-3">
          <%= product.price %>
        </div>
      </div>
    </li>
  <% end %>
</ul>
</div>
```

Note the use of the sanitize() method for the description. This allows us to safely[1] add HTML stylings to make the descriptions more interesting for our customers.

We also used the image_tag() helper method. This generates an HTML <img> tag using its argument as the image source. We'll need to place this image in the app/assets/images directory. You've already downloaded it, so you can copy it there now.

depot> `cp db/images/logo.svg app/assets/images/`

A page refresh brings up the display shown in the following screenshot. It's still pretty basic, and it seems to be missing something. The customer happens to be walking by as we ponder this, and she points out that she'd also like to see a decent-looking banner and sidebar on public-facing pages.

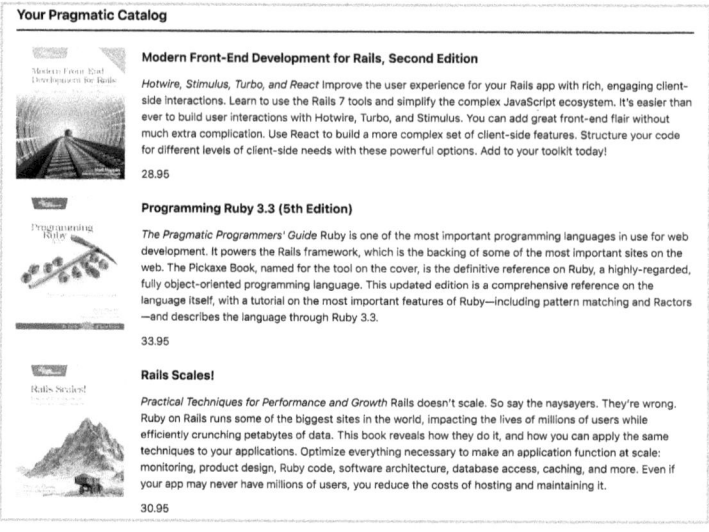

At this point in the real world, we'd probably want to call in the design folks. But Pragmatic Web Designer is off getting inspiration on a beach somewhere and won't be back until later in the year, so let's put a placeholder in for now. It's time for another iteration.

---

1. https://owasp.org/www-community/attacks/xss/

Iteration C2: Adding a Page Layout

The pages in a typical website often share a similar layout; the designer will have created a standard template that's used when content is placed. Our job is to modify this page to add decoration to each of the store pages.

If you look at the .html.erb files we've created so far, you won't find any reference to style sheets. You won't even find the HTML <head> section where such references would normally live. Instead, Rails keeps a separate file that's used to create a standard page environment for the entire application. This file, called application.html.erb, is a Rails layout and lives in the layouts directory: we can change the look and feel of the entire site by editing this one file. This makes us feel better about putting a placeholder page layout in for now; we can update it when the designer eventually returns from the islands.

Let's update this file to define a banner and a sidebar:

```erb
rails80/depot_e/app/views/layouts/application.html.erb
<!DOCTYPE html>
<html>
  <head>
➤   <title><%= content_for(:title) || "Pragprog Books Online Store" %></title>
      <meta name="viewport" content="width=device-width,initial-scale=1">
      <meta name="apple-mobile-web-app-capable" content="yes">
      <meta name="mobile-web-app-capable" content="yes">
      <%= csrf_meta_tags %>
      <%= csp_meta_tag %>

      <%= yield :head %>

      <%# Enable PWA manifest for installable apps (make sure to enable in
          config/routes.rb too!) %>
      <%#= tag.link rel: "manifest", href: pwa_manifest_path(format: :json) %>

      <link rel="icon" href="/icon.png" type="image/png">
      <link rel="icon" href="/icon.svg" type="image/svg+xml">
      <link rel="apple-touch-icon" href="/icon.png">

      <%# Includes all stylesheet files in app/assets/stylesheets %>
      <%= stylesheet_link_tag :app, "data-turbo-track": "reload" %>
      <%= javascript_importmap_tags %>
  </head>

  <body>
➤   <header class="bg-green-700">
➤     <%= image_tag 'logo.svg', alt: 'The Pragmatic Bookshelf' %>
➤     <h1><%= @page_title %></h1>
➤   </header>
➤
➤   <section class="flex">
```

```
      <nav class="bg-green-900 p-6">
        <ul class="text-gray-300 leading-8">
          <li><a href="/">Home</a></li>
          <li><a href="/questions">Questions</a></li>
          <li><a href="/news">News</a></li>
          <li><a href="/contact">Contact</a></li>
        </ul>
      </nav>

      <main class="container mx-auto mt-4 px-5 flex">
        <%= yield %>
      </main>
    </section>
  </body>
</html>
```

Apart from the usual HTML gubbins, this layout has a number of Rails-specific items. The Rails stylesheet_link_tag() helper method generates a <link> tag to both Tailwind and our application's style sheets and specifies an option to enable Turbo,[2] which transparently works behind the scenes to speed up page changes within an application.

Finally, the csrf_meta_tags() and csp_meta_tag() methods set up all the behind-the-scenes data needed to prevent cross-site request forgery attacks, which will be important once we add forms in Chapter 12, Task G: Check Out!, on page 165.

Inside the body, we set the page heading to the value in the @page_title instance variable. By default, this is blank, meaning there won't be an H1 rendered, but any controller that sets the variable @page_title can override this. The real magic, however, takes place when we invoke yield. This causes Rails to substitute in the page-specific content—the stuff generated by the view invoked by this request. Here, this'll be the catalog page generated by index.html.erb.

The page design is fairly minimal, though we've added a lot of padding, margins, and other speccing directives to ensure a decent layout for the side nav and main content. Some of the sizes we've used might seem strange (for example, mt-4 and px-5), but everything should work out. Anytime we need padding, margin, or any other size, we'll use one of a few hand-picked sizes that ensure our layout is always decent.

Refresh the page, and the browser window looks something like the screenshot shown on page 107. It won't win any design awards, but it'll show our customer roughly what the final page will look like.

---

2. https://turbo.hotwired.dev/

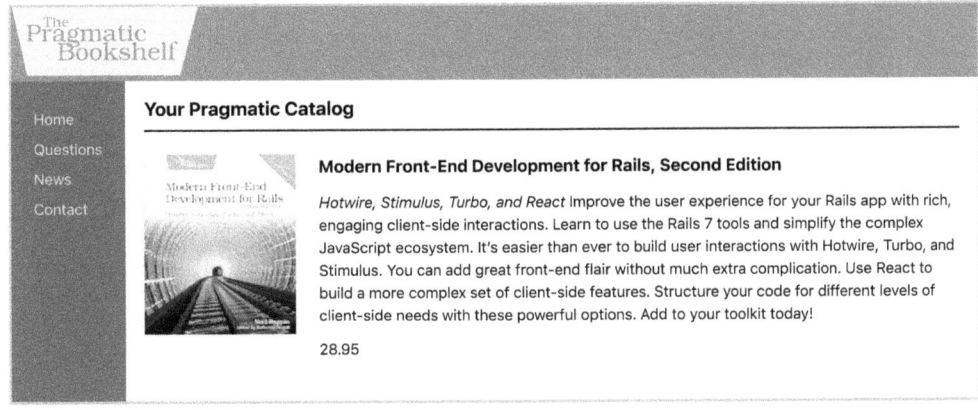

Looking at this page, we spot a minor problem with how prices are displayed. The database stores the price as a number, but we'd like to show it as dollars and cents. A price of 12.34 should be shown as $12.34, and 13 should display as $13.00. We'll tackle that next.

Iteration C3: Using a Helper to Format the Price

Ruby provides a sprintf() function that can be used to format prices. We could place logic that makes use of this function directly in the view. For example, we could say this:

```
<%= sprintf("$%0.02f", product.price) %>
```

That would work, but it embeds knowledge of currency formatting into the view. If we display prices of products in several places and want to internationalize the application later, this would be a maintenance problem.

Instead, let's use a helper method to format the price as a currency. Rails has an appropriate one built in, called number_to_currency().

Using our helper in the view is just a matter of invoking it as a regular method; in the index template, this is the code we start with:

```
<%= product.price %>
```

We can change it to the following:

rails80/depot_e/app/views/store/index.html.erb
```
<%= number_to_currency(product.price) %>
```

When we refresh, we see a nicely formatted price, as shown in the screenshot on page 108.

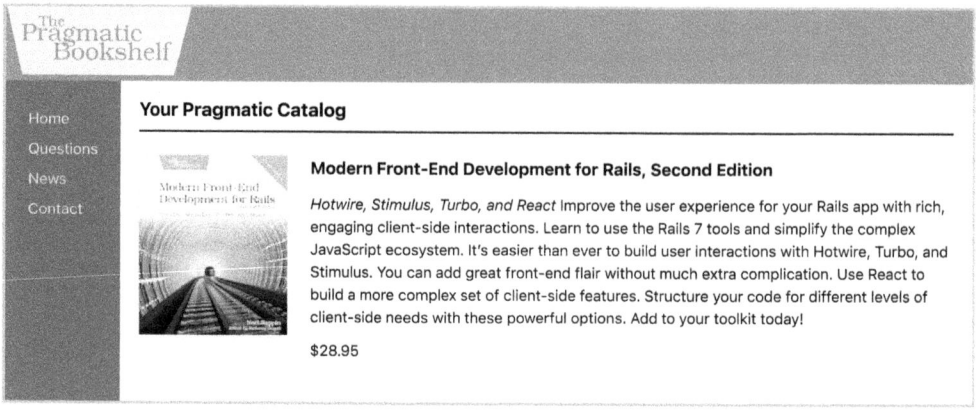

Although it looks nice enough, we're starting to get a nagging feeling that we really should be running and writing tests for all this new functionality, particularly after our experience of adding logic to our model.

Iteration C4: Functional Testing of Controllers

Now for the moment of truth. Before we focus on writing new tests, we need to determine if we've broken anything. Remembering our experience after we added validation logic to our model, with some trepidation we run our tests again:

depot> **bin/rails test**

This time, all is well. We added a lot, but we didn't break anything. That's a relief, but our work isn't done yet; we still need tests for what we just added.

The unit testing of models that we did previously seemed straightforward enough. We called a method and compared what it returned against what we expected it to return. But now we're dealing with a server that processes requests and a user viewing responses in a browser. What we need is *functional* tests that verify that the model, view, and controller work well together. Never fear—Rails has you covered.

First, let's take a look at what Rails generated for us:

```
rails80/depot_d/test/controllers/store_controller_test.rb
require "test_helper"

class StoreControllerTest < ActionDispatch::IntegrationTest
  test "should get index" do
    get store_index_url
    assert_response :success
  end
end
```

The should get index test gets the index and asserts that a successful response is expected. That certainly seems straightforward enough. That's a reasonable beginning, but we also want to verify that the response contains our layout, our product information, and our number formatting. Let's see what that looks like in code:

rails80/depot_e/test/controllers/store_controller_test.rb
```ruby
require "test_helper"

class StoreControllerTest < ActionDispatch::IntegrationTest
  test "should get index" do
    get store_index_url
    assert_response :success
➤   assert_select "nav a", minimum: 4
➤   assert_select "main ul li", 3
➤   assert_select "h2", "The Pragmatic Programmer"
➤   assert_select "div", /\$[,\d]+\.\d\d/
  end
end
```

The four lines we added take a look *into* the HTML that's returned, using CSS selector notation. As a refresher, selectors that start with a number sign (#) match on id attributes; selectors that start with a dot (.) match on class attributes; and selectors that contain no prefix match on element names.

So the first select test looks for an element named a that's contained in a nav element. This test verifies that a minimum of four such elements is present. Pretty powerful stuff, assert_select(), eh?

The next three lines verify that all of our products are displayed. The first verifies that there are three li elements inside a ul, which is itself inside the main element. The next line verifies that there's an h2 element with the title of the Ruby book that we'd entered previously. The fourth line verifies that the price is formatted correctly. These assertions are based on the test data that we put inside our fixtures:

rails80/depot_e/test/fixtures/products.yml
```yaml
# Read about fixtures at
# https://api.rubyonrails.org/classes/ActiveRecord/FixtureSet.html

one:
  title: MyString
  description: MyText
  price: 9.99

two:
  title: MyString
  description: MyText
  price: 9.99
```

```
pragprog:
  title:        The Pragmatic Programmer
  description:
    Your Journey To Mastery, 20th Anniversary Edition (2nd Edition)
  price:        39.99
```

Maybe you noticed that the type of test that assert_select() performs varies based on the type of the second parameter. If it's a number, it's treated as a quantity. If it's a string, it's treated as an expected result. Another useful type of test is a regular expression, which is what we use in our final assertion. We verify that there's a price that has a value that contains a dollar sign followed by any number (but at least one), commas, or digits; followed by a decimal point; followed by two digits.

One final point before we move on: both validation and functional tests will test the behavior of controllers only; they won't retroactively affect any objects that already exist in the database or in fixtures. In the previous example, two products contain the same title. Such data will cause no problems and will go undetected up to the point when such records are modified and saved.

We've touched on only a few things that assert_select() can do. More information can be found in the online documentation.[3]

That's a lot of verification in a few lines of code. We can see that it works by rerunning just the functional tests (after all, that's all we changed):

depot> `bin/rails test:controllers`

Now, not only do we have something recognizable as a storefront, but we also have tests that ensure that all of the pieces—the model, view, and controller—are all working together to produce the desired result. Although this sounds like a lot, with Rails it wasn't much at all. In fact, it was mostly HTML and CSS and not much in the way of code or tests. Before moving on, let's make sure that it'll stand up to the onslaught of customers we're expecting.

Iteration C5: Caching of Partial Results

If everything goes as planned, this page will definitely be a high-traffic area for the site. To respond to requests for this page, we'd need to fetch every product from the database and render each one. We can do better than that. After all, the catalog doesn't change that often, so there's no need to start from scratch on each request.

So we can see what we're doing, we're first going to modify the configuration for the development environment to turn on caching. To make this easy, Rails

---

3. https://github.com/rails/rails-dom-testing

provides a handy command to toggle caching on and off in the development environment:

depot> `bin/rails dev:cache`

Note that this command will cause your server to automatically restart.

Next we need to plan our attack. Thinking about it, we only need to rerender things if a product changed, and even then we need to render only the products that actually changed. So we need to make two small changes to our template.

First, we mark the sections of our template that we need to update if any product changes, and then inside that section we mark the subsection that we need in order to update any specific product that changed:

rails80/depot_e/app/views/store/index.html.erb
```erb
<div class="w-full">
<% if notice.present? %>
  <p class="py-2 px-3 bg-green-50 mb-5 text-green-500 font-medium rounded-lg
           inline-block" id="notice">
    <%= notice %>
  </p>
<% end %>

<h1 class="font-bold text-xl mb-6 pb-2 border-b-2">
  Your Pragmatic Catalog
</h1>

<ul>
➤   <% cache @products do %>
      <% @products.each do |product| %>
➤       <% cache product do %>
          <li class='flex mb-6'>
            <%= image_tag(product.image,
              class: 'object-contain w-40 h-48 shadow mr-6') %>

            <div>
              <h2 class="font-bold text-lg mb-3"><%= product.title %></h2>

              <p>
                <%= sanitize(product.description) %>
              </p>

              <div class="mt-3">
                <%= number_to_currency(product.price) %>
              </div>
            </div>
          </li>
➤       <% end %>
      <% end %>
➤   <% end %>
</ul>
</div>
```

In addition to bracketing the sections, we identify the data to associate with each: the complete set of products for the overall store and the individual product we're rendering with the entry. Whenever the specified data changes, the section will be rerendered.

Bracketed sections can be nested to arbitrary depth, which is why those in the Rails community have come to refer to this as "Russian doll" caching.[4]

With this, we're done! Rails takes care of all of the rest, including managing the storage and deciding when to invalidate old entries. If you're interested, you can turn all sorts of knobs and make choices as to which backing store to use for the cache. It's nothing you need to worry about now, but it might be worth bookmarking the overview page of Caching with Rails in the Ruby on Rails Guides.[5]

As far as verifying that this works is concerned, you're going to get some insight into the work the server is doing behind the scenes. Go back to your server window and watch what happens when you refresh the page. The first time you load the page, you should see some SQL that's loading the products like `Product Load (0.2ms) SELECT "products".* FROM "products" ORDER BY "products"."title" ASC`. When you refresh the page again, it will still work, but you *won't* see that SQL run. You *should* see some SQL that Rails runs to check if its cache is outdated, like so: `SELECT COUNT(*) AS "size", MAX("products"."updated_at") AS timestamp FROM "products"`.

If you still aren't convinced, you can check your log/development.log file. In there you should see log messages that look like this:

```
Read  fragment views/store/index:f6d3d1696e62859f692c4ae9e7980d0f/…
Write fragment views/store/index:f6d3d1696e62859f692c4ae9e7980d0f/…
Read  fragment views/store/index:f6d3d1696e62859f692c4ae9e7980d0f/…
Write fragment views/store/index:f6d3d1696e62859f692c4ae9e7980d0f/…
Read  fragment views/store/index:f6d3d1696e62859f692c4ae9e7980d0f/…
Write fragment views/store/index:f6d3d1696e62859f692c4ae9e7980d0f/…
Read  fragment views/products/2-20170611204944059695/cb43383298…
```

Once you're satisfied that caching is working, turn caching off in development so that further changes to the template will always be visible immediately:

depot> `bin/rails dev:cache`

Once again, wait for the server to restart, and verify that changes to the template show up as quickly as you save them.

---

4. http://37signals.com/svn/posts/3113-how-key-based-cache-expiration-works
5. http://guides.rubyonrails.org/caching_with_rails.html

What We Just Did

We put together the basis of the store's catalog display. The steps were as follows:

1. Create a new controller to handle customer-centric interactions.

2. Implement the default index() action.

3. Add a call to the order() method within the Store controller to control the order in which the items on the website are listed.

4. Implement a view (a .html.erb file) and a layout to contain it (another .html.erb file).

5. Use a helper to format prices the way we want.

6. Make use of a CSS style sheet.

7. Write functional tests for our controller.

8. Implement fragment caching for portions of the page.

It's time to check it all in and move on to the next task—namely, making a shopping cart!

Playtime

Here's some stuff to try on your own:

- Add a date and time to the sidebar. It doesn't have to update; just show the value at the time the page was displayed.

- Experiment with setting various number_to_currency helper method options, and see the effect on your catalog listing.

- Write some functional tests for the product management application using assert_select. The tests will need to be placed into the test/controllers/products_controller_test.rb file.

- A reminder: the end of an iteration is a good time to save your work using Git. If you've been following along, you have the basics you need at this point.

In this chapter, you'll see:
- Sessions and session management
- Adding relationships among models
- Adding a button to add a product to a cart

CHAPTER 9

Task D: Cart Creation

Now that we have the ability to display a catalog containing all our wonderful products, it would be nice to be able to sell them. Our customer agrees, so we've jointly decided to implement the shopping cart functionality next. This is going to involve a number of new concepts, including sessions, relationships among models, and adding a button to the view—so let's get started.

Iteration D1: Finding a Cart

As users browse our online catalog, they will (we hope) select products to buy. The convention is that each item selected will be added to a virtual shopping cart, held in our store. At some point, our buyers will have everything they need and will proceed to our site's checkout, where they'll pay for the stuff in their carts.

This means that our application will need to keep track of all the items added to the cart by the buyer. To do that, we'll keep a cart in the database and store its unique identifier, cart.id, in the session. Every time a request comes in, we can recover that identifier from the session and use it to find the cart in the database.

Let's go ahead and create a cart:

```
depot> bin/rails generate scaffold Cart
 ...
depot> bin/rails db:migrate
== 20250420000003 CreateCarts: migrating ======================================
-- create_table(:carts)
   -> 0.0016s
== 20250420000003 CreateCarts: migrated (0.0016s) =============================
```

Rails makes the current session look like a hash to the controller, so we'll store the ID of the cart in the session by indexing it with the :cart_id symbol:

```ruby
# rails80/depot_f/app/controllers/concerns/current_cart.rb
module CurrentCart
  private

    def set_cart
      @cart = Cart.find(session[:cart_id])
    rescue ActiveRecord::RecordNotFound
      @cart = Cart.create
      session[:cart_id] = @cart.id
    end
end
```

The set_cart() method starts by getting the :cart_id from the session object and then attempts to find a cart corresponding to this ID. If such a cart record isn't found (which will happen if the ID is nil or invalid for any reason), this method will proceed to create a new Cart and then store the ID of the created cart into the session.

Note that we place the set_cart() method in a CurrentCart module and place that module in a new file in the app/controllers/concerns directory.[1] This treatment allows us to share common code (even as little as a single method!) among controllers.

Additionally, we mark the method as private, which prevents Rails from ever making it available as an action on the controller.

Iteration D2: Connecting Products to Carts

We're looking at sessions because we need somewhere to keep our shopping cart. We'll cover sessions in more depth in Rails Sessions, on page 372, but for now let's move on to implement the cart.

Let's keep things simple. A cart contains a set of products. Based on the Initial guess at application data diagram on page 63, combined with a brief chat with our customer, we can now generate the Rails models and populate the migrations to create the corresponding tables:

```
depot> bin/rails generate scaffold LineItem product:references cart:belongs_to
 ...
depot> bin/rails db:migrate
== 20250420000004 CreateLineItems: migrating =====================================
-- create_table(:line_items)
   -> 0.0023s
== 20250420000004 CreateLineItems: migrated (0.0024s) ============================
```

---

1. https://signalvnoise.com/posts/3372-put-chubby-models-on-a-diet-with-concerns

The database now has a place to store the references among line items, carts, and products. If you look at the generated definition of the LineItem class, you can see the definitions of these relationships:

rails80/depot_f/app/models/line_item.rb
```ruby
class LineItem < ApplicationRecord
  belongs_to :product
  belongs_to :cart
end
```

The belongs_to() method defines an accessor method—in this case, carts() and products()—but more importantly it tells Rails that rows in line_items are the children of rows in carts and products. No line item can exist unless the corresponding cart and product rows exist. A great rule of thumb for where to put belongs_to declarations is this: if a table has any columns whose values consist of ID values for another table (this concept is known by database designers as *foreign keys*), the corresponding model should have a belongs_to for each.

What do these various declarations do? Basically, they add navigation capabilities to the model objects. Because Rails added the belongs_to declaration to LineItem, we can now retrieve its Product and display the book's title:

```ruby
li = LineItem.find(...)
puts "This line item is for #{li.product.title}"
```

To be able to traverse these relationships in both directions, we need to add some declarations to our model files that specify their inverse relations.

Open the cart.rb file in app/models, and add a call to has_many():

rails80/depot_f/app/models/cart.rb
```ruby
class Cart < ApplicationRecord
➤   has_many :line_items, dependent: :destroy
end
```

That has_many :line_items part of the directive is fairly self-explanatory: a cart (potentially) has many associated line items. These are linked to the cart because each line item contains a reference to its cart's ID. The dependent: :destroy part indicates that the existence of line items is dependent on the existence of the cart. If we destroy a cart, deleting it from the database, we want Rails also to destroy any line items that are associated with that cart.

Now that the Cart is declared to have many line items, we can reference them (as a collection) from a cart object:

```ruby
cart = Cart.find(...)
puts "This cart has #{cart.line_items.count} line items"
```

Now, for completeness, we should add a has_many directive to our Product model. After all, if we have lots of carts, each product might have many line items referencing it. This time, we make use of validation code to prevent the removal of products that are referenced by line items:

```
rails80/depot_f/app/models/product.rb
class Product < ApplicationRecord
  has_many :line_items

  before_destroy :ensure_not_referenced_by_any_line_item

  #...

  private

    # ensure that there are no line items referencing this product
    def ensure_not_referenced_by_any_line_item
      unless line_items.empty?
        errors.add(:base, "Line Items present")
        throw :abort
      end
    end
end
```

Here we declare that a product has many line items and define a *hook* method named ensure_not_referenced_by_any_line_item(). A hook method is a method that Rails calls automatically at a given point in an object's life. In this case, the method will be called before Rails attempts to destroy a row in the database. If the hook method throws :abort, the row isn't destroyed.

Note that we have direct access to the errors object. This is the same place that the validates() method stores error messages. Errors can be associated with individual attributes, but in this case we associate the error with the base object.

Before moving on, add a test to ensure that a product in a cart can't be deleted:

```
rails80/depot_f/test/controllers/products_controller_test.rb
  test "should destroy product" do
    assert_raises ActiveRecord::RecordNotDestroyed do
      delete product_url(products(:two))
    end

    assert Product.exists?(products(:two).id)
  end
```

And change the fixture to make sure that product two is in both carts:

```
rails80/depot_f/test/fixtures/line_items.yml
# Read about fixtures at
# https://api.rubyonrails.org/classes/ActiveRecord/FixtureSet.html
```

```
one:
  product: two
  cart: one
two:
  product: two
  cart: two
```

We'll have more to say about intermodel relationships starting in Specifying Relationships in Models, on page 322.

Iteration D3: Adding a Button

Now that that's done, it's time to add an Add to Cart button for each product.

We don't need to create a new controller or even a new action. Taking a look at the actions provided by the scaffold generator, we find index(), show(), new(), edit(), create(), update(), and destroy(). The one that matches this operation is create(). (new() may sound similar, but its use is to get a form that's used to solicit input for a subsequent create() action.)

Once this decision is made, the rest follows. What are we creating? Certainly not a Cart or even a Product. What we're creating is a LineItem. Looking at the comment associated with the create() method in app/controllers/line_items_controller.rb, you see that this choice also determines the URL to use (/line_items) and the HTTP method (POST).

This choice even suggests the proper UI control to use. When we added links before, we used link_to(), but links default to using HTTP GET. We want to use POST, so we'll add a button this time; this means we'll be using the button_to() method.

We could connect the button to the line item by specifying the URL, but again we can let Rails take care of this for us by simply appending _path to the controller's name. In this case, we'll use line_items_path.

However, there's a problem with this: how will the line_items_path method know *which* product to add to our cart? We'll need to pass it the ID of the product corresponding to the button. All we need to do is add the :product_id option to the line_items_path() call. We can even pass in the product instance itself—Rails knows to extract the ID from the record in circumstances such as these.

In all, the *one* line that we need to add to our index.html.erb looks like this:

```
rails80/depot_f/app/views/store/index.html.erb
<div class="w-full">
<% if notice.present? %>
```

```erb
    <p class="py-2 px-3 bg-green-50 mb-5 text-green-500 font-medium rounded-lg
        inline-block" id="notice">
      <%= notice %>
    </p>
<% end %>

<h1 class="font-bold text-xl mb-6 pb-2 border-b-2">
  Your Pragmatic Catalog
</h1>

<ul>
  <% cache @products do %>
    <% @products.each do |product| %>
      <% cache product do %>
        <li class='flex mb-6'>
          <%= image_tag(product.image,
              class: 'object-contain w-40 h-48 shadow mr-6') %>

          <div>
            <h2 class="font-bold text-lg mb-3"><%= product.title %></h2>

            <p>
              <%= sanitize(product.description) %>
            </p>

            <div class="mt-3">
              <%= number_to_currency(product.price) %>

➤             <%= button_to "Add to Cart",
➤                 line_items_path(product_id: product),
➤                 form_class: "inline",
➤                 class: 'ml-4 rounded-lg py-1 px-2
➤                         text-white bg-green-600' %>
            </div>
          </div>
        </li>
      <% end %>
    <% end %>
  <% end %>
</ul>
</div>
```

We also need to deal with two formatting issues. button_to creates an HTML <form> wrapping the <button>. HTML <form> is normally a block element that appears on the next line. We'd like to place them next to the price. This is no problem as Rails lets you specify both the form_class as well as the button class.

Now our index page looks like the screenshot shown on page 121. But before we push the button, we need to modify the create() method in the line items controller to expect a product ID as a form parameter. Here's where we start to see how important the id field is in our models. Rails identifies model objects (and the corresponding database rows) by their id fields. If we pass an ID to create(), we're uniquely identifying the product to add.

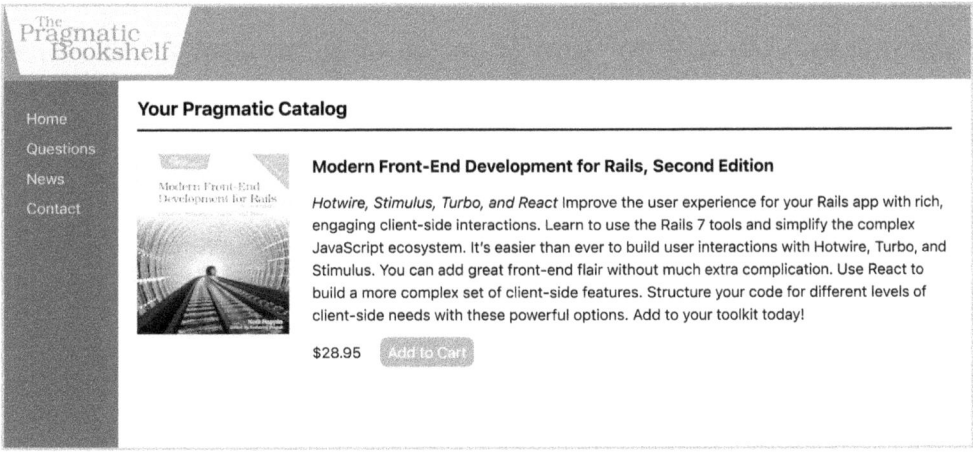

Why the create() method? The default HTTP method for a link is a GET, and for a button is a POST. Rails uses these conventions to determine which method to call. Refer to the comments inside the app/controllers/line_items_controller.rb file to see other conventions. We'll be making extensive use of these conventions inside the Depot application.

Now let's modify the LineItemsController to find the shopping cart for the current session (creating one if one isn't there already), add the selected product to that cart, and display the cart contents.

We use the CurrentCart concern we implemented in Iteration D1 on page 116 to find (or create) a cart in the session:

```
rails80/depot_f/app/controllers/line_items_controller.rb
class LineItemsController < ApplicationController
  include CurrentCart
  before_action :set_cart, only: %i[ create ]
  before_action :set_line_item, only: %i[ show edit update destroy ]

  # GET /line_items or /line_items.json
  #...
end
```

We include the CurrentCart module and declare that the set_cart() method is to be involved before the create() action. We explore action callbacks in depth in Callbacks, on page 378, but for now all you need to know is that Rails provides the ability to wire together methods that are to be called before, after, or even around controller actions.

In fact, as you can see, the generated controller already uses this facility to set the value of the @line_item instance variable before the show(), edit(), update(), or destroy() actions are called.

Now that we know that the value of @cart is set to the value of the current cart, all we need to modify is a few lines of code in the create() method in app/controllers/line_items_controller.rb. to build the line item itself:

rails80/depot_f/app/controllers/line_items_controller.rb
```ruby
  def create
➤   product = Product.find(params[:product_id])
➤   @line_item = @cart.line_items.build(product: product)

    respond_to do |format|
      if @line_item.save
➤       format.html { redirect_to @line_item.cart,
          notice: "Line item was successfully created." }
        format.json { render :show,
          status: :created, location: @line_item }
      else
        format.html { render :new,
          status: :unprocessable_entity }
        format.json { render json: @line_item.errors,
          status: :unprocessable_entity }
      end
    end
  end
```

We use the params object to get the :product_id parameter from the request. The params object is important inside Rails applications. It holds all of the parameters passed in a browser request. We store the result in a local variable because there's no need to make this available to the view.

We then pass that product we found into @cart.line_items.build. This causes a new line item relationship to be built between the @cart object and the product. You can build the relationship from either end, and Rails takes care of establishing the connections on both sides.

We save the resulting line item into an instance variable named @line_item.

The remainder of this method takes care of handling errors, which we'll cover in more detail in Iteration E2: Handling Errors, on page 132, (as well as handling JSON requests, which we don't need per se but that were added by the Rails generator). But for now, we want to modify only one more thing: once the line item is created, we want to redirect users to the cart instead of back to the line item. Since the line item object knows how to find the cart object, all we need to do is add .cart to the method call.

Confident that the code works as intended, we try the Add to Cart buttons in our browser. And the following screenshot shows what we see.

This is a bit underwhelming. We have scaffolding for the cart, but when we created it we didn't provide any attributes, so the view doesn't have anything to show. For now, let's add a trivial template that shows the title of each book in the cart. Update the file views/carts/_cart.html.erb like so:

```
rails80/depot_f/app/views/carts/_cart.html.erb
<div id="<%= dom_id cart %>">
➤   <h2 class="font-bold text-lg mb-3">Your Pragmatic Cart</h2>
➤
➤   <ul class="list-disc list-inside">
➤     <% cart.line_items.each do |item| %>
➤       <li><%= item.product.title %></li>
➤     <% end %>
➤   </ul>
</div>
```

You may be wondering about the underscore in the file name and where the cart variable comes from. Don't worry, we'll cover all this and more when we get to Partial Templates, on page 144, but for now it's enough to know that this is the file that Rails uses to render a single cart.

So, with everything plumbed together, let's go back and click the Add to Cart button again and see our view displayed, as in the following screenshot.

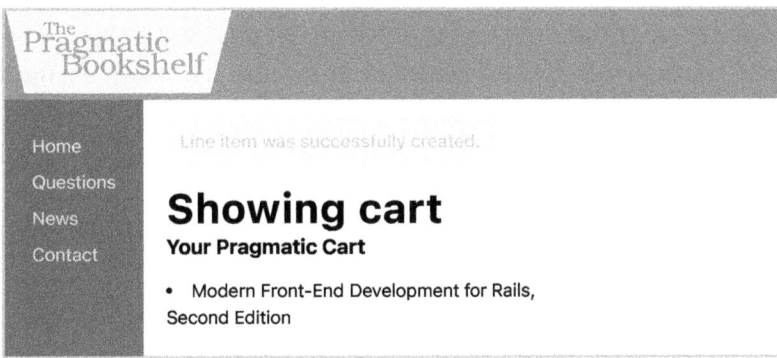

Go back to http://localhost:3000/, the main catalog page, and add a different product to the cart. You'll see the original two entries plus our new item in your cart. It looks like we have sessions working.

We changed the function of our controller, so we know that we need to update the corresponding functional test.

For starters, we only need to pass a product ID on the call to post. Next, we have to deal with the fact that we're no longer redirecting to the line items page. We're instead redirecting to the cart, where the cart ID is internal state data residing in a cookie. Because this is an integration test, instead of focusing on how the code is implemented, we should focus on what users see after following the redirect: a page with a heading identifying that they're looking at a cart, with a list item corresponding to the product they added.

We do this by updating test/controllers/line_items_controller_test.rb:

rails80/depot_g/test/controllers/line_items_controller_test.rb
```ruby
  test "should create line_item" do
    assert_difference("LineItem.count") do
➤     post line_items_url, params: { product_id: products(:pragprog).id }
    end

➤   follow_redirect!

➤   assert_select "h2", "Your Pragmatic Cart"
➤   assert_select "li", "The Pragmatic Programmer"
  end
```

We now rerun this set of tests:

depot> **bin/rails test test/controllers/line_items_controller_test.rb**

It's time to show our customer, so we call her over and proudly display our handsome new cart. Somewhat to our dismay, she makes that *tsk-tsk* sound that customers make just before telling you that you clearly don't get something.

Real shopping carts, she explains, don't show separate lines for two of the same product. Instead, they show the product line once with a quantity of 2. It looks like we're lined up for our next iteration.

What We Just Did

It's been a busy, productive day so far. We added a shopping cart to our store, and along the way we dipped our toes into some neat Rails features:

- We created a Cart object in one request and successfully located the same cart in subsequent requests by using a session object.

- We added a private method and placed it in a concern, making it accessible to all of our controllers.
- We created relationships between carts and line items, and relationships between line items and products, and we were able to navigate using these relationships.
- We added a button that causes a product to be posted to a cart, causing a new line item to be created.

Playtime

Here's some stuff to try on your own:

- Add a new variable to the session to record how many times the user has accessed the store controller's index action. Note that the first time this page is accessed, your count won't be in the session. You can test for this with code like this:

```
if session[:counter].nil?
  ...
```

  If the session variable isn't there, you need to initialize it. Then you'll be able to increment it.

- Pass this counter to your template, and display it at the top of the catalog page. Hint: the pluralize helper (There's a method to pluralize nouns: on page 394) might be useful for forming the message you display.

- Reset the counter to zero whenever the user adds something to the cart.

- Change the template to display the counter only if the count is greater than five.

In this chapter, you'll see:
- Modifying the schema and existing data
- Error diagnosis and handling
- The flash
- Logging

CHAPTER 10

Task E: A Smarter Cart

Although we have rudimentary cart functionality implemented, we have much to do. To start with, we need to recognize when customers add multiples of the same item to the cart. Once that's done, we'll also have to make sure that the cart can handle error cases and communicate problems encountered along the way to the customer or system administrator, as appropriate.

Iteration E1: Creating a Smarter Cart

Associating a count with each product in our cart is going to require us to modify the line_items table. We've used migrations before; for example, we used a migration in Applying the Migration, on page 68, to update the schema of the database. While that was as part of creating the initial scaffolding for a model, the basic approach is the same:

```
depot> bin/rails generate migration add_quantity_to_line_items quantity:integer
```

Rails can tell from the name of the migration that you're adding columns to the line_items table and can pick up the names and data types for each column from the last argument. The two patterns that Rails matches on are AddXXXToTABLE and RemoveXXXFromTABLE, where the value of XXX is ignored; what matters is the list of column names and types that appears after the migration name.

The only thing Rails can't tell is what a reasonable default is for this column. In many cases, a null value would do, but let's make it the value 1 for existing carts by modifying the migration before we apply it:

rails80/depot_g/db/migrate/20250420000005_add_quantity_to_line_items.rb
```ruby
class AddQuantityToLineItems < ActiveRecord::Migration[8.0]
  def change
➤   add_column :line_items, :quantity, :integer, default: 1
  end
end
```

Once it's complete, we run the migration:

```
depot> bin/rails db:migrate
```

Now we need a smart add_product() method in our Cart, one that checks if our list of items already includes the product we're adding; if it does, it bumps the quantity, and if it doesn't, it builds a new LineItem:

rails80/depot_g/app/models/cart.rb
```ruby
def add_product(product)
  current_item = line_items.find_by(product_id: product.id)
  if current_item
    current_item.quantity += 1
  else
    current_item = line_items.build(product_id: product.id)
  end
  current_item
end
```

The find_by() method is a streamlined version of the where() method. Instead of returning an array of results, it returns either an existing LineItem or nil.

We also need to modify the line item controller to use this method:

rails80/depot_g/app/controllers/line_items_controller.rb
```ruby
  def create
    product = Product.find(params[:product_id])
➤   @line_item = @cart.add_product(product)

    respond_to do |format|
      if @line_item.save
        format.html { redirect_to @line_item.cart,
          notice: "Line item was successfully created." }
        format.json { render :show,
          status: :created, location: @line_item }
      else
        format.html { render :new,
          status: :unprocessable_entity }
        format.json { render json: @line_item.errors,
          status: :unprocessable_entity }
      end
    end
  end
```

We make two small changes to the _cart template to use this new information:

rails80/depot_g/app/views/carts/_cart.html.erb
```erb
<div id="<%= dom_id cart %>">
  <h2 class="font-bold text-lg mb-3">Your Pragmatic Cart</h2>
➤   <ul class="list-none list-inside">
```

```erb
      <% cart.line_items.each do |item| %>
        <li><%= item.quantity %> &times; <%= item.product.title %></li>
      <% end %>
    </ul>
</div>
```

In addition to displaying the quantity for each line item, we remove the bullets that precede each item in the unordered list by changing list-disc to list-none. This shows one of many benefits to using a CSS framework to make our work more agile. When we make this change, we know not only that this change applies to this particular view; we also know that this change does *not* affect any other view—assurances we don't always have when authoring CSS style sheets.

Now that all the pieces are in place, we can go back to the store page and click the Add to Cart button for a product that's already in the cart. What we're likely to see is a mixture of individual products listed separately and a single product listed with a quantity of two. This is because we added a quantity of one to existing columns instead of collapsing multiple rows when possible. What we need to do next is migrate the data.

We start by creating a migration:

depot> `bin/rails generate migration combine_items_in_cart`

This time, Rails can't infer what we're trying to do, so we can't rely on the generated change() method. What we need to do instead is to replace this method with separate up() and down() methods. First, here's the up() method:

rails80/depot_g/db/migrate/20250420000006_combine_items_in_cart.rb
```ruby
def up
  # replace multiple items for a single product in a cart with a
  # single item
  Cart.all.each do |cart|
    # count the number of each product in the cart
    sums = cart.line_items.group(:product_id).sum(:quantity)

    sums.each do |product_id, quantity|
      if quantity > 1
        # remove individual items
        cart.line_items.where(product_id: product_id).delete_all

        # replace with a single item
        item = cart.line_items.build(product_id: product_id)
        item.quantity = quantity
        item.save!
      end
    end
  end
end
```

This is easily the most extensive code you've seen so far. Let's look at it in small pieces:

- We start by iterating over each cart.
- For each cart, we get a sum of the quantity fields for each of the line items associated with this cart, grouped by product_id. The resulting sums will be a list of ordered pairs of product_ids and quantity.
- We iterate over these sums, extracting the product_id and quantity from each.
- In cases where the quantity is greater than one, we delete all of the individual line items associated with this cart and this product and replace them with a single line item with the correct quantity.

Note how easily and elegantly Rails enables you to express this algorithm.

With this code in place, we apply this migration like any other migration:

depot> `bin/rails db:migrate`

We can see the results by looking at the cart, shown in the following screenshot.

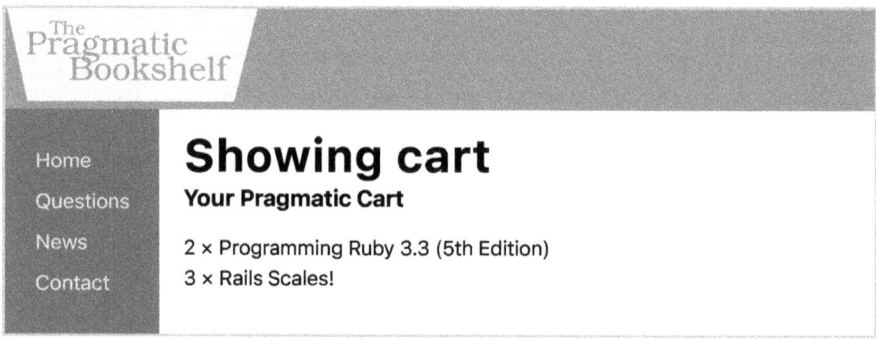

Although we have reason to be pleased with ourselves, we're not done yet. An important principle of migrations is that each step needs to be reversible, so we implement a down() too. This method finds line items with a quantity of greater than one; adds new line items for this cart and product, each with a quantity of one; and, finally, deletes the line item:

rails80/depot_g/db/migrate/20250420000006_combine_items_in_cart.rb
```
def down
  # split items with quantity>1 into multiple items
  LineItem.where("quantity>1").each do |line_item|
    # add individual items
```

```
      line_item.quantity.times do
        LineItem.create(
          cart_id: line_item.cart_id,
          product_id: line_item.product_id,
          quantity: 1
        )
      end
      # remove original item
      line_item.destroy
    end
  end
end
```

Now, we can just as easily roll back our migration with a single command:

depot> **bin/rails db:rollback**

Rails provides a Rake task to allow you to check the status of your migrations:

depot> **bin/rails db:migrate:status**
```
database: storage/development.sqlite3

 Status   Migration ID    Migration Name
--------------------------------------------------
   up     20160407000001  Create products
   up     20160407000002  Create carts
   up     20160407000003  Create line items
   up     20160407000004  Add quantity to line items
  down    20160407000005  Combine items in cart
```

Now, we can modify and reapply the migration or even delete it entirely. To inspect the results of the rollback, we have to move the migration file out of the way so Rails doesn't think it should apply it. You can do that via mv, for example. If you do that, the cart should look like the following screenshot:

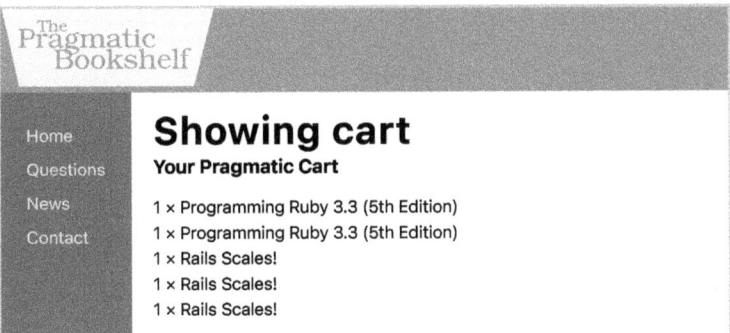

Once we move the migration file back and reapply the migration (with the bin/rails db:migrate command), we have a cart that maintains a count for each of the products it holds, and we have a view that displays that count.

Since we changed the output the application produces, we need to update the tests to match. Note that what the user sees isn't the string × but the Unicode character ×. If you can't find a way to enter that character using your keyboard and operating system combination, you can use the escape sequence \u00D7[1] instead (also note the use of double quotes, as this is needed in Ruby to enter the escape sequence):

rails80/depot_h/test/controllers/line_items_controller_test.rb
```
  test "should create line_item" do
    assert_difference("LineItem.count") do
      post line_items_url, params: { product_id: products(:pragprog).id }
    end

    follow_redirect!

    assert_select "h2", "Your Pragmatic Cart"
➤   assert_select "li", "1 \u00D7 The Pragmatic Programmer"
  end
```

Happy that we have something presentable, we call our customer over and show her the result of our morning's work. She's pleased—she can see the site starting to come together. However, she's also troubled, having just read an article in the trade press on the way e-commerce sites are being attacked and compromised daily. She read that one kind of attack involves feeding requests with bad parameters into web applications, hoping to expose bugs and security flaws. She noticed that the link to the cart looks like carts/nnn, where nnn is our internal cart ID. Feeling malicious, she manually types this request into a browser, giving it a cart ID of wibble. She's not impressed when our application displays the page shown in the screenshot on page 133.

This seems fairly unprofessional. So our next iteration will be spent making the application more resilient.

Iteration E2: Handling Errors

It's apparent from the page shown in the screenshot on page 133 that our application raised an exception at line 63 of the carts controller. Your line number might be different, as we have some book-related formatting stuff in our source files. If you go to that line, you'll find the following code:

```
@cart = Cart.find(params[:id])
```

If the cart can't be found, Active Record raises a RecordNotFound exception, which we clearly need to handle. The question arises—how?

---

[1] http://www.fileformat.info/info/unicode/char/00d7/index.htm

> **ActiveRecord::RecordNotFound in CartsController#show**
>
> Couldn't find Cart with 'id'=wibble
>
> Extracted source (around line **#63**):
>
> ```
> 61      # Use callbacks to share common setup or constraints between actions.
> 62      def set_cart
> 63        @cart = Cart.find(params.expect(:id))
> 64      end
> 65
> 66      # Only allow a list of trusted parameters through.
> ```
>
> Rails.root: /Users/rubys/git/awdwr8/work
>
> Application Trace | Framework Trace | Full Trace
> app/controllers/carts_controller.rb:63:in 'CartsController#set_cart'
>
> **Request**
>
> **Parameters**:
>
> `{"id" => "wibble"}`
>
> Toggle session dump
>
> Toggle env dump

We could silently ignore it. From a security standpoint, this is probably the best move, because it gives no information to a potential attacker. However, it also means that if we ever have a bug in our code that generates bad cart IDs, our application will appear to the outside world to be unresponsive—no one will know that an error occurred.

Instead, we'll take two actions when an exception is raised. First, we'll log the fact to an internal log file using the Rails logger facility.[2] Second, we'll redisplay the catalog page along with a short message (something along the lines of "Invalid cart") to the user, who can then continue to use our site.

Rails has a convenient way of dealing with errors and error reporting. It defines a structure called a *flash*. A flash is a bucket (actually closer to a Hash) in which you can store stuff as you process a request. The contents of the flash are available to the next request in this session before being deleted automatically. Typically, the flash is used to collect error messages. For example, when our show() method detects that it was passed an invalid cart ID, it can store that error message in the flash area and redirect to the index() action to redisplay the catalog. The view for the index action can extract the error and display it at the top of the catalog page. The flash information is accessible within the views via the flash accessor method.

Why can't we store the error in any old instance variable? Remember that after a redirect is sent by our application to the browser, the browser sends a new request back to our application. By the time we receive that request, our application has moved on; all the instance variables from previous requests are long gone. The flash data is stored in the session to make it available between requests.

Armed with this background about flash data, we can create an invalid_cart() method to report on the problem:

```ruby
rails80/depot_h/app/controllers/carts_controller.rb
class CartsController < ApplicationController
  before_action :set_cart, only: %i[ show edit update destroy ]
➤ rescue_from ActiveRecord::RecordNotFound, with: :invalid_cart
  # GET /carts or /carts.json
  # ...
  private
  # ...
➤   def invalid_cart
➤     logger.error "Attempt to access invalid cart #{params[:id]}"
➤     redirect_to store_index_url, notice: "Invalid cart"
➤   end
end
```

The rescue_from clause intercepts the exception raised by Cart.find(). In the handler, we do the following:

---

2. http://guides.rubyonrails.org/debugging_rails_applications.html#the-logger

- Use the Rails logger to record the error. Every controller has a logger attribute. Here we use it to record a message at the error logging level.

- Redirect to the catalog display by using the redirect_to() method. The :notice parameter specifies a message to be stored in the flash as a notice. Why redirect rather than display the catalog here? If we redirect, the user's browser will end up displaying the store URL rather than http://.../cart/wibble. We expose less of the application this way. We also prevent the user from retriggering the error by clicking the Reload button.

With this code in place, we can rerun our customer's problematic query by entering the following URL:

http://localhost:3000/carts/wibble

We don't see a bunch of errors in the browser now. Instead, the catalog page is displayed with the error message shown in the following screenshot.

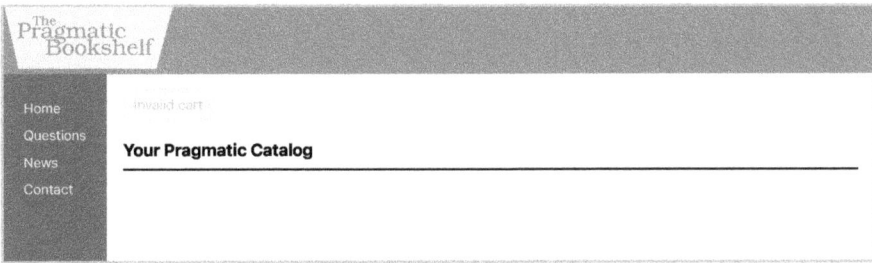

If we look at the end of the log file (development.log in the log directory), we see our message:

```
Started GET "/carts/wibble" for ::1 at 2024-06-20 19:59:26 -0400
Processing by CartsController#show as HTML
  Parameters: {"id"=>"wibble"}
  ^[[1m^[[36mCart Load (0.4ms)^[[0m  ^[[1m^[[34mSELECT "carts".* FROM "carts"
  ↳ app/controllers/carts_controller.rb:71:in `set_cart'
Attempt to access invalid cart wibble
Redirected to http://localhost:3003/
Completed 302 Found in 6ms (ActiveRecord: 0.3ms (1 query, 0 cached) | GC:
```

On Unix machines, we'd probably use a command such as tail or less to view this file. On Windows, you can use your favorite editor. It's often a good idea to keep a window open to show new lines as they're added to this file. In Unix, you'd use tail -f. You can download a tail command for Windows[3] or get a GUI-based

---

3. http://gnuwin32.sourceforge.net/packages/coreutils.htm

tool.[4] Finally, some OS X users use Console.app to track log files. Just say open development.log at the command line.

This being the Internet, we can't worry only about our published web forms; we have to worry about every possible interface, because malicious crackers can get underneath the HTML we provide and attempt to provide additional parameters. Invalid carts aren't our biggest problem here; we also want to prevent access to *other people's carts*.

As always, your controllers are your first line of defense. Let's go ahead and remove cart_id from the list of parameters that are permitted:

rails80/depot_h/app/controllers/line_items_controller.rb
```
    def line_item_params
➤     params.expect(line_item: [ :product_id ])
    end
```

We can see this in action by rerunning our controller tests:

```
bin/rails test:controllers
```

No tests fail, but we should clean this up anyway:

rails80/depot_h/test/controllers/line_items_controller_test.rb
```
  test "should update line_item" do
➤   patch line_item_url(@line_item),
➤     params: { line_item: { product_id: @line_item.product_id } }
    assert_redirected_to line_item_url(@line_item)
  end
```

```
bin/rails test:controllers
```

Sensing the end of an iteration, we call our customer over and show her that the error is now properly handled. She is delighted and continues to play with the application. She notices a minor problem on our new cart display: there's no way to empty items out of a cart. This minor change will be our next iteration. We should make it before heading home.

Iteration E3: Finishing the Cart

We know by now that to implement the empty-cart function, we have to add a link to the cart and modify the destroy() method in the carts controller to clean up the session.

Start with the template and use the button_to() method to add a button:

---

4. http://tailforwin32.sourceforge.net/

```
rails80/depot_h/app/views/carts/_cart.html.erb
<div id="<%= dom_id cart %>">
  <h2 class="font-bold text-lg mb-3">Your Pragmatic Cart</h2>

  <ul class="list-none list-inside">
    <% cart.line_items.each do |item| %>
      <li><%= item.quantity %> &times; <%= item.product.title %></li>
    <% end %>
  </ul>
</div>
➤         <%= button_to 'Empty Cart', cart, method: :delete,
➤ class: 'ml-4 rounded-lg py-1 px-2 text-white bg-green-600' %>
```

In the controller, let's modify the destroy() method to ensure that the user is deleting his or her own cart (think about it!) and to remove the cart from the session before redirecting to the index page with a notification message:

```
rails80/depot_h/app/controllers/carts_controller.rb
  def destroy
➤   @cart.destroy! if @cart.id == session[:cart_id]
➤   session[:cart_id] = nil

    respond_to do |format|
➤     format.html { redirect_to store_index_path, status: :see_other,
➤       notice: "Your cart is currently empty" }
      format.json { head :no_content }
    end
  end
```

And we update the corresponding test in test/controllers/carts_controller_test.rb:

```
rails80/depot_i/test/controllers/carts_controller_test.rb
  test "should destroy cart" do
➤   post line_items_url, params: { product_id: products(:pragprog).id }
➤   @cart = Cart.find(session[:cart_id])
➤
    assert_difference("Cart.count", -1) do
      delete cart_url(@cart)
    end

➤   assert_redirected_to store_index_url
  end
```

Now when we view our cart and click the Empty Cart button, we're taken back to the catalog page and see the message shown in the screenshot on page 138.

We can remove the flash message that's autogenerated when a line item is added:

```ruby
rails80/depot_i/app/controllers/line_items_controller.rb
def create
  product = Product.find(params[:product_id])
  @line_item = @cart.add_product(product)

  respond_to do |format|
    if @line_item.save
      format.html { redirect_to @line_item.cart }
      format.json { render :show,
        status: :created, location: @line_item }
    else
      format.html { render :new,
        status: :unprocessable_entity }
      format.json { render json: @line_item.errors,
        status: :unprocessable_entity }
    end
  end
end
```

Finally, we get around to tidying up the cart display. The <li>-based approach makes it hard to style. A table-based layout would be easier. Replace app/views/carts/_cart.html.erb with the following:

```erb
rails80/depot_i/app/views/carts/_cart.html.erb
<div id="<%= dom_id cart %>">
  <h2 class="font-bold text-lg mb-3">Your Cart</h2>

  <table class="table-auto">
    <% cart.line_items.each do |line_item| %>
      <tr>
        <td class="text-right"><%= line_item.quantity %></td>
        <td>&times;</td>
        <td class="pr-2">
          <%= line_item.product.title %>
        </td>
        <td class="text-right font-bold">
```

```erb
        <%= number_to_currency(line_item.total_price) %>
      </td>
    </tr>
  <% end %>

  <tfoot>
    <tr>
      <th class="text-right pr-2 pt-2" colspan="3">Total:</th>
      <td class="text-right pt-2 font-bold border-t-2 border-black">
        <%= number_to_currency(cart.total_price) %>
      </td>
    </tr>
  </tfoot>
</table>

<%= button_to 'Empty Cart', cart, method: :delete,
  class: 'ml-4 rounded-lg py-1 px-2 text-white bg-green-600' %>
</div>
```

To make this work, we need to add a method to both the LineItem and Cart models that returns the total price for the individual line item and entire cart, respectively. Here is the line item, which involves only simple multiplication:

rails80/depot_i/app/models/line_item.rb
```ruby
def total_price
  product.price * quantity
end
```

We implement the Cart method using the nifty Array::sum() method to sum the prices of each item in the collection:

rails80/depot_i/app/models/cart.rb
```ruby
def total_price
  line_items.sum { |item| item.total_price }
end
```

The following screenshot shows a nicer-looking cart.

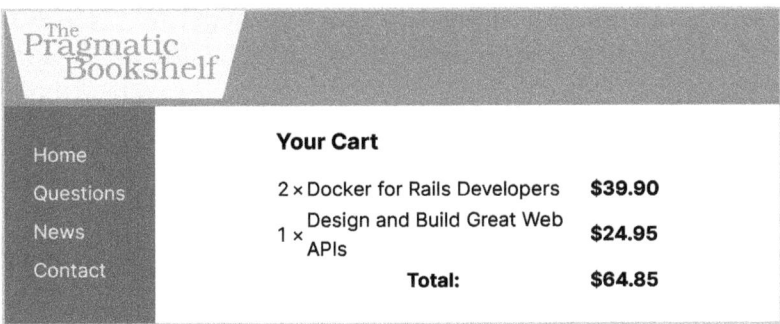

Finally, we update our test cases to match the current output:

rails80/depot_i/test/controllers/line_items_controller_test.rb
```
test "should create line_item" do
  assert_difference("LineItem.count") do
    post line_items_url, params: { product_id: products(:pragprog).id }
  end

  follow_redirect!

➤  assert_select "h2", "Your Cart"
➤  assert_select "td", "The Pragmatic Programmer"
end
```

What We Just Did

Our shopping cart is now something the client is happy with. Along the way, we covered the following:

- Adding a column to an existing table, with a default value
- Migrating existing data into the new table format
- Providing a flash notice of an error that was detected
- Using the logger to log events
- Removing a parameter from the permitted list
- Deleting a record
- Adjusting the way a table is rendered, using Tailwind CSS classes

But, just as we think we've wrapped up this functionality, our customer wanders over with a copy of *Information Technology and Golf Weekly*. Apparently, it has an article about the Hotwire style of browser interface, where stuff gets updated on the fly. Hmmm…let's look at that tomorrow.

Playtime

Here's some stuff to try on your own:

- Create a migration that copies the product price into the line item, and change the add_product() method in the Cart model to capture the price whenever a new line item is created. Add prices to the line_items.yml fixture.

- Write unit tests that add both unique products and duplicate products to a cart. Assert how many products should be in the cart in each instance. Note that you'll need to modify the fixture to refer to products and carts by name—for example, product: pragprog.

- Check products and line items for other places where a user-friendly error message would be in order.

- Add the ability to delete individual line items from the cart. This will require buttons on each line, and such buttons will need to be linked to the destroy() action in the LineItemsController.

- We prevented accessing other users' carts in the LineItemsController, but you can still see other carts by navigating directly to a URL like http://localhost/carts/3. See if you can prevent accessing any cart other than the one currently stored in the session.

In this chapter, you'll see:
- Using partial templates
- Rendering into the page layout
- Updating pages dynamically with TurboStreams
- Testing the TurboStream updates
- Highlighting changes with CSS Animations
- Broadcasting changes with Action Cable

CHAPTER 11

Task F: Hotwiring the Storefront

Our customer wants us to make the storefront more interactive. After we ask her what she means, we come to realize that what she wants is for the page to update in place—no bouncing between pages, but to have the page dynamically update as the cart is being filled.

Back in the old days (up until 1994 or so), browsers were treated as dumb devices. When you wrote a browser-based application, you'd send stuff to the browser and then forget about that session. At some point, the user would fill in some form fields or click a hyperlink, and your application would get woken up by an incoming request. It would render a complete page back to the user, and the whole tedious process would start afresh. That's exactly how our Depot application behaves so far.

But it turns out that browsers aren't really that dumb. (Who knew?) They can run code. All modern browsers can run JavaScript. And it turns out that the JavaScript in the browser can interact behind the scenes with the application on the server, updating the stuff the user sees as a result.

Originally introduced in Rails 7 is a collection of web frameworks included by default that collectively goes by the name Hotwire,[1] which stands for HTML Over The Wire. Clever, huh? The general idea is that instead of always building entire HTML pages to send to the client, you build HTML fragments or partials and send the results to the client, which will integrate those fragments into the page that already is being displayed.

So let's Hotwire our shopping cart. Rather than having a separate shopping cart page, let's put the current cart display into the catalog's sidebar. Then we'll use Hotwire to update the cart in the sidebar without redisplaying the whole page.

---

1. https://hotwired.dev/

Whenever you work with Hotwire, it's good to start with the non-Hotwire version of the application and then gradually introduce Hotwire features. That's what we'll do here. For starters, let's move the cart from its own page and put it in the sidebar.

Iteration F1: Moving the Cart

Currently, our cart is rendered by the show action in the CartController and the corresponding .html.erb template. We'd like to move that rendering into the sidebar. This means it'll no longer be in its own page. Instead, we'll render it in the layout that displays the overall catalog. You can do that using *partial templates*.

Partial Templates

Programming languages let you define *methods*. A method is a chunk of code with a name: invoke the method by the name, and the corresponding chunk of code gets run. And, of course, you can pass parameters to a method, which lets you write a piece of code that can be used in many different circumstances.

Think of Rails partial templates (*partials* for short) like a method for views. A partial is simply a chunk of a view in its own separate file. You can invoke (aka *render*) a partial from another template or from a controller, and the partial will render itself and return the results of that rendering. As with methods, you can pass parameters to a partial, so the same partial can render different results.

We'll use partials twice in this iteration. First let's look at the cart display:

```erb
rails80/depot_i/app/views/carts/_cart.html.erb
<div id="<%= dom_id cart %>">
  <h2 class="font-bold text-lg mb-3">Your Cart</h2>

  <table class="table-auto">
    <% cart.line_items.each do |line_item| %>
      <tr>
        <td class="text-right"><%= line_item.quantity %></td>
        <td>&times;</td>
        <td class="pr-2">
          <%= line_item.product.title %>
        </td>
        <td class="text-right font-bold">
          <%= number_to_currency(line_item.total_price) %>
        </td>
      </tr>
    <% end %>

    <tfoot>
      <tr>
        <th class="text-right pr-2 pt-2" colspan="3">Total:</th>
        <td class="text-right pt-2 font-bold border-t-2 border-black">
```

```erb
      <%= number_to_currency(cart.total_price) %>
      </td>
    </tr>
  </tfoot>
</table>

<%= button_to 'Empty Cart', cart, method: :delete,
    class: 'ml-4 rounded-lg py-1 px-2 text-white bg-green-600' %>
</div>
```

It creates a list of table rows, one for each item in the cart. Whenever you find yourself iterating like this, stop and ask yourself, is this too much logic in a template? It turns out we can abstract away the loop by using partials. To do this, make use of the fact that you can pass a collection to the method that renders partial templates, and that method will automatically invoke the partial once for each item in the collection. Let's rewrite our cart view to use this feature:

rails80/depot_j/app/views/carts/_cart.html.erb
```erb
<div id="<%= dom_id cart %>">
  <h2 class="font-bold text-lg mb--3">Your Cart</h2>

  <table class="table-auto">
➤   <%= render cart.line_items %>

    <tfoot>
      <tr>
        <th class="text-right pr-2 pt-2" colspan="3">Total:</th>
        <td class="text-right pt-2 font-bold border-t-2 border-black">
          <%= number_to_currency(cart.total_price) %>
        </td>
      </tr>
    </tfoot>
  </table>

  <%= button_to 'Empty Cart', cart, method: :delete,
      class: 'ml-4 rounded-lg py-1 px-2 text-white bg-green-600' %>
</div>
```

That's a lot simpler. The render() method will iterate over any collection that's passed to it. The partial template is simply another template file (by default in the same directory as the object being rendered and with the name of the table as the name). However, to keep the names of partials distinct from regular templates, Rails automatically prepends an underscore to the partial name when looking for the file. That means the partial is named _line_item.html.erb and can be found in the app/views/line_items directory:

rails80/depot_j/app/views/line_items/_line_item.html.erb
```erb
<tr>
  <td class="text-right"><%= line_item.quantity %></td>
  <td>&times;</td>
  <td class="pr-2">
```

```erb
      <%= line_item.product.title %>
    </td>
    <td class="text-right font-bold">
      <%= number_to_currency(line_item.total_price) %>
    </td>
  </tr>
```

Something subtle is going on here. Inside the partial template, we refer to the current object by using the variable name that matches the name of the template. In this case, the partial is named line_item, so inside the partial we expect to have a variable called line_item.

So now we've tidied up the cart display, but that hasn't moved it into the sidebar. To do that, let's revisit our layout. Since we already have a partial template that displays the cart, all we need to do is include this new partial in the sidebar:

rails80/depot_k/app/views/layouts/application.html.erb
```erb
<!DOCTYPE html>
<html>
  <head>
  <title><%= content_for(:title) || "Pragprog Books Online Store" %></title>
    <meta name="viewport" content="width=device-width,initial-scale=1">
    <meta name="apple-mobile-web-app-capable" content="yes">
    <meta name="mobile-web-app-capable" content="yes">
    <%= csrf_meta_tags %>
    <%= csp_meta_tag %>

    <%= yield :head %>

    <%# Enable PWA manifest for installable apps (make sure to enable in
        config/routes.rb too!) %>
    <%= tag.link rel: "manifest", href: pwa_manifest_path(format: :json) %>

    <link rel="icon" href="/icon.png" type="image/png">
    <link rel="icon" href="/icon.svg" type="image/svg+xml">
    <link rel="apple-touch-icon" href="/icon.png">

    <%# Includes all stylesheet files in app/assets/stylesheets %>
    <%= stylesheet_link_tag :app, "data-turbo-track": "reload" %>
    <%= javascript_importmap_tags %>
  </head>

  <body>
    <header class="bg-green-700">
      <%= image_tag 'logo.svg', alt: 'The Pragmatic Bookshelf' %>
      <h1><%= @page_title %></h1>
    </header>

    <section class="flex">
      <nav class="bg-green-900 p-6">
➤       <div id="cart" class="bg-white rounded p--2">
➤         <%= render @cart %>
➤       </div>
```

```erb
      <ul class="text-gray-300 leading-8">
        <li><a href="/">Home</a></li>
        <li><a href="/questions">Questions</a></li>
        <li><a href="/news">News</a></li>
        <li><a href="/contact">Contact</a></li>
      </ul>
    </nav>

    <main class="container mx-auto mt-4 px-5 flex">
      <%= yield %>
    </main>
  </section>
</body>
</html>
```

As black lettering on a green background would be hard to read, we also added an HTML <div> element that wraps the cart with a white background, rounded corners, and some padding.

Next, we have to make a small change to the store controller. We're invoking the layout while looking at the store's index action, and that action doesn't currently set @cart. That's a quick change:

rails80/depot_k/app/controllers/store_controller.rb
```ruby
class StoreController < ApplicationController
  include CurrentCart
  before_action :set_cart
  def index
    @products = Product.order(:title)
  end
end
```

If you display the catalog after adding something to your cart, you should see something like the following screenshot.

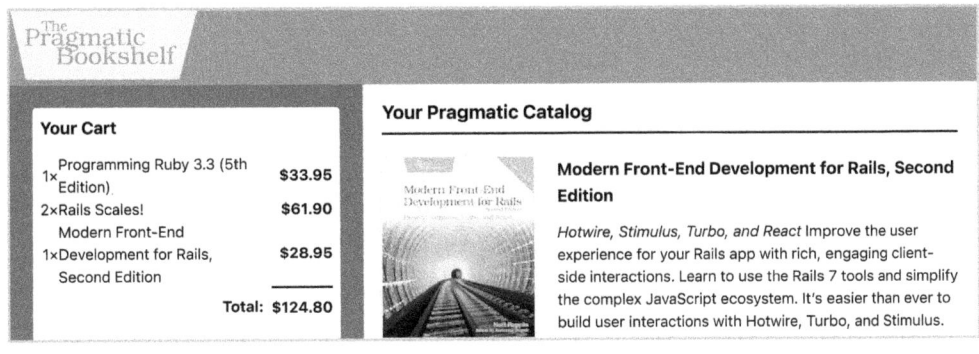

Let's just wait for the Webby Award nomination.

Changing the Flow

Now that we're displaying the cart in the sidebar, we can change the way that the Add to Cart button works. Rather than display a separate cart page, all it has to do is refresh the main index page.

The change is straightforward. At the end of the create action, we redirect the browser back to the index:

rails80/depot_k/app/controllers/line_items_controller.rb
```ruby
  def create
    product = Product.find(params[:product_id])
    @line_item = @cart.add_product(product)

    respond_to do |format|
      if @line_item.save
➤       format.html { redirect_to store_index_url }
        format.json { render :show,
          status: :created, location: @line_item }
      else
        format.html { render :new,
          status: :unprocessable_entity }
        format.json { render json: @line_item.errors,
          status: :unprocessable_entity }
      end
    end
  end
```

At this point, we rerun our tests and see a number of failures:

```
$ bin/rails test
Running 30 tests in a single process (parallelization threshold is 50)
Run options: --seed 58541

# Running:

...E

Error:
ProductsControllerTest#test_should_show_product:
ActionView::Template::Error: 'nil' is not an ActiveModel-compatible
object. It must implement :to_partial_path.
app/views/layouts/application.html.erb:25
```

If we try to display the products index by visiting http://localhost:3000/products in the browser, we see the error shown in the screenshot on page 149.

This information is helpful. The message identifies the template file that was being processed at the point where the error occurs (app/views/layouts/application.html.erb), the line number where the error occurred, and an excerpt from the template of lines around the error. From this, we see that the expression

> **ArgumentError in Products#index**
>
> Showing /Users/rubys/git/awdwr8/work/app/views/layouts/application.html.erb where line #38 raised:
>
> 'nil' is not an ActiveModel-compatible object. It must implement #to_partial_path.
>
> Extracted source (around line #38):

being evaluated at the point of error is @cart.line_items, and the message produced is 'nil' is not an ActiveModel-compatible object.

So, @cart is apparently nil when we display an index of our products. That makes sense, because it's set only in the store controller. We can even verify this using the web console provided at the bottom of the web page. Now that we know what the problem is, the fix is to avoid displaying the cart at all unless the value is set:

rails80/depot_l/app/views/layouts/application.html.erb
```erb
<nav class="bg-green-900 p-6">
➤   <% if @cart and not @cart.line_items.empty? %>
    <div id="cart" class="bg-white rounded p-2">
      <%= render @cart %>
    </div>
➤   <% end %>
  <ul class="text-gray-300 leading-8">
    <li><a href="/">Home</a></li>
    <li><a href="/questions">Questions</a></li>
    <li><a href="/news">News</a></li>
    <li><a href="/contact">Contact</a></li>
  </ul>
</nav>
```

With this change in place, our tests now pass once again. Imagine what could have happened. A change in one part of an application made to support a new requirement breaks a function implemented in another part of the application. If you're not careful, this can happen in a small application like Depot. Even if you're careful, this will happen in a large application.

Keeping tests up-to-date is an important part of maintaining your application. Rails makes this as easy as possible to do. Agile programmers make testing an integral part of their development efforts. Many even go so far as to write their tests first, before the first line of code is written.

So now we have a store with a cart in the sidebar. When we click to add an item to the cart, the page is redisplayed with an updated cart. But if our catalog is large, that redisplay might take a while. It uses bandwidth, and it uses server resources. Fortunately, we can use Turbo to make this better.

Iteration F2: Creating a Hotwired Cart

Turbo[2] is one of the Hotwire frameworks. Turbo lets us write code that runs in the browser and interacts with our server-based application. In our case, we'd like to make the Add to Cart buttons invoke the server create action on the LineItems controller in the background. The server can then send down just the HTML for the cart, and we can replace the cart in the sidebar with the server's updates.

Now, normally we'd do this by writing JavaScript that runs in the browser and by writing server-side code that communicates with this JavaScript (possibly using a technology such as JavaScript Object Notation [JSON]). The good news is that, with Rails, all this is hidden from us. We can use Ruby to do everything we need to do (and with a whole lot of support from some Rails helper methods).

The trick when adding Turbo to an application is to take small steps. So let's start with the most basic one. Let's change it so that our application responds with the HTML fragment containing the cart.

Because Rails includes Turbo by default, our client application is already ready. Behind the scenes it included text/vnd.turbo-stream.html in Accept header in form requests, so all we need to do is provide a turbo stream response.

We do this by adding a call to respond_to() telling it that we want to respond with a format of .turbo_stream:

```
rails80/depot_I/app/controllers/line_items_controller.rb
  def create
    product = Product.find(params[:product_id])
    @line_item = @cart.add_product(product)

    respond_to do |format|
      if @line_item.save
➤       format.turbo_stream do
➤         render turbo_stream: turbo_stream.replace(
➤           :cart,
```

---

2. https://turbo.hotwired.dev/

```
              partial: 'layouts/cart',
              locals: { cart: @cart }
            )
        end
        format.html { redirect_to store_index_url }
        format.json { render :show,
          status: :created, location: @line_item }
      else
        format.html { render :new,
          status: :unprocessable_entity }
        format.json { render json: @line_item.errors,
          status: :unprocessable_entity }
      end
    end
  end
```

The way to read this code is as follows: whenever we get a request that accepts a turbo stream response, we render a turbo stream response consisting of turbo stream replace, specifying an HTML element ID of cart as the element to be replaced, and rendering the partial, which can be found in app/views/layouts/_cart.html.erb using the value of @cart as the value of cart.

When receiving a turbo stream response, Turbo instructs the browser to stick the HTML fragment contained in the response into the browser's internal representation of the structure and content of the document being displayed—namely, the Document Object Model (DOM). By manipulating the DOM, we cause the display to change in front of the user's eyes.

Best of all, if the browser's request does *not* specify that it will accept a turbo stream response (perhaps because JavaScript was disabled?), what it will get instead is the HTML response, which in this case is a redirect to the store.

Now let's create the partial that this code references. Starting with code we extract from app/views/layouts/application.html.erb, add an HTML id attribute so that Turbo can identify the portion of the display that needs to be replaced. As we do this, we take care to ensure that the id is present even when the cart isn't displayed, which we do by adding an else clause:

rails80/depot_m/app/views/layouts/_cart.html.erb
```erb
<% if cart and not cart.line_items.empty? %>
  <div id="cart" class="bg-white rounded p-2">
    <%= render cart %>
  </div>
<% else %>
  <div id="cart"></div>
<% end %>
```

Finally, we update the template that we extracted this from to make use of the new partial:

rails80/depot_m/app/views/layouts/application.html.erb
```erb
<!DOCTYPE html>
<html>
  <head>
    <title><%= content_for(:title) || "Pragprog Books Online Store" %></title>
    <meta name="viewport" content="width=device-width,initial-scale=1">
    <meta name="apple-mobile-web-app-capable" content="yes">
    <meta name="mobile-web-app-capable" content="yes">
    <%= csrf_meta_tags %>
    <%= csp_meta_tag %>

    <%= yield :head %>

    <%# Enable PWA manifest for installable apps (make sure to enable in
        config/routes.rb too!) %>
    <%#= tag.link rel: "manifest", href: pwa_manifest_path(format: :json) %>

    <link rel="icon" href="/icon.png" type="image/png">
    <link rel="icon" href="/icon.svg" type="image/svg+xml">
    <link rel="apple-touch-icon" href="/icon.png">

    <%# Includes all stylesheet files in app/assets/stylesheets %>
    <%= stylesheet_link_tag :app, "data-turbo-track": "reload" %>
    <%= javascript_importmap_tags %>
  </head>

  <body>
    <header class="bg-green-700">
      <%= image_tag 'logo.svg', alt: 'The Pragmatic Bookshelf' %>
      <h1><%= @page_title %></h1>
    </header>

    <section class="flex">
      <nav class="bg-green-900 p-6">
►       <%= render partial: 'layouts/cart', locals: {cart: @cart } %>

        <ul class="text-gray-300 leading-8">
          <li><a href="/">Home</a></li>
          <li><a href="/questions">Questions</a></li>
          <li><a href="/news">News</a></li>
          <li><a href="/contact">Contact</a></li>
        </ul>
      </nav>

      <main class="container mx-auto mt-4 px-5 flex">
        <%= yield %>
      </main>
    </section>
  </body>
</html>
```

Does it work? At first, it's hard to tell the difference. But after emptying the cart and adding another book to the cart we see an obviously not-empty cart alongside a message that it currently is empty, as illustrated in the following screenshot.

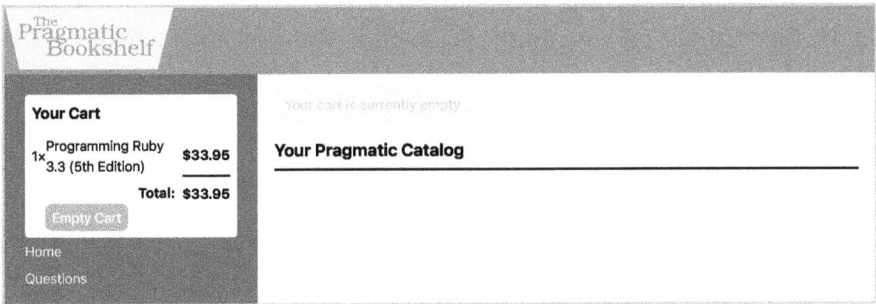

What's going on here is that we updated the cart (Yay!), but didn't update the notice (Boo!). This failure is something agile folks call failing fast and is something to be celebrated. So far in this iteration we literally added one call to format.turbo_stream and we got the cart updated dynamically and learned a lot.

What did we learn? Well for starters, we need a partial for every area of the screen that we wish to dynamically update, the HTML in that partial needs to contain a unique HTML ID element, and we need to update the controller to return turbo streams.

Let's apply this to the notice. First, we extract the notice from app/views/store/index.html.erb into a separate partial. While we're here, we add an else clause to ensure that there always is an HTML element with an ID of notice present on the page, even if its content is empty.

```
rails80/depot_m/app/views/store/_notice.html.erb
<% if notice.present? %>
  <p class="py-2 px-3 bg-green-50 mb-5 text-green-500 font-medium rounded-lg
            inline-block" id="notice">
    <%= notice %>
  </p>
<% else %>
  <div id="notice"></div>
<% end %>
```

And then we update the original template to make use of this partial, keeping things DRY:

```
rails80/depot_m/app/views/store/index.html.erb
<div class="w-full">
➤ <%= render 'notice' %>
```

```
<h1 class="font-bold text-xl mb-6 pb-2 border-b-2">
  Your Pragmatic Catalog
</h1>
```

Remembering from the test failures from the last iteration that the cart may not be present in the layout, we add an else clause there too. And while we're at it, we tidy things up and make it so that the cart isn't visible when it's empty:

rails80/depot_m/app/views/layouts/application.html.erb
```
<nav class="bg-green-900 p-6">
➤  <%= render partial: 'layouts/cart', locals: {cart: @cart } %>

  <ul class="text-gray-300 leading-8">
    <li><a href="/">Home</a></li>
    <li><a href="/questions">Questions</a></li>
    <li><a href="/news">News</a></li>
    <li><a href="/contact">Contact</a></li>
  </ul>
</nav>
```

Now that the partials are in place, we need to send two turbo stream replace instructions in response to a line item create. We actually can send an array of responses within the partial, but that feels messy, so we instead create a new template. As this will be the template for turbo stream LineItem create responses, the natural place to put this is in app/views/line_items/create.turbo_stream.erb:

rails80/depot_m/app/views/line_items/create.turbo_stream.erb
```
<%= turbo_stream.replace 'notice' do %>
  <%= render partial: 'store/notice' %>
<% end %>

<%= turbo_stream.replace 'cart' do %>
  <%= render partial: 'layouts/cart', locals: {cart: @cart} %>
<% end %>
```

Whether you create the turbo stream response inline in your controller or make use of an HTML template is a matter of personal taste, but generally a template is recommended, particularly when multiple items are in the response.

All that's remaining is to update the controller. Since we followed the default naming conventions for the template, we don't need to pass any arguments to the format.turbo_stream call.

```
rails80/depot_m/app/controllers/line_items_controller.rb
def create
  product = Product.find(params[:product_id])
  @line_item = @cart.add_product(product)

  respond_to do |format|
    if @line_item.save
➤     format.turbo_stream
      format.html { redirect_to store_index_url }
      format.json { render :show,
        status: :created, location: @line_item }
    else
      format.html { render :new,
        status: :unprocessable_entity }
      format.json { render json: @line_item.errors,
        status: :unprocessable_entity }
    end
  end
end
```

The Customer Is Never Satisfied

We're feeling pretty pleased with ourselves. We changed a handful of lines of code, and our boring old Web 1.0 application now sports Hotwire speed stripes. We breathlessly call the client over to come look. Without saying anything, we proudly click Add to Cart and look at her, eager for the praise we know will come. Instead, she looks surprised. "You called me over to show me a bug?" she asks. "You click that button, and nothing happens."

We patiently explain that, in fact, a lot happened. Just look at the cart in the sidebar. See? When we add something, the quantity changes from 4 to 5.

"Oh," she says, "I didn't notice that." And if she didn't notice the page update, it's likely that our users won't either. It's time for some user interface hacking.

Iteration F3: Highlighting Changes

A common way to highlight changes made to a page is the (now) infamous Yellow Fade Technique.[3] It highlights an element in a browser: by default it flashes the background yellow and then gradually fades it back to white. The user clicks the Add to Cart button, and the count updates to two as the line flares brighter. It then fades back to the background color over a short period of time.

---

3. https://signalvnoise.com/archives/000558.php

While Tailwind provides an extensive set of utility CSS classes to cover most needs, there comes a time when you need something more. For us, now is that time.

You can implement this with CSS animations.[4] In CSS animations, a class uses the animation attribute to reference a particular animation. The animation itself is defined as a series of keyframes that describe the style of an element at various points in the animation. The animation is executed by the browser when the page loads or when the class is applied to an element. This sounds complicated, but for our case we only need to define the starting and ending states of the element.

Let's see the CSS first. We'll place it inside app/assets/stylesheets/line_items.css. You can name the file whatever you like as long as it ends in css and is placed in this directory, and it will be made available to your entire application. Generally it makes sense to group related things into separate files.

rails80/depot_n/app/assets/stylesheets/line_items.css
```css
@keyframes line-item-highlight {
  0% {
    background: #8f8;
  }
  100% {
    background: none;
  }
}
.line-item-highlight {
  animation: line-item-highlight 1s;
}
```

The @keyframes directive defines an animation, in this case named line-item-highlight. Inside that declaration, we specify what the state of the DOM element should be at various points in the animation. At the start of the animation (0%), the element should have a background color of bright green, which is the highlight color. At the end of the animation (100%), it should have no background color.

Next we define a CSS class named line-item-highlight that uses the animation attribute. It accepts the name of the animation (which we just defined) and an animation time, which we've set at one second (note that you don't have to name the CSS class the same as the animation, but it can help keep it all straight if you do).

---

4. https://developer.mozilla.org/en-US/docs/Web/CSS/CSS_Animations/Using_CSS_animations

The last step is to use this class on the recently added item. To do that, our ERB template needs to know which item is the most recently added item. Set that inside LineItemsController:

```ruby
rails80/depot_o/app/controllers/line_items_controller.rb
  def create
    product = Product.find(params[:product_id])
    @line_item = @cart.add_product(product)

    respond_to do |format|
      if @line_item.save
➤       format.turbo_stream { @current_item = @line_item }
        format.html { redirect_to store_index_url }
        format.json { render :show,
          status: :created, location: @line_item }
      else
        format.html { render :new,
          status: :unprocessable_entity }
        format.json { render json: @line_item.errors,
          status: :unprocessable_entity }
      end
    end
  end
```

In the _line_item.html.erb partial, we then check to see if the item we're rendering is the one that just changed. If so, we give it the animation class we just defined:

```erb
rails80/depot_o/app/views/line_items/_line_item.html.erb
➤ <% if line_item == @current_item %>
➤ <tr class="line-item-highlight">
➤ <% else %>
➤ <tr>
➤ <% end %>
    <td class="text-right"><%= line_item.quantity %></td>
    <td>&times;</td>
    <td class="pr-2">
      <%= line_item.product.title %>
    </td>
    <td class="text-right font-bold">
      <%= number_to_currency(line_item.total_price) %>
    </td>
  </tr>
```

As a result of these two minor changes, the <tr> element of the most recently changed item in the cart will be tagged with class="line-item-highlight". When the browser receives this rendered HTML and inserts it into the DOM, the browser will see that the most recently added line item has the class line-item-highlight, which will trigger the animation. No JavaScript needed!

With that change in place, reload the page, then click any Add to Cart button, and you'll see that the changed item in the cart glows a light green before fading back to merge with the background.

We're not done yet. We haven't tested any of our Hotwire additions, such as what happens when we click the Add to Cart button. Rails provides the help we need to do that too.

We already have a should create line_item test, so let's add another one called should create line_item via turbo-stream:

rails80/depot_o/test/controllers/line_items_controller_test.rb
```
test "should create line_item via turbo-stream" do
  assert_difference("LineItem.count") do
    post line_items_url, params: { product_id: products(:pragprog).id },
      as: :turbo_stream
  end

  assert_response :success
  assert_match /<tr class="line-item-highlight">/, @response.body
end
```

This test differs in the name of the test, the addition of as: :turbo_stream—and in the expected results. Instead of a redirect, we expect a successful response containing a call to replace the HTML for the cart.

Iteration F4: Broadcasting Updates with Action Cable

As we saw with the products index page in Iteration A3: Making the Page Update in Real Time, on page 78, it's possible to send information from our Rails app to our users' browsers without a direct request. The technology that enables this is called WebSockets.[5] Prior to Rails 5, setting this up was fairly involved, but Rails 5 introduced Action Cable, which simplifies pushing data to all connected browsers.

We can use Action Cable and WebSockets to broadcast price updates to the users browsing the catalog. To see why we'd want to, bring up the Depot application in two browser windows or tabs. In the first window, display the catalog. Then, in the second window, update the price of an item. Return to the first window and add that item to the cart. At this point, the cart shows the updated price, but the catalog shows the original price, as illustrated in the screenshot on page 159.

We discuss this with our customer. She agrees to honor the price at the time the item was placed in the cart, but she wants the catalog being displayed to

---

5. https://www.w3.org/TR/websockets/

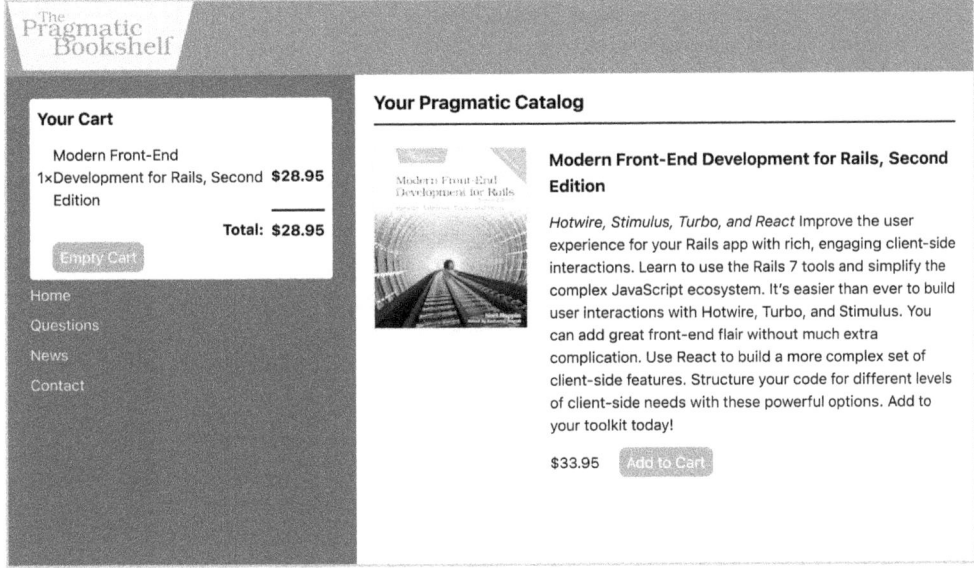

be up-to-date. At this point, we've reached the limits of what Turbo Streams can do for us, and we don't want to do full-page refreshes. We need a way to push partial updates to the browser.

In 2011, the Internet Engineering Task Force (IETF) published a Standards Track document describing a two-way WebSocket protocol.[6] Action Cable provides both a client-side JavaScript framework and a server-side Ruby framework that together seamlessly integrate the WebSocket protocol into the rest of your Rails application. This enables features like real-time updates to be easily added to your Rails application in a manner that performs well and is scalable.

Making use of Action Cable is a three-step process: create a channel, broadcast some data, and receive the data. And by now, it should be no surprise that Rails has a generator that does most of the work (for two out of the three steps, anyway):

```
depot> bin/rails generate channel products
      invoke  test_unit
      create    test/channels/products_channel_test.rb
   identical  app/channels/application_cable/channel.rb
   identical  app/channels/application_cable/connection.rb
      create  app/channels/products_channel.rb
      create  app/javascript/channels/index.js
      create  app/javascript/channels/consumer.js
```

---

6. https://tools.ietf.org/html/rfc6455

```
    append  app/javascript/application.js
    append  config/importmap.rb
    create  app/javascript/channels/products_channel.js
      gsub  app/javascript/channels/products_channel.js
    append  app/javascript/channels/index.js
```

The way to create a channel is by updating the file created in the app/channels/ directory:

rails80/depot_o/app/channels/products_channel.rb
```ruby
class ProductsChannel < ApplicationCable::Channel
  def subscribed
➤   stream_from "store/products"
  end

  def unsubscribed
    # Any cleanup needed when channel is unsubscribed
  end
end
```

What's important here is the name of the class (ProductsChannel) and the name of the stream (products). It's possible for a channel to support multiple streams (for example, a chat application can have multiple rooms), but we only need one stream for now.

Channels can have security implications, so by default Rails only allows access from the localhost when running in development mode. If you're doing development with multiple machines, you must disable this check. Do this by uncommenting the following line in config/environments/development.rb:

```ruby
config.action_cable.disable_request_forgery_protection = true
```

We'll be sending only data over this channel, and not processing commands, so this is safe to do.

As with before, we begin by separating out the product information from the store index template into a partial, and wrapping it with an HTML element with an id attribute.

rails80/depot_o/app/views/store/_product.html.erb
```erb
➤ <%= turbo_frame_tag(dom_id(product)) do %>
    <li class='flex mb-6'>
      <%= image_tag(product.image,
        class: 'object-contain w-40 h-48 shadow mr-6') %>
      <div>
        <h2 class="font-bold text-lg mb-3"><%= product.title %></h2>
        <p>
          <%= sanitize(product.description) %>
        </p>
```

```erb
      <div class="mt-3">
        <%= number_to_currency(product.price) %>
        <%= button_to "Add to Cart",
            line_items_path(product_id: product),
            form_class: "inline",
            class: 'ml-4 rounded-lg py-1 px-2
                    text-white bg-green-600' %>
      </div>
    </div>
  </li>
➤ <% end %>
```

We use the handy turbo_frame_tag() helper to create the HTML element, as well as the dom_id() helper to create a unique id for every product.

Next, we make two changes to the template from which this was extracted. First, we add a call to turbo_stream_from() to identify what channel we'll subscribe to. Next we make use of the partial that we just created.

rails80/depot_o/app/views/store/index.html.erb
```erb
<div class="w-full">
<%= render 'notice' %>

<h1 class="font-bold text-xl mb-6 pb-2 border-b-2">
  Your Pragmatic Catalog
</h1>
➤
➤ <%= turbo_stream_from 'products' %>

<ul>
  <% cache @products do %>
    <% @products.each do |product| %>
      <% cache product do %>
➤         <%= render partial: 'product', object: product %>
      <% end %>
    <% end %>
  <% end %>
</ul>
</div>
```

All that remains to be done is to broadcast the HTML for a product every time an update is made:

rails80/depot_o/app/controllers/products_controller.rb
```ruby
  def update
    respond_to do |format|
      if @product.update(product_params)
        format.html { redirect_to @product,
          notice: "Product was successfully updated." }
        format.json { render :show, status: :ok, location: @product }
➤
```

```
      @product.broadcast_replace_later_to "store/products",
        partial: "store/product"
      else
        format.html { render :edit,
          status: :unprocessable_entity }
        format.json { render json: @product.errors,
          status: :unprocessable_entity }
      end
    end
  end
```

We're calling broadcast_replace_later_to() because we want the messages to go out asynchronously, and generally after this request completes. We specify the channel and the partial to be used.

To start the Action Cable process (and to pick up the configuration change if that was done), we need to restart the server. The first time you visit the Depot page you'll see additional messages on the server window (information slightly abbreviated to fit within the book margins):

```
Started GET "/cable" for 127.0.0.1
Started GET "/cable/" [WebSocket] for 127.0.0.1
Successfully upgraded to WebSocket
Started GET "/cable" for 127.0.0.1
ProductsChannel is transmitting the subscription confirmation
ProductsChannel is streaming from products
Started GET "/cable/" [WebSocket] for 127.0.0.1
Successfully upgraded to WebSocket
Turbo::StreamsChannel is transmitting the subscription confirmation
Turbo::StreamsChannel is streaming from products
```

Again, update the price of a book in one browser window and watch the catalog update instantly in any other browser window that shows the Depot store.

What We Just Did

In this iteration, we added Hotwire support to our cart:

- We moved the shopping cart into the sidebar. We then arranged for the create action to redisplay the catalog page.

- We used as: :turbo_stream to indicate to the LineItemsController.create() that the client supports Turbo Streams.

- We then used an ERB partial template to return only the portions of the page that need to be replaced.

- We used Action Cable and Turbo Frames to update the catalog display whenever a product changes.

- We wrote a test that verifies not only the creation of a line item but also the content of the response that's returned from such a request.

The key point to take away is the incremental style of Hotwire development. Start with a conventional application and then add Ajax features, one by one. Hotwire applications can be hard to debug; by adding it slowly to an application, you make it easier to track down what changed if your application stops working. And, as you saw, starting with a conventional application makes it easier to support both Hotwire and non-Hotwire behavior in the same codebase.

Finally, here are a couple of hints. First, if you plan to do a lot of Hotwire development, you'll probably need to get familiar with your browser's JavaScript debugging facilities and with its DOM inspectors, such as Firefox's DevTools, Google Chrome's Developer Tools, Safari's Web Inspector, or Opera's Dragonfly. And, second, the NoScript plugin for Firefox makes checking JavaScript/no JavaScript a one-click breeze. Others find it useful to run two different browsers when they're developing—with JavaScript enabled in one and disabled in the other. Then, as new features are added, poking at it with both browsers will ensure that your application works regardless of the state of JavaScript.

Playtime

Here's some stuff to try on your own:

- The cart is currently hidden when the user empties it by redrawing the entire catalog. Can you change the application to remove it using a Turbo Stream request, so the page doesn't reload?

- Add a button next to each item in the cart. When clicked, it should invoke an action to decrement the quantity of the item, deleting it from the cart when the quantity reaches zero. Get it working without using Turbo first and then add the Turbo goodness.

- Make images clickable. In response to a click, add the associated product to the cart.

- When a product changes, highlight the product that changed in response to receiving a broadcast message.

In this chapter, you'll see:
- Linking tables with foreign keys
- Using belongs_to, has_many, and :through
- Creating forms based on models (form_with)
- Linking forms, models, and views

CHAPTER 12

Task G: Check Out!

Let's take stock. So far, we've put together a basic product administration system, we've implemented a catalog, and we have a pretty spiffy-looking shopping cart. So now we need to let the buyer actually purchase the contents of that cart. Let's implement the checkout function.

We're not going to go overboard here. For now, all we'll do is capture the customer's contact information and payment details. Using these, we'll construct an order in the database. Along the way, we'll be looking a bit more at models, validation, and form handling.

Iteration G1: Capturing an Order

An order is a set of line items, along with details of the purchase transaction. Our cart already contains line_items, so all we need to do is add an order_id column to the line_items table and create an orders table based on the Initial guess at application data diagram on page 63, combined with a brief chat with our customer.

First we create the order model and update the line_items table:

```
depot> bin/rails generate scaffold Order name address:text email \
        pay_type:integer
depot> bin/rails generate migration add_order_to_line_item order:references
```

Note that we didn't specify any data type for two of the four columns. This is because the data type defaults to string. This is yet another small way in which Rails makes things easier for you in the most common case without making things any more cumbersome when you need to specify a data type.

Also note that we defined pay_type as an integer. While this is an efficient way to store data that can only store discrete values, storing data in this way requires keeping track of which values are used for which payment type. Rails can do this for you through the use of enum declarations placed in the model class. Add this code to app/models/order.rb:

rails80/depot_o/app/models/order.rb
```ruby
class Order < ApplicationRecord
  enum :pay_type, {
    "Check"          => 0,
    "Credit card"    => 1,
    "Purchase order" => 2
  }
end
```

Finally, we need to modify the second migration to indicate that cart_id can be null in records. This is done by modifying the existing add_reference line to say null: true and adding a new change_column line to enable nulls in the cart_id column.

rails80/depot_o/db/migrate/20250420000009_add_order_to_line_item.rb
```ruby
class AddOrderToLineItem < ActiveRecord::Migration[8.0]
  def change
    add_reference :line_items, :order, null: true, foreign_key: true
    change_column :line_items, :cart_id, :integer, null: true
  end
end
```

Now that we've created the migrations, we can apply them:

```
depot> bin/rails db:migrate
== 20250420000007 CreateOrders: migrating =================================
-- create_table(:orders)
   -> 0.0007s
== 20250420000007 CreateOrders: migrated (0.0022s) ========================

== 20250420000008 AddOrderToLineItem: migrating ===========================
-- add_reference(:line_items, :order, {:null=>true, :foreign_key=>true})
   -> 0.0058s
-- change_column(:line_items, :cart_id, :integer, {:null=>true})
   -> 0.0046s
== 20250420000008 AddOrderToLineItem: migrated (0.0246s) ==================
```

Because the database didn't have entries for these two new migrations in the schema_migrations table, the db:migrate task applied both migrations to the database. We could, of course, have applied them separately by running the migration task after creating the individual migrations.

Creating the Order Capture Form

Now that we have our tables and our models as we need them, we can start the checkout process. First, we need to add a Checkout button to the shopping cart. Because it'll create a new order, we'll link it back to a new action in our order controller:

```erb
# rails80/depot_o/app/views/carts/_cart.html.erb
<div id="<%= dom_id cart %>">
  <h2 class="font-bold text-lg mb-3">Your Cart</h2>

  <table class="table-auto">
    <%= render cart.line_items %>

    <tfoot>
      <tr>
        <th class="text-right pr-2 pt-2" colspan="3">Total:</th>
        <td class="text-right pt-2 font-bold border-t-2 border-black">
          <%= number_to_currency(cart.total_price) %>
        </td>
      </tr>
    </tfoot>
  </table>

  <div class="flex mt-1">
    <%= button_to 'Empty Cart', cart, method: :delete,
      class: 'ml-4 rounded-lg py-1 px-2 text-white bg-green-600' %>
    <%= button_to 'Checkout', new_order_path, method: :get,
      class: 'ml-4 rounded-lg py-1 px-2 text-black bg-green-200' %>
  </div>
</div>
```

We wrapped the buttons in a div and used a flex layout so that they'll appear side by side.

The first thing we want to do is check to make sure that there's something in the cart. This requires us to have access to the cart. Planning ahead, we'll also need this when we create an order:

```ruby
# rails80/depot_o/app/controllers/orders_controller.rb
class OrdersController < ApplicationController
  include CurrentCart
  before_action :set_cart, only: %i[ new create ]
  before_action :ensure_cart_isnt_empty, only: %i[ new ]
  before_action :set_order, only: %i[ show edit update destroy ]

  # GET /orders or /orders.json
  #...

  private
    def ensure_cart_isnt_empty
      if @cart.line_items.empty?
        redirect_to store_index_url, notice: "Your cart is empty"
      end
    end
end
```

If nothing is in the cart, we redirect the user back to the storefront, provide a notice of what we did, and return immediately. This prevents people from navigating directly to the checkout option and creating empty orders. Note that we tucked this handling of an exception case into a before_action method. This enables the main line processing logic to remain clean.

And we add a test for requires item in cart and modify the existing test for should get new to ensure that the cart contains an item:

rails80/depot_o/test/controllers/orders_controller_test.rb
```
➤    test "requires item in cart" do
➤      get new_order_url
➤      assert_redirected_to store_index_path
➤      assert_equal "Your cart is empty", flash[:notice]
➤    end

     test "should get new" do
➤      post line_items_url, params: { product_id: products(:pragprog).id }
➤
       get new_order_url
       assert_response :success
     end
```

Now we want the new action to present users with a form, prompting them to enter the information in the orders table: the user's name, address, email address, and payment type. This means we'll need to display a Rails template containing a form. The input fields on this form will have to link to the corresponding attributes in a Rails model object, so we need to create an empty model object in the new action to give these fields something to work with.

As always with HTML forms, the trick is populating any initial values into the form fields and then extracting those values out into our application when the user clicks the submit button.

In the controller, the order variable is set to reference a new Order model object. This is done because the view populates the form from the data in this object. As it stands, that's not particularly interesting. Because it's a new model object, all the fields will be empty. However, consider the general case. Maybe we want to edit an existing order. Or maybe the user has tried to enter an order but the data has failed validation. In these cases, we want any existing data in the model shown to the user when the form is displayed. Passing in the empty model object at this stage makes all these cases consistent. The view can always assume it has a model object available. Then, when the user clicks the submit button, we'd like the new data from the form to be extracted into a model object back in the controller.

Fortunately, Rails makes this relatively painless. It provides us with a bunch of *form helper* methods. These helpers interact with the controller and with the models to implement an integrated solution for form handling. Before we start on our final form, let's look at a small example:

```erb
<%= form_with(model: order) do |form| %>
  <p>
    <%= form.label :name, "Name:" %>
    <%= form.text_field :name, size: 40 %>
  </p>
<% end %>
```

This code does two powerful things for us. First, the form_with() helper on the first line sets up an HTML form that knows about Rails routes and models. The argument, model: order, tells the helper which instance variable to use when naming fields and sending the form data back to the controller.

The second powerful feature of the code is how it creates the form fields themselves. You can see that form_with() sets up a Ruby block environment (that ends on the last line of the listing with the end keyword). Within this block, you can put normal template stuff (such as the <p> tag). But you can also use the block's parameter (form in this case) to reference a form context. We use this context to add a text field with a label by calling text_field() and label(), respectively. Because the text field is constructed in the context of form_with, it's automatically associated with the data in the order object. This association means that submitting the form will set the right names and values in the data available to the controller, but it will also pre-populate the form fields with any values already existing on the model.

All these relationships can be confusing. It's important to remember that Rails needs to know both the *names* and the *values* to use for the fields associated with a model. The combination of form_with and the various field-level helpers (such as text_field) gives it this information.

Now we can update the template for the form that captures a customer's details for checkout. It's invoked from the new action in the order controller, so the template is called new.html.erb, found in the app/views/orders directory:

rails80/depot_o/app/views/orders/new.html.erb
```erb
<% content_for :title, "New order" %>

<div class="md:w-2/3 w-full">
  <h1 class="font-bold text-4xl">Please Enter Your Details</h1>

  <%= render "form", order: @order %>
</div>
```

In this file, we've updated the h1 and removed the link back to the orders index. This template makes use of a partial named _form. We take a peek at that file and see many long lines repeating the same class definitions.

```erb
<div class="my-5">
  <%= form.label :name %>
  <%= form.text_field :name, class: [
    "block shadow-sm rounded-md border outline-hidden px-3 py-2 mt-2 w-full",
    { "border-gray-400 focus:outline-blue-600": order.errors[:name].none?,
      "border-red-400 focus:outline-red-600": order.errors[:name].any? } ] %>
</div>
```

That's quite a mouthful. The class= attribute is an array. The first element of the array is a list of class names. The second element of the array is a hash of class names and conditions. If the condition is true, the class names are added to the list of classes. If the condition is false, the class names aren't added. The net result is a gray border if there are no errors and a red border if there are errors. An outline is also defined, but hidden, which appears to be an oversight.[1]

Let's introduce a pair of CSS rules so that we can clean this up:

rails80/depot_o/app/assets/tailwind/application.css
```css
@import "tailwindcss";

.input-field {
  @apply
  block shadow-sm rounded-md border px-3 py-2 mt-2 w-full
  border-gray-400 focus:outline-blue-600
}

.field_with_errors .input-field {
  @apply
  border-red-400 focus:outline-red-600
}
```

There is a lot to unpack in this short little file:

- The @apply directive[2] is a Tailwind CSS feature that enables you to combine a set of utility classes into a single CSS class.

- The field_with_errors[3] class is a Rails feature that is added to form fields that have errors. This class is used to style the form fields differently when there are errors.

- With CSS, the most specific rule wins. In this case, the .field_with_errors .input-field rule is more specific than the .input-field rule, so classes included in it will take precedence. There is no need to repeat the classes in the less

---

1. https://github.com/rails/tailwindcss-rails/issues/489M
2. https://tailwindcss.com/docs/functions-and-directives#apply-directive
3. https://guides.rubyonrails.org/active_record_validations.html#displaying-validation-errors-in-views

specific .input-field rule as they will be applied to elements that include this class.

With this change in place, we can simplify the form template:

```erb
<div class="my-5">
  <%= form.label :name %>
  <%= form.text_field :name, class: "input-field" %>
</div>
```

There are many reasons to consider factoring out repeated definitions into a style sheet: perhaps it's to reduce repetition to ease maintenance, perhaps it's to reduce visual clutter so that you can focus on the structure of the document, or perhaps it's merely to keep the number of columns down so that it will fit on the printed page. Any of these are good reasons, and they all apply here.

Once we've replaced the class attributes for the form.text_field and wrapped other lines to fit on the page, we make a second set of changes:

rails80/depot_o/app/views/orders/_form.html.erb
```erb
<%= form_with(model: order, class: "contents") do |form| %>
  <% if order.errors.any? %>
    <div id="error_explanation" class="bg-red-50 text-red-500 px-3 py-2
      font-medium rounded-md mt-3">
      <h2><%= pluralize(order.errors.count, "error") %>
      prohibited this order from being saved:</h2>

      <ul class="list-disc ml-6">
        <% order.errors.each do |error| %>
          <li><%= error.full_message %></li>
        <% end %>
      </ul>
    </div>
  <% end %>

  <div class="my-5">
    <%= form.label :name %>
    <%= form.text_field :name, class: "input-field" %>
  </div>

  <div class="my-5">
    <%= form.label :address %>
    <%= form.textarea :address, rows: 4, class: "input-field" %>
  </div>

  <div class="my-5">
    <%= form.label :email %>
    <%= form.email_field :email, class: "input-field" %>
  </div>

  <div class="my-5">
```

```erb
    <%= form.label :pay_type %>
    <%= form.select :pay_type, Order.pay_types.keys,
                    { prompt: 'Select a payment method' },
                    class: "input-field" %>
  </div>

  <div class="inline">
    <%= form.submit 'Place Order', class: "w-full sm:w-autorounded-md
        px-3.5 py-2.5 bg-green-200 hover:bg-blue-500 text-black
        inline-block font-medium cursor-pointer" %>
  </div>
<% end %>
```

Rails has form helpers for all the different HTML-level form elements. In the preceding code we use text_field, email_field, and text_area helpers to capture the customer's name, email, and address. We'll cover form helpers in more depth in Generating Forms, on page 383.

The only tricky thing in there is the code associated with the selection list. We use the keys defined for the pay_type enum for the list of available payment options. We also pass the :prompt parameter, which adds a dummy selection containing the prompt text.

We also adjust the background and text color of the submit button as well as the text for the button itself.

We're ready to play with our form. Add some stuff to your cart, then click the Checkout button. You should see something like the following screenshot.

Looking good! Before we move on, let's finish the new action by adding some validation. We'll change the Order model to verify that the customer enters data for all the input fields. We'll also validate that the payment type is one of the accepted values:

```ruby
rails80/depot_o/app/models/order.rb
class Order < ApplicationRecord
  # ...
➤  validates :name, :address, :email, presence: true
➤  validates :pay_type, inclusion: pay_types.keys
end
```

Some folks might be wondering why we bother to validate the payment type, given that its value comes from a drop-down list that contains only valid values. We do it because an application can't assume that it's being fed values from the forms it creates. Nothing is stopping a malicious user from submitting form data directly to the application, bypassing our form. If the user sets an unknown payment type, that user might conceivably get our products for free.

Note that we already loop over the @order.errors at the top of the page. This'll report validation failures.

Since we modified validation rules, we need to modify our test fixture to match:

```yaml
rails80/depot_o/test/fixtures/orders.yml
# Read about fixtures at
# https://api.rubyonrails.org/classes/ActiveRecord/FixtureSet.html

one:
➤  name: Dave Thomas
  address: MyText
➤  email: dave@example.org
➤  pay_type: Check
two:
  name: MyString
  address: MyText
  email: MyString
  pay_type: 1
```

Furthermore, for an order to be created, a line item needs to be in the cart, so we need to modify the line items test fixture too:

```yaml
rails80/depot_o/test/fixtures/line_items.yml
# Read about fixtures at
# https://api.rubyonrails.org/classes/ActiveRecord/FixtureSet.html

one:
  product: two
  cart: one
  price: 1
```

```
    two:
➤     product: pragprog
➤     order: one
      price: 1
```

Note that if you didn't choose to do the optional exercises in Playtime, on page 140, you need to modify all of the references to products and carts at this time and *not* add price to the line items.

Feel free to make other changes, but only the first is currently used in the functional tests. For these tests to pass, we'll need to implement the model.

Capturing the Order Details

Let's implement the create() action in the controller. This method has to do the following:

1. Capture the values from the form to populate a new Order model object.
2. Add the line items from our cart to that order.
3. Validate and save the order. If this fails, display the appropriate messages, and let the user correct any problems.
4. Once the order is successfully saved, delete the cart, redisplay the catalog page, and display a message confirming that the order has been placed.

We define the relationships themselves, first from the line item to the order:

rails80/depot_o/app/models/line_item.rb
```
class LineItem < ApplicationRecord
➤   belongs_to :order, optional: true
    belongs_to :product
➤   belongs_to :cart, optional: true

    def total_price
      price * quantity
    end
end
```

And then we define the relationship from the order to the line item, once again indicating that all line items that belong to an order are to be destroyed whenever the order is destroyed:

rails80/depot_o/app/models/order.rb
```
class Order < ApplicationRecord
➤   has_many :line_items, dependent: :destroy
    # ...
end
```

The method ends up looking something like this:

```
rails80/depot_o/app/controllers/orders_controller.rb
def create
  @order = Order.new(order_params)
➤ @order.add_line_items_from_cart(@cart)

  respond_to do |format|
    if @order.save
➤     Cart.destroy(session[:cart_id])
➤     session[:cart_id] = nil
➤     format.html { redirect_to store_index_url, notice:
➤       "Thank you for your order." }
      format.json { render :show, status: :created,
        location: @order }
    else
      format.html { render :new, status: :unprocessable_entity }
      format.json { render json: @order.errors,
        status: :unprocessable_entity }
    end
  end
end
```

We start by creating a new Order object and initialize it from the form data. The next line adds into this order the items that are already stored in the cart; we'll write the method to do that in a minute.

Next, we tell the order object to save itself (and its children, the line items) to the database. Along the way, the order object will perform validation (but we'll get to that in a minute).

If the save succeeds, we do two things. First, we ready ourselves for this customer's next order by deleting the cart from the session. Then we redisplay the catalog, using the redirect_to() method to display a cheerful message. If, instead, the save fails, we redisplay the checkout form with the current cart.

In the create action, we assumed that the order object contains the add_line_items_from_cart() method, so let's implement that method now:

```
rails80/depot_p/app/models/order.rb
class Order < ApplicationRecord
  # ...
➤ def add_line_items_from_cart(cart)
➤   cart.line_items.each do |item|
➤     item.cart_id = nil
➤     line_items << item
➤   end
➤ end
end
```

> ### Joe asks:
> ### Aren't You Creating Duplicate Orders?
>
> Joe is concerned to see our controller creating Order model objects in two actions: new and create. He's wondering why this doesn't lead to duplicate orders in the database.
>
> The answer is that the new action creates an Order object *in memory* simply to give the template code something to work with. Once the response is sent to the browser, that particular object gets abandoned, and it'll eventually be reaped by Ruby's garbage collector. It never gets close to the database.
>
> The create action also creates an Order object, populating it from the form fields. This object *does* get saved in the database. So model objects perform two roles: they map data into and out of the database, but they're also regular objects that hold business data. They affect the database only when you tell them to, typically by calling save().

For each item that we transfer from the cart to the order, we need to do two things. First we set the cart_id to nil to prevent the item from going poof when we destroy the cart.

Then we add the item itself to the line_items collection for the order. Notice we didn't have to do anything special with the various foreign-key fields, such as setting the order_id column in the line item rows to reference the newly created order row. Rails does that knitting for us using the has_many() and belongs_to() declarations we added to the Order and LineItem models. Appending each new line item to the line_items collection hands the responsibility for key management over to Rails. We also need to modify the test to reflect the new redirect:

rails80/depot_p/test/controllers/orders_controller_test.rb
```
  test "should create order" do
    assert_difference("Order.count") do
      post orders_url, params: { order: { address: @order.address,
        email: @order.email, name: @order.name,
        pay_type: @order.pay_type } }
    end
➤   assert_redirected_to store_index_url
  end
```

So, as a first test of all of this, click the Place Order button on the checkout page without filling in any of the form fields. You should see the checkout page redisplayed along with error messages complaining about the empty fields, as shown in screenshot on page 177.

If we fill in data, as shown in the following screenshot, and click Place Order, we should be taken back to the catalog, as shown in next the screenshot.

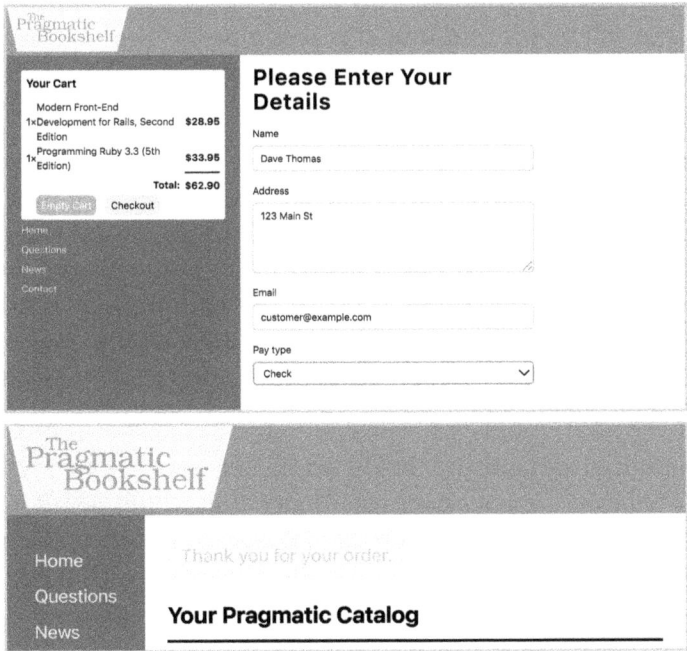

But did it work? Let's look in the database, using the Rails command dbconsole, which tells Rails to open an interactive shell to whatever database we have configured.

```
depot> bin/rails dbconsole
SQLite version 3.36.0 2021-06-18 18:58:49
Enter ".help" for instructions
sqlite> .mode line
sqlite> select * from orders;
           id = 1
         name = Dave Thomas
      address = 123 Main St
        email = customer@example.com
     pay_type = 0
   created_at = 2022-01-12 16:41:35.897275
   updated_at = 2022-01-12 16:41:48.065263
sqlite> select * from line_items;
```

```
              id = 10
      product_id = 3
         cart_id =
      created_at = 2022-01-12 16:41:46.548932
      updated_at = 2022-01-12 16:41:48.065780
        quantity = 1
           price = 19.95
        order_id = 1
sqlite> .quit
```

Although what you see will differ on details such as version numbers and dates (and price will be present only if you completed the exercises defined in Playtime, on page 140), you should see a single order and one or more line items that match your selections.

Our customer is enthusiastic about our progress, but after playing with the new checkout feature for a few minutes, she has a question: how does a user enter payment details? It's a great question, since there isn't a way to do that. Making that possible is somewhat tricky because each payment method requires different details. If users want to pay with a credit card, they need to enter a card number and expiration date. If they want to pay with a check, we'll need a routing number and an account number. And for purchase orders, we need the purchase order number.

Although we could put all five fields on the screen at once, the customer immediately balks at the poor user experience that would result. Can we show the appropriate fields, depending on what payment type is chosen? Changing elements of a user interface dynamically is certainly possible with some JavaScript but is beyond what we can do with Turbo alone.

Iteration G2: Adding Fields Dynamically to a Form

We need a dynamic form that changes what fields are shown based on what pay type the user has selected. We could cobble something together with jQuery, but Rails includes another framework from the Hotwire set of frameworks that's well-suited to this task: Stimulus.[4] Let's put it to use!

Creating a Stimulus Controller

Our starting point is clearly the existing order form. The plan is to add some *additonal fields*, cause those fields to be *hidden* on initial display, and finally, to expose the fields associated with selected pay type whenever the selection changes.

---

4. https://stimulus.hotwired.dev/

Let's focus intially on the behavior we want to implement, then on the markup. With Stimulus, the behavior is placed inside a controller, so let's generate one:

```
depot> bin/rails generate stimulus payment
      create  app/javascript/controllers/payment_controller.js
```

What we have is a single file. That's where we place our logic:

rails80/depot_p/app/javascript/controllers/payment_controller.js
```
import { Controller } from "@hotwired/stimulus"

// Connects to data-controller="payment"
export default class extends Controller {
➤   static targets = [ "selection", "additionalFields" ]
➤
➤   initialize() {
➤     this.showAdditionalFields()
➤   }
➤
➤   showAdditionalFields() {
➤     let selection = this.selectionTarget.value
➤
➤     for (let fields of this.additionalFieldsTargets) {
➤       fields.disabled = fields.hidden = (fields.dataset.type != selection)
➤     }
➤   }
}
```

This has three parts:

- First, we declare a list of targets. Targets identify HTML elements that our controller will interact with. Our targets are a selection element and additional fields. We simply list our targets here without specifying how many of each we expect.

- Next, we define the initialization logic, which could implement as a loop over the targets, hiding each, but it turns out that we can take advantage of the code that shows additional fields. This has the additional benefit of gracefully handing the case where the browser restores the value of some form fields when the user manually refreshes the browser window.

- Finally, we define the code that shows the additional fields. We start by getting the value of the selection. We then iterate over the additional fields. Inside the iteration, we either disable and hide each set of fields or enable and show each set based on whether or not the type of those fields matches the selection.

This all sounds straightforward but won't completely make sense until we see the markup. So the next step is to define the additional fields.

Defining Additional Fields

Paying online from your checking account involves providing a routing code and an account number. Let's add these fields to a new partial:

```
rails80/depot_p/app/views/orders/_check.html.erb
<fieldset data-payment-target="additionalFields" data-type="Check">
  <div class="my-5">
    <%= form.label :routing_number %>
    <%= form.text_field :routing_number, class: "input-field" %>
  </div>

  <div class="my-5">
    <%= form.label :account_number %>
    <%= form.password_field :account_number, class: "input-field" %>
  </div>
</fieldset>
```

The first line defines a payment target of additionalFields as well as a type of Check. This matches up with the controller, which defined additionalFields as a target and matches the fields.dataset.type against the value from the selection target.

The remainder of this file is familiar: it defines the two new fields exactly as we have been defining them all along. The only new thing is the reference to a password_field, which causes most browsers to hide the text as you're entering it.

Next up, we need to define fields for a credit card number and an expiration date. We put them into a second partial:

```
rails80/depot_p/app/views/orders/_cc.html.erb
<fieldset data-payment-target="additionalFields" data-type="Credit card">
  <div class="my-5">
    <%= form.label :credit_card_number %>
    <%= form.password_field :credit_card_number, class: "input-field" %>
  </div>

  <div class="my-5">
    <%= form.label :expiration_date %>
    <%= form.text_field :expiration_date, class: "input-field",
      size:9, placeholder: "e.g. 03/22" %>
  </div>
</fieldset>
```

No surprises here. Finally, we need a purchase order number field, which we put into a third partial:

```
rails80/depot_p/app/views/orders/_po.html.erb
<fieldset data-payment-target="additionalFields" data-type="Purchase order">
  <div class="my-5">
    <%= form.label :po_number %>
```

```erb
      <%= form.number_field :po_number, class: "input-field" %>
    </div>
</fieldset>
```

Now that we're done with the additional fields, it's time to update the form itself:

```erb
rails80/depot_p/app/views/orders/_form.html.erb
<%= form_with(model: order, class: "contents") do |form| %>
  <% if order.errors.any? %>
    <div id="error_explanation" class="bg-red-50 text-red-500 px-3 py-2
      font-medium rounded-md mt-3">
      <h2><%= pluralize(order.errors.count, "error") %>
      prohibited this order from being saved:</h2>

      <ul class="list-disc ml-6">
        <% order.errors.each do |error| %>
          <li><%= error.full_message %></li>
        <% end %>
      </ul>
    </div>
  <% end %>

  <div class="my-5">
    <%= form.label :name %>
    <%= form.text_field :name, class: "input-field" %>
  </div>

  <div class="my-5">
    <%= form.label :address %>
    <%= form.textarea :address, rows: 4, class: "input-field" %>
  </div>

  <div class="my-5">
    <%= form.label :email %>
    <%= form.email_field :email, class: "input-field" %>
  </div>

➤  <div data-controller="payment">
    <div class="my-5">
      <%= form.label :pay_type %>
      <%= form.select :pay_type, Order.pay_types.keys,
                    { prompt: 'Select a payment method' },
➤                   'data-payment-target' => 'selection',
➤                   'data-action' => 'payment#showAdditionalFields',
                    class: "input-field" %>
    </div>

➤    <%= render partial: 'check', locals: {form: form} %>
➤    <%= render partial: 'cc', locals: {form: form} %>
➤    <%= render partial: 'po', locals: {form: form} %>
➤  </div>

  <div class="inline">
```

```erb
    <%= form.submit 'Place Order', class: "w-full sm:w-auto
        rounded-md px-3.5 py-2.5 bg-green-200 hover:bg-blue-500 text-black
        inline-block font-medium cursor-pointer" %>
  </div>
<% end %>
```

This file has three sets of changes.

- First, we wrap all of the elements that are to be controlled by the payment Stimulus controller with a div element containing a data-controller field naming the controller.

- Next, we identify the form.select element as the selection target for the payment controller and associate an action by naming the method to be called when the selection changes.

- Finally, we render the three partials that we just created.

With both the code and markup now in place, we revisit the browser to see the results shown in the screenshots on page 183.

If that isn't what you're seeing, here are some things to check:

- Your browser's console is always a great resource and where you'll find both syntax and runtime errors in your JavaScript code.

- Check for typos in your markup and in the portions of the payment Stimulus controller that need to match your markup. Remember that generally the default is to do nothing. If the controller doesn't match, then no code will be executed. If no additional fields are found, the loop won't hide anything.

- Feel free to add calls to console.log inside your Stimulus controller.

For the times when you really want to run all of your tests with a single command, Rails has this covered too: try running bin/rails test:all.

What We Just Did

In a fairly short amount of time, we did the following:

- We created a form to capture details for the order and linked it to a new order model.

- We added validation and used helper methods to display errors to the user.

- We provided a feed so the administrator can monitor incoming orders.

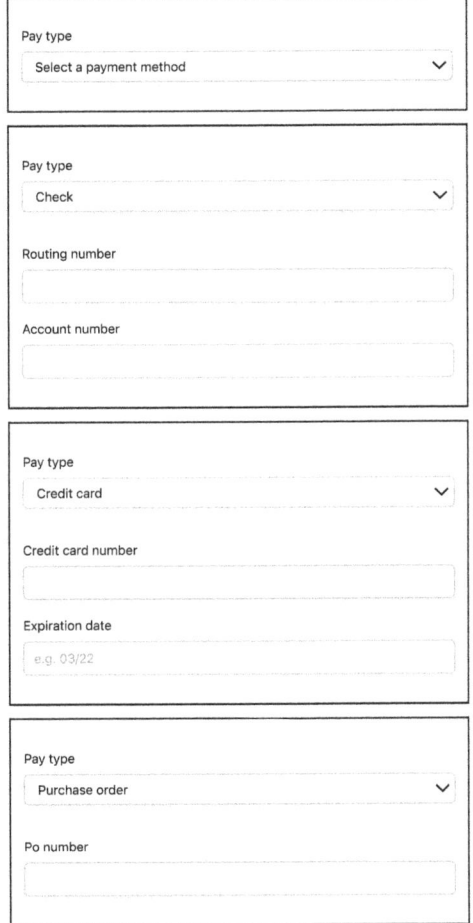

Playtime

Here's some stuff to try on your own:

• Get HTML- and JSON-formatted views working for who_bought requests. Experiment with including the order information in the JSON view by rendering @product.to_json(include: :orders). Do the same thing for XML using ActiveModel::Serializers::Xml.[5]

• What happens if you click the Checkout button in the sidebar while the checkout screen is already displayed? Can you find a way to disable the button in this circumstance?

---

5. https://github.com/rails/activemodel-serializers-xml#readme

- The list of possible payment types is currently stored as a constant in the Order class. Can you move this list into a database table? Can you still make validation work for the field?

Iteration G3: Testing Our JavaScript Functionality

Now that we have application-level functionality in JavaScript code, we're going to need to have tests in place to ensure that the function not only works as intended but continues to work as we make changes to the application.

Testing this functionality involves a lot of steps: visiting the store, selecting an item, adding that item to the cart, clicking checkout, filling in a few fields, and selecting a payment type. And from a testing perspective, we're going to need both a Rails server and a browser.

To accomplish this, Rails makes use of the popular Google Chrome web browser and Capybara,[6] which is a tool that drives this automation. Microsoft Edge and Mozilla's Firefox are also supported, as is Apple's Safari once Allow Remote Automation is enabled via the Develop menu. The choice of browser is controlled by the application_system_test_case.rb file in the test directory.

rails80/depot_p/test/application_system_test_case.rb
```ruby
require "test_helper"

class ApplicationSystemTestCase < ActionDispatch::SystemTestCase
➤   driven_by :selenium, using: :headless_chrome, screen_size: [ 1400, 1400 ]
end
```

Should you wish to test with a different browser, this is the place where you would indicate which browser to use. :edge, :firefox, and :safari are all supported.

Tests that pull together a complete and integrated version of the software are called *system tests*, and that's exactly what we'll be doing: we'll be testing a full end-to-end scenario with a web browser, web server, our application, and a database.

Let's run the existing system tests using bin/rails test:system. Oh dear, there are about a dozen failures—which isn't all that surprising, given that we've ignored these tests up to this point.

The output indicates screenshot images have been placed into the /tmp/screenshots directory, and taking a look at a few of them, we feel a bit like archaeologists. The tests verify the operation of the code as originally scaffolded—most importantly before we added product validation logic in Iteration

---

6. https://github.com/teamcapybara/capybara#readme

Iteration G3: Testing Our JavaScript Functionality • 185

B1: Validating!, on page 85, and before we moved the cart in Changing the Flow, on page 148.

We could fix these errors, but we would end up with tests that largely duplicate tests we already have. Let's clean things up and write an entirely new test—one that takes advantage of the fact that we're interacting with a real browser that runs the JavaScript code that we provided.

```
$ rm test/system/carts_test.rb
$ rm test/system/line_items_test.rb
$ rm test/system/products_test.rb
```

Now we're ready to write the test we came here to write, which is that our JavaScript is working when it's run in a web browser. We start by describing the actions and checks we want performed in test/system/orders_test.rb, which already has some tests in it from the scaffold:

rails80/depot_p/test/system/orders_test.rb
```ruby
require "application_system_test_case"

class OrdersTest < ApplicationSystemTestCase
  test "check dynamic fields" do
    visit store_index_url

    click_on "Add to Cart", match: :first

    click_on "Checkout"

    assert has_no_field? "Routing number"
    assert has_no_field? "Account number"
    assert has_no_field? "Credit card number"
    assert has_no_field? "Expiration date"
    assert has_no_field? "Po number"

    select "Check", from: "Pay type"

    assert has_field? "Routing number"
    assert has_field? "Account number"
    assert has_no_field? "Credit card number"
    assert has_no_field? "Expiration date"
    assert has_no_field? "Po number"

    select "Credit card", from: "Pay type"

    assert has_no_field? "Routing number"
    assert has_no_field? "Account number"
    assert has_field? "Credit card number"
    assert has_field? "Expiration date"
    assert has_no_field? "Po number"

    select "Purchase order", from: "Pay type"

    assert has_no_field? "Routing number"
    assert has_no_field? "Account number"
    assert has_no_field? "Credit card number"
```

```
    assert has_no_field? "Expiration date"
    assert has_field? "Po number"
  end
end
```

As you can see, it's largely a repetition of a few lines of code with minor variations, prefaced by a few discrete steps: visit() a URL, find the :first button with the text "Add to Cart" and click_on() it. Then click_on() the button labeled "Checkout". We then select() various pay types and verify what fields we expect to see and what fields we expect *not* to see.

At this point in the test, we check an assumption that the routing number field isn't on the page yet. We do this using has_no_field?() and pass it "Routing number", which is a the text the user would see if they had selected Check as the Pay type. We repeat this for all the other fields that the user could eventually see but at this point should be hidden.

In general, be careful when using has_no_field?() as there are an uncountable number of fields the form doesn't have, and any typo will cause such a test to pass. In this case we're safe, as the test contains matching has_field?() method calls.

After that, we select() the value "Check" from the "Pay type" selector and then assert that the routing number text field showed up, using has_field(). We repeat this for each combination of Pay type and field. Four groups of five assertions, for a total of twenty asssertions. Whew!

Capybara makes all of this possible using a compact, readable API that requires very little code. For additional information and more methods, we suggest that you familiarize yourself with the domain-specific language (DSL) that Capybara provides.[7]

Now let's run the test we just wrote:

```
$ bin/rails test:system
Running 5 tests in a single process (parallelization threshold is 50)
Run options: --seed 55897

# Running:

Capybara starting Puma...
* Version 5.5.2 , codename: Zawgyi
* Min threads: 0, max threads: 4
* Listening on tcp://127.0.0.1:56776
Capybara starting Puma...
* Version 3.12.1 , codename: Llamas in Pajamas
```

---

7. https://github.com/teamcapybara/capybara#the-dsl

```
* Min threads: 0, max threads: 4
* Listening on tcp://127.0.0.1:43749
.....
Finished in 4.065668s, 1.2298 runs/s, 5.9031 assertions/s.

5 runs, 24 assertions, 0 failures, 0 errors, 0 skips
```

When you run this, you'll notice a number of things. First, a web server is started on your behalf, and then a browser is launched and the actions you requested are performed. Once the test is complete, both are stopped and the results of the test are reported back to you. All this is based on your instructions as to what actions and tests are to be performed, and it's then expressed clearly and succinctly as a system test.

Note that system tests tend to take a bit longer to execute than model or controller tests, which is why they're not run as a part of bin/rails test. But all in all, these tests aren't all that slow, and they can test things that can't be tested in any other way, so system tests are a valuable tool to have in our toolchest.

What We Just Did

- We replaced a static form_select field with a dynamic list of form fields that change instantly based on user selection.

- We wrote a Stimulus controller that attached to the HTML to make the dynamic changes happen.

- We used Capybara to system-test this functionality.

Playtime

Here's some stuff to try on your own:

- While new fields were added to the form, they have yet to be added to the database. Generate a migration to add the fields, and add them to the order_parameters() method.

- Add a test to verify that the Add to Cart and Empty Cart buttons reveal and hide the cart, respectively.

- Add a test of the highlight feature you added in Iteration F3: Highlighting Changes, on page 155. The Capybara have_css() method[8] may be useful here.

---

8. https://rubydoc.info/github/jnicklas/capybara/Capybara%2FRSpecMatchers:have_css

In this chapter, you'll see:
- Sending email
- Running background code with Active Job
- System testing background jobs and email

CHAPTER 13

Task H: Sending Emails and Processing Payments Efficiently

At this point, we have a website that responds to requests and provides feeds that allow sales of individual titles to be checked periodically. The customer is happier but still not satisfied. The first bit of feedback is that users aren't getting confirmation emails of their purchases. The second is around payment processing. The customer has arranged for us to integrate with a payment processor that can handle all forms of payment we want to support, but the processor's API is very slow. The customer wants to know if that will slow down the site.

Sending email is a common need for any web application, and Rails has you covered via Action Mailer,[1] which you'll learn in this chapter. Dealing with the slow payment-processing API requires learning about the library Action Mailer is built on, Active Job.[2] Active Job allows you to run code in a background process so that the user doesn't have to wait for it to complete. Sending email is slow, which is why Action Mailer uses Active Job to offload the work. This is a common technique you'll use often when developing web applications. Let's take it one step at a time and learn how to send email.

Iteration H1: Sending Confirmation Emails

Sending email in Rails has three basic parts: configuring how email is to be sent, determining when to send the email, and specifying what you want to say. We'll cover each of these three in turn.

---

1. http://guides.rubyonrails.org/action_mailer_basics.html
2. http://guides.rubyonrails.org/active_job_basics.html

Configuring Email

Email configuration is part of a Rails application's environment and involves a Rails.application.configure block. If you want to use the same configuration for development, testing, and production, add the configuration to environment.rb in the config directory; otherwise, add different configurations to the appropriate files in the config/environments directory.

Inside the block, you need to have one or more statements. You first have to decide how you want mail delivered:

```
config.action_mailer.delivery_method = :smtp
```

Alternatives to :smtp include :sendmail and :test.

The :smtp and :sendmail options are used when you want Action Mailer to attempt to deliver email. You'll clearly want to use one of these methods in production.

The :test setting is great for unit and functional testing, which we'll make use of in Testing Email, on page 195. Email won't be delivered; instead, it'll be appended to an array (accessible via the ActionMailer::Base.deliveries attribute). This is the default delivery method in the test environment. Interestingly, though, the default in development mode is :smtp. If you want Rails to deliver email during the development of your application, this is good. If you'd rather disable email delivery in development mode, edit the development.rb file in the config/environments directory and add the following lines:

```
Rails.application.configure do
config.action_mailer.delivery_method = :test
  end
```

The :sendmail setting delegates mail delivery to your local system's sendmail program, which is assumed to be in /usr/sbin. This delivery mechanism isn't particularly portable, because sendmail isn't always installed in this directory for every operating system. It also relies on your local sendmail supporting the -i and -t command options.

You achieve more portability by leaving this option at its default value of :smtp. If you do so, you'll need also to specify some additional configuration to tell Action Mailer where to find an SMTP server to handle your outgoing email. This can be the machine running your web application, or it can be a separate box (perhaps at your ISP if you're running Rails in a noncorporate environment). Your system administrator will be able to give you the settings for these parameters. You may also be able to determine them from your own mail client's configuration.

The following are typical settings for Gmail: adapt them as you need.

```ruby
Rails.application.configure do
  config.action_mailer.delivery_method = :smtp

  config.action_mailer.smtp_settings = {
    address:        "smtp.gmail.com",
    port:           587,
    domain:         "domain.of.sender.net",
    authentication: "plain",
    user_name:      "dave",
    password:       "secret",
    enable_starttls_auto: true
  }
end
```

As with all configuration changes, you'll need to restart your application if you make changes to any of the environment files.

Sending Email

Now that we have everything configured, let's write some code to send emails.

By now you shouldn't be surprised that Rails has a generator script to create *mailers*. In Rails, a mailer is a class that's stored in the app/mailers directory. It contains one or more methods, with each method corresponding to an email template. To create the body of the email, these methods in turn use views (in the same way that controller actions use views to create HTML and XML). So let's create a mailer for our store application. We'll use it to send two different types of email: one when an order is placed and a second when the order ships. The rails generate mailer command takes the name of the mailer class along with the names of the email action methods:

```
depot> bin/rails generate mailer Order received shipped
      create    app/mailers/order_mailer.rb
      invoke    tailwindcss
      create      app/views/order_mailer
      create      app/views/order_mailer/received.text.erb
      create      app/views/order_mailer/received.html.erb
      create      app/views/order_mailer/shipped.text.erb
      create      app/views/order_mailer/shipped.html.erb
      invoke    test_unit
      create      test/mailers/order_mailer_test.rb
      create      test/mailers/previews/order_mailer_preview.rb
```

Notice that we create an OrderMailer class in app/mailers and two template files, one for each email type, in app/views/order_mailer. (We also create a test file; we'll look into this in Testing Email, on page 195.)

Each method in the mailer class is responsible for setting up the environment for sending an email. Let's look at an example before going into detail. Here's the code that was generated for our OrderMailer class, with one default changed:

```
rails80/depot_q/app/mailers/order_mailer.rb
class OrderMailer < ApplicationMailer
➤   default from: "Sam Ruby <depot@example.com>"
  # Subject can be set in your I18n file at config/locales/en.yml
  # with the following lookup:
  #
  #   en.order_mailer.received.subject
  #
  def received
    @greeting = "Hi"

    mail to: "to@example.org"
  end

  # Subject can be set in your I18n file at config/locales/en.yml
  # with the following lookup:
  #
  #   en.order_mailer.shipped.subject
  #
  def shipped
    @greeting = "Hi"

    mail to: "to@example.org"
  end
end
```

If you're thinking to yourself that this looks like a controller, that's because it does. It includes one method per action. Instead of a call to render(), there's a call to mail(). This method accepts a number of parameters including :to (as shown), :cc, :from, and :subject, each of which does pretty much what you'd expect it to do. Values that are common to all mail() calls in the mailer can be set as defaults by simply calling default, as is done for :from at the top of this class. Feel free to tailor this to your needs.

The comments in this class also indicate that subject lines are already enabled for translation, a subject we'll cover in Chapter 15, Task J: Internationalization, on page 225. For now, we'll simply use the :subject parameter.

As with controllers, templates contain the text to be sent, and controllers and mailers can provide values to be inserted into those templates via instance variables.

Email Templates

The generate script created two email templates in app/views/order_mailer, one for each action in the OrderMailer class. These are regular .erb files. We'll use them to create plain-text emails (you'll see later how to create HTML email). As with the templates we use to create our application's web pages, the files contain a combination of static text and dynamic content. We can customize the template in received.text.erb; this is the email that's sent to confirm an order:

rails80/depot_q/app/views/order_mailer/received.text.erb
```
Dear <%= @order.name %>

Thank you for your recent order from The Pragmatic Store.

You ordered the following items:

<%= render @order.line_items -%>

We'll send you a separate e-mail when your order ships.
```

The partial template that renders a line item formats a single line with the item quantity and the title. Because we're in a template, all the regular helper methods, such as truncate(), are available:

rails80/depot_q/app/views/line_items/_line_item.text.erb
```
<%= sprintf("%2d x %s",
            line_item.quantity,
            truncate(line_item.product.title, length: 50)) %>
```

We now have to go back and fill in the received() method in the OrderMailer class:

rails80/depot_qa/app/mailers/order_mailer.rb
```ruby
def received(order)
  @order = order

  mail to: order.email, subject: "Pragmatic Store Order Confirmation"
end
```

What we did here is add order as an argument to the method-received call, add code to copy the parameter passed into an instance variable, and update the call to mail() specifying where to send the email and what subject line to use.

Generating Emails

Now that we have our template set up and our mailer method defined, we can use them in our regular controllers to create and/or send emails. Note that just calling the method we defined isn't enough; we also need to tell Rails to actually send the email. The reason this doesn't happen automatically is that Rails can't be 100 percent sure if you want to deliver the email right this moment, while the user waits, or later, in a background job.

Generally, you don't want the user to have to wait for emails to get sent, because this can take a while. Instead, we'll send it in a background job (which we'll learn more about later in the chapter) by calling deliver_later() (to send the email right now, you'd use deliver_now()).[3]

```ruby
rails80/depot_qa/app/controllers/orders_controller.rb
def create
  @order = Order.new(order_params)
  @order.add_line_items_from_cart(@cart)

  respond_to do |format|
    if @order.save
      Cart.destroy(session[:cart_id])
      session[:cart_id] = nil
      OrderMailer.received(@order).deliver_later
      format.html { redirect_to store_index_url, notice:
        "Thank you for your order." }
      format.json { render :show, status: :created,
        location: @order }
    else
      format.html { render :new, status: :unprocessable_entity }
      format.json { render json: @order.errors,
        status: :unprocessable_entity }
    end
  end
end
```

And we need to update shipped() as we did for received():

```ruby
rails80/depot_qa/app/mailers/order_mailer.rb
def shipped(order)
  @order = order

  mail to: order.email, subject: "Pragmatic Store Order Shipped"
end
```

Now we have enough of the basics in place that you can place an order and have a plain email sent to yourself, assuming you didn't disable the sending of email in development mode. Let's spice up the email with a bit of formatting.

Delivering Multiple Content Types

Some people prefer to receive email in plain-text format, while others like the look of an HTML email. Rails supports this directly, allowing you to send email messages that contain alternative content formats, allowing users (or their email clients) to decide which they'd prefer to view.

In the preceding section, we created a plain-text email. The view file for our received action was called received.text.erb. This is the standard Rails naming convention. We can also create HTML-formatted emails.

---

3. http://api.rubyonrails.org/classes/ActionMailer/MessageDelivery.html#method-i-deliver_now

Let's try this with the order-shipped notification. We don't need to modify any code—we simply need to create a new template:

rails80/depot_qa/app/views/order_mailer/shipped.html.erb
```erb
<h3>Pragmatic Order Shipped</h3>
<p>
  This is just to let you know that we've shipped your recent order:
</p>
<table>
  <tr><th colspan="2">Qty</th><th>Description</th></tr>
<%= render @order.line_items -%>
</table>
```

We don't need to modify the partial, because the existing one will do just fine:

rails80/depot_qa/app/views/line_items/_line_item.html.erb
```erb
<% if line_item == @current_item %>
<tr class="line-item-highlight">
<% else %>
<tr>
<% end %>
  <td class="text-right"><%= line_item.quantity %></td>
  <td>&times;</td>
  <td class="pr-2">
    <%= line_item.product.title %>
  </td>
  <td class="text-right font-bold">
    <%= number_to_currency(line_item.total_price) %>
  </td>
</tr>
```

But for email templates, Rails provides a bit more naming magic. If you create multiple templates with the same name but with different content types embedded in their filenames, Rails will send all of them in one email, arranging the content so that the email client can distinguish each.

This means you'll want to either update or delete the plain-text template that Rails provided for the shipped notifier.

Testing Email

When we used the generate script to create our order mailer, it automatically constructed a corresponding order_test.rb file in the application's test/mailers directory. It's pretty straightforward; it simply calls each action and verifies selected portions of the email produced. Because we've tailored the email, let's update the test case to match:

```ruby
rails80/depot_qa/test/mailers/order_mailer_test.rb
require "test_helper"

class OrderMailerTest < ActionMailer::TestCase
  test "received" do
    mail = OrderMailer.received(orders(:one))
    assert_equal "Pragmatic Store Order Confirmation", mail.subject
    assert_equal [ "dave@example.org" ], mail.to
    assert_equal [ "depot@example.com" ], mail.from
    assert_match /1 x The Pragmatic Programmer/, mail.body.encoded
  end

  test "shipped" do
    mail = OrderMailer.shipped(orders(:one))
    assert_equal "Pragmatic Store Order Shipped", mail.subject
    assert_equal [ "dave@example.org" ], mail.to
    assert_equal [ "depot@example.com" ], mail.from
    assert_match %r{
      <td[^>]*>1</td>\s*
      <td>&times;</td>\s*
      <td[^>]*>\s*The\sPragmatic\sProgrammer\s*</td>
    }x, mail.body.encoded
  end
end
```

The test method instructs the mail class to create (but not to send) an email, and we use assertions to verify that the dynamic content is what we expect. Note the use of assert_match() to validate just part of the body content. Your results may differ depending on how you tailored the default :from line in your OrderMailer.

Note that it's also possible to have your Rails application receive emails. We'll cover that in Chapter 16, Task K: Receive Emails and Respond with Rich Text, on page 247.

Now that we've implemented our mailer and tested it, let's move on to that pesky slow payment processor. To deal with that, we'll put our API calls into a job that can be run in the background so the user doesn't have to wait.

Iteration H2: Connecting to a Slow Payment Processor with Active Job

The code inside the controllers is relatively fast and returns a response to the user quickly. This means we can reliably give users feedback by checking and validating their orders and the users won't have to wait too long for a response.

The more we add to the controller, the slower it'll become. Slow controllers create several problems. First, the user must wait a long time for a response even though the processing that's going on might not be relevant to the user experience. In the previous section, we set up sending email. The user certainly needs to get that email but doesn't need to wait for Rails to format and send it just to show a confirmation in the browser.

The second problem caused by slow code is *timeouts*. A timeout is when Rails, a web server, or a browser decides that a request has taken too long and terminates it. This is jarring to the user *and* to the code because it means the code is interrupted at a potentially odd time. What if we've recorded the order but haven't sent the email? The customer won't get a notification.

In the common case of sending email, Rails handles sending it in the background. We use deliver_later() to trigger sending an email, and Rails executes that code in the background. This means that users don't have to wait for email to be sent before we render a response. This is a great hidden benefit to Rails' integrated approach to building a web app.

Rails achieves this using Active Job, which is a generic framework for running code in the background. We'll use this framework to connect to the slow payment processor.

To make this change, you'll implement the integration with the payment processor as a method inside Order, then have the controller use Active Job to execute that method in a background job. Because the end result will be somewhat complex, you'll write a system test to ensure everything is working together.

Moving Logic into the Model

It's way outside the scope of this book to integrate with an actual payment processor, so we've cooked up a fake one named Pago, along with an implementation, which we'll see in a bit. First, this is the API it provides and a sketch of how you can use it:

```
payment_result = Pago.make_payment(
  order_id: order.id,
  payment_method: :check,
  payment_details: { routing: xxx, account: yyy }
)
```

The fake implementation does some basic validations of the parameters, prints out the payment details it received, pauses for a few seconds, and returns a structure that responds to succeeded?().

rails80/depot_qb/lib/pago.rb
```
require "ostruct"
class Pago
  def self.make_payment(order_id:,
```

```ruby
                        payment_method:,
                        payment_details:)
    case payment_method
    when :check
      Rails.logger.info "Processing check: " +
        payment_details.fetch(:routing).to_s + "/" +
        payment_details.fetch(:account).to_s
    when :credit_card
      Rails.logger.info "Processing credit_card: " +
        payment_details.fetch(:cc_num).to_s + "/" +
        payment_details.fetch(:expiration_month).to_s + "/" +
        payment_details.fetch(:expiration_year).to_s
    when :po
      Rails.logger.info "Processing purchase order: " +
        payment_details.fetch(:po_num).to_s
    else
      raise "Unknown payment_method #{payment_method}"
    end

    sleep 3 unless Rails.env.test?
    Rails.logger.info "Done Processing Payment"
    OpenStruct.new(succeeded?: true)
  end
end
```

If you aren't familiar with OpenStruct, it's part of Ruby's standard library and provides a quick-and-dirty way to make an object that responds to the methods given to its constructor.[4] In this case, we can call succeeded?() on the return value from make_payment(). OpenStruct is handy for creating realistic objects from prototype or faked-out code like Pago.

With the payment API in hand, you need logic to adapt the payment details that you added in Defining Additional Fields, on page 180, to Pago's API. You'll also move the call to OrderMailer into this method, because you don't want to send the email if there was a problem collecting payment.

In a Rails app, when a bit of logic becomes more complex than a line or two of code, you want to move that out of the controller and into a model. You'll create a new method in Order called charge!() that will handle all this logic.

To prepare for this, we first define a pay_type_params() method in the controller that will capture the parameters to be passed to the model. We put this new method in the bottom of the controller, in the private section:

rails80/depot_qb/app/controllers/orders_controller.rb
```ruby
def pay_type_params
  if order_params[:pay_type] == "Credit card"
```

---

4. https://ruby-doc.org/stdlib-2.4.1/libdoc/ostruct/rdoc/OpenStruct.html

```ruby
      params.require(:order).permit(:credit_card_number, :expiration_date)
    elsif order_params[:pay_type] == "Check"
      params.require(:order).permit(:routing_number, :account_number)
    elsif order_params[:pay_type] == "Purchase order"
      params.require(:order).permit(:po_number)
    else
      {}
    end
end
```

The method will be somewhat long and has to do three things. First, it must adapt the pay_type_params that you just created to the parameters that Pago requires. Second, it should make the call to Pago to collect payment. Finally, it must check to see if the payment succeeded and, if so, send the confirmation email. Here's what the method looks like:

rails80/depot_qb/app/models/order.rb
```ruby
➤ require "pago"

  class Order < ApplicationRecord
    enum :pay_type, {
      "Check"          => 0,
      "Credit card"    => 1,
      "Purchase order" => 2
    }
    has_many :line_items, dependent: :destroy
    # ...
    validates :name, :address, :email, presence: true
    validates :pay_type, inclusion: pay_types.keys
    def add_line_items_from_cart(cart)
      cart.line_items.each do |item|
        item.cart_id = nil
        line_items << item
      end
    end
➤   def charge!(pay_type_params)
➤     payment_details = {}
➤     payment_method = nil
➤
➤     case pay_type
➤     when "Check"
➤       payment_method = :check
➤       payment_details[:routing] = pay_type_params[:routing_number]
➤       payment_details[:account] = pay_type_params[:account_number]
➤     when "Credit card"
➤       payment_method = :credit_card
➤       month, year = pay_type_params[:expiration_date].split(//)
➤       payment_details[:cc_num] = pay_type_params[:credit_card_number]
➤       payment_details[:expiration_month] = month
➤       payment_details[:expiration_year] = year
```

```
      when "Purchase order"
        payment_method = :po
        payment_details[:po_num] = pay_type_params[:po_number]
      end

      payment_result = Pago.make_payment(
        order_id: id,
        payment_method: payment_method,
        payment_details: payment_details
      )

      if payment_result.succeeded?
        OrderMailer.received(self).deliver_later
      else
        raise payment_result.error
      end
    end
  end
```

If you weren't concerned with how slow Pago's API is, you'd change the code in the create() method of OrdersController to call charge!():

```
if @order.save
  Cart.destroy(session[:cart_id])
  session[:cart_id] = nil
  @order.charge!(pay_type_params) # do not do this
  format.html { redirect_to store_index_url, notice:
    'Thank you for your order.' }
```

Since you already know the call to Pago will be slow, you want it to happen in a background job so that users can see the confirmation message in their browser immediately without having to wait for the charge to actually happen. To do this, you must create an Active Job class, implement that class to call charge!(), and then add code to the controller to execute this job. The flow looks like the figure shown on page 201.

Creating an Active Job Class

Rails provides a generator to create a shell of a job class for us. Create the job using it like so:

```
> bin/rails generate job charge_order
    invoke  test_unit
    create    test/jobs/charge_order_job_test.rb
    create  app/jobs/charge_order_job.rb
```

The argument charge_order tells Rails that the job's class name should be ChargeOrderJob.

Iteration H2: Connecting to a Slow Payment Processor with Active Job • 201

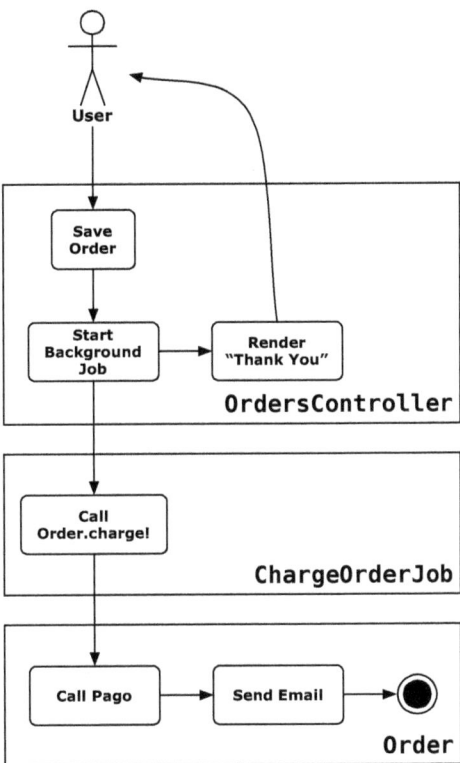

You've implemented the logic in the charge!() method of Order, so what goes in the newly created ChargeOrderJob? The purpose of job classes like ChargeOrderJob is to act as a glue between the controller—which wants to run some logic later—and the actual logic in the models.

Here's the code that implements this:

```ruby
rails80/depot_qb/app/jobs/charge_order_job.rb
class ChargeOrderJob < ApplicationJob
  queue_as :default

➤  def perform(order, pay_type_params)
➤    order.charge!(pay_type_params)
  end
end
```

Next, you need to fire this job in the background from the controller.

Queuing a Background Job

Because background jobs run in parallel to the code in the controller, the code you write to initiate the background job isn't the same as calling a method. When you call a method, you expect that method's code to be executed while you wait. Background jobs are different. They often go to a queue, where they wait to be executed outside the controller. Thus, when we talk about executing code in a background job, we often use the phrase "queue the job."

To queue a job using Active Job, use the method perform_later() on the job class and pass it the arguments you want to be given to the perform() method you implemented above. Here's where to do that in the controller (note that this replaces the call to OrderMailer, since that's now part of the charge!() method):

rails80/depot_qb/app/controllers/orders_controller.rb
```ruby
def create
  @order = Order.new(order_params)
  @order.add_line_items_from_cart(@cart)

  respond_to do |format|
    if @order.save
      Cart.destroy(session[:cart_id])
      session[:cart_id] = nil
      ChargeOrderJob.perform_later(@order, pay_type_params.to_h)
      format.html { redirect_to store_index_url, notice:
        "Thank you for your order." }
      format.json { render :show, status: :created,
        location: @order }
    else
      format.html { render :new, status: :unprocessable_entity }
      format.json { render json: @order.errors,
        status: :unprocessable_entity }
    end
  end
end
```

With this in place, you can now add an item to the cart, check out, and see everything working just as we did before, with the addition of seeing the calls to Pago. If you look at the Rails log when you check out, you should see some logging, like so (formatted to fit the page):

```
[ActiveJob] Enqueued ChargeOrderJob
  (Job ID: 79da671e-865c-4d51-a1ff-400208c6dbd1)
    to Async(default) with arguments:
      #<GlobalID:0x007fa294a43ce0 @uri=#<URI::GID gid://depot/Order/9>>,
      {"routing_number"=>"23412341234", "account_number"=>"345356345"}
[ActiveJob] [ChargeOrderJob] [79da671e-865c-4d51-a1ff-400208c6dbd1]
    Performing ChargeOrderJob
      (Job ID: 79da671e-865c-4d51-a1ff-400208c6dbd1) from
    Async(default) with arguments:
    #<GlobalID:0x007fa294a01570 @uri=#<URI::GID gid://depot/Order/9>>,
      {"routing_number"=>"23412341234", "account_number"=>"345356345"}
[ActiveJob] [ChargeOrderJob] [79da671e-865c-4d51-a1ff-400208c6dbd1]
    Processing check: 23412341234/345356345
```

This shows the guts of how Active Job works and is useful for debugging if things aren't working right.

Speaking of debugging and possible failures, this interaction really should have a test.

System Testing the Checkout Flow

In Iteration G3: Testing Our JavaScript Functionality, on page 184, you wrote a system test that uses a real browser to simulate user interaction. To test the entire flow of checking out, communicating with the payment processor, and sending an email, you'll add a second test.

To test the full, end-to-end workflow, including execution of Active Jobs, you want to do the following:

1. Add a book to the cart.
2. Fill in the checkout form completely (including selecting a pay type).
3. Submit the order.
4. Process all background jobs.
5. Check that the order was created properly.
6. Check that email was sent.

You should already be familiar with how to write most parts of this test. Processing background jobs and checking mail, however, are new. Rails provides helpers for us, so the test will be short and readable when you're done. One of those helpers is available by mixing in the ActiveJob::TestHelper module:

rails80/depot_qb/test/system/orders_test.rb
```ruby
class OrdersTest < ApplicationSystemTestCase
➤   include ActiveJob::TestHelper
```

This provides the method perform_enqueued_jobs(), which you'll use in your test:

rails80/depot_qb/test/system/orders_test.rb
```ruby
test "check order and delivery" do
  LineItem.delete_all
  Order.delete_all

  visit store_index_url

  click_on "Add to Cart", match: :first

  click_on "Checkout"

  fill_in "Name", with: "Dave Thomas"
  fill_in "Address", with: "123 Main Street"
  fill_in "Email", with: "dave@example.com"

  select "Check", from: "Pay type"
  fill_in "Routing number", with: "123456"
```

```
    fill_in "Account number", with: "987654"

    click_button "Place Order"
    assert_text "Thank you for your order"

    perform_enqueued_jobs
    perform_enqueued_jobs
    assert_performed_jobs 2

    orders = Order.all
    assert_equal 1, orders.size

    order = orders.first
    assert_equal "Dave Thomas",        order.name
    assert_equal "123 Main Street",    order.address
    assert_equal "dave@example.com",   order.email
    assert_equal "Check",              order.pay_type
    assert_equal 1, order.line_items.size

    mail = ActionMailer::Base.deliveries.last
    assert_equal [ "dave@example.com" ],                 mail.to
    assert_equal "Sam Ruby <depot@example.com>",         mail[:from].value
    assert_equal "Pragmatic Store Order Confirmation",   mail.subject
end
```

This test reads almost like English. Since you now need to submit the form and assert that an order was created, you start by clearing out any orders in the test database that might be hanging around from previous test runs.

Next, you add an item to the cart, check out and fill in the pay type details, place your order, and verify that you get a *Thank you* response.

Since this test is about the user's experience end-to-end, you don't need to look at the jobs that have been queued—instead we need to make sure they are executed. It's sufficient to assert the *results* of those jobs having been executed. To that end, the method perform_enqueued_jobs() will perform any jobs that get enqueued inside the block of code given to it. Since our ChangeOrderJob enqueues a mail job, clearing the queue once isn't enough, so we clear it twice. After this, we verify that exactly two jobs were executed.

Next, check that an order was created in the way you expect by locating the created order and asserting that the values provided in the checkout form were properly saved.

Lastly, you need to check that the mail was sent. In the test environment, Rails doesn't actually deliver mail but instead saves it in an array available via ActionMailer::Base.deliveries(). The objects in there respond to various methods that allow you to examine the email.

> **Joe asks:**
> ## How Are Background Jobs Run in Development or Production?
>
> When running the application locally, the background jobs are executed and emails are sent by Rails. By default, Rails uses an in-memory queue to manage the jobs. This is fine for development, but it could be a problem in production. If your app were to crash before all background jobs were processed or before emails were sent, those jobs would be lost and unrecoverable.
>
> In production, you'd need to use a different *back end*, as detailed in the Active Job Rails Guide.[a] Sidekiq is a popular open source back end that works great.[b] Setting it up is a bit tricky since you must have access to a Redis database to store the waiting jobs.[c] If you're using Postgres for your Active Records, Queue Classic is another option for a back end that doesn't require Redis—it uses your existing Postgres database.[d]
>
> ---
> a. http://guides.rubyonrails.org/active_job_basics.html#job-execution
> b. http://sidekiq.org/
> c. https://redis.io/
> d. https://github.com/QueueClassic/queue_classic/tree/3-1-stable

If you run this test via bin/rails test test/system/orders_test.rb, it should pass. You've now tested a complex workflow using the browser, background jobs, and email.

What We Just Did

Without much code and with just a few templates, we've managed to pull off the following:

- We configured our development, test, and production environments for our Rails application to enable the sending of outbound emails.

- We created and tailored a mailer that can send confirmation emails in both plain-text and HTML formats to people who order our products.

- We used Active Job to execute slow-running code in the background so the user doesn't have to wait.

- We enhanced a system test to cover the entire end-to-end workflow, including verifying that the background job executed and the email was sent.

Playtime

Here's some stuff to try on your own:

- Add a ship_date column to the orders table, and send a notification when this value is updated by the OrdersController.

- Update the application to send an email to the system administrator—namely, yourself—when an application failure occurs, such as the one we handled in Iteration E2: Handling Errors, on page 132.

- Modify Pago to sometimes return a failure (OpenStruct.new(succeeded?: false)), and handle that by sending a different email with the details of the failure.

- Add system tests for all of the above.

In this chapter, you'll see:
- Using the authentication generator
- Generating scaffolding for an existing model
- Using more validations
- Using rails console
- Using database transactions
- Writing an Active Record hook

CHAPTER 14

Task I: Logging In

We have a happy customer: in a short time, we've jointly put together a basic shopping cart that she can start showing to her users. She'd like to see just one more change. Right now, anyone can access the administrative functions. She'd like us to add a basic user administration system that would force you to log in to get into the administration parts of the site.

Chatting with our customer, it seems as if we don't need a particularly sophisticated security system for our application. We just need to recognize a number of people based on email addresses and passwords. Once recognized, these folks can use all of the administration functions.

Iteration I1: Authenticating Users

Building a user administration system is a common task in web applications. Rails provides a generator to help you get started. The code it generates is a good starting point, and takes care of important details like storing passwords securely. It builds upon sessions, mailers, and jobs, which we've seen in previous chapters.

We start by running the generator:

```
depot> bin/rails generate authentication
```

This creates three models: Session, User, and Current. It creates controllers for sessions and passwords and a controller concern for authentication. Finally, it creates views for passwords and their associated mailer. The one task it leaves to you is the task of defining the user. We could create this from scratch, but we'll use the scaffold generator to get us started and tell it to *not* modify what was produced by the authentication generator. The existing user model defines the user's email address and password; we just need to add the user's name.

```
depot> bin/rails generate scaffold User \
  name:string email_address:string password:digest \
  --skip-collision-check --skip
```

We declare the password as a digest type, which will automatically handle HTTP Digest authentication[1] for us—another one of the nice extra touches that Rails provides.

Because we skipped the collision check, we need to manually update the migration:

rails80/depot_r/db/migrate/20250420000011_create_users.rb
```ruby
class CreateUsers < ActiveRecord::Migration[8.0]
  def change
    create_table :users do |t|
      t.string :name, null: false
      t.string :email_address, null: false
      t.string :password_digest, null: false

      t.timestamps
    end
    add_index :users, :email_address, unique: true
  end
end
```

And then run the migration:

```
depot> bin/rails db:migrate
```

Next, we have to flesh out the user model:

rails80/depot_r/app/models/user.rb
```ruby
class User < ApplicationRecord
  validates :name, presence: true, uniqueness: true
  validates :email_address, presence: true, uniqueness: true
  has_secure_password
  has_many :sessions, dependent: :destroy

  normalizes :email_address, with: ->(e) { e.strip.downcase }
end
```

We check that the name and email addresses are present and unique (that is, no two users can have the same name or email address in the database).

Then there's the mysterious has_secure_password().

You know those forms that prompt you to enter a password and then make you reenter it in a separate field so they can validate that you typed what you

---

[1]. https://api.rubyonrails.org/classes/ActionController/HttpAuthentication/Digest.html

thought you typed? That's exactly what has_secure_password() does for you: it tells Rails to validate that the two passwords match.

A user is defined to have many sessions, and those sessions are to be destroyed when the user is destroyed. Finally, email addresses are normalized to lowercase before being stored in the database.

Finally, you need to restart your server as a new gem was installed by the authentication generator.

With this code in place, we have the ability to present both a password and a password confirmation field in a form, as well as the ability to authenticate a user, given a name and a password. Not bad for two commands and three lines of code.

But now we have an embarrassing problem: there are no administrative users in the database, so we can't log in.

Fortunately, we can quickly add a user to the database from the command line. If you invoke the rails console command, Rails invokes Ruby's irb utility, but it does so in the context of your Rails application. That means you can interact with your application's code by typing Ruby statements and looking at the values they return.

We can use this to invoke our user model directly, having it add a user into the database for us:

```
depot> bin/rails console
Loading development environment (Rails 8.0.2)
work(dev)* User.create(name: "dave",
work(dev)>   email_address: "dave@example.org", password: "secret")
work(dev)> exit
```

With this in place, we can now log in as the user dave with the password secret:

If the blue button offends you, the file to change is app/views/sessions/new.html.erb.

You can also use this interface to send a password reset email. In development mode, you can save the emails into files by editing the config/environments/development.rb file.

rails80/depot_r/config/environments/development.rb
```ruby
# Save emails as files in tmp/mails
config.action_mailer.delivery_method = :file
```

We also have a small problem in that all of our controller tests are now failing. We can fix this by defining a method in the test helper to log in as a user:

rails80/depot_r/test/test_helper.rb
```ruby
ENV["RAILS_ENV"] ||= "test"
require_relative "../config/environment"
require "rails/test_help"

module ActiveSupport
  class TestCase
    # Run tests in parallel with specified workers
    parallelize(workers: :number_of_processors)

    # Setup all fixtures in test/fixtures/*.yml for all tests in
    # alphabetical order.
    fixtures :all

    # Add more helper methods to be used by all tests here...
    def login_as(user)
      get users_path
      post session_path, params: {
        email_address: user.email_address,
        password: "password"
      }
    end
  end
end
```

And then each controller test needs to be updated to call this method:

rails80/depot_r/test/controllers/carts_controller_test.rb
```ruby
  setup do
    @cart = carts(:one)
    login_as users(:one)
  end
```

rails80/depot_r/test/controllers/line_items_controller_test.rb
```ruby
  setup do
    @line_item = line_items(:one)
    login_as users(:one)
  end
```

```
rails80/depot_r/test/controllers/orders_controller_test.rb
    setup do
      @order = orders(:one)
➤     login_as users(:one)
    end
```

```
rails80/depot_r/test/controllers/products_controller_test.rb
    setup do
      @product = products(:one)
      @title = "The Great Book #{rand(1000)}"
➤     login_as users(:one)
    end
```

```
rails80/depot_r/test/controllers/store_controller_test.rb
    def setup
➤     login_as users(:one)
    end
```

```
rails80/depot_r/test/controllers/users_controller_test.rb
    setup do
      @user = users(:one)
➤     login_as @user
    end
```

We need to update the test fixtures to add names to the users.

```
rails80/depot_r/test/fixtures/users.yml
<% password_digest = BCrypt::Password.create("password") %>

one:
➤   name: one
    email_address: one@example.com
    password_digest: <%= password_digest %>
two:
➤   name: two
    email_address: two@example.com
    password_digest: <%= password_digest %>
```

Once the tests are passing again, we can move on to the next step: adding the ability to administer users.

Administering Our Users

Now we turn our attention to the scaffolding we created for our users. Let's go through it and make some tweaks as necessary.

We start with the controller. It defines the standard methods: index(), show(), new(), edit(), create(), update(), and destroy(). By default, Rails omits the unintelligible password hash from the view. This means that in the case of users, there isn't much to show() except a name and an email. So let's avoid the redirect to showing the user after a create operation. Instead, let's redirect to the user's index and add the username to the flash notice:

rails80/depot_r/app/controllers/users_controller.rb
```ruby
  def create
    @user = User.new(user_params)

    respond_to do |format|
      if @user.save
➤       format.html { redirect_to users_url,
➤         notice: "User #{@user.name} was successfully created." }
        format.json { render :show, status: :created, location: @user }
      else
        format.html { render :new, status: :unprocessable_entity }
        format.json { render json: @user.errors,
          status: :unprocessable_entity }
      end
    end
  end
```

Let's do the same for an update operation:

```ruby
  def update
    respond_to do |format|
      if @user.update(user_params)
➤       format.html { redirect_to users_url,
➤         notice: "User #{@user.name} was successfully updated." }
        format.json { render :show, status: :ok, location: @user }
      else
        format.html { render :edit, status: :unprocessable_entity }
        format.json { render json: @user.errors,
          status: :unprocessable_entity }
      end
    end
  end
```

While we're here, let's also order the users returned in the index by name:

```ruby
  def index
➤   @users = User.order(:name)
  end
```

Now that the controller changes are done, let's attend to the view. We need to update the form used to create a new user and to update an existing user. Note this form is already set up to show the password and password confirmation fields. We'll make a few aesthetic changes so the form looks nice and matches the look and feel of the site.

rails80/depot_r/app/views/users/_form.html.erb
```erb
<%= form_with(model: user, class: "contents") do |form| %>
  <% if user.errors.any? %>
```

```erb
    <div id="error_explanation" class="bg-red-50 text-red-500 px-3 py-2
                                       font-medium rounded-md mt-3">
      <h2><%= pluralize(user.errors.count, "error") %>
          prohibited this user from being saved:</h2>

      <ul class="list-disc ml-6">
        <% user.errors.each do |error| %>
          <li><%= error.full_message %></li>
        <% end %>
      </ul>
    </div>
  <% end %>

➤ <h2>Enter User Details</h2>
➤
  <div class="my-5">
➤   <%= form.label :name, 'Name:' %>
➤   <%= form.text_field :name, class: [
➤     "block shadow-sm rounded-md border px-3 py-2 mt-2 w-full",
➤     {"border-gray-400 focus:outline-blue-600":
➤        user.errors[:name].none?,
➤     "border-red-400 focus:outline-red-600":
➤        user.errors[:name].any?}] %>
  </div>

  <div class="my-5">
    <%= form.label :email_address %>
➤   <%= form.text_field :email_address, class: [
➤     "block shadow-sm rounded-md border px-3 py-2 mt-2 w-full",
➤     {"border-gray-400 focus:outline-blue-600":
➤        user.errors[:email_address].none?,
➤     "border-red-400 focus:outline-red-600":
➤        user.errors[:email_address].any?}] %>
  </div>

  <div class="my-5">
➤   <%= form.label :password, 'Password:' %>
➤   <%= form.password_field :password, class: "input-field" %>
  </div>

  <div class="my-5">
➤   <%= form.label :password_confirmation, 'Confirm:' %>

➤   <%= form.password_field :password_confirmation,
➤                           id: :user_password_confirmation,
➤                           class: "input-field" %>
  </div>

  <div class="inline">
    <%= form.submit class: "w-full sm:w-auto rounded-md px-3.5 py-2.5 bg-blue-600
        hover:bg-blue-500 text-white inline-block font-medium cursor-pointer" %>
  </div>
<% end %>
```

Let's try it. Navigate to http://localhost:3000/users/new. For a stunning example of page design, see the following screenshot.

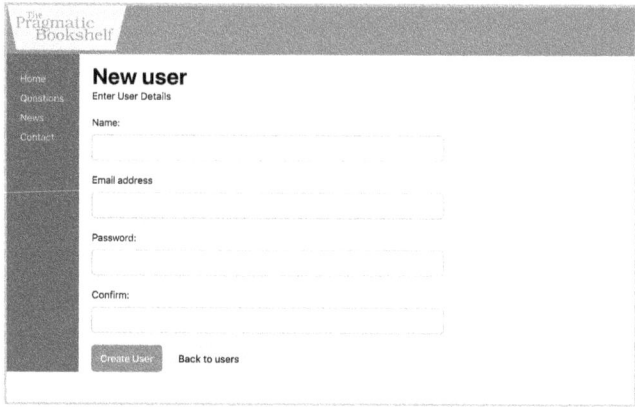

After Create User is clicked, the index is redisplayed with a cheery flash notice. If we look in our database, you'll see that we've stored the user details:

```
depot> sqlite3 -line storage/development.sqlite3 "select * from users"
           id = 1
         name = dave
email_address = dave@example.org
password_digest = $2a$12$p1HwU98TtNu.j/UBv74e4.ljjpvWdPk4tN6kTkWxp1QVV7UyR73em
   created_at = 2025-04-20 14:43:27.934633
   updated_at = 2025-04-20 14:43:27.934633

           id = 2
         name = sam
email_address = sam@example.org
password_digest = $2a$12$UQrQxRNRatkzGpwhnUQ3X.QjUQr57bcCui01wXYMjlosZO0rIzLLK
   created_at = 2025-04-20 14:43:35.232745
   updated_at = 2025-04-20 14:43:35.232745
```

As we've done before, we need to update our tests to reflect the validation and redirection changes we've made. First we update the test for the create() method:

rails80/depot_r/test/controllers/users_controller_test.rb
```
  test "should create user" do
    assert_difference("User.count") do
➤     post users_url, params: { user: {
➤       email_address: "sam@example.org",
➤       name: "sam",
➤       password: "secret",
➤       password_confirmation: "secret" } }
    end
➤   assert_redirected_to users_url
  end
```

Because the redirect on the update() method changed too, the update test also needs to change:

```
test "should update user" do
  patch user_url(@user), params: { user: {
    email_address: @user.email_address,
    name: @user.name,
    password: "secret",
    password_confirmation: "secret" } }
➤ assert_redirected_to users_url
end
```

Note the use of dynamically computed values in the fixture, specifically for the value of password_digest. This code was also inserted by the scaffolding command and uses the same function that Rails uses to compute the password.[2]

At this point, we can administer our users; and only authenticated users can access our site. Now we need to open things up so that customers can access the store.

Iteration I2: Administration pages

Finally, it's about time to add the index page—the first screen that administrators see when they log in. Let's make it useful. We'll have it display the total number of orders in our store. Create the template in the index.html.erb file in the app/views/admin directory. (This template uses the pluralize() helper, which in this case generates the order or orders string, depending on the cardinality of its first parameter.)

rails80/depot_r/app/views/admin/index.html.erb
```
<div class="w-full">
  <h1 class="mx-auto text-lg font-bold">Welcome</h1>

  <p>
    It's <%= Time.now %>.
    We have <%= pluralize(@total_orders, "order") %>.
  </p>
</div>
```

The index() action sets up the count:

rails80/depot_r/app/controllers/admin_controller.rb
```
class AdminController < ApplicationController
  def index
➤   @total_orders = Order.count
  end
end
```

---

2. https://github.com/rails/rails/blob/5-1-stable/activemodel/lib/active_model/secure_password.rb

We have one more task to do before we can use this. Whereas previously we relied on the scaffolding generator to create our model and routes for us, this time we simply generated a controller because there's no database-backed model for this controller. Unfortunately, without the scaffolding conventions to guide it, Rails has no way of knowing which actions are to respond to GET requests, which are to respond to POST requests, and so on, for this controller. We need to provide this information by editing our config/routes.rb file:

rails80/depot_r/config/routes.rb
```ruby
Rails.application.routes.draw do
  get "admin" => "admin#index"
  resources :users
  resource :session
  resources :passwords, param: :token
  resources :orders
  resources :line_items
  resources :carts
  root "store#index", as: "store_index"
  resources :products
  # Define your application routes per the DSL in
  # https://guides.rubyonrails.org/routing.html

  # Reveal health status on /up that returns 200 if the app boots with no
  # exceptions, otherwise 500.
  # Can be used by load balancers and uptime monitors to verify that the
  # app is live.
  get "up" => "rails/health#show", as: :rails_health_check

  # Render dynamic PWA files from app/views/pwa/*
  # (remember to link manifest in application.html.erb)
  # get "manifest" => "rails/pwa#manifest", as: :pwa_manifest
  # get "service-worker" => "rails/pwa#service_worker", as: :pwa_service_worker

  # Defines the root path route ("/")
  # root "posts#index"
end
```

We've touched this before, when we added a root statement in Iteration C1: Creating the Catalog Listing, on page 101. What the generate command adds to this file are fairly generic get statements for each action specified.

Now we change where logged-in users are redirected to after logging in:

rails80/depot_r/app/controllers/concerns/authentication.rb
```ruby
    def after_authentication_url
      session.delete(:return_to_after_authenticating) || admin_url
    end
```

With these routes in place, we can experience the joy of logging in as an administrator. Visit http://localhost:3000/admin and log in as dave@example.org with the password secret. You'll be redirected to the administrative index page. See the following screenshot.

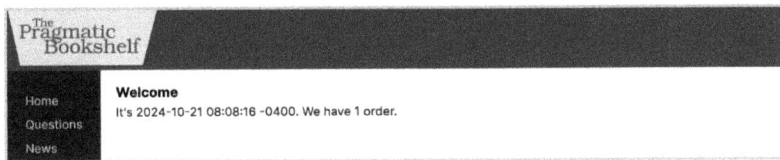

We need to replace the functional tests in the admin controller to match what we just implemented: a logged-in user can access the admin index page, and a session that isn't logged in gets redirected to the login page.

rails80/depot_r/test/controllers/admin_controller_test.rb
```
require "test_helper"

class AdminControllerTest < ActionDispatch::IntegrationTest
  test "should get index if logged in as admin" do
    login_as users(:one)
    get admin_url
    assert_response :success
  end

  test "should be redirected if not logged in" do
    get admin_url
    assert_redirected_to new_session_url
  end
end
```

We show our customer where we are, but she points out that customers can no longer access the store. We need to fix that.

Iteration I3: Permitting Access

We want people without an administrative login to be able to purchase our products. This, too, can be accomplished with very little code.

We could go back and change things so that we mark only those methods that specifically need authorization. Such an approach, called *denylisting*, is prone to errors of omission. A much better approach is to *allowlist*—list methods or controllers for which authorization is *not* required. We do this by inserting an allow_unauthenticated_access() call within the StoreController:

rails80/depot_r/app/controllers/store_controller.rb
```
class StoreController < ApplicationController
➤  allow_unauthenticated_access
```

And we do it again for the SessionsController class.

We're not done yet; we need to allow people to create, update, and delete carts:

rails80/depot_r/app/controllers/carts_controller.rb
```
class CartsController < ApplicationController
  allow_unauthenticated_access only: %i[ create update destroy ]
```

And we allow them to create line items:

rails80/depot_r/app/controllers/line_items_controller.rb
```
class LineItemsController < ApplicationController
  allow_unauthenticated_access only: %i[ create ]
```

We also allow them to create orders (which includes access to the new form):

rails80/depot_r/app/controllers/orders_controller.rb
```
class OrdersController < ApplicationController
  allow_unauthenticated_access only: %i[ new create ]
```

With the authorization logic in place, we can navigate to http://localhost:3000/ without requiring a login. But if we navigate to http://localhost:3000/products, we're redirected to the login screen instead.

We show our customer the results of our efforts and are rewarded with a big smile and a request: could we add a sidebar and put links to the user and product administration stuff in it? You betcha!

Iteration I4: Adding a Sidebar, More Administration

Let's start with adding links to various administration functions to the sidebar in the layout and have them show up only if a :user_id is in the session:

rails80/depot_r/app/views/layouts/application.html.erb
```
<!DOCTYPE html>
<html>
  <head>
    <title><%= content_for(:title) || "Pragprog Books Online Store" %></title>
    <meta name="viewport" content="width=device-width,initial-scale=1">
    <meta name="apple-mobile-web-app-capable" content="yes">
    <meta name="mobile-web-app-capable" content="yes">
    <%= csrf_meta_tags %>
    <%= csp_meta_tag %>

    <%= yield :head %>

    <%# Enable PWA manifest for installable apps (make sure to enable in
        config/routes.rb too!) %>
    <%= tag.link rel: "manifest", href: pwa_manifest_path(format: :json) %>

    <link rel="icon" href="/icon.png" type="image/png">
    <link rel="icon" href="/icon.svg" type="image/svg+xml">
    <link rel="apple-touch-icon" href="/icon.png">

    <%# Includes all stylesheet files in app/assets/stylesheets %>
```

```erb
    <%= stylesheet_link_tag :app, "data-turbo-track": "reload" %>
    <%= javascript_importmap_tags %>
  </head>

  <body>
    <header class="bg-green-700">
      <%= image_tag 'logo.svg', alt: 'The Pragmatic Bookshelf' %>
      <h1><%= @page_title %></h1>
    </header>

    <section class="flex">
      <nav class="bg-green-900 p-6">
        <%= render partial: 'layouts/cart', locals: {cart: @cart } %>

        <ul class="text-gray-300 leading-8">
          <li><a href="/">Home</a></li>
          <li><a href="/questions">Questions</a></li>
          <li><a href="/news">News</a></li>
          <li><a href="/contact">Contact</a></li>
        </ul>

➤       <hr class="my-2">
➤
➤       <ul class="text-gray-300 leading-8">
➤       <% if authenticated? %>
➤         <li><%= link_to 'Orders',   orders_path   %></li>
➤         <li><%= link_to 'Products', products_path %></li>
➤         <li><%= link_to 'Users',    users_path    %></li>
➤         <li><%= button_to 'Logout', session_path, method: :delete %></li>
➤       <% else %>
➤         <li><%= link_to 'Login', new_session_path %></li>
➤       <% end %>
        </ul>
      </nav>

      <main class="container mx-auto mt-4 px-5 flex">
        <%= yield %>
      </main>
    </section>
  </body>
</html>
```

Now it's all starting to come together. We can log in, and by clicking a link in the sidebar, we can see a list of users. Let's see if we can break something.

Would the Last Admin to Leave…

We bring up the user list screen that looks something like the screenshot shown on page 220.

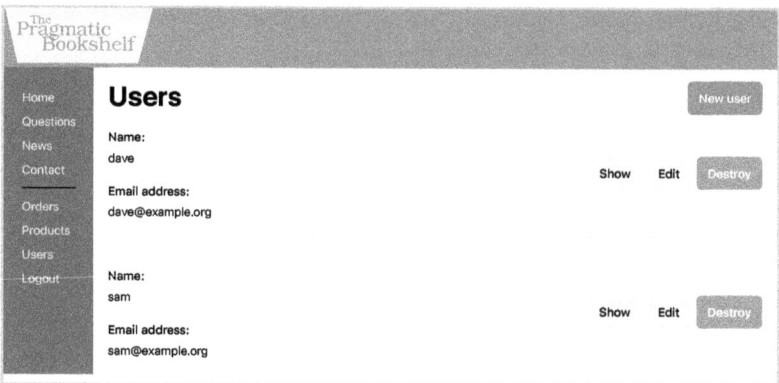

If we click the Show this user link, we see the following:

Now click the Destroy this user link to delete that user. Sure enough, our user is removed. But to our surprise, we're then presented with the login screen instead. We just deleted the only administrative user from the system. When the next request came in, the authentication failed, so the application refused to let us in. We have to log in again before using any administrative functions.

We once again make use of rails console.

```
depot> bin/rails console
Loading development environment (Rails 8.0.2)
work(dev)> User.create(name: 'dave', email: 'dave@example.org',
work(dev)*    password: 'secret', password_confirmation: 'secret')
=> #<User:0x2933060 ... >
work(dev)> User.count
=> 1
work(dev)> exit
```

Panic over. We can now log back in to the application. But how can we stop this from happening again? We have several ways. For example, we could write code that prevents you from deleting your own user. That doesn't quite work: in theory, A could delete B at just the same time that B deletes A. Let's try a different approach. We'll delete the user inside a database transaction. Transactions provide an all-or-nothing proposition, stating that each work unit performed in a database must either complete in its entirety or none of them will have any effect whatsoever. If no users are left after we've deleted the user, we'll roll the transaction back, restoring the user we just deleted.

To do this, we'll use an Active Record hook method. We've already seen one of these: the validate hook is called by Active Record to validate an object's state. It turns out that Active Record defines sixteen or so hook methods, each called at a particular point in an object's life cycle. We'll use the after_destroy() hook, which is called after the SQL delete is executed. If a method by this name is publicly visible, it'll conveniently be called in the same transaction as the delete—so if it raises an exception, the transaction will be rolled back. The hook method looks like this:

rails80/depot_t/app/models/user.rb
```ruby
class User < ApplicationRecord
  validates :name, presence: true, uniqueness: true
  validates :email_address, presence: true, uniqueness: true
  has_secure_password
  has_many :sessions, dependent: :destroy

  normalizes :email_address, with: ->(e) { e.strip.downcase }

➤ after_destroy :ensure_an_admin_remains
➤
➤ class Error < StandardError
➤ end
➤
➤ private
➤   def ensure_an_admin_remains
➤     if User.count.zero?
➤       raise Error.new "Can't delete last user"
➤     end
➤   end
end
```

The key concept is the use of an exception to indicate an error when the user is deleted. This exception serves two purposes. First, because it's raised inside a transaction, it causes an automatic rollback. By raising the exception if the users table is empty after the deletion, we undo the delete and restore that last user.

Second, the exception signals the error back to the controller, where we use a rescue_from block to handle it and report the error to the user in the notice. If you want only to abort the transaction but not otherwise signal an exception, raise an ActiveRecord::Rollback exception instead, because this is the only exception that won't be passed on by ActiveRecord::Base.transaction:

```
rails80/depot_t/app/controllers/users_controller.rb
def destroy
  @user.destroy!

  respond_to do |format|
    format.html { redirect_to users_path, status: :see_other,
      notice: "User #{@user.name} deleted" }
    format.json { head :no_content }
  end
end

rescue_from "User::Error" do |exception|
  redirect_to users_url, notice: exception.message
end
```

This code still has a potential timing issue: it's still possible for two administrators each to delete the last two users if their timing is right. Fixing this would require more database wizardry than we have space for here.

The login system described in this chapter is pretty basic, but sufficient for many applications. Applications with more complex requirements generally use a gem to do this.

A number of plugins are available that provide ready-made solutions that are more comprehensive than the authentication logic shown here and often don't require significantly more code and effort on your part to use. Devise[3] is a common and popular gem that does this.

What We Just Did

By the end of this iteration, we've done the following:

- We used has_secure_password to store an encrypted version of the password into the database.

- We controlled access to the administration functions using before action callbacks to invoke an authorize() method.

- We used rails console to interact directly with a model (and dig us out of a hole after we deleted the last user).

- We used a transaction to help prevent deletion of the last user.

Playtime

Here's some stuff to try on your own:

---

3. https://github.com/plataformatec/devise

- Modify the user update function to require and validate the current password before allowing a user's password to be changed.

- The system test in test/system/users_test.rb was generated by the scaffolding generator we used at the start of the chapter. Those tests don't pass. See if you can get them to pass without breaking the other system tests. You'll recall we created the module AuthenticationHelpers and included it in all of the system tests by default, so you might need to change the code to *not* do that so that you can properly test the login functionality.

  When the system is freshly installed on a new machine, no administrators are defined in the database, and hence no administrator can log on. But if no administrator can log on, then no one can create an administrative user.

  Change the code so that if no administrator is defined in the database, any username works to log on (allowing you to quickly create a real administrator).

- Experiment with rails console. Try creating products, orders, and line items. Watch for the return value when you save a model object—when validation fails, you'll see false returned. Find out why by examining the errors:

```
>> prd = Product.new
=> #<Product id: nil, title: nil, description: nil, image_url:
nil, created_at: nil, updated_at: nil, price:
#<BigDecimal:246aa1c,'0.0',4(8)>>
>> prd.save
=> false
>> prd.errors.full_messages
=> ["Image url must be a URL for a GIF, JPG, or PNG image",
    "Image url can't be blank", "Price should be at least 0.01",
    "Title can't be blank", "Description can't be blank"]
```

- We've gotten our tests working by performing a login, but we haven't yet written tests that verify that access to sensitive data requires login. Write at least one test that verifies this by calling logout() and then attempting to fetch or update some data that requires authentication.

In this chapter, you'll see:
- Localizing templates
- Database design considerations for I18n

CHAPTER 15

Task J: Internationalization

Now we have a basic cart working, and our customer starts to inquire about languages other than English, noting that her company has a big push on for expansion in emerging markets. Unless we can present something in a language that visitors to our customer's website will understand, our customer will be leaving money on the table. We can't have that.

The first problem is that none of us are professional translators. The customer reassures us that this isn't something we need to concern ourselves with because that part of the effort will be outsourced. All we need to worry about is *enabling* translation. Furthermore, we don't have to worry about the administration pages yet because all the administrators speak English. What we have to focus on is the store.

That's a relief—but still a tall order. We'll need to define a way to enable the user to select a language, we'll have to provide the translations themselves, and we'll have to change the views to use these translations. But we're up to the task, and—armed with a bit of remembered high-school Spanish—we set off to work.

Joe asks:
If We Stick to One Language, Do We Need to Read This Chapter?

The short answer is no. In fact, many Rails applications are for a small or homogeneous group and never need translating. That being said, pretty much everybody who does find that they need translation agrees that it's best if this is done early. So unless you're sure that translation won't ever be needed, it's our recommendation that you at least understand what would be involved so that you can make informed decisions.

Iteration J1: Selecting the Locale

We start by creating a new configuration file that encapsulates our knowledge of what locales are available and which one is to be used as the default:

```
rails80/depot_t/config/initializers/i18n.rb
#encoding: utf-8
I18n.default_locale = :en

LANGUAGES = [
  [ "English",                    "en" ],
  [ "Espa&ntilde;ol".html_safe,  "es" ]
]
```

This code is doing two things.

The first thing it does is use the I18n module to set the default locale. I18n is a funny name, but it sure beats typing out *internationalization* all the time. Internationalization, after all, starts with an *i*, ends with an *n*, and has eighteen letters in between.

Then the code defines a list of associations between display names and locale names. Unfortunately, all we have available at the moment is a U.S. keyboard, and Español has a character that can't be directly entered via our keyboard. Different operating systems have different ways of dealing with this, and often the easiest way is to copy and paste the correct text from a website. If you do this, make sure your editor is configured for UTF-8. Meanwhile, we've opted to use the HTML equivalent of the *n con tilde* character in Spanish. If we didn't do anything else, the markup itself would be shown. But by calling html_safe, we inform Rails that the string is safe to be interpreted as containing HTML.

For Rails to pick up this configuration change, the server needs to be restarted.

Since each page that's translated will have an en and an es version (for now—more will be added later), it makes sense to include this in the URL. Let's plan to put the locale up front, make it optional, and have it default to the current locale, which in turn will default to English.

To implement this cunning plan, let's start by modifying config/routes.rb:

```ruby
# rails80/depot_t/config/routes.rb
Rails.application.routes.draw do
  get "admin" => "admin#index"
  get "up" => "rails/health#show", as: :rails_health_check

  resources :users
  resources :products
  resource :session
  resources :passwords, param: :token

➤ scope "(:locale)" do
    resources :orders
    resources :line_items
    resources :carts
➤   root "store#index", as: "store_index", via: :all
➤ end
end
```

We've nested our resources and root declarations inside a scope declaration for :locale. Furthermore, :locale is in parentheses, which is the way to say that it's optional. Note that we didn't choose to put the administrative and session functions inside this scope, because it's not our intent to translate them at this time.

What this means is that http://localhost:3000/ will use the default locale (namely, English) and therefore be routed exactly the same as http://localhost:3000/en. http://localhost:3000/es will route to the same controller and action, but we'll want this to cause the locale to be set differently.

At this point, we've made a lot of changes to config.routes, and with the nesting and all the optional parts to the path, the gestalt might be hard to visualize. Never fear—when running a server in development mode, Rails provides a visual aid. All you need to do is navigate to http://localhost:3000/rails/info/routes, and you'll see a list of all your routes. You can even filter the list, as shown in the screenshot shown on page 228, to quickly find the route you're interested in. More information on the fields shown in this table can be found in the description of rake routes on page 352.

With the routing in place, we're ready to extract the locale from the parameters and make it available to the application. To do this, we need to create a before_action callback. The logical place to do this is in the common base class for all of our controllers, which is ApplicationController:

Helper (Path / Url)	HTTP Verb	Path	Controller#Action	Source Location
		/assets	Propshaft::Server	propshaft (1.1.0) lib/propshaft/railtie.rb:47
admin_path	GET	/admin(.:format)	admin#index	/Users/rubys/git/awdwr8/work/config/routes.rb:2
rails_health_check_path	GET	/up(.:format)	rails/health#show	/Users/rubys/git/awdwr8/work/config/routes.rb:3
users_path	GET	/users(.:format)	users#index	/Users/rubys/git/awdwr8/work/config/routes.rb:5
	POST	/users(.:format)	users#create	/Users/rubys/git/awdwr8/work/config/routes.rb:5
new_user_path	GET	/users/new(.:format)	users#new	/Users/rubys/git/awdwr8/work/config/routes.rb:5
edit_user_path	GET	/users/:id/edit(.:format)	users#edit	/Users/rubys/git/awdwr8/work/config/routes.rb:5

rails80/depot_t/app/controllers/application_controller.rb
```ruby
class ApplicationController < ActionController::Base
  before_action :set_i18n_locale_from_params
  # ...
  def set_i18n_locale_from_params
    if params[:locale]
      if I18n.available_locales.map(&:to_s).include?(params[:locale])
        I18n.locale = params[:locale]
      else
        flash.now[:notice] =
          "#{params[:locale]} translation not available"
        logger.error flash.now[:notice]
      end
    end
  end
end
```

This set_i18n_locale_from_params does pretty much what it says: it sets the locale from the params, but only if there's a locale in the params; otherwise, it leaves the current locale alone. Care is taken to provide a message for both the user and the administrator when a failure occurs.

Iteration J1: Selecting the Locale • 229

With this in place, we can see the results in the following screenshot of navigating to http://localhost:3000/en.

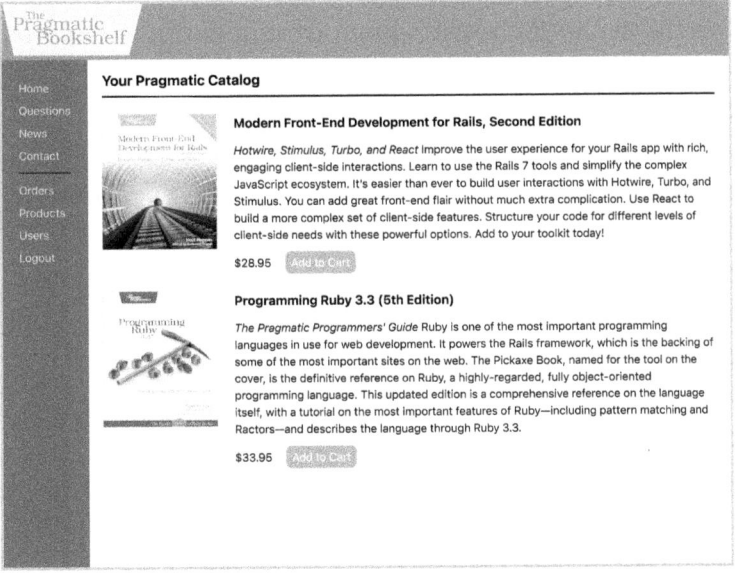

At this point, the English version of the page is available both at the root of the website and at pages that start with /en. If you try another language code, say "es" (or Spanish), you can see that an error message appears saying no translations are available. The following screenshot shows what this might look like when navigating to http://localhost:3000/es:

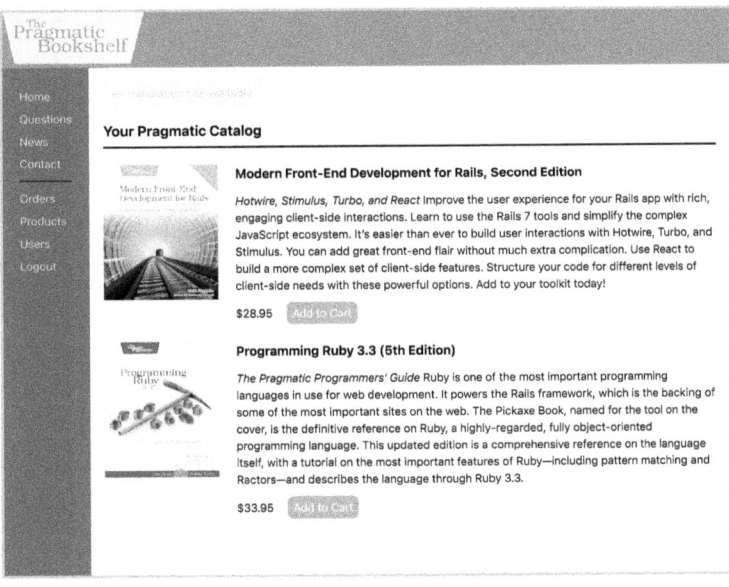

Iteration J2: Translating the Storefront

Now it's time to begin providing the translated text. Let's start with the layout since it's pretty visible. We replace any text that needs to be translated with calls to I18n.translate. Not only is this method conveniently aliased as I18n.t, but a helper named t is provided.

The parameter to the translate function is a unique dot-qualified name. We can choose any name we like, but if we use the t helper function provided, names that start with a dot will first be expanded using the name of the template.

So, let's do that:

```erb
rails80/depot_t/app/views/layouts/application.html.erb
<!DOCTYPE html>
<html>
  <head>
    <title><%= content_for(:title) || "Pragprog Books Online Store" %></title>
    <meta name="viewport" content="width=device-width,initial-scale=1">
    <meta name="apple-mobile-web-app-capable" content="yes">
    <meta name="mobile-web-app-capable" content="yes">
    <%= csrf_meta_tags %>
    <%= csp_meta_tag %>

    <%= yield :head %>

    <%# Enable PWA manifest for installable apps (make sure to enable in
        config/routes.rb too!) %>
    <%#= tag.link rel: "manifest", href: pwa_manifest_path(format: :json) %>

    <link rel="icon" href="/icon.png" type="image/png">
    <link rel="icon" href="/icon.svg" type="image/svg+xml">
    <link rel="apple-touch-icon" href="/icon.png">

    <%# Includes all stylesheet files in app/assets/stylesheets %>
    <%= stylesheet_link_tag :app, "data-turbo-track": "reload" %>
    <%= javascript_importmap_tags %>
  </head>

  <body>
    <header class="bg-green-700">
      <%= image_tag 'logo.svg', alt: 'The Pragmatic Bookshelf' %>
      <h1><%= @page_title %></h1>
    </header>

    <section class="flex">
      <nav class="bg-green-900 p-6">
        <%= render partial: 'layouts/cart', locals: {cart: @cart } %>

        <ul class="text-gray-300 leading-8">
          <li><a href="/"><%= t('.home') %></a></li>
```

```erb
➤       <li><a href="/questions"><%= t('.questions') %></a></li>
➤       <li><a href="/news"><%= t('.news') %></a></li>
➤       <li><a href="/contact"><%= t('.contact') %></a></li>
      </ul>

      <hr class="my-2">

      <ul class="text-gray-300 leading-8">
      <% if authenticated? %>
        <li><%= link_to 'Orders',   orders_path  %></li>
        <li><%= link_to 'Products', products_path %></li>
        <li><%= link_to 'Users',    users_path   %></li>
        <li><%= button_to 'Logout', session_path, method: :delete %></li>
      <% else %>
        <li><%= link_to 'Login', new_session_path %></li>
      <% end %>
      </ul>
    </nav>

    <main class="container mx-auto mt-4 px-5 flex">
      <%= yield %>
    </main>
  </section>
 </body>
</html>
```

Since this view is named layouts/application.html.erb, the English mappings will expand to en.layouts.application. Here's the corresponding locale file:

rails80/depot_t/config/locales/en.yml
```yaml
en:
  layouts:
    application:
      title:      "The Pragmatic Bookshelf"
      home:       "Home"
      questions:  "Questions"
      news:       "News"
      contact:    "Contact"
```

Here it is in Spanish:

rails80/depot_t/config/locales/es.yml
```yaml
es:
  layouts:
    application:
      title:      "Biblioteca de Pragmatic"
      home:       "Inicio"
      questions:  "Preguntas"
      news:       "Noticias"
      contact:    "Contacto"
```

The format is YAML, the same as the one used to configure the databases. YAML consists of indented names and values, where the indentation in this case matches the structure that we created in our names.

To get Rails to recognize new YAML files, the server needs to be restarted.

Navigating to http://localhost:3000/es now will show some translated text, as shown in the following screenshot.

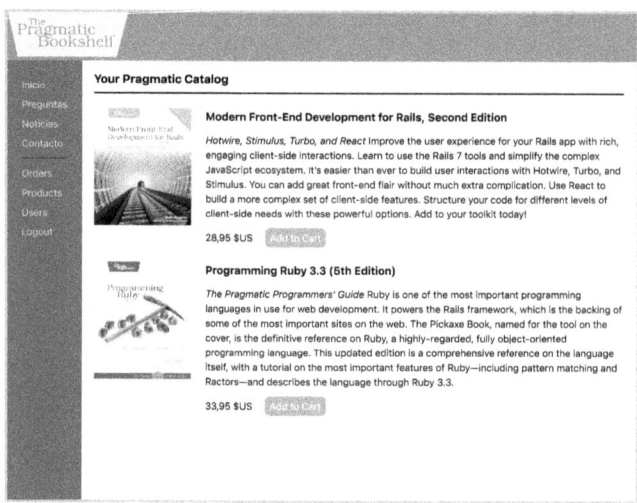

Next to be updated is the main title as well as the Add to Cart button. The first can be found in the store index template:

```
rails80/depot_s/app/views/store/index.html.erb
<div class="w-full">
<%= render 'notice' %>

<h1 class="font-bold text-xl mb-6 pb-2 border-b-2">
  <%= t('.title_html') %>
</h1>
```

The button can be found in the store product partial:

```
rails80/depot_s/app/views/store/_product.html.erb
        <%= button_to t(".add_html"),
            line_items_path(product_id: product),
            form_class: "inline",
            class: 'ml-4 rounded-lg py-1 px-2
                text-white bg-green-600' %>
```

And here's the corresponding updates to the locales files, first in English:

```
rails80/depot_t/config/locales/en.yml
en:
  store:
    index:
      title_html:   "Your Pragmatic Catalog"
    product:
      add_html:     "Add to Cart"
```

And here it is in Spanish:

```
rails80/depot_t/config/locales/es.yml
es:
  store:
    index:
      title_html:   "Su Cat&aacute;logo de Pragmatic"
    product:
      add_html:     "A&ntilde;adir al Carrito"
```

Note that since title_html and add_html end in the characters _html, we're free to use HTML entity names for characters that don't appear on our keyboard. If we didn't name the translation key this way, what you'd end up seeing on the page is the markup. This is yet another convention that Rails has adopted to make your coding life easier. Rails will also treat names that contain html as a component (in other words, the string .html.) as HTML key names.

By refreshing the page in the browser window, we see the results shown in the following screenshot.

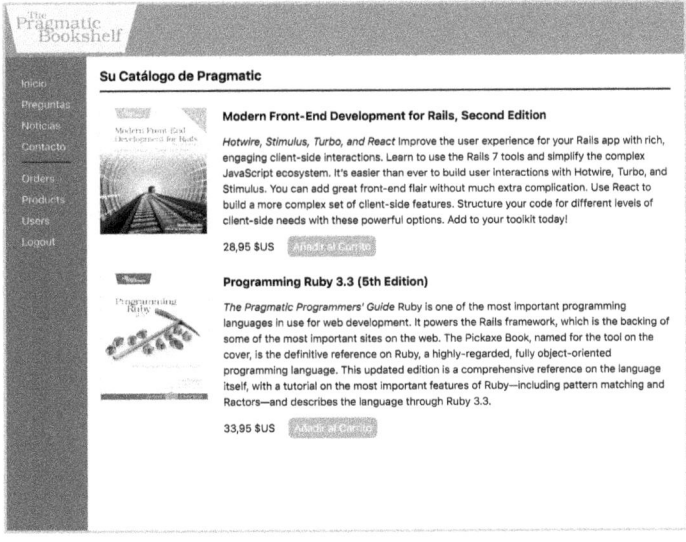

Feeling confident, we move on to the cart partial, replacing text that needs translation as well as adding the locale to the new_order_path:

```
rails80/depot_t/app/views/carts/_cart.html.erb
<div id="<%= dom_id cart %>">
  <h2 class="font-bold text-lg mb-3"><%= t('.title') %></h2>

  <table class="table-auto">
    <%= render cart.line_items %>

    <tfoot>
      <tr>
        <th class="text-right pr-2 pt-2" colspan="3">Total:</th>
        <td class="text-right pt-2 font-bold border-t-2 border-black">
          <%= number_to_currency(cart.total_price) %>
        </td>
      </tr>
    </tfoot>
  </table>

  <div class="flex mt-1">
    <%= button_to t('.empty'), cart, method: :delete,
      class: 'ml-4 rounded-lg py-1 px-2 text-white bg-green-600' %>

    <%= button_to t('.checkout'), new_order_path(locale: I18n.locale),
      method: :get,
      class: 'ml-4 rounded-lg py-1 px-2 text-black bg-green-200' %>
  </div>
</div>
```

And again, here are the translations:

```
rails80/depot_t/config/locales/en.yml
en:

  carts:
    cart:
      title:       "Your Cart"
      empty:       "Empty cart"
      checkout:    "Checkout"
```

```
rails80/depot_t/config/locales/es.yml
es:

  carts:
    cart:
      title:       "Carrito de la Compra"
      empty:       "Vaciar Carrito"
      checkout:    "Comprar"
```

Refreshing the page, we see the cart title and buttons have been translated, as shown in the following screenshot.

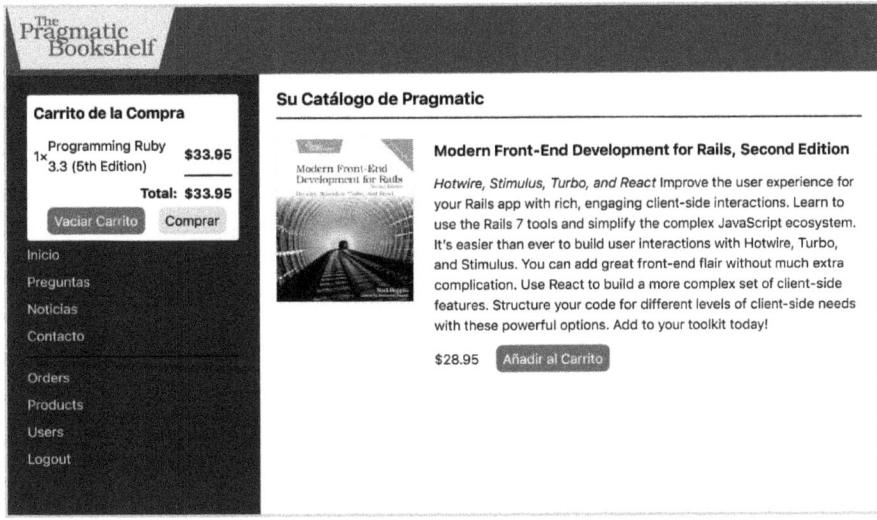

Something to appreciate here—the logic to render the cart is rendered in two places: first in the storefront and second in response to pushing the Añadir al Carrito (Add to Cart) button via Turbo/Hotwire. Since both make use of the same partial and are rendered on the server, the cart renders in Spanish no matter which path we take.

We now notice our next problem. Languages aren't the only thing that varies from locale to locale; currencies do too. And the customary way that numbers are presented varies too.

So first we check with our customer and we verify that we're not worrying about exchange rates at the moment (whew!), because that'll be taken care of by the credit card and/or wire companies, but we do need to display the string USD or $US after the value when we're showing the result in Spanish.

Another variation is the way that numbers themselves are displayed. Decimal values are delimited by a comma, and separators for the thousands place are indicated by a dot.

Currency is a lot more complicated than it first appears, with lots of decisions to be made. Fortunately, Rails knows to look in your translations file for this information; all we need to do is supply it.

Here it is for en:

rails80/depot_t/config/locales/en.yml
```
en:

  number:
    currency:
      format:
        unit:       "$"
        precision:  2
        separator:  "."
        delimiter:  ","
        format:     "%u%n"
```

Here it is for es:

rails80/depot_t/config/locales/es.yml
```
es:

  number:
    currency:
      format:
        unit:       "$US"
        precision:  2
        separator:  ","
        delimiter:  "."
        format:     "%n %u"
```

We've specified the unit, precision, separator, and delimiter for number.currency.format. That much is pretty self-explanatory. The format is a bit more involved: %n is a placeholder for the number;   is a nonbreaking space character, preventing this value from being split across multiple lines; and %u is a placeholder for the unit. See the following screenshot for the result.

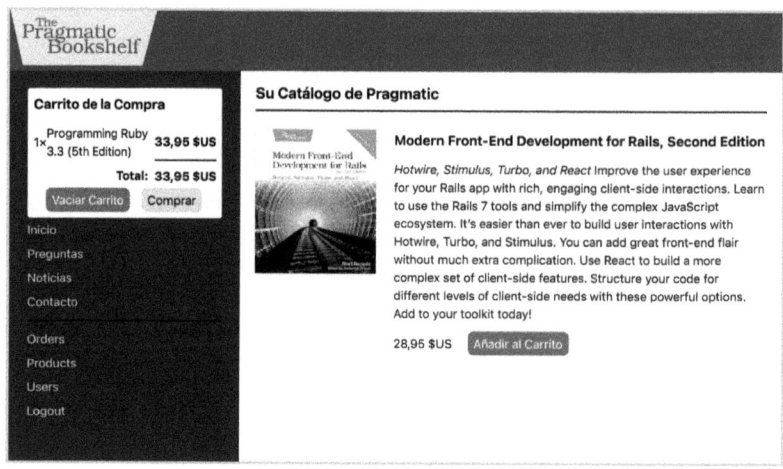

Iteration J3: Translating Checkout

Now we're entering the homestretch. The new order page is next:

rails80/depot_t/app/views/orders/new.html.erb
```erb
<% content_for :title, "New order" %>

<div class="md:w-2/3 w-full">
  <h1 class="font-bold text-4xl"><%= t('.legend') %></h1>

  <%= render "form", order: @order %>
</div>
```

Here's the form that's used by this page, updated to ensure that the locale is passed along with any requests, and to translate the fields and submit button:

rails80/depot_t/app/views/orders/_form.html.erb
```erb
<%= form_with(model: order, class: "contents",
  url: orders_path(locale: I18n.locale)) do |form| %>

  <% if order.errors.any? %>
    <div id="error_explanation" class="bg-red-50 text-red-500 px-3 py-2
      font-medium rounded-md mt-3">
      <h2><%= pluralize(order.errors.count, "error") %>
      prohibited this order from being saved:</h2>

      <ul class="list-disc ml-6">
        <% order.errors.each do |error| %>
          <li><%= error.full_message %></li>
        <% end %>
      </ul>
    </div>
  <% end %>

  <div class="my-5">
    <%= form.label :name, t('.name') %>
    <%= form.text_field :name, class: "input-field" %>
  </div>

  <div class="my-5">
    <%= form.label :address, t('.address_html') %>
    <%= form.textarea :address, rows: 4, class: "input-field" %>
  </div>

  <div class="my-5">
    <%= form.label :email, t('.email') %>
    <%= form.email_field :email, class: "input-field" %>
  </div>

  <div data-controller="payment">
    <div class="my-5">
      <%= form.label :pay_type, t(".pay_type") %>
      <%= form.select :pay_type,
        Order.pay_types.keys.map {|key| [t(".pay_types.#{key}"), key] },
                    { prompt: t('.pay_prompt_html') },
```

```erb
                    'data-payment-target' => 'selection',
                    'data-action' => 'payment#showAdditionalFields',
                    class: "input-field" %>
    </div>

    <%= render partial: 'check', locals: {form: form} %>
    <%= render partial: 'cc', locals: {form: form} %>
    <%= render partial: 'po', locals: {form: form} %>
  </div>

  <div class="inline">

➤   <%= form.submit t('.submit'),
      class: "w-full sm:w-autorounded-md
        px-3.5 py-2.5 bg-green-200 hover:bg-blue-500 text-black
        inline-block font-medium cursor-pointer" %>
  </div>
<% end %>
```

That covers the form elements that Rails is rendering, but what about the Stimulus-controlled additional payment details we added in Defining Additional Fields, on page 180? Once again, the ability to have everything rendered by the server from a common set of templates makes this concern go away. First, we update the credit card fields:

rails80/depot_t/app/views/orders/_cc.html.erb
```erb
<fieldset data-payment-target="additionalFields" data-type="Credit card">
  <div class="my-5">
➤   <%= form.label :credit_card_number, t('.cc_number') %>
    <%= form.password_field :credit_card_number, class: "input-field" %>
  </div>

  <div class="my-5">
➤   <%= form.label :expiration_date, t('.expiration_date') %>
    <%= form.text_field :expiration_date, class: "input-field",
      size:9, placeholder: "e.g. 03/22" %>
  </div>
</fieldset>
```

Next, we do the check fields:

rails80/depot_t/app/views/orders/_check.html.erb
```erb
<fieldset data-payment-target="additionalFields" data-type="Check">
  <div class="my-5">
➤   <%= form.label :routing_number, t('.routing_number') %>
    <%= form.text_field :routing_number, class: "input-field" %>
  </div>

  <div class="my-5">
➤   <%= form.label :account_number, t('.account_number') %>
    <%= form.password_field :account_number, class: "input-field" %>
  </div>
</fieldset>
```

And finally, update the purchase order fields:

rails80/depot_t/app/views/orders/_po.html.erb
```erb
<fieldset data-payment-target="additionalFields" data-type="Purchase order">
  <div class="my-5">
➤    <%= form.label :po_number, t('.po_number') %>
    <%= form.number_field :po_number, class: "input-field" %>
  </div>
</fieldset>
```

With those done, here are the corresponding locale definitions:

rails80/depot_t/config/locales/en.yml
```yaml
en:
  orders:
    new:
      legend:          "Please Enter Your Details"
      form:
        name:            "Name"
        address_html:    "Address"
        email:           "E-mail"
        pay_type:        "Pay with"
        pay_prompt_html: "Select a payment method"
        submit:          "Place Order"
        pay_types:
          "Check":           "Check"
          "Credit card":     "Credit Card"
          "Purchase order":  "Purchase Order"
      check:
        routing_number: "Routing #"
        account_number: "Account #"
      cc:
        cc_number: "CC #"
        expiration_date: "Expiry"
      po:
        po_number: "PO #"
```

rails80/depot_t/config/locales/es.yml
```yaml
orders:
  new:
    legend:          "Por favor, introduzca sus datos"
    form:
      name:            "Nombre"
      address_html:    "Direcci&oacute;n"
      email:           "E-mail"
      pay_type:        "Forma de pago"
      pay_prompt_html: "Seleccione un método de pago"
      submit:          "Realizar Pedido"
      pay_types:
        "Check":           "Cheque"
        "Credit card":     "Tarjeta de Crédito"
```

```
    "Purchase order":  "Orden de Compra"
check:
  routing_number: "# de Enrutamiento"
  account_number: "# de Cuenta"
cc:
  cc_number: "Número"
  expiration_date: "Expiración"
po:
  po_number: "Número"
```

See the following screenshot for the completed form.

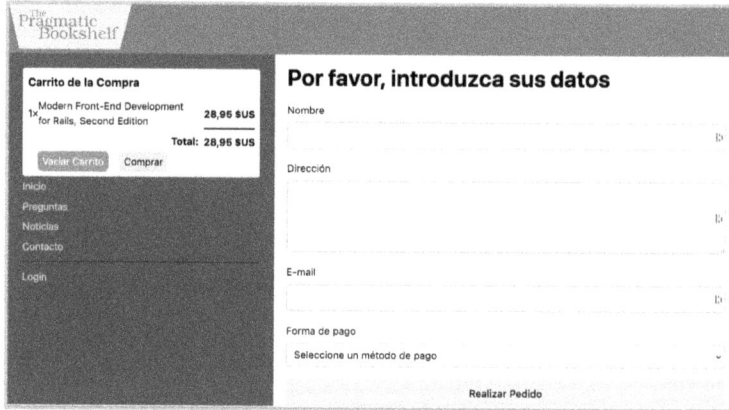

All looks good until we click the Realizar Pedido button prematurely and see the results shown in the following screenshot.

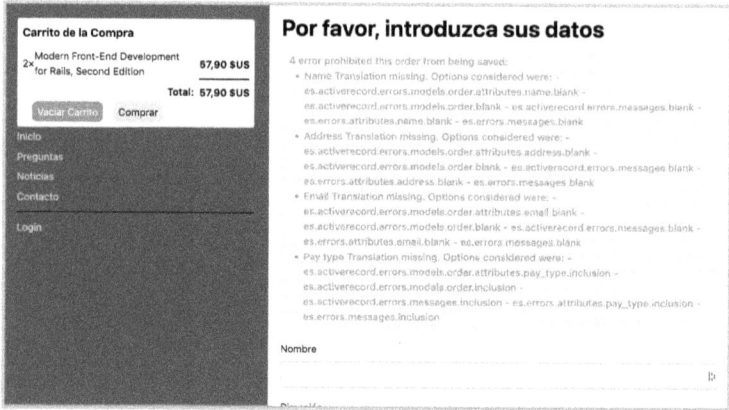

The error messages that Active Record produces can also be translated; what we need to do is supply the translations:

Iteration J3: Translating Checkout

```
rails80/depot_t/config/locales/es.yml
es:
  activerecord:
    errors:
      messages:
        inclusion: "no está incluido en la lista"
        blank:     "no puede quedar en blanco"
  errors:
    template:
      body:      "Hay problemas con los siguientes campos:"
      header:
        one:     "1 error ha impedido que este %{model} se guarde"
        other:   "%{count} errores han impedido que este %{model} se guarde"
```

Although you can create these with many trips to Google Translate, the Rails i18n gem's GitHub repo contains a lot of translations for common strings in many languages.[1]

Note that messages with counts typically have two forms: errors.template.header.one is the message that's produced when there's one error, and errors.template.header.other is produced otherwise. This gives the translators the opportunity to provide the correct pluralization of nouns and to match verbs with the nouns.

Since we once again made use of HTML entities, we want these error messages to be displayed as is (or in Rails parlance, *raw*). We also need to translate the error messages. So, again, we modify the form:

```
rails80/depot_u/app/views/orders/_form.html.erb
➤ <%= form_with(model: order, class: "contents",
➤     url: orders_path(locale: I18n.locale)) do |form| %>

    <% if order.errors.any? %>
      <div id="error_explanation" class="bg-red-50 text-red-500 px-3 py-2
        font-medium rounded-md mt-3">
➤       <h2><%=raw t('errors.template.header', count: @order.errors.count,
➤         model: t('activerecord.models.order')) %>.</h2>
➤       <p><%= t('errors.template.body') %></p>

        <ul class="list-disc ml-6">
          <% order.errors.each do |error| %>
➤           <li><%=raw error.full_message %></li>
          <% end %>
        </ul>
      </div>
    <% end %>
<!-- ... -->
```

---

1. https://github.com/svenfuchs/rails-i18n/tree/master/rails/locale

Note that we're passing the count and model name (which is, itself, enabled for translation) on the translate call for the error template header. With these changes in place, we try again and see improvement, see the following screenshot.

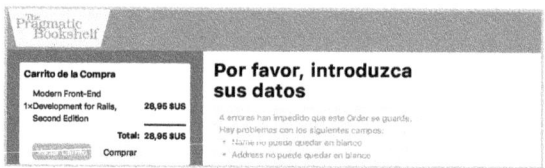

That's better, but the names of the model and the attributes bleed through the interface. This is OK in English, because the names we picked work for English. We need to provide translations for each model. This, too, goes into the YAML file:

```
rails80/depot_u/config/locales/es.yml
es:
  activerecord:
    models:
      order:      "pedido"
    attributes:
      order:
        address:   "Direcci&oacute;n"
        name:      "Nombre"
        email:     "E-mail"
        pay_type:  "Forma de pago"
```

Note that there's no need to provide English equivalents for this, because those messages are built into Rails. We're pleased to see the model and attribute names translated in the following screenshot; we fill out the form, we submit the order, and we get a "Thank you for your order" message.

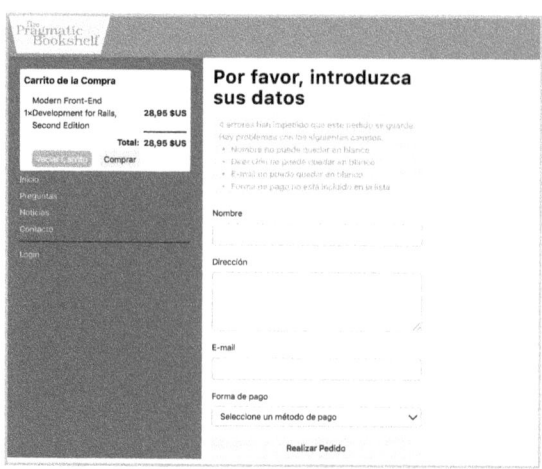

We need to update the flash messages and add the locale to the store_index_url:

rails80/depot_u/app/controllers/orders_controller.rb
```ruby
  def create
    @order = Order.new(order_params)
    @order.add_line_items_from_cart(@cart)

    respond_to do |format|
      if @order.save
        Cart.destroy(session[:cart_id])
        session[:cart_id] = nil
        ChargeOrderJob.perform_later(@order, pay_type_params.to_h)
➤       format.html { redirect_to store_index_url(locale: I18n.locale),
➤         notice: I18n.t(".thanks") }
        format.json { render :show, status: :created,
          location: @order }
      else
        format.html { render :new, status: :unprocessable_entity }
        format.json { render json: @order.errors,
          status: :unprocessable_entity }
      end
    end
  end
```

Next, we adjust the test to match:

rails80/depot_u/test/controllers/orders_controller_test.rb
```ruby
  test "should create order" do
    assert_difference("Order.count") do
      post orders_url, params: { order: { address: @order.address,
        email: @order.email, name: @order.name,
        pay_type: @order.pay_type } }
    end

➤   assert_redirected_to store_index_url(locale: "en")
  end
```

Finally, we provide the translations:

rails80/depot_u/config/locales/en.yml
```yaml
en:

  thanks:         "Thank you for your order"
```

rails80/depot_u/config/locales/es.yml
```yaml
es:

  thanks:         "Gracias por su pedido"
```

See the cheery message in the screenshot shown on page 244.

Iteration J4: Adding a Locale Switcher

We've completed the task, but we need to advertise its availability more. We spy some unused area in the top-right side of the layout, so we add a form immediately before the image_tag:

```
rails80/depot_u/app/views/layouts/application.html.erb
    <header class="bg-green-700">
➤     <aside data-controller="locale">
➤       <%= form_with url: store_index_path, class: 'locale' do %>
➤         <%= select_tag 'set_locale',
➤             options_for_select(LANGUAGES, I18n.locale.to_s),
➤             class: 'text-white',
➤             onchange: 'this.form.submit()' %>
➤         <%= submit_tag 'submit', data: {'locale-target' => 'submit'} %>
➤       <% end %>
➤     </aside>
      <%= image_tag 'logo.svg', alt: 'The Pragmatic Bookshelf' %>
      <h1><%= @page_title %></h1>
    </header>
```

The url specifies the path to the store as the page to be redisplayed when the form is submitted. A class attribute lets us associate the form with some CSS.

The select_tag is used to define the input field for this form—namely, locale. It's an options list based on the LANGUAGES array we set up in the configuration file, with the default being the current locale (also made available via the I18n module). We also set up an onchange event handler, which submits this form whenever the value changes. This works only if JavaScript is enabled, but it's handy. For cases where JavaScript isn't enabled, we've also put a submit_tag() in so there's a button the user can press to switch locales.

That said, since we don't need the submit button if JavaScript is enabled, it might be nice to hide it. The simplest way to do that is to write some JavaScript to do the hiding. If JavaScript is disabled, the JavaScript won't execute and the button remains to allow those users to submit the form. You'll notice we included a data-controller attribute on the aside element, and a locale-target on the submit_tag() in preceding the code. This allows us to locate that exact submit button in JavaScript.

Once again, we start by generating a stimulus controller:

```
depot> bin/rails generate stimulus locale
```

Now we update this code to set the style.display for the submit button to "none", which is the programmatic way of setting the CSS display property to none.

rails80/depot_u/app/javascript/controllers/locale_controller.js
```
import { Controller } from "@hotwired/stimulus"

// Connects to data-controller="locale"
export default class extends Controller {
➤   static targets = [ "submit" ]
➤
➤   initialize() {
➤     this.submitTarget.style.display = 'none'
➤   }
}
```

Next, we modify the root route to accept POST requests, as that's the default for forms:

rails80/depot_u/config/routes.rb
```
scope "(:locale)" do
  resources :orders
  resources :line_items
  resources :carts
  root "store#index", as: "store_index", via: :all
end
```

Finally, we modify the store controller to redirect to the store path for a given locale if the :set_locale form is used:

rails80/depot_u/app/controllers/store_controller.rb
```
  def index
➤   if params[:set_locale]
➤     redirect_to store_index_url(locale: params[:set_locale])
➤   else
      @products = Product.order(:title)
➤   end
  end
```

For the actual selector, see the screenshot on page 246. We can now switch back and forth between languages with a single mouse click.

At this point, we can place orders in two languages, and our thoughts turn to deployment. But because it's been a busy day, it's time to put down our tools and relax. We'll start on deployment in the morning.

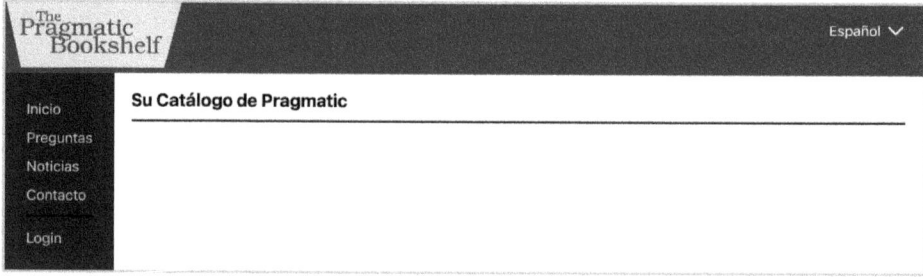

What We Just Did

By the end of this iteration, we've done the following:

- We set the default locale for our application and provided means for the user to select an alternative locale.

- We created translation files for text fields, currency amounts, errors, and model names.

- We altered layouts and views to call out to the I18n module by way of the t() helper to translate textual portions of the interface.

Playtime

Here's some stuff to try on your own:

- Add a locale column to the products database and adjust the index view to select only the products that match the locale. Adjust the products view so that you can view, enter, and alter this new column. Enter a few products in each locale and test the resulting application.

- Determine the current exchange rate between U.S. dollars and euros, and localize the currency display to display euros when ES_es is selected.

In this chapter, you'll see:
- Receiving email with Action Mailbox
- Writing and storing rich text with Action Text
- Managing cloud storage with Active Storage

CHAPTER 16

Task K: Receive Emails and Respond with Rich Text

We've now got a fully functioning store, internationalized for global domination, but what if a customer has a problem they can't solve using our site? With Rails, we can easily do what most e-commerce sites do, which is allow customers to email us so we can solve their problem and write them back with a solution.

Hopefully, you've come to expect by now that Rails has us covered. We sent emails to our customers in Iteration H1: Sending Confirmation Emails, on page 189, but Rails includes a powerful way to *receive* emails called Action Mailbox.[1] You'll learn how that works in this chapter. You'll also learn how to create richly formatted text in your replies by using a rich-text editing system included with Rails called Action Text.[2]

Both Action Text and Action Mailbox rely on another Rails library called Active Storage. Active Storage is an abstraction around cloud storage systems like Amazon's S3. Both incoming emails and rich-text attachments are stored in the cloud using Active Storage. We'll explain why as we go.

Iteration K1: Receiving Support Emails with Action Mailbox

Configuring Rails to receive emails requires three steps: initially setting up Action Mailbox, setting up Active Storage to hold the raw emails we receive, and implementing a *mailbox*, which is like a controller that handles incoming emails.

---

1. https://guides.rubyonrails.org/action_mailbox_basics.html
2. https://guides.rubyonrails.org/action_text_overview.html

Setting Up Action Mailbox

To set up Action Mailbox in our app, we'll run a Rake task that will create some configuration files, a base mailbox class we'll inherit from, and some database tables that Rails will use to store information about incoming emails. Let's run the Rake task:

```
> bin/rails action_mailbox:install
Copying application_mailbox.rb to app/mailboxes
      create  app/mailboxes/application_mailbox.rb
Copied migration
  20250420000011_create_active_storage_tables.active_storage.rb
    from active_storage
Copied migration
  20250420000012_create_action_mailbox_tables.action_mailbox.rb
    from action_mailbox
```

Note that a) we've reformatted our output to fit the pages in the book and b) since there were two migrations created and migration filenames have a date and timestamp in them, your filenames won't exactly match ours. Next, we'll add the tables that the Rake task created to our development and test databases:

```
> bin/rails db:migrate
== 20250420191846 CreateActiveStorageTables: migrating ======================
-- create_table(:active_storage_blobs, {})
   -> 0.0015s
-- create_table(:active_storage_attachments, {})
   -> 0.0013s
== 20250420191846 CreateActiveStorageTables: migrated (0.0029s) =============

== 20250420191847 CreateActionMailboxTables: migrating ======================
-- create_table(:action_mailbox_inbound_emails)
   -> 0.0017s
== 20250420191847 CreateActionMailboxTables: migrated (0.0017s) =============
```

In the real world, we'd also need to configure Action Mailbox for our particular incoming email service provider. The Rails Guide[3] is the best place to look for how to do that. We won't set one up here since setting up accounts with services like Amazon SES or Mailgun is somewhat involved (though once you have your account set up, configuring Rails to use it is a snap). For our immediate needs, Rails provides a way to simulate sending emails, which we'll see in a moment.

---

3. https://guides.rubyonrails.org/action_mailbox_basics.html#configuration

The way Action Mailbox works is that all incoming emails get stored in a cloud storage system like Amazon's S3. Rails includes a library called Active Storage that abstracts away the details of the cloud service you're using.

Active Storage Configuration

As with your real-world email provider, your real-world cloud storage provider will require specific configuration in Rails, which we'll do in Configure Active Storage, on page 286. For development purposes, we'll use the disk-based service that works with our local disk. This will allow us to fully use Active Storage locally, which means Action Mailbox can work locally.

Rails has already preconfigured the development and test environments for you to use Active Storage.

If you take a peek in config/environments/development.rb, you'll see:

rails80/depot_ta/config/environments/development.rb
```
  # Store uploaded files on the local file system
  # (see config/storage.yml for options).
➤ config.active_storage.service = :local
```

We'll explain what :local means in a moment. And you'll see a similar line in config/environments/test.rb but using the :test service instead:

rails80/depot_ta/config/environments/test.rb
```
  # Store uploaded files on the local file system in a temporary directory.
➤ config.active_storage.service = :test
```

The definition of those symbols is contained in config/storage.yml:

rails80/depot_ta/config/storage.yml
```
test:
  service: Disk
➤ root: <%= Rails.root.join("tmp/storage") %>

local:
  service: Disk
➤ root: <%= Rails.root.join("storage") %>
```

The root keys in this file match the values used in the files in config/environments. In this case, both :local and :test are configured to use Active Storage's disk-based service, with our development environment (:local) using the directory storage that's in the root of our project and the test environment (:test) using tmp/storage.

With this setup, when we receive an email, the entire payload gets written to our storage service, and as we'll see in a moment, we can access parts of that email to trigger whatever logic we need in our Rails app. The reason Rails does this is that emails can be large (especially if they have attachments), and you don't necessarily want to store very large objects in a relational database. It's much more common to store such data to disk or with a cloud storage provider and store a reference to that object in the database.

Now that we've done the one-time setup, let's create a mailbox to receive our support request emails from customers.

Creating a Mailbox to Receive Emails

Action Mailbox works by routing incoming emails to a mailbox. A mailbox is a subclass of ApplicationMailbox with a method named process() that's called for each email routed to that mailbox. The way emails get routed is similar to how web requests get routed in config/routes.rb. For email, you'll tell Rails what sorts of emails you want routed where.

We want emails to support@example.com to get routed to a mailbox so we can handle them. The way to do that is to insert a call to the method routing() inside ApplicationMailbox:

rails80/depot_ta/app/mailboxes/application_mailbox.rb
```ruby
class ApplicationMailbox < ActionMailbox::Base
  # routing /something/i => :somewhere
  routing "support@example.com" => :support
end
```

This tells Rails that any email to (or cc'd to) support@example.com should be handled by the class SupportMailbox. We can create that class using a Rails generator:

```
> bin/rails generate mailbox support
      create  app/mailboxes/support_mailbox.rb
      invoke  test_unit
      create    test/mailboxes/support_mailbox_test.rb
```

If you look at app/mailboxes/support_mailbox.rb, you'll see a few lines of code, notably an empty method called process():

```ruby
class SupportMailbox < ApplicationMailbox
  def process
  end
end
```

Now, every email we receive at support@example.com will trigger a call to process() in SupportMailbox. Inside the process() method, we have access to the special variable mail. This is an instance of Mail::Message[4] and allows us to access the various bits of an email you might expect to have, such as who sent it, the subject, and the contents.

Before getting too far along, let's see how this works by adding some puts() calls into our mailbox:

```
rails80/depot_ta/app/mailboxes/support_mailbox.rb
class SupportMailbox < ApplicationMailbox
  def process
➤    puts "START SupportMailbox#process:"
➤    puts "From : #{mail.from_address}"
➤    puts "Subject: #{mail.subject}"
➤    puts "Body : #{mail.body}"
➤    puts "END SupportMailbox#process:"
  end
end
```

Since we didn't configure a real email provider, how do we trigger our mailbox locally? The answer is a special UI included with Rails called a *conductor*.

Using the Conductor to Send Emails Locally

Action Mailbox includes a special developer-only UI we can use to send emails to ourselves. This allows us to see our mailbox working end-to-end without having to configure a real email provider. To see it, start up your server (or restart it if it's already running).

Navigate to http://localhost:3000/rails/conductor/action_mailbox/inbound_emails and you should see a bare-bones UI that includes a link labeled "New inbound email by form":

> **All inbound emails**
>
> New inbound email by form | New inbound email by source
> **Message ID Status**

Click that link, and you should see a very basic UI to write an email, as shown in the screenshot on page 252.

---

4. https://www.rubydoc.info/github/mikel/mail/Mail/Message

Deliver new inbound email

From
`customer@example.com`
To
`support@example.com`
CC

BCC

X-Original-To

In-Reply-To

Subject
`I need help!`
Body
```
I can't find my order.  It's #12345
```

Attachments
[Choose Files] No file chosen
[Deliver inbound email]

Fill this in, remembering to use support@example.com as the To email so that the email gets routed to your mailbox. If you then click "Deliver inbound email" and flip back to where you ran your server, you should see, among other log output, the puts() you inserted:

```
START SupportMailbox#process:
From   : test@somewhere.com
Subject: I need help!
Body   : I can't find my order. It's #12345
END SupportMailbox#process:
```

Now that we see how all the parts fit together, let's write the real code to store the request for help from the customer (as well as how to test our mailbox with a unit test).

Iteration K2: Storing Support Requests from Our Mailbox

As we mentioned above, the purpose of mailboxes is to allow us to execute code on every email we receive. Because emails come in whenever the sender sends them, we'll need to store the details of a customer support request somewhere for an administrator to handle later. To that end, we'll create a new model called SupportRequest that will hold the relevant details of the request, and have the process() method of SupportMailbox create an instance for each email we get (in the final section of this chapter, we'll display these in a UI so an admin can respond).

Creating a Model for Support Requests

We want our model to hold the sender's email, the subject and body of the email, and a reference to the customer's most recent order if there's one on file. First, let's create the model using a Rails generator:

```
> bin/rails generate model support_request
      invoke  active_record
      create    db/migrate/20250420000014_create_support_requests.rb
      create    app/models/support_request.rb
      invoke    test_unit
      create      test/models/support_request_test.rb
      create      test/fixtures/support_requests.yml
```

This created a migration for us, which is currently empty (remember that migration filenames have a date and time in them, so your filename will be slightly different). Let's fill that in.

rails80/depot_tb/db/migrate/20250420000014_create_support_requests.rb
```
class CreateSupportRequests < ActiveRecord::Migration[8.0]
  def change
    create_table :support_requests do |t|
➤     t.string :email, comment: "Email of the submitter"
➤     t.string :subject, comment: "Subject of their support email"
➤     t.text :body, comment: "Body of their support email"
➤     t.references :order,
➤                  foreign_key: true,
➤                  comment: "their most recent order, if applicable"
      t.timestamps
    end
  end
end
```

With this in place, we can create this table via bin/rails db:migrate:

```
> bin/rails db:migrate
== 20250420121503 CreateSupportRequests: migrating ===========================
-- create_table(:support_requests)
   -> 0.0016s
== 20250420121503 CreateSupportRequests: migrated (0.0017s) ==================
```

We'll also need to adjust the model itself to optionally reference an order:

rails80/depot_tb/app/models/support_request.rb
```ruby
class SupportRequest < ApplicationRecord
➤   belongs_to :order, optional: true
end
```

And we'll need to create the inverse relationship in the Order model:

rails80/depot_tb/app/models/order.rb
```ruby
class Order < ApplicationRecord
  enum :pay_type, {
    "Check"          => 0,
    "Credit card"    => 1,
    "Purchase order" => 2
  }
  has_many :line_items, dependent: :destroy
➤  has_many :support_requests, dependent: :nullify
  # ...
```

Now, we can create instances of SupportRequest from our mailbox.

Creating Support Requests from Our Mailbox

Our mailbox needs to do two things. First, it needs to create an instance of SupportRequest for each email that comes in. But it also needs to connect that request to the user's most recent order, if there's one in our database (this will allow our admin to quickly reference the order that might be causing trouble).

As you recall, all orders have an email associated with them. So, to get the most recent order for an email, we can use where() to search all orders by email: order() to order the results by the create data and first() to grab the most recent one. With that, we can use the methods on mail we saw earlier to create the SupportRequest.

Here's the code we need in app/mailboxes/support_mailbox.rb (which replaces the calls to puts() we added before):

rails80/depot_tb/app/mailboxes/support_mailbox.rb
```ruby
class SupportMailbox < ApplicationMailbox
  def process
```

```
      recent_order = Order.where(email: mail.from_address.to_s).
                       order("created_at desc").
                       first
    SupportRequest.create!(
      email: mail.from_address.to_s,
      subject: mail.subject,
      body: mail.body.to_s,
      order: recent_order
    )
  end
end
```

> **Why Don't We Access Emails Directly When Needed?**
>
> It might seem easier to simply access the customer emails whenever we need them rather than pluck out the data we want and store it in a database. There are two reasons not to do this.
>
> The first and most practical reason is about separation of concerns. Our support requests only need part of what is in the emails, but they also might need more metadata than the customer sends us. To keep our code organized and clean, it's better to store what we need explicitly.
>
> The second reason is one of Rails' famously held opinions. Rails arranges for all emails to be deleted after thirty days. The reasoning is that emails contain personal data that we don't want to hold onto unnecessarily.
>
> Protecting the personal data of your customers is a good practice, and it's one that's more and more required by law. For example, the European General Data Protection Regulation (GDPR) requires, among other things, that you delete any personal data you have within one month of a request to do so. By auto-deleting personal data every thirty days, you automatically comply with this requirement.[a]
>
> ---
>
> a. We're not lawyers, so please don't take this sidebar as legal advice!

Now, restart your server and navigate to the conductor at http://localhost:3000/rails/conductor/action_mailbox/inbound_emails. Click "Deliver new inbound email" and send another email (remember to send it to support@example.com).

Now, quit your server and start up the Rails console. This will allow us to check that a new SupportRequest was created (remember we have to format this to fit in the book, so your output will be on fewer, longer lines):

```
> bin/rails console
irb(main):001:0> SupportRequest.first
   (1.5ms)  SELECT sqlite_version(*)
  SupportRequest Load (0.1ms)
```

```
      SELECT "support_requests".* FROM "support_requests"
        ORDER BY "support_requests"."id" ASC LIMIT ?  [["LIMIT", 1]]
=> #<SupportRequest
       id: 1,
       email: "chris@somewhere.com",
       subject: "Missing book!",
       body: "I can't find my book that I ordered. Please help!",
       order_id: nil,
       created_at: "2021-01-19 12:29:17",
       updated_at: "2021-01-19 12:29:17">
```

You should see the data you entered into the conductor saved in the SupportRequest instance. You can also try this using the email of an order you have in your system to verify it locates the most recent order. Of course, manually checking our code isn't ideal. We would like to have an automated test. Fortunately, Rails provides a simple way to test our mailboxes, which you'll learn about now.

Testing Our Mailbox

When we used the generator to create our mailbox, you probably noticed the file test/mailboxes/support_mailbox_test.rb gets created. This is where we'll write our test. Since we generally know how to write tests, all we need to know now is how to trigger an email. ActionMailbox provides the method, receive_inbound_email_from_mail(), which we can use in our tests to do just that.

We need two tests to cover the functionality of our mailbox. The first is to send an email from a customer without an order and verify we created a SupportRequest instance. The second is to send an email from a customer who *does* have orders and verify that the SupportRequest instance is correctly connected to their most recent order.

The first test is most straightforward since we don't need any test setup, so we'll create a new test() block inside test/mailboxes/support_mailbox_test.rb:

```
rails80/depot_tb/test/mailboxes/support_mailbox_test.rb
require "test_helper"

class SupportMailboxTest < ActionMailbox::TestCase
➤   test "we create a SupportRequest when we get a support email" do
➤     receive_inbound_email_from_mail(
➤       to: "support@example.com",
➤       from: "chris@somewhere.net",
➤       subject: "Need help",
➤       body: "I can't figure out how to check out!!"
➤     )
➤
➤     support_request = SupportRequest.last
➤     assert_equal "chris@somewhere.net", support_request.email
```

```ruby
➤       assert_equal "Need help", support_request.subject
➤       assert_equal "I can't figure out how to check out!!", support_request.body
➤       assert_nil support_request.order
➤     end
    end
```

If we run this test now, it should pass:

> **bin/rails test test/mailboxes/support_mailbox_test.rb**
Run options: --seed 26908

Running:

.

Finished in 0.322222s, 3.1035 runs/s, 12.4138 assertions/s.
1 runs, 4 assertions, 0 failures, 0 errors, 0 skips

Great! For the second test, we'll need to create a few orders before we send the email. You'll recall from Test Fixtures, on page 92, that we can use fixtures to set up test data in advance. We have one we can use already, but ideally, we'd have a total of two orders for the user sending the email and a third order from another user. That would validate that we're both searching for the right user *and* selecting the most recent order.

Let's add two new fixtures to test/fixtures/orders.yml

```
rails80/depot_tb/test/fixtures/orders.yml
# Read about fixtures at
# https://api.rubyonrails.org/classes/ActiveRecord/FixtureSet.html
one:
  name: Dave Thomas
  address: MyText
  email: dave@example.org
  pay_type: Check

➤ another_one:
➤   name: Dave Thomas
➤   address: 123 Any St
➤   email: dave@example.org
➤   pay_type: Check
➤   created_at: <%= 2.days.ago %>
➤
➤ other_customer:
➤   name: Chris Jones
➤   address: 456 Somewhere Ln
➤   email: chris@nowhere.net
➤   pay_type: Check
two:
  name: MyString
  address: MyText
```

```
    email: MyString
    pay_type: 1
```

Note how we're using ERB inside our fixture. This code is executed when we request a fixture, and we're using it to force an older creation date for one of our orders. By default, Rails sets created_at on models it creates from fixtures to the current time. When we ask Rails to create that particular fixture with orders(:another_one), it will execute the code inside the <%= and %>, effectively setting the created_at value to the date as of two days ago.

With these fixtures available, we can write our second test:

rails80/depot_tb/test/mailboxes/support_mailbox_test.rb
```
require "test_helper"

class SupportMailboxTest < ActionMailbox::TestCase

  # previous test

➤  test "we create a SupportRequest with the most recent order" do
➤    recent_order = orders(:one)
➤    older_order  = orders(:another_one)
➤    non_customer = orders(:other_customer)
➤
➤    receive_inbound_email_from_mail(
➤      to: "support@example.com",
➤      from: recent_order.email,
➤      subject: "Need help",
➤      body: "I can't figure out how to check out!!"
➤    )
➤
➤    support_request = SupportRequest.last
➤    assert_equal recent_order.email, support_request.email
➤    assert_equal "Need help", support_request.subject
➤    assert_equal "I can't figure out how to check out!!", support_request.body
➤    assert_equal recent_order, support_request.order
➤  end

end
```

Next, rerun the test, and we should see our new test is passing:

```
> bin/rails test test/mailboxes/support_mailbox_test.rb
Run options: --seed 47513

# Running:

..

Finished in 0.384217s, 5.2054 runs/s, 20.8216 assertions/s.
2 runs, 8 assertions, 0 failures, 0 errors, 0 skips
```

Nice! We can now confidently write code to handle incoming emails and test it with an automated test. Now, what do we do with these SupportRequest instances we're creating? We'd like to allow an administrator to respond to them. We could do that with plain text, but let's learn about another part of Rails called Action Text that will allow us to author rich text we can use to respond.

Iteration K3: Responding with Rich Text

To allow our admins to respond to support requests, we'll need to make a new UI for them to see the requests that need a response, a way for them to provide a response, and then some code to email the customer back. We know how to do all of these things, but this is a great opportunity to learn about Action Text, which is a Rails library that allows us to easily provide a richtext editing experience. We can use this to allow our admins to write a fully formatted response and not just plain text.

Let's first quickly create the UI where we'll see the support requests and edit them. This should be old hat for you by now, so we'll go quickly. Add a new route to config/routes.rb for the index() and update() methods:

```ruby
rails80/depot_tb/config/routes.rb
Rails.application.routes.draw do
  get "admin" => "admin#index"
  get "up" => "rails/health#show", as: :rails_health_check

➤ resources :support_requests, only: %i[ index update ]

  resources :users
  resources :products
  resource :session
  resources :passwords, param: :token

  scope "(:locale)" do
    resources :orders
    resources :line_items
    resources :carts
    root "store#index", as: "store_index", via: :all
  end
end
```

Now, create app/controllers/support_requests_controller.rb and implement index() (we'll see update() in a moment):

```ruby
rails80/depot_tb/app/controllers/support_requests_controller.rb
➤ class SupportRequestsController < ApplicationController
➤   def index
➤     @support_requests = SupportRequest.all
➤   end
➤
➤ end
```

Next, we'll create the view in app/views/support_requests/index.html.erb:

```
rails80/depot_tb/app/views/support_requests/index.html.erb
<ul>
  <% @support_requests.each do |support_request| %>
    <li>
      <h1 class="text-2xl font-bold">
        On <%= support_request.created_at.to_formatted_s(:long) %>
        <code><%= support_request.email %></code> writes:
      </h1>
      <blockquote class="ml-4">
        <h2 class="font-bold"><%= support_request.subject %></h2>
        <%= support_request.body %>
      </blockquote>
      <% if support_request.order %>
        <h3 class="mt-4 text-xl font-bold">Recent Order</h3>
        <dl>
          <dt>Name</dt>
          <dd class="ml-4"><%= support_request.order.name %></dd>

          <dt>Email</dt>
          <dd  class="ml-4"><%= support_request.order.email %></dd>

          <dt>Address</dt>
          <dd class="ml-4"><%= support_request.order.address %></dd>

          <dt>PayType</dt>
          <dd class="ml-4"><%= support_request.order.pay_type %></dd>

          <dt>Line Items</dt>
          <dd>
            <ul class="ml-4 list-disc">
              <% support_request.order.line_items.each do |line_item| %>
                <li>
                  <%= line_item.product.title %>
                  (<%= line_item.product.price %>)
                </li>
              <% end %>
            </ul>
          </dd>
        </dl>
      <% else %>
        <h3 class="notice">No associated order</h3>
      <% end %>
      <%= form_with(model: support_request,
                    local: true,
                    class: "depot_form") do |form| %>
        <div class="field">
          <%= form.label :response, "Write Response" %>
          <%= form.rich_textarea :response, id: :support_request_response %>
        </div>
```

```erb
          <div class="actions">
            <%= form.submit "Send Response" %>
          </div>
      <% end %>
      <hr>
    </li>
  <% end %>
</ul>
```

Restart your server, create a few orders and, using the Rails conductor we saw earlier, create a few support tickets. Be sure that at least one of them is from an email you used to create an order. When you've done that, navigate to http://localhost:3000/admin and log in. Once you've done *that*, navigate to http://localhost:3000/support_requests and you should see the UI you just created with your support requests rendered:

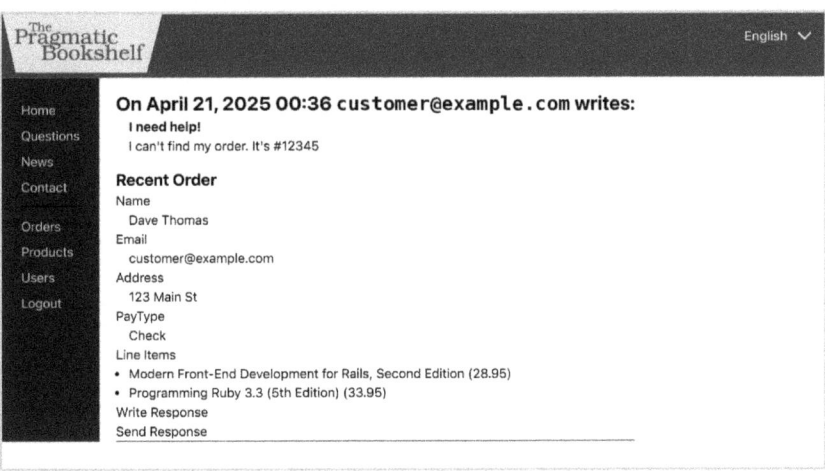

It's not pretty, but it'll work for now. Next, we need to add the ability to write a response. If we were OK with plain text, we would make a new attribute on SupportRequest to hold the response, then wire up a form to write it, just like we've done several times. With rich text, it works a bit differently.

Action Text stores the rich text in its own table outside of the model's. In our SupportRequest model, we'll tell Rails that we have a rich-text field that we want Action Text to manage by using the has_rich_text() method, like so:

rails80/depot_tc/app/models/support_request.rb
```ruby
class SupportRequest < ApplicationRecord
  belongs_to :order, optional: true
  has_rich_text :response
end
```

This method (and the rest of Action Text) won't work without some setup, which we can do with the Rake task action_text:install:

```
> bin/rails action_text:install
      append  app/javascript/application.js
      append  config/importmap.rb
      create  app/assets/stylesheets/actiontext.css
      append  app/assets/stylesheets/application.tailwind.css
      create  app/views/active_storage/blobs/_blob.html.erb
      create  app/views/layouts/action_text/contents/_content.html.erb
Ensure image_processing gem has been enabled so image uploads will work
(remember to bundle!)
        gsub  Gemfile
       rails  railties:install:migrations FROM=active_storage,action_text
Copied migration 20250420145849_create_action_text_tables.action_text.rb
 from action_text
      invoke  test_unit
      create    test/fixtures/action_text/rich_texts.yml
```

Because this changed the Gemfile, we need to run bundle install:

```
> bin/bundle install
```

You'll notice that the generator created a database migration. This is for the tables that Action Text uses to store the rich text itself.

Let's add those by running the db:migrate task:

```
> bin/rails db:migrate
== 20250420120454 CreateActionTextTables: migrating =======================
-- create_table(:action_text_rich_texts, {:id=>:primary_key})
   -> 0.0016s
== 20250420120454 CreateActionTextTables: migrated (0.0017s) ==============
```

With all of that back-end setup out of the way, we can now make our UI. We'll create this in the same way we've created other forms in our app, with the exception of the text area. Instead of using the text_area() form helper to make a regular HTML textarea tag, we'll use rich_textarea(), which will set up the Trix editor for us, enabling the UI part of Action Text.

Add this to app/views/support_requests/index.html.erb:

rails80/depot_tc/app/views/support_requests/index.html.erb
```erb
<ul>
  <% @support_requests.each do |support_request| %>
    <li>
      <h1 class="text-2xl font-bold">
        On <%= support_request.created_at.to_formatted_s(:long) %>
        <code><%= support_request.email %></code> writes:
      </h1>
      <blockquote class="ml-4">
```

```erb
      <h2 class="font-bold"><%= support_request.subject %></h2>
      <%= support_request.body %>
    </blockquote>
    <% if support_request.order %>
      <h3 class="mt-4 text-xl font-bold">Recent Order</h3>
      <dl>
        <dt>Name</dt>
        <dd class="ml-4"><%= support_request.order.name %></dd>

        <dt>Email</dt>
        <dd  class="ml-4"><%= support_request.order.email %></dd>

        <dt>Address</dt>
        <dd class="ml-4"><%= support_request.order.address %></dd>

        <dt>PayType</dt>
        <dd class="ml-4"><%= support_request.order.pay_type %></dd>

        <dt>Line Items</dt>
        <dd>
          <ul class="ml-4 list-disc">
            <% support_request.order.line_items.each do |line_item| %>
              <li>
                <%= line_item.product.title %>
                (<%= line_item.product.price %>)
              </li>
            <% end %>
          </ul>
        </dd>
      </dl>
    <% else %>
      <h3 class="notice">No associated order</h3>
    <% end %>
➤   <% if support_request.response.blank? %>
➤     <%= form_with(model: support_request,
➤                   local: true,
➤                   class: "depot_form") do |form| %>
➤       <div class="field">
➤         <%= form.label :response, "Write Response" %>
➤         <%= form.rich_textarea :response, id: :support_request_response %>
➤       </div>
➤       <div class="actions">
➤         <%= form.submit "Send Response" %>
➤       </div>
➤     <% end %>
➤   <% else %>
➤     <h4>Our response:</h4>
➤     <p>
➤       <blockquote>
➤         <%= support_request.response %>
➤       </blockquote>
➤     </p>
```

```erb
      <% end %>
        <hr>
      </li>
    <% end %>
  </ul>
```

Note that we check to see if the support request has a response, and if it does, we render it. As we'll see, this has been enhanced by Action Text.

Next, we implement update() in our controller:

```ruby
# rails80/depot_tc/app/controllers/support_requests_controller.rb
class SupportRequestsController < ApplicationController
  def index
    @support_requests = SupportRequest.all
  end

  def update
    support_request = SupportRequest.find(params[:id])
    support_request.update(response: params.require(:support_request)[:response])
    SupportRequestMailer.respond(support_request).deliver_now
    redirect_to support_requests_path
  end
end
```

You learned how to send emails in Chapter 13, Task H: Sending Emails, on page 189, but when dealing with rich text and the need to send a plain-text email, we have to strip out the rich text. So, let's set up the mailer to respond to the user, and when we create the plain-text template, we'll see how to strip out the rich text. We'll start this off by creating the mailer using the Rails generator:

```
> bin/rails generate mailer support_request respond
      create  app/mailers/support_request_mailer.rb
      invoke  erb
      create    app/views/support_request_mailer
      create    app/views/support_request_mailer/respond.text.erb
      create    app/views/support_request_mailer/respond.html.erb
      invoke  test_unit
      create    test/mailers/support_request_mailer_test.rb
      create    test/mailers/previews/support_request_mailer_preview.rb
```

Our mailer will look similar to the mailers we've created in the past. This is what your app/mailers/support_request_mailer.rb should look like:

```ruby
# rails80/depot_tc/app/mailers/support_request_mailer.rb
class SupportRequestMailer < ApplicationMailer
  # Subject can be set in your I18n file at config/locales/en.yml
  # with the following lookup:
  #
```

```
    #     en.support_request_mailer.respond.subject
    #
    default from: "support@example.com"

  def respond(support_request)
    @support_request = support_request
    mail to: @support_request.email, subject: "Re: #{@support_request.subject}"
  end
end
```

For the views, we'll show our response and quote the user's original email. As we saw in our web view, Rails will handle rendering the rich text for us, so the HTML mail view in app/views/support_request_mailer/respond.html.erb will look fairly straightforward:

rails80/depot_tc/app/views/support_request_mailer/respond.html.erb
```
<%= @support_request.response %>
<hr>
<blockquote>
  <%= @support_request.body %>
</blockquote>
```

We also want to include a plain-text version, since not everyone wants rich text in their emails. In the case of a plain-text email, we want to strip out the rich text from our response. Action Text provides a method to do that, called to_plain_text(), which we can use in app/views/support_request_mailer/respond.text.erb:

rails80/depot_tc/app/views/support_request_mailer/respond.text.erb
```
<%= @support_request.response.to_plain_text %>

---

<%= @support_request.body %>
```

The last step is to add a call to our mailer when we update the SupportRequest:

```
class SupportRequestsController < ApplicationController
  def index
    @support_requests = SupportRequest.all
  end

  def update
    support_request = SupportRequest.find(params[:id])
    support_request.update(response: params.require(:support_request)[:response])
    SupportRequestMailer.respond(support_request).deliver_now
      redirect_to support_requests_path
  end
end
```

Now, start up your server, and assuming you've created some support requests, you should see a rich-text editor instead of a plain old text area:

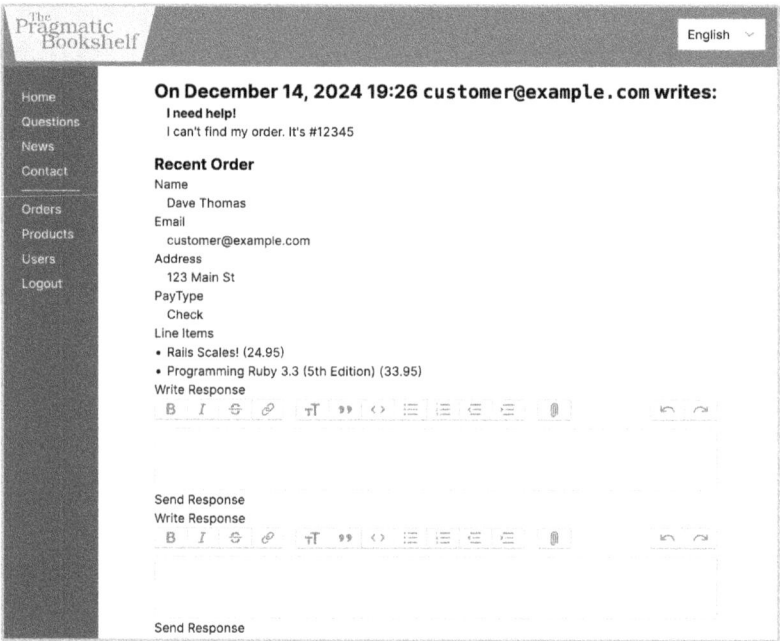

You can see in the following screenshot that we've added rich text to the text area using the editor's controls. Try that in your environment, then click Send Response. The page will refresh, and because we've now saved a response with this SupportRequest, you'll see the rich text rendered…in rich text!

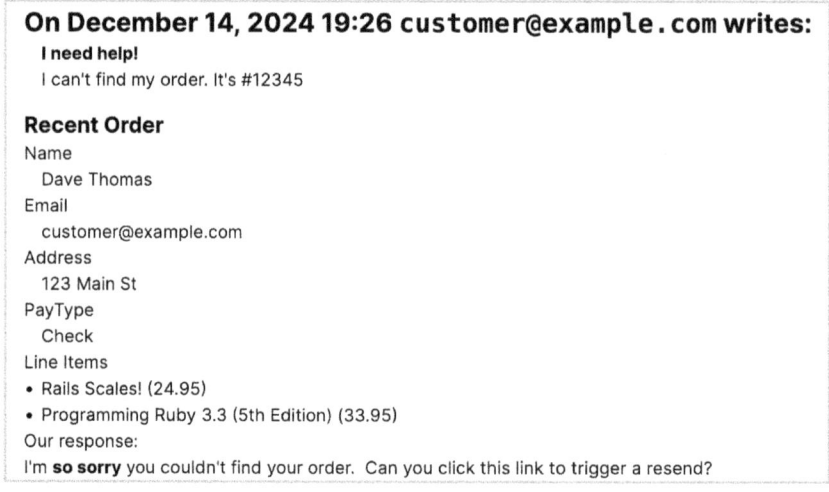

You'll also see the mail printed out in your log, and you should see that the plain-text part of the email is free of formatting.

What We Just Did

- We configured and set up Action Mailbox to allow our app to receive support emails. We saw how to configure Rails to inspect each incoming email and route it to the right bit of code, called a mailbox.

- We also configured Active Storage, which Rails uses to store the raw emails it processes. With this setup, we could easily access cloud storage for any other purpose we might need.

- We used Action Text to enable rich-text editing for responding to support requests. With just a few lines of code, we have a cross-browser rich-text editing experience that works.

- We stripped out the rich text to send a plain-text email of our rich-text response.

Playtime

Here are some things you can try on your own:

- Modify the product editor to allow products to have rich text.

- Change the support request to find all orders for the email, not just the most recent.

In this chapter, you'll see:
- Running our application in a Docker container
- Using Kamal to deploy our application on a host machine
- Monitoring your application and backups

CHAPTER 17

Task L: Deployment and Production

Deployment is supposed to mark a happy point in the lifetime of our application. It's when we take the code that we've so carefully crafted and upload it to a server so that other people can use it. It's when the beer, champagne, and hors d'oeuvres are supposed to flow. Shortly thereafter, our application will be written about in *Hacker News*, and we'll become overnight sensations in the geek community.

But the reality is that it often takes quite a bit of up-front planning to pull off a smooth and repeatable deployment of your application.

In this chapter, we'll take the Depot application that we've been working on and deploy it to a server. We'll start by deploying it locally, and then move on to deploying it to a cloud provider, and finally we'll add backups and monitoring to our application.

Iteration L1: Deploying Locally

In the past, there was a bewildering number of options available for deployment: Ansible, Capistrano, Chef, and Puppet were all popular choices. But starting with Rails 7.1, Docker has become the official default for deployment.

If you're not familiar with Docker images, you can find out more in *Docker for Rails Developers [Ise19]*. Meanwhile, all you need to know is that they're essentially self-contained and portable runtimes that can be deployed by pretty much any cloud-hosting provider. This means you can build and test your deployment locally and then choose your cloud provider later, and even change your mind and move hosts at any time.

You control what goes into a Docker image by creating a Dockerfile. Helpfully, Rails provides a Dockerfile for you to start with. We won't be changing it, so if you're in a hurry, you can skip to Orchestrate the Deployment, on page 274 and refer back to this later.

Base Image

We'll look at the Dockerfile in three parts. We'll start with the base image:

```
rails80/depot_td/Dockerfile
# syntax=docker/dockerfile:1
# check=error=true

# This Dockerfile is designed for production, not development. Use with
#   Kamal or build'n'run by hand:
# docker build -t work .
# docker run -d -p 80:80 \
#    -e RAILS_MASTER_KEY=<value from config/master.key> --name work work

# For a containerized dev environment, see Dev Containers:
#    https://guides.rubyonrails.org/getting_started_with_devcontainer.html

# Make sure RUBY_VERSION matches the Ruby version in .ruby-version
ARG RUBY_VERSION=3.4.3
FROM docker.io/library/ruby:$RUBY_VERSION-slim AS base

# Rails app lives here
WORKDIR /rails

# Install base packages
RUN apt-get update -qq && \
    apt-get install --no-install-recommends -y curl libjemalloc2 \
      libvips sqlite3 && \
    rm -rf /var/lib/apt/lists /var/cache/apt/archives

# Set production environment
ENV RAILS_ENV="production" \
    BUNDLE_DEPLOYMENT="1" \
    BUNDLE_PATH="/usr/local/bundle" \
    BUNDLE_WITHOUT="development"
```

This part contains five *instructions*, each of which by convention is capitalized. The first instruction is ARG, which defines a variable that can be used in subsequent instructions. The second instruction is FROM, which specifies the base image to build upon. Taken together, they instruct Docker to start with an image that has Ruby 3.4.3 installed. You can find the image on Docker Hub.[1]

The third instruction is WORKDIR, which creates and sets the current working directory.

---

1. https://hub.docker.com/_/ruby

The fourth instruction is RUN, which runs a series of commands. The first command updates the package list, and the second installs a number of packages. The third command cleans up files that are no longer necessary.

While the full ruby image contains everything you *might* need, including plenty that you'll never use, ruby:slim doesn't contain things that will be needed to generate your demo application—things like make and git.

Scanning the list of Debian Bookworm packages,[2] you can find libjemalloc2 and curl, but it takes some perseverance. The last time I ran a count, there were 58,733 packages on that list. Sifting through thousands of packages to find what you need is too cumbersome. Instead, when you have failed to include what you need, it's better to paste the resulting error message in your favorite search engine and review the answer in places like StackOverflow.

For the curious, these are some of the packages:

- curl is a command-line tool for transferring data with URLs.
- libjemalloc2 is a library that speeds up memory-hungry applications.
- libvips is a fast image-processing library.
- sqlite3 is the command line interface to Sqlite3.

The way to install packages on Debian is to use a tool named apt-get.

The final instruction in this part is ENV, which sets a number of environment variables.

Overall, the docker portions (ARG, FROM, RUN, WORKDIR, and ENV) are very straightforward.

The parts that need explaining are the operating system parts like apt-get and build-essential. This will remain true as you continue your journey: the hard part isn't learning Docker, but rather getting to know what for many of you is an entirely new operating system—in this case, Debian Linux.

Build Image

The next part is the *build* image. As you might expect, this is where the application is built.

rails80/depot_td/Dockerfile
```
# Throw-away build stage to reduce size of final image
FROM base AS build

# Install packages needed to build gems
RUN apt-get update -qq && \
```

---

2. https://packages.debian.org/stable/allpackages

```
    apt-get install --no-install-recommends -y build-essential git \
      libyaml-dev pkg-config && \
    rm -rf /var/lib/apt/lists /var/cache/apt/archives
# Install application gems
COPY Gemfile Gemfile.lock ./
RUN bundle install && \
    rm -rf ~/.bundle/ "${BUNDLE_PATH}"/ruby/*/cache \
      "${BUNDLE_PATH}"/ruby/*/bundler/gems/*/.git && \
    bundle exec bootsnap precompile --gemfile
# Copy application code
COPY . .

# Precompile bootsnap code for faster boot times
RUN bundle exec bootsnap precompile app/ lib/

# Precompiling assets for production without requiring secret
#    RAILS_MASTER_KEY
RUN SECRET_KEY_BASE_DUMMY=1 ./bin/rails assets:precompile
```

This FROM instruction specifies that the previous image is to be used as the base for this step. The importance of this will become clear when we get to the final image.

Next, we install some packages that are needed to build the application:

- build-essential is a package that installs the basic tools needed to compile software.
- git is a version control system.
- pkg-config is a helper tool used when compiling software.

Next, is a COPY instruction which copies the Gemfile and Gemfile.lock from your application to the image. This is done separately from the rest of the application code to take advantage of Docker's caching mechanism. If neither of these files has changed, Docker will use the cached image from the previous build. If either of these files has changed, Docker will rebuild the image from this point on.

The next instruction will run bundle install to install the gems needed by the application. This step may take a while, which is why it's important to only be run if the Gemfile or Gemfile.lock file havs changed. It will also run bootsnap precompile on the Gemfile to speed up the start time of the application.[3]

Once this is complete, the rest of your application is copied to the image. Then, bootsnap is run again, this time on the application code and libraries.

---

3. https://github.com/Shopify/bootsnap?tab=readme-ov-file#bootsnap-for-rails

The final step is to run rails assets:precompile to precompile the assets for the application. This is a step that's only needed when deploying the application. In development, the assets are served dynamically from the app/assets directory. The setting of SECRET_KEY_BASE is a work-around to Rails requiring a master key even on commands that won't make use of it.

Deploy Image

The last image in any Dockerfile is the image that will be run when the container is started. Note that this step too specifies the original image is to be used as the base. This avoids the inclusion of all of the build tools in the final image.

```
rails80/depot_td/Dockerfile
# Final stage for app image
FROM base

# Copy built artifacts: gems, application
COPY --from=build "${BUNDLE_PATH}" "${BUNDLE_PATH}"
COPY --from=build /rails /rails

# Run and own only the runtime files as a non-root user for security
RUN groupadd --system --gid 1000 rails && \
    useradd rails --uid 1000 --gid 1000 --create-home --shell \
      /bin/bash && \
    chown -R rails:rails db log storage tmp
USER 1000:1000

# Entrypoint prepares the database.
ENTRYPOINT ["/rails/bin/docker-entrypoint"]

# Start server via Thruster by default, this can be overwritten at
#   runtime
EXPOSE 80
CMD ["./bin/thrust", "./bin/rails", "server"]
```

Next, the installed gems and the application code are copied from the build image to the final deploy image.

A non-root user is then created, and only specific directories are owned by that user. This is a security measure to prevent an attacker from gaining access to the entire system if they manage to break out of the application.

An ENTRYPOINT is defined that will set up the application. This is a separate script that will set up libjemalloc2 and then run the database preparation commands.

EXPOSE 80 identifies the port that the Thruster HTTP/2 proxy will be listening on.

Finally, the CMD instruction specifies the command that will be run when the container is started. In this case, it runs Thruster. The last two entries in the CMS list are arguments to Thruster, which is the command to start the Rails server and the parameter to pass to Rails. Note that this is *not* the bin/dev command as that command is only used in development.

Using Thruster as an HTTP/2 Proxy

Thruster is a high-performance HTTP/2 proxy that can be used to serve your application. It's a good choice for serving Rails applications as it can handle the large number of connections that Rails can generate.

Thruster serves three purposes:

- It can serve static files quickly. It does this by making direct use of operating system functionality and implementing compression.

- It serves as an HTTP/2 proxy. Puma implements HTTP 1.1 and Puma's threads can only handle one request at a time. HTTP 2 allows clients to make multiple concurrent requests that are multiplexed, which is a fancy term for saying that responses can come back in any order.

- It can provide certificate management. This is used in single-machine Kamal deployments to provide SSL.

Orchestrate the Deployment

To run this image, we'll need to associate various paths on our machine with paths in the container. We'll also need to set up a network so that the web service can communicate with the database service. And we'll need to pass in the master key that we created earlier. We can do all this on the command line, but it's easier to use a file to orchestrate the deployment. We can do that all by creating a docker-compose.yml:

```
rails80/depot_td/docker-compose.yml
services:
  web:
    build: .
    volumes:
      - ./log:/rails/log
      - ./storage:/rails/storage
    ports:
      - "3000:3000"
    secrets:
      - source: master_key
        target: /rails/config/master.key
```

```
secrets:
  master_key:
    file: ./config/master.key
```

Note that docker-compose.yml is useful for deploying locally. Production deployments generally won't use this file, but overall the principles will be very similar.

This file starts with build. The value of the period . here means that the Dockerfile used to build this image can be found in the current directory.

Then, there's a volumes element that, in this case, maps the log directory in the container to our local log directory and the storage directory in the container to our local storage directory.

Next, there's a ports element. This maps port 3000 on our development machine to port 3000 in the container. This means that we'll be able to access our application as http://localhost:3000 once it's up and running.

Managing Secrets

When we defined our seed data back in Iteration A2: Making Prettier Listings, on page 74, our database didn't have any users. After we added our first user in Chapter 14, Task I: Logging In, on page 207, we added code to require a valid login to access pages that update the database.

This means that, if we were to deploy a new installation starting with the seed data alone, we would be locked out of our own application. That's not good. So let's fix it!

Adding an initial user to our seed data solves the problem, but checking in a password into our version control and deploying it's hardly secure. Fortunately, Rails has provided a way to encrypt secrets such as this one. Rails calls such secrets credentials.

We get started by editing our credentials:

```
$ EDITOR='code --wait' bin/rails credentials:edit
```

Feel free to replace the editor with vim or another editor of your choice.

You'll see that Rails has already defined one credential that's used to encrypt cookies, which is how Rails implements sessions such as the one used to track a user's cart. Leave that credential alone, and add another one to the file:

```
dave_password: secret
```

When you save the file, Rails will update config/credentials.yml.enc using the master key defined in config/master.key. The encoded file can be checked into version control and shared publicly. The key, however, needs to be kept private.

Now that we have a credential defined, let's make use of it by adding the following to db/seeds.rb:

rails80/depot_td/db/seeds.rb
```ruby
User.create! name: 'dave',
  password: Rails.application.credentials.dave_password
```

So far, we've defined a credential and made use of it. The one task remaining is to set things up to deploy the master key at runtime. The following lines in docker-compose.yml take care of this:

rails80/depot_td/docker-compose.yml
```yaml
services:
  web:
    secrets:
      - source: master_key
        target: /rails/config/master.key
secrets:
  master_key:
    file: ./config/master.key
```

The general pattern of placing a secret in a file, listing all of the secrets you'll be using in one place, and then referencing individual secrets by the containers that use them is common in cloud deployments. Rails makes it easy in that there's only one secret you need for Rails applications, namely a master key. That key can be used to unlock all of the credentials that you'll need.

Configuring SSL

When you deploy your application to the web, you'll want to use SSL. SSL is a protocol that encrypts the data between the client and the server. But for now, we're going to disable SSL. This is because we're deploying to a local machine. SSL isn't needed for local deployments.

In config/environments/production.rb edit the following line to disable SSL:

```ruby
# Force all access to the app over SSL, use Strict-Transport-Security,
# and use secure cookies.
config.force_ssl = !ENV["RAILS_MASTER_KEY"].nil?
```

Note that this checks for a RAILS_MASTER_KEY environment variable. This will be set when you deploy using Kamal or Cloud hosting providers. It won't be set when you deploy locally.

Getting Up and Running

We've covered a lot of ground. Whether you skimmed or read every word in the preceding sections, you can see that a lot of thought and expertise has gone into the creation of the Dockerfile that Rails provides.

Now it's time to get things up and running. The first thing we need to do is install Docker itself. You can get it at the Docker website.[4]

Next, we use docker to build our image for the web service with a single command:

```
$ docker compose build
```

This command will take a while. It will download an image. And most of the remaining time will be spent installing gems. If you run the same command again, it'll run quickly as nothing needs to be redone. If you change any file *other* than your Gemfile, the image will be updated quickly with the change. If you change the Gemfile, run bundle update, and then rerun docker compose build. This will take longer as it will rerun the bundle install step on a fresh image.

Next, we start the web container with a single command:

```
$ docker compose up
```

Normally, this command will be run with the --detach or -d option, which will run the containers in the background, but for now it's helpful to see the output.

At this point, your application is up and running! It can be accessed at http://localhost:3000/.

Using Console to Look at a Live Application

We've already created a large amount of functionality in our application's model classes. Of course, we created these to be used by our application's controllers—but we can also interact with them directly. The gateway to this world is the rails console script. We can launch it on our server with this:

```
$ docker compose exec web bin/rails console
Loading production environment (Rails 8.0.2)
work(prod)> p = Product.last
```

---

4. https://docs.docker.com/get-docker/

```
=> #<Product:0x0000ffff745c3f18 id: 3>
work(prod)> p.title
=> "Modern CSS with Tailwind"
work(prod)> p.price = 29.00
=> 29.0
work(prod)> p.save
=> true
```

Once we have a console session open, we can poke and prod all the various methods in our models. We can create, inspect, and delete records. In a way, it's like having a root console for your application.

Now that we've deployed to our local machine, we can move on to conquering the world. By placing our application into a container, we've made it portable. It can be deployed to any cloud provider. It can be deployed to your own server. It can be deployed to a Raspberry Pi. It can be deployed to a Kubernetes cluster. The possibilities are endless.

Iteration L2: Deployment to the Cloud

Deploying to production isn't hard at all; it's just a number of small steps. And these steps will go quicker if you do them in the correct order and start with a code base that you've deployed locally first. But first, let's review what resources are available:

- kamal-deploy.org[5] contains a 32-minute video demonstrating the creation and deployment of a simple application to a Hetzner server.
- Kamal docs[6] contains some reference material that may be useful.
- *Kamal Handbook: The Missing Manual*[7] is a short and practical book and, at the time of this writing, the only book on the subject.

What follows is neither a video nor a manual, but rather a recipe. And like most recipes, it starts with assembling your ingredients. Along the way, we will share some general ideas of what prices you can expect to pay for each. We'll also list a number of popular choices. These lists are neither endorsements nor meant to be exhaustive.

We're going to start with a single machine, running Sqlite3. Later, in Horizontal Scaling, on page 292, we'll outline the steps you need to take to scale to multiple machines, running PostgreSQL or another database.

---

5. https://kamal-deploy.org/
6. https://kamal-deploy.org/docs/
7. https://kamalmanual.com/handbook/

Assemble Your Ingredients

While in theory you can assemble ingredients in any order, things might go faster if you do them in the order shown. Think of this as a scavenger hunt, where sometimes the item you pick up is needed for your next clue.

SSH Key

SSH keys are used to authenticate you to a server. You can think of them as a password that you don't have to remember.

You probably already have one, but if not, create one. GitHub has some good docs on the subject.[8] It generally is a good idea to have a separate ssh key for each activity anyway.

```
$ ssh-keygen -t ed25519 -C "your_email@example.com"
```

SSH keys are free.

Machine

A machine is a computer that you can access over the Internet. You can think of it as a computer that you rent by the month (and in some cases, by the hour). You can also time-share a machine with others by requesting a Virtual Private Server (VPS).

Most Kamal demos start with Hetzner.[9] Digital Ocean posts a list of alternatives.[10]

For demo or hobby purposes head to Hetzner Cloud. You can get a VPS starting at less than $10 a month. Such a machine could handle up to around 20 requests per second.[11]

For production purposes head to Hetzner Robot and consider a dedicated machine. Here you'll need to work out your application profile before deciding on a machine configuration. It's probably a good idea to start fairly small, and then load test once you're deployed. You can then add any upgrades you need.

Sign up, provide your public ssh key, and select the latest LTS version of Ubuntu (24.04). In all, this process will take about 15 minutes, and you'll end up with an IPv4 address.

---

8. https://docs.github.com/en/authentication/connecting-to-github-with-ssh/generating-a-new-ssh-key-and-adding-it-to-the-ssh-agent
9. https://www.hetzner.com/
10. https://www.digitalocean.com/resources/articles/hetzner-alternatives
11. https://fractaledmind.github.io/2023/12/23/rubyconftw/

Before proceeding, click the Firewall tab, select the WebServer template, and click Apply and Save.

You'll also want Object Storage. You'll find this is priced both on the size you store and the bandwidth you use each month. While you can add this later, it's needed to store your book cover images. Be aware that although there are free quotas, you're charged for every hour you have at least one Bucket, even if it's empty.

Domain Name

A domain name is a human-readable name that points to an ip address. This is what your users will put in the URL bar of their browser.

CloudFlare[12] is a domain registrar that prices domains at or close to cost and has other benefits. Shopify posts a list of alternatives.[13]

After any initial teaser rates, plan to spend $10 to $25 a year for a domain name. (Vanity names can be considerably more.)

Once you've obtained your domain name, go into the DNS settings and create an A record with your ip address as the content. If you're using CloudFlare, disable the "orange cloud" by clicking the Proxied setting for now—if needed, you can add that back later.

Container Registry

Kamal works by building a Docker image and pushing it to a registry, and then pulling that image onto your deployment machines.

DockerHub[14] is effectively the default container registry and can range from free to $24/user/month. quay.io,[15] gcr.io,[16] public.ecr.aws,[17] ghcr.io,[18] and Gitlab[19] are alternatives. You can also use CNCF's Distribution Registry[20] to self-host a registry.

Realistically, you can get a container registry for a small number of personal projects for free.

---

12. https://www.cloudflare.com/products/registrar/
13. https://www.shopify.com/blog/best-domain-registrars#
14. https://hub.docker.com/
15. https://quay.io/
16. https://cloud.google.com/artifact-registry/docs
17. https://gallery.ecr.aws/
18. https://docs.github.com/en/packages/working-with-a-github-packages-registry/working-with-the-container-registry
19. https://docs.gitlab.com/ee/user/packages/container_registry/
20. https://distribution.github.io/distribution/

When done, you'll end up with a rather opaque registry password that you'll need later.

Password Manager (Optional but Highly Recommended)

A password manager is a tool that stores your passwords in an encrypted form. If you're working as a team, a password manager can be used to share secrets.

Password managers supported by Kamal are 1Password[21] LastPass,[22] Bitwarden,[23] AWS Secrets Manager,[24] and Doppler.[25] Plan for $2 to $10/user/month, unless you decide to self-host, which is an option with Bitwarden.[26]

It's not recommended, but you can directly put your passwords into .kamal/secrets, just be sure to add this file to your .gitignore and .dockerignore files.

Builder (Optional)

Kamal can use Docker to build your images locally, but there are at least two good reasons why you wouldn't want to do so:

- If you're developing on ARM64 (like Apple Silicon), but you want to deploy on AMD64 (x86 64-bit), the build can be quite slow[27] and buggy.[28]

- If you have an asymmetric network connection (where downloads are faster than uploads), you may benefit from a configuration where you only upload your changed source to another server, where that server is responsible for uploading the considerably larger resulting Docker image.

A builder is just a host you have ssh access to that's running Docker—preferably running the target instruction set architecture. You already have exactly that: you commissioned a server and Kamal will automatically install Docker on it for you.

There are more choices in Iteration L2: Deployment to the Cloud, on page 278, but you don't need to worry about them at the moment. Now that you finished your preparations, the next part will move quickly.

---

21. https://1password.com/
22. https://www.lastpass.com/
23. https://bitwarden.com/
24. https://aws.amazon.com/secrets-manager/
25. https://www.doppler.com/
26. https://bitwarden.com/help/self-host-an-organization/
27. https://kamal-deploy.org/docs/configuration/builder-examples/#using-remote-builder-for-single-arch
28. https://github.com/docker/for-mac/issues/5342#issuecomment-779133157

Recipe

You've gathered your ingredients, and now it's time to start cooking. Much of the data you've gathered gets deposited into two files.

First up is config/deploy.yml.

```yaml
# rails80/depot_td/config/deploy.yml
# Name of your application. Used to uniquely configure containers.
service: depot

# Name of the container image.
image: samruby/depot

# Deploy to these servers.
servers:
  web:
    - 192.168.0.1
  # job:
  #   hosts:
  #     - 192.168.0.1
  #   cmd: bin/jobs

# Enable SSL auto certification via Let's Encrypt and allow for multiple apps
# on a single web server.  Remove this section when using multiple web
# servers and ensure you terminate SSL at your load balancer.
#
# Note: If using Cloudflare, set encryption mode in SSL/TLS setting to "Full"
# to enable CF-to-app encryption.
proxy:
  ssl: true
  host: depot.example.com

# Credentials for your image host.
registry:
  # Specify the registry server, if you're not using Docker Hub
  # server: registry.digitalocean.com / ghcr.io / ...
  username: samruby

  # Always use an access token rather than real password when possible.
  password:
    - KAMAL_REGISTRY_PASSWORD

# Inject ENV variables into containers (secrets come from .kamal/secrets).
env:
  secret:
    - RAILS_MASTER_KEY
    - ACCESS_KEY_ID
    - SECRET_ACCESS_KEY
    - ENDPOINT_URL_S3
    - REGION
    - BUCKET_NAME
  clear:
    # Run the Solid Queue Supervisor inside the web server's Puma process to
```

```yaml
      # do jobs.  When you start using multiple servers, you should split out
      # job processing to a dedicated machine.
      SOLID_QUEUE_IN_PUMA: true

      # Set number of processes dedicated to Solid Queue (default: 1)
      # JOB_CONCURRENCY: 3

      # Set number of cores available to the application on each server
      # (default: 1).
      # WEB_CONCURRENCY: 2

      # Match this to any external database server to configure Active Record
      # correctly. Use work-db for a db accessory server on same machine via
      #  local kamal docker network.

      # Log everything from Rails
      # RAILS_LOG_LEVEL: debug

  # Aliases are triggered with "bin/kamal <alias>".
  # You can overwrite arguments on invocation:
  # "bin/kamal logs -r job" will tail logs from the first server
  # in the job section.
  aliases:
    console: app exec --interactive --reuse "bin/rails console"
    shell: app exec --interactive --reuse "bash"
    logs: app logs -f
    dbc: app exec --interactive --reuse "bin/rails dbconsole"


  # Use a persistent storage volume for sqlite database files
  # and local Active Storage files.
➤ # Recommended to change this to a mounted volume path that is backed
➤ # up off server.
  volumes:
    - "work_storage:/rails/storage"


  # Bridge fingerprinted assets, like JS and CSS, between versions to avoid
  # hitting 404 on in-flight requests. Combines all files from new and old
  # version inside the asset_path.
  asset_path: /rails/public/assets

  # Configure the image builder.
  builder:
    arch: amd64
➤   context: .
➤   remote: ssh://root@192.168.0.1
➤   local: false

    # # Build image via remote server (useful for faster amd64 builds on
    # # arm64 computers)
    # remote: ssh://docker@docker-builder-server
    #
    # # Pass arguments and secrets to the Docker build process
    # args:
    #   RUBY_VERSION: ruby-3.4.3
```

```
  # secrets:
  #   - GITHUB_TOKEN
  #   - RAILS_MASTER_KEY
# Configure logging
logging:
  driver: local
  options:
    max-size: 20m
    max-file: 5

  # Use a different ssh user than root
  # ssh:
  #   user: app

  # Use accessory services (secrets come from .kamal/secrets).
  # accessories:
  #   db:
  #     image: mysql:8.0
  #     host: 192.168.0.2
  #     # Change to 3306 to expose port to the world instead of just
  #     # local network.
  #     port: "127.0.0.1:3306:3306"
  #     env:
  #       clear:
  #         MYSQL_ROOT_HOST: '%'
  #       secret:
  #         - MYSQL_ROOT_PASSWORD
  #     files:
  #       - config/mysql/production.cnf:/etc/mysql/my.cnf
  #       - db/production.sql:/docker-entrypoint-initdb.d/setup.sql
  #     directories:
  #       - data:/var/lib/mysql
  #   redis:
  #     image: redis:7.0
  #     host: 192.168.0.2
  #     port: 6379
  #     directories:
  #       - data:/data
```

Kamal provides full documentation on this file.[29] Here are the fields you'll be updating:

- service and image are completely up to you. service is the container name prefix, and image is where the containers will be pushed.

- You put the ip address of your host in this file twice, once as the deployment target and once as your builder.

---

29. https://kamal-deploy.org/docs/configuration/overview/

- You put your domain name in the proxy section; https certificates will be provided for you using Let's Encrypt.[30]

- In the registry section you put your server (defaults to Docker Hub), username, and password. This can either be inline or a reference to a secret.

- In the secret section you list your S3 secrets. Alternatively, they can be placed in your credentials file.[31] Some of these values (for example, ENDPOINT_ID, REGION, and BUCKET_NAME) could be passed in the clear instead.

- Volume is used to retain your data across deployments: it maps a directory in your container to a directory on your host machine. We're not changing it, but note the recommendation in the comment above it ("Recommended to change this to a mounted volume path that is backed up off server").

- The default for building is to use your last git commit. Initially, it's sometimes easier to deploy the files as they exist on your development machine until things are working. That's what "context: ." does. This does mean that at times you'll deploy changes and not commit them. For this reason, it's recommended that you delete this line once you're comfortable with your setup.

- The remainder of the builder section specifies to do remote builds on your deployment machine. If you have a separate builder, you can specify that here.

- For logging, you can keep the default (json-file) or go with Docker's recommendation (local).[32] Either way, you likely will want to adjust max-size and/or max-file.

While not related to data you've captured, aliases[33] are useful for commands that you're likely to repeat.

Secrets

In your config/deploy.yml you listed your secrets but not their values. Those values are extracted using a script that you can find in .kamal/secrets.

rails80/depot_td/.kamal/secrets
```
# Secrets defined here are available for reference under registry/password,
# env/secret, builder/secrets, and accessories/*/env/secret in
```

---

30. https://letsencrypt.org/
31. https://guides.rubyonrails.org/security.html#custom-credentials/url
32. https://docs.docker.com/engine/logging/configure/
33. https://kamal-deploy.org/docs/configuration/aliases/

```
# config/deploy.yml. All secrets should be pulled from either password
# manager, ENV, or a file. DO NOT ENTER RAW CREDENTIALS HERE! This file
# needs to be safe for git.

# Example of extracting secrets from 1password (or another compatible
# pw manager)
SECRETS=$(kamal secrets fetch --adapter 1password --account your-account  \
    --from Vault/Item KAMAL_REGISTRY_PASSWORD RAILS_MASTER_KEY \
    ACCESS_KEY_ID SECRET_ACCESS_KEY ENDPOINT_URL REGION BUCKET_NAME)

KAMAL_REGISTRY_PASSWORD=$(kamal secrets extract KAMAL_REGISTRY_PASSWORD
                        ${SECRETS})
RAILS_MASTER_KEY=$(kamal secrets extract RAILS_MASTER_KEY ${SECRETS})
ACCESS_KEY_ID=$(kamal secrets extract ACCESS_KEY_ID ${SECRETS})
SECRET_ACCESS_KEY=$(kamal secrets extract SECRET_ACCESS_KEY ${SECRETS})
ENDPOINT_URL=$(kamal secrets extract ENDPOINT_URL ${SECRETS})
REGION=$(kamal secrets extract REGION ${SECRETS})
BUCKET_NAME=$(kamal secrets extract BUCKET_NAME ${SECRETS})

# Use a GITHUB_TOKEN if private repositories are needed for the image
# GITHUB_TOKEN=$(gh config get -h github.com oauth_token)

# Grab the registry password from ENV
# KAMAL_REGISTRY_PASSWORD=$KAMAL_REGISTRY_PASSWORD

# Improve security by using a password manager.
# Never check config/master.key into git!
# RAILS_MASTER_KEY=$(cat config/master.key)
```

This file has examples of three ways to get your secrets: from a password manager, from the environment, or from a file. A password manager is the most secure and the one we recommend.

Uncomment out this section, select the appropriate adapter,[34] and add the S3 secrets, unless you added them to config/credentials.yml.enc.

Now place all of the secrets you gathered while assembling your ingredients into your password manager. You can find the MASTER_KEY in your Rails app at config/master.key.

While it's possible to list your secrets here, it's strongly discouraged. If you chose to do it anyway, be sure to add this file to your .gitignore and .dockerignore files.

Configure Active Storage

Active Storage is the Rails way to store files. The Depot application uses it to store book cover images. Configure it using the environment variables you extracted from your password manager:

---

34. https://kamal-deploy.org/docs/commands/secrets/

```
rails80/depot_td/config/storage.yml
test:
  service: Disk
  root: <%= Rails.root.join("tmp/storage") %>

local:
  service: Disk
  root: <%= Rails.root.join("storage") %>
➤ hetzner:
➤   service: S3
➤   access_key_id: <%= ENV["ACCESS_KEY_ID"] %>
➤   secret_access_key: <%= ENV["SECRET_ACCESS_KEY"] %>
➤   endpoint: <%= ENV["ENDPOINT_URL"] %>
➤   region: <%= ENV["REGION"] %>
➤   bucket: <%= ENV["BUCKET_NAME"] %>

# Use bin/rails credentials:edit to set the AWS secrets
# (as aws:access_key_id|secret_access_key)
# amazon:
#   service: S3
#   access_key_id: <%= Rails.application.credentials
                          .dig(:aws, :access_key_id) %>
#   secret_access_key: <%= Rails.application.credentials
                              .dig(:aws, :secret_access_key) %>
#   region: us-east-1
#   bucket: your_own_bucket-<%= Rails.env %>

# Remember not to checkin your GCS keyfile to a repository
# google:
#   service: GCS
#   project: your_project
#   credentials: <%= Rails.root.join("path/to/gcs.keyfile") %>
#   bucket: your_own_bucket-<%= Rails.env %>

# Use bin/rails credentials:edit to set the Azure Storage secret
# (as azure_storage:storage_access_key)
# microsoft:
#   service: AzureStorage
#   storage_account_name: your_account_name
#   storage_access_key: <%= Rails.application.credentials
                    .dig(:azure_storage, :storage_access_key) %>
#   container: your_container_name-<%= Rails.env %>

# mirror:
#   service: Mirror
#   primary: local
#   mirrors: [ amazon, google, microsoft ]
```

Note that if you used the Rails credentials file, you can use the Rails.application.credentials hash to extract these values. The amazon example in this file uses this approach.

Finally, update your config/environments/production.rb to use the S3 service:

rails80/depot_td/config/environments/production.rb
```
➤    # Store uploaded files in S3 object storage
➤    #   (see config/storage.yml for options)
➤    config.active_storage.service = :hetzner
```

First Deploy

Congratulations! You've gathered all the ingredients necessary for your first deploy. You've configured Kamal and also Active Storage.

With all this in place, your first deploy is as simple as this:

```
$ bin/kamal setup
```

Messages will scroll by as commands are executed and can be useful to help you spot any problems.

This command does the following:

- Installs Docker on your host
- Builds your image
- Pushes your image to your registry
- Pulls your image onto your host
- Starts your container, passing in your secrets
- Runs your migrations and seed your database
- Waits for your health check to pass
- Configures your proxy to forward requests to your container
- Sets up your SSL certificate

Subsequent deploys can be done via this:

```
$ bin/kamal deploy
```

Once we put an application into production, we need to take care of a few chores to keep the application running smoothly. These chores aren't automatically taken care of for us, but luckily we can automate them.

Iteration L3: Moving to Production

Running in production is so much more than just deploying your application. It's about keeping your application running smoothly and keeping your data safe. If your server goes down, a new one can be started in minutes. If your data is lost, it's lost forever.

Backing Up Your Database

If you look at your config/database.yml, you'll see that it contains definitions for four databases: primary, cache, queue, and cable. These are stored in a storage directory, which is mapped to a directory on your host machine. This is where your data is stored. It's quite possible to back up all four, but for now we're going to focus on the primary database. The primary database is the one that contains your users, products, and orders. It's the one that you can't afford to lose. Because you set up a volume, your data is safe as long as your host machine is running. But what if your host machine goes down?

Docker stores its data in a directory called /var/lib/docker. Inside that directory is a directory called volumes. You created a volume called work_storage. Inside the volumes directory is a file named production.sqlite3. This is your database.

Litestream[35] is a tool that can be used to back up your database. It's free and open source. It's easy to set up and can be used to back up to the S3 Object Storage you've already set up. It can also be used to restore your database to a point in time.

We could run it in your Kamal container or as a Kamal accessory, but instead, we're going to run it on your host machine. This ensures it's always running and we don't have to worry about multiple instances of it running as you deploy new versions of your application.

Following Litestream's installation instructions,[36] we first need to install Litestream. SSH into your host, and run the following commands:

```
apt-get update
apt-get install -y wget
export LITESTREAM=https://github.com/benbjohnson/litestream/releases/download
wget $LITESTREAM/v0.3.13/litestream-v0.3.13-linux-amd64.deb
dpkg -i litestream-v0.3.13-linux-amd64.deb
rm litestream-v0.3.13-linux-amd64.deb
```

Now find the ACCESS_KEY_ID, SECRET_ACCESS_KEY, ENDPOINT_URL, REGION, and BUCKET_NAME in your password manager. Then run nano /etc/litestream.yml. Replace the file with the following, substituting in the values you found in your password manager:

```
# This is the configuration file for litestream.
#
# For more details, see: https://litestream.io/reference/config/
#
dbs:
```

---

35. https://litestream.io/
36. https://litestream.io/install/debian/

```
      - path: /var/lib/docker/volumes/work_storage/production.sqlite3
        replicas:
          - type: s3
            access-key-id: ACCESS_KEY_ID
            secret-access-key: SECRET_ACCESS_KEY
            endpoint: ENDPOINT_URL
            region: REGION
            bucket: BUCKET_NAME
            path: storage/production.sqlite3
```

Exit nano by pressing Ctrl-X, and then press Y to save the file.

Now start the Litestream service:

```
systemctl enable litestream
systemctl start litestream
```

Once configured, Litestream is pretty much set and forget. It will back up your database after every write and can be used to restore your database to a point in time. The Litestream reference[37] is a good place to start if you want to learn more.

Making Logs Searchable

When you deploy your application to production, you'll want to be able to find information contained in your logs. This is especially true if you have a lot of users, as you'll want to be able to quickly find and fix any issues that arise.

Kamal provides a command to watch your logs in real time: bin/kamal app logs --follow. This is useful if you're actively watching at the time of a failure.

Docker captures logs and places them in /var/lib/docker/containers/*/local-logs/*.log. You can use a tool like grep to search these logs, but it's not very user-friendly. You also have to know which container to look in.

Kamal (by default) keeps the last five containers, so if you deploy infrequently your logs may have gaps, and if you deploy too frequently, you may not have log entries that span enough time.

A more robust approach is to send your logs to a service like DataDog,[38] Elastic Search,[39] or Loki.[40] These services can be used to search your logs, and can be used to create alerts when certain conditions are met.

---

37. https://litestream.io/reference/
38. https://www.datadoghq.com/
39. https://www.elastic.co/
40. https://grafana.com/oss/loki/

Most come with some sort of free tier and can be set up in minutes. Prices are generally based on the amount of data you send them. Some can be self-hosted, but if you go this route, you'll want to set up a separate machine to run them on.

Vector[41] is a tool that can be used to send your logs to a number of services and filter your logs before they are sent.

To install Vector, SSH into your host, and run the following command:

```
apt-get install -y vector
```

Once installed, you'll need to configure Vector. Vector is configured using a file named /etc/vector.yaml. Instructions for a number of services can be found in the Vector documentation.[42]

Run nano /etc/vector.yaml, and replace the file with the following:

```yaml
sources:
  docker:
    type: "docker_logs"
sinks:
  nats:
    inputs:
      - "docker"
    type: "console"
    encoding:
      codec: "text"
```

Fill in the definition of the sink based on the service you selected. Exit nano by pressing Ctrl-X, and then press Y to save the file. You can run Vector by running the following command:

```
vector --config vector.yaml
```

Visit your application's website and perform some actions. You should see the logs in your console. Next, edit /etc/vetor.yaml once again and replace the definition of the sink based on the service you selected. Finally, give Vector permission to access Docker's information, and start the Vector service:

```
usermod -aG docker vector
systemctl enable vector
systemctl start vector
```

---

41. https://vector.dev/
42. https://vector.dev/docs/reference/configuration/sinks/

Note that the service you choose can be one that you write yourself. Vector can be used to send logs to Nats,[43] which you can subscribe to in a service that you write yourself. Vector can even be used to send logs to multiple services at once.

Additional Monitoring Tools

AppSignal.[44] Honeybadger,[45] New Relic,[46] Rollbar,[47] Sentry,[48] and Scout[49] are tools that can be used to monitor your application's performance and create alerts when certain conditions are met.

Mobi/dev has a list of security considerations and tools.[50]

The host you select will often offer tools to prevent DDoS attack and monitor your server's performance. You'll want to enable these.

Horizontal Scaling

As your needs increase, you can move to bigger and bigger servers.[51] At some point you may need more, or simply want resiliency, or perhaps want to serve requests close to users.

This generally means that you'll need to convert from Sqlite3 to a database like PostgreSQL. For this, you'll want a *managed* PostgreSQL solution. Trust me on this.

- In your Dockerfile replace sqlite3 with libpq-dev postgresql-client.
- The active record guides[52] recommend updating config/database.yml, but it generally is easier to set a DATABASE_URL secret.[53]

There is a tool named pgloader[54] that you can use to copy your Sqlite3 database to PostgreSQL.

---

43. https://nats.io/
44. https://appsignal.com/
45. https://www.honeybadger.io/
46. https://newrelic.com/
47. https://rollbar.com/
48. https://sentry.io/
49. https://scoutapm.com/
50. https://mobidev.biz/blog/security-considerations-for-ruby-on-rails-applications
51. https://x.com/dhh/status/1799107964412056012
52. https://guides.rubyonrails.org/v5.0/configuring.html#configuring-a-postgresql-database
53. https://guides.rubyonrails.org/v5.0/configuring.html#configuring-a-database
54. https://github.com/dimitri/pgloader?tab=readme-ov-file#pgloader

Once you define a second application machine, you'll need to add a load balancer to route requests between machines. This generally is a paid feature.[55] You'll also need an SSL certificate[56] for your load balancer, as Kamal's ssl[57] is only for one server.

As PostgreSQL requests tend to have a higher latency per request than Sqlite3, you likely will need to tune your application. Look for places where you execute a query and iterate over the results, and inside the iteration you traverse over relationships—this will generally require multiple queries. You can avoid this using includes,[58] preloads,[59] or eager-load.[60]

See *High Performance PostgreSQL for Rails [Atk24]* for more information on how to scale your application with PostgreSQL.

Although our job is just starting when we first deploy our application to production, we've completed our tour of the Depot application. After we recap what we did in this chapter, let's look back at what we've accomplished in remarkably few lines of code.

What We Just Did

We covered a lot of ground in this chapter. We took our code that ran locally on our development machine for a single user and placed it on a different machine where it could be accessed worldwide. We also took steps to ensure that our data would be safe.

To accomplish this, we used a number of products:

- We used the Dockerfile provided by Rails as a starting point and deployed our application in a container.
- We configured Kamal to deploy our application to a server.
- We used LiteStream and Vector to back up our data and make our logs searchable.

Playtime

Here's some stuff to try on your own:

---

55. https://www.hetzner.com/cloud/load-balancer/
56. https://www.cloudflare.com/learning/ssl/what-is-an-ssl-certificate/
57. https://kamal-deploy.org/docs/configuration/proxy/#ssl
58. https://apidock.com/rails/ActiveRecord/QueryMethods/includes
59. https://apidock.com/rails/v5.2.3/ActiveRecord/QueryMethods/preload
60. https://apidock.com/rails/v5.2.3/ActiveRecord/QueryMethods/eager_load

- While our data is backed up in S3, it's not truly backed up off-site. On a separate machine (which can be your laptop), install rclone[61] and use rclone sync to extract a copy of your data. Set up a cron job to run this command daily.

- While Rails selected some good defaults for rubocop, ruby gems doesn't follow them. Try running rubocop -A to correct this, or tell rubocop to ignore this error in the .rubocop.yml:

rails80/depot_td/.rubocop.yml
```
# Avoid flagging bundler added statements
Style/HashSyntax:
  Exclude:
    - Gemfile
```

---

61. https://rclone.org/

In this chapter, you'll see:
- Reviewing Rails concepts: model, view, controller, configuration, testing, and deployment
- Documenting what we've done

CHAPTER 18

Depot Retrospective

Congratulations! By making it this far, you've obtained a solid understanding of the basics of every Rails application. There's much more to learn, which we'll pick back up again in Part III. For now, relax, and let's recap what you've seen in Part II.

Rails Concepts

In Chapter 3, The Architecture of Rails Applications, on page 33, we introduced models, views, and controllers. Now let's see how we applied each of these concepts in the Depot application. Then let's explore how we used configuration, testing, and deployment.

Model

Models are where all of the persistent data retained by your application is managed. In developing the Depot application, we created five models: Cart, LineItem, Order, Product, SupportRequest, and User.

By default, all models have id, created_at, and updated_at attributes. To our models, we added attributes of type string (examples: title, name), integer (quantity), text (description, address), and decimal (price), as well as foreign keys (product_id, cart_id). We even created a virtual attribute that's never stored in the database—namely, a password.

We created has_many and belongs_to relationships that we can use to navigate among our model objects, such as from Carts to LineItems to Products.

We employed migrations to update the databases, not only to introduce new schema information but also to modify existing data. We demonstrated that they can be applied in a fully reversible manner.

The models we created weren't merely passive receptacles for our data. For starters, they actively validate the data, preventing errors from propagating. We created validations for presence, inclusion, numericality, range, uniqueness, format, and confirmation (and length, too, if you completed the exercises). We created custom validations for ensuring that deleted products aren't referenced by any line item. We used an Active Record hook to ensure that an administrator always remains and used a transaction to roll back incomplete updates on failure.

We also created logic to add a product to a cart, add all line items from a cart to an order, encrypt and authenticate a password, and compute various totals.

Finally, we created a default sort order for products for display purposes.

View

Views control the way our application presents itself to the external world. By default, Rails scaffolding provides edit, index, new, and show, as well as a partial named form that's shared between edit and new. We modified a number of these and created new partials for carts and line items.

In addition to the model-backed resource views, we created entirely new views for admin, sessions, and the store itself.

We updated an overall layout to establish a common look and feel for the entire site. We updated a style sheet. We made use of partials and added JavaScript to take advantage of Hotwire and WebSocket technologies to make our website more interactive.

We localized the customer views for display in both English and Spanish.

Not all of the views were designed for browsers: we created views for email too, and those views were able to share partials for displaying line items.

Controller

By the time we were done, we created nine controllers: one each for the six models and the three additional ones to support the views for admin, sessions, and the store itself.

These controllers interacted with the models in a number of ways, from finding and fetching data and putting it into instance variables to updating models and saving data entered via forms. When done, we either redirected to another action or rendered a view.

We limited the set of permitted parameters on the line item controller.

We created callback actions that were run before selected actions to find the cart, set the language, and authorize requests. We placed logic common to a number of controllers into a concern—namely, the CurrentCart module.

We managed sessions, keeping track of the logged-in user (for administrators) and carts (for customers). We kept track of the current locale used for internationalization of our output. We captured errors, logged them, and informed the user via notices.

We employed fragment caching on the storefront.

We also sent confirmation emails on receipt of an order.

Configuration

Conventions keep to a minimum the amount of configuration required for a Rails application, but we did do a bit of customization.

We modified our database configuration to use PostgreSQL in production.

We defined routes for our resources, admin and session controllers, and the *root* of our website—namely, our storefront.

We created an initializer for i18n purposes and updated the locales information for both English (en) and Spanish (es).

We created seed data for our database.

We created a Docker configuration for local deployment, including the definition of a secret.

We updated the Kamal configuration to use our builder, docker repository, DNS name, IP address, object storage secrets, and to configure logging; we placed our secrets in a password manager and updated .kamal/secrets to reference them. We configured Active Storage.

Testing

We maintained and enhanced tests throughout.

We employed unit tests to validation methods. We also tested increasing the quantity on a given line item.

Rails provided basic tests for all our scaffolded controllers, which we maintained as we made changes. We added tests along the way for things such as Ajax and ensuring that a cart has items before we create an order.

We used fixtures to provide test data to fuel our tests.

We created an integration test to test an end-to-end scenario involving a user adding product to a cart, entering an order, and receiving a confirmation email.

Deployment

We assembled our ingredients:

- Obtained an SSH key
- Acquired a machine
- Purchased a Domain Name
- Selected a Container Registry
- Used a Password Manager
- Set up a Builder

We deployed using Kamal.

We installed litestream and vector to provide backups and monitoring.

Documenting What We've Done

To complete our retrospective, let's see how much code we've written. There's a Rails command for that too:

```
% bin/rails stats
+----------------------+--------+--------+---------+---------+-----+--------+
| Name                 | Lines  |  LOC   | Classes | Methods | M/C | LOC/M  |
+----------------------+--------+--------+---------+---------+-----+--------+
| Controllers          |   670  |   462  |    11   |    71   |  6  |    4   |
| Helpers              |    16  |    16  |     0   |     0   |  0  |    0   |
| Jobs                 |    18  |     8  |     2   |     1   |  0  |    6   |
| Models               |   191  |   126  |    10   |     8   |  0  |   13   |
| Mailers              |    53  |    28  |     4   |     4   |  1  |    5   |
| Mailboxes            |    22  |    16  |     2   |     1   |  0  |   14   |
| Channels             |    31  |    25  |     3   |     4   |  1  |    4   |
| Views                |  1158  |   908  |     0   |     1   |  0  |  906   |
| Stylesheets          |   470  |   417  |     0   |     0   |  0  |    0   |
| JavaScript           |    82  |    51  |     0   |     0   |  0  |    0   |
| Libraries            |    34  |    33  |     1   |     1   |  1  |   31   |
| Controller tests     |   389  |   269  |     7   |    42   |  6  |    4   |
| Helper tests         |     0  |     0  |     0   |     0   |  0  |    0   |
| Job tests            |     7  |     3  |     1   |     0   |  0  |    0   |
| Model tests          |   145  |   102  |     6   |     9   |  1  |    9   |
| Mailer tests         |    64  |    49  |     5   |     7   |  1  |    5   |
| Mailbox tests        |    58  |    32  |     1   |     2   |  2  |   14   |
| Channel tests        |     8  |     3  |     1   |     0   |  0  |    0   |
| Integration tests    |     0  |     0  |     0   |     0   |  0  |    0   |
| System tests         |   137  |    99  |     2   |     6   |  3  |   14   |
| Model specs          |    58  |    36  |     0   |     0   |  0  |    0   |
+----------------------+--------+--------+---------+---------+-----+--------+
| Total                |  3611  |  2683  |    56   |   157   |  2  |   15   |
+----------------------+--------+--------+---------+---------+-----+--------+
  Code LOC: 2090     Test LOC: 593     Code to Test Ratio: 1:0.3
```

Think about it: you've accomplished a lot and with not all that much code. And much of it was generated for you. This is the magic of Rails.

Part III

Rails in Depth

In this chapter, you'll see:
- The directory structure of a Rails application
- Naming conventions
- Adding Rake tasks
- Configuration

CHAPTER 19

Finding Your Way Around Rails

Having survived our Depot project, you're now prepared to dig deeper into Rails. For the rest of the book, we'll go through Rails topic by topic (which pretty much means module by module). You've seen most of these modules in action before. We'll cover not only what each module does but also how to extend or even replace the module and why you might want to do so.

The chapters in Part III cover all the major subsystems of Rails: Active Record, Active Resource, Action Pack (including both Action Controller and Action View), and Active Support. This is followed by an in-depth look at migrations.

Then we're going to delve into the interior of Rails and show how the components are put together, how they start up, and how they can be replaced. Having shown how the parts of Rails can be put together, we'll complete this book with a survey of a number of popular replacement parts, many of which can be used outside of Rails.

We need to set the scene first. This chapter covers all the high-level stuff you need to know to understand the rest: directory structures, configuration, and environments.

Where Things Go

Rails assumes a certain runtime directory layout and provides application and scaffold generators, which will create this layout for you. For example, if we generate *my_app* using the command rails new my_app, the top-level directory for our new application appears as shown in the figure on page 304.

```
my_app/
    app/
        | Model, view, and controller files go here.
    bin/
        | Wrapper scripts
    config/
        | Configuration and database connection parameters.
    config.ru - Rack server configuration.
    db/
        | Schema and migration information.
    Gemfile - Gem Dependencies.
    Gemfile.lock - snapshot of Gem Dependencies.
    lib/
        | Shared code.
    log/
        | Log files produced by your application.
    public/
        | Web-accessible directory. Your application runs from here.
    Rakefile - Build script.
    README.md - Installation and usage information.
    storage/
        | Attachments uploaded with Active Storage
    test/
        | Unit, functional, and integration tests, fixtures, and mocks.
    tmp/
        | Runtime temporary files.
    vendor/
        | Imported code.
```

> **Joe asks:**
> ### So, Where's Rails?
>
> One of the interesting aspects of Rails is how componentized it is. From a developer's perspective, you spend all your time dealing with high-level modules such as Active Record and Action View. There's a component called Rails, but it sits below the other components, silently orchestrating what they do and making them all work together seamlessly. Without the Rails component, not much would happen. But at the same time, only a small part of this underlying infrastructure is relevant to developers in their day-to-day work. We'll cover the parts that *are* relevant in the rest of this chapter.

Let's start with the text files in the top of the application directory:

- config.ru configures the Rack Webserver Interface, either to create Rails Metal applications or to use Rack Middlewares in your Rails application. These are discussed further in the Rails Guides.[1]

---

1. http://guides.rubyonrails.org/rails_on_rack.html

- Gemfile specifies the dependencies of your Rails application. You've already seen this in use when the bcrypt-ruby gem was added to the Depot application. Application dependencies also include the database, web server, and even scripts used for deployment.

    Technically, this file isn't used by Rails but rather by your application. You can find calls to the Bundler[2] in the config/application.rb and config/boot.rb files.

- Gemfile.lock records the specific versions for each of your Rails application's dependencies. This file is maintained by Bundler and should be checked into your repository.

- Rakefile defines tasks to run tests, create documentation, extract the current structure of your schema, and more. Type rake -T at a prompt for the full list. Type rake -D task to see a more complete description of a specific task.

- README contains general information about the Rails framework.

Let's look at what goes into each directory (although not necessarily in order).

A Place for Our Application

Most of our work takes place in the app directory. The main code for the application lives below the app directory, as shown in the figure on page 306. We'll talk more about the structure of the app directory as we look at the various Rails modules such as Active Record, Action Controller, and Action View in more detail later in the book.

A Place for Our Tests

As we've seen in Iteration B2: Unit Testing of Models, on page 89, Iteration C4: Functional Testing of Controllers, on page 108, and Iteration G3: Testing Our JavaScript Functionality, on page 184, Rails has ample provisions for testing your application, and the test directory is the home for all testing-related activities, including fixtures that define data used by our tests.

A Place for Supporting Libraries

The lib directory holds application code that doesn't fit neatly into a model, view, or controller. For example, you may have written a library that creates PDF receipts that your store's customers can download. These receipts are sent directly from the controller to the browser (using the send_data() method). The code that creates these PDF receipts will sit naturally in the lib directory.

---

2. https://github.com/bundler/bundler

```
app/
    assets/
        builds/
            tailwind.css
        config/
            manifest.js
        images/
            rails.png
        stylesheets/
            application.css
            application.tailwind.css
    channels/
        application_cable/
        products_channel.rb
    controllers/
        application_controller.rb
        products_controller.rb
        concerns/
            current_cart.rb
    helpers/
        application_helper.rb
        products_helper.rb
    javascript/
        controllers/
            locale_controller.js
    mailboxes/
    mailers/
        notifier.rb
    models/
        product.rb
    views/
        layouts/
```

The lib directory is also a good place to put code that's shared among models, views, or controllers. Maybe you need a library that validates a credit card number's checksum, that performs some financial calculation, or that works out the date of Easter. Anything that isn't directly a model, view, or controller should be slotted into lib.

Don't feel that you have to stick a bunch of files directly into the lib directory. Feel free to create subdirectories in which you group related functionality under lib. For example, on the Pragmatic Programmer site, the code that generates receipts, customs documentation for shipping, and other PDF-formatted documentation is in the directory lib/pdf_stuff.

In previous versions of Rails, the files in the lib directory were automatically included in the load path used to resolve require statements. This is now an

option that you need to explicitly enable. To do so, place the following in
config/application.rb:

```
config.autoload_paths += %W(#{Rails.root}/lib)
```

Once you have files in the lib directory and the lib added to your autoload
paths, you can use them in the rest of your application. If the files contain
classes or modules and the files are named using the lowercase form of the
class or module name, then Rails will load the file automatically. For example,
we might have a PDF receipt writer in the file receipt.rb in the directory lib/pdf_stuff.
As long as our class is named PdfStuff::Receipt, Rails will be able to find and load
it automatically.

For those times where a library can't meet these automatic loading conditions,
you can use Ruby's require mechanism. If the file is in the lib directory, you
can require it directly by name. For example, if our Easter calculation library
is in the file lib/easter.rb, we can include it in any model, view, or controller
using this:

```
require "easter"
```

If the library is in a subdirectory of lib, remember to include that directory's
name in the require statement. For example, to include a shipping calculation
for airmail, we might add the following line:

```
require "shipping/airmail"
```

A Place for Our Rake Tasks

You'll also find an empty tasks directory under lib. This is where you can write
your own Rake tasks, allowing you to add automation to your project. This
isn't a book about Rake, so we won't elaborate, but here's a simple example.

Rails provides a Rake task to tell you the latest migration that's been performed. But it may be helpful to see a list of *all* the migrations that have been
performed. We'll write a Rake task that prints the versions listed in the
schema_migration table. These tasks are Ruby code, but they need to be placed
into files with the extension .rake. We'll call ours db_schema_migrations.rake:

```
rails80/depot_u/lib/tasks/db_schema_migrations.rake
namespace :db do
  desc "Prints the migrated versions"
  task schema_migrations: :environment do
    puts ActiveRecord::Base.connection.select_values(
      "select version from schema_migrations order by version")
  end
end
```

We can run this from the command line just like any other Rake task:

```
depot> bin/rails db:schema_migrations
(in /Users/rubys/Work/...)
20250420000001
20250420000002
20250420000003
20250420000004
20250420000005
20250420000006
20250420000007
```

Consult the Rake documentation at https://github.com/ruby/rake#readme for more information on writing Rake tasks.

A Place for Our Logs

As Rails runs, it produces a bunch of useful logging information. This is stored (by default) in the log directory. Here you'll find three main log files, called development.log, test.log, and production.log. The logs contain more than just trace lines; they also contain timing statistics, cache information, and expansions of the database statements executed.

Which file is used depends on the environment in which your application is running (and we'll have more to say about environments when we talk about the config directory in A Place for Configuration, on page 309).

A Place for Static Web Pages

The public directory is the external face of your application. The web server takes this directory as the base of the application. In here you place *static* (in other words, unchanging) files, generally related to the running of the server.

A Place for Script Wrappers

If you find it helpful to write scripts that are launched from the command line and perform various maintenance tasks for your application, the bin directory is the place to put wrappers that call those scripts.

This directory also holds the Rails script. This is the script that's run when you run the rails command from the command line. The first argument you pass to that script determines the function Rails will perform:

console
> Allows you to interact with your Rails application methods.

dbconsole
> Allows you to directly interact with your database via the command line.

destroy
>   Removes autogenerated files created by generate.

generate
>   A code generator. Out of the box, it will create controllers, mailers, models, scaffolds, and web services. Run generate with no arguments for usage information on a particular generator; here's an example:
>
>   ```
>   bin/rails generate migration
>   ```

new
>   Generates Rails application code.

runner
>   Executes a method in your application outside the context of the Web. This is the noninteractive equivalent of rails console. You could use this to invoke cache expiry methods from a cron job or handle incoming email.

server
>   Runs your Rails application in a self-contained web server, using the web server listed in your Gemfile, or WEBrick if none is listed. We've been using Puma in our Depot application during development.

A Place for Temporary Files

It probably isn't a surprise that Rails keeps its temporary files tucked in the tmp directory. You'll find subdirectories for cache contents, sessions, and sockets in here. Generally these files are cleaned up automatically by Rails, but occasionally if things go wrong, you might need to look in here and delete old files.

A Place for Third-Party Code

The vendor directory is where third-party code lives. You can install Rails and all of its dependencies into the vendor directory.

If you want to go back to using the system-wide version of gems, you can delete the vendor/cache directory.

A Place for Configuration

The config directory contains files that configure Rails. In the process of developing Depot, we configured a few routes, configured the database, created an initializer, modified some locales, and defined deployment instructions. The rest of the configuration was done via Rails conventions.

Before running your application, Rails loads and executes config/environment.rb and config/application.rb. The standard environment set up automatically by these files includes the following directories (relative to your application's base directory) in your application's load path:

- The app/controllers directory and its subdirectories
- The app/models directory
- The vendor directory and the lib contained in each plugin subdirectory
- The directories app, app/helpers, app/mailers, and app/*/concerns

Each of these directories is added to the load path only if it exists.

In addition, Rails will load a per-environment configuration file. This file lives in the environments directory and is where you place configuration options that vary depending on the environment.

This is done because Rails recognizes that your needs, as a developer, are very different when writing code, testing code, and running that code in production. When writing code, you want lots of logging, convenient reloading of changed source files, in-your-face notification of errors, and so on. In testing, you want a system that exists in isolation so you can have repeatable results. In production, your system should be tuned for performance, and users should be kept away from errors.

The switch that dictates the runtime environment is external to your application. This means that no application code needs to be changed as you move from development through testing to production. When starting a server with the bin/rails server command, we use the -e option:

```
depot> bin/rails server -e development
depot> bin/rails server -e test
depot> bin/rails server -e production
```

If you have special requirements, such as if you favor having a *staging* environment, you can create your own environments. You'll need to add a new section to the database configuration file and a new file to the config/environments directory.

What you put into these configuration files is entirely up to you. You can find a list of configuration parameters you can set in the Configuring Rails Applications guide.[3]

---

3. http://guides.rubyonrails.org/configuring.html

Naming Conventions

Newcomers to Rails are sometimes puzzled by the way it automatically handles the naming of things. They're surprised that they call a model class Person and Rails somehow knows to go looking for a database table called people. In this section, you'll learn how this implicit naming works.

The rules here are the default conventions used by Rails. You can override all of these conventions using configuration options.

Mixed Case, Underscores, and Plurals

We often name variables and classes using short phrases. In Ruby, the convention is to have variable names where the letters are all lowercase and words are separated by underscores. Classes and modules are named differently: there are no underscores, and each word in the phrase (including the first) is capitalized. (We'll call this *mixed case*, for fairly obvious reasons.) These conventions lead to variable names such as order_status and class names such as LineItem.

Rails takes this convention and extends it in two ways. First, it assumes that database table names, such as variable names, have lowercase letters and underscores between the words. Rails also assumes that table names are always plural. This leads to table names such as orders and third_parties.

On another axis, Rails assumes that files are named using lowercase with underscores.

Rails uses this knowledge of naming conventions to convert names automatically. For example, your application might contain a model class that handles line items. You'd define the class using the Ruby naming convention, calling it LineItem. From this name, Rails would automatically deduce the following:

- The corresponding database table will be called line_items. That's the class name, converted to lowercase, with underscores between the words, and pluralized.

- Rails would also know to look for the class definition in a file called line_item.rb (in the app/models directory).

Rails controllers have additional naming conventions. If our application has a store controller, then the following happens:

- Rails assumes the class is called StoreController and that it's in a file named store_controller.rb in the app/controllers directory.

- Rails also looks for a helper module named StoreHelper in the file store_helper.rb located in the app/helpers directory.
- It will look for view templates for this controller in the app/views/store directory.
- It will by default take the output of these views and wrap them in the layout template contained in the file store.html.erb or store.xml.erb in the directory app/views/layouts.

All these conventions are shown in the following tables.

Model Naming	
Table	line_items
File	app/models/line_item.rb
Class	LineItem

Controller Naming	
URL	http://../store/list
File	app/controllers/store_controller.rb
Class	StoreController
Method	list
Layout	app/views/layouts/store.html.erb

View Naming	
URL	http://../store/list
File	app/views/store/list.html.erb (or .builder)
Helper	module StoreHelper
File	app/helpers/store_helper.rb

There's one extra twist. In normal Ruby code you have to use the require keyword to include Ruby source files before you reference the classes and modules in those files. Since Rails knows the relationship between filenames and class names, require isn't normally necessary in a Rails application. The first time you reference a class or module that isn't known, Rails uses the naming conventions to convert the class name to a filename and tries to load that file behind the scenes. The net effect is that you can typically reference (say) the name of a model class, and that model will be automatically loaded into your application.

Grouping Controllers into Modules

So far, all our controllers have lived in the app/controllers directory. It's sometimes convenient to add more structure to this arrangement. For example, our store might end up with a number of controllers performing related but disjoint administration functions. Rather than pollute the top-level namespace, we might choose to group them into a single admin namespace.

> **David says:**
> ## Why Plurals for Tables?
>
> Because it sounds good in conversation. Really. "Select a Product from products." And "Order has_many :line_items."
>
> The intent is to bridge programming and conversation by creating a domain language that can be shared by both. Having such a language means cutting down on the mental translation that otherwise confuses the discussion of a *product description* with the client when it's really implemented as *merchandise body*. These communications gaps are bound to lead to errors.
>
> Rails sweetens the deal by giving you most of the configuration for free if you follow the standard conventions. Developers are thus rewarded for doing the right thing, so it's less about giving up "your ways" and more about getting productivity for free.

Rails does this using a simple naming convention. If an incoming request has a controller named (say) admin/book, Rails will look for the controller called book_controller in the directory app/controllers/admin. That is, the final part of the controller name will always resolve to a file called *name*_controller.rb, and any leading path information will be used to navigate through subdirectories, starting in the app/controllers directory.

Imagine that our program has two such groups of controllers (say, admin/*xxx* and content/*xxx*) and that both groups define a book controller. There'd be a file called book_controller.rb in both the admin and content subdirectories of app/controllers. Both of these controller files would define a class named BookController. If Rails took no further steps, these two classes would clash.

To deal with this, Rails assumes that controllers in subdirectories of the directory app/controllers are in Ruby modules named after the subdirectory. Thus, the book controller in the admin subdirectory would be declared like this:

```
class Admin::BookController < ActionController::Base
  # ...
end
```

The book controller in the content subdirectory would be in the Content module:

```
class Content::BookController < ActionController::Base
  # ...
end
```

The two controllers are therefore kept separate inside your application.

The templates for these controllers appear in subdirectories of app/views. Thus, the following is the view template corresponding to this request:

`http://my.app/admin/book/edit/1234`

And it will be in this file:

`app/views/admin/book/edit.html.erb`

You'll be pleased to know that the controller generator understands the concept of controllers in modules and lets you create them with commands such as this:

myapp> **bin/rails generate controller Admin::Book action1 action2 ...**

What We Just Did

Everything in Rails has a place, and we systematically explored each of those nooks and crannies. In each place, files and the data contained in them follow naming conventions, and we covered that too. Along the way, we filled in a few missing pieces:

- We added a Rake task to print the migrated versions.
- We showed how to configure each of the Rails execution environments.

Next up are the major subsystems of Rails, starting with the largest, Active Record.

In this chapter, you'll see:
- The establish_connection method
- Tables, classes, columns, and attributes
- IDs and relationships
- Create, read, update, and delete operations
- Callbacks and transactions

CHAPTER 20

Active Record

Active Record is the object-relational mapping (ORM) layer supplied with Rails. It's the part of Rails that implements your application's model.

In this chapter, we'll build on the mapping data to rows and columns that we did in Depot. Then we'll look at using Active Record to manage table relationships and in the process cover create, read, update, and delete operations (commonly referred to in the industry as CRUD methods). Finally, we'll dig into the Active Record object life cycle (including callbacks and transactions).

Defining Your Data

In Depot, we defined a number of models, including one for an Order. This particular model has a number of attributes, such as an email address of type String. In addition to the attributes that we defined, Rails provided an attribute named id that contains the primary key for the record. Rails also provides several additional attributes, including attributes that track when each row was last updated. Finally, Rails supports relationships between models, such as the relationship between orders and line items.

When you think about it, Rails provides a lot of support for models. Let's examine each in turn.

Organizing Using Tables and Columns

Each subclass of ApplicationRecord, such as our Order class, wraps a separate database table. By default, Active Record assumes that the name of the table associated with a given class is the plural form of the name of that class. If the class name contains multiple capitalized words, the table name is assumed to have underscores between these words, as shown in the table on page 316.

Classname	Table Name
Order	orders
TaxAgency	tax_agencies
Batch	batches
Diagnosis	diagnoses
LineItem	line_items
Person	people
Datum	data
Quantity	quantities

These rules reflect Rails' philosophy that class names should be singular while the names of tables should be plural.

Although Rails handles most irregular plurals correctly, occasionally you may stumble across one that's incorrect. If you encounter such a case, you can add to Rails' understanding of the idiosyncrasies and inconsistencies of the English language by modifying the inflection file provided:

rails80/depot_u/config/initializers/inflections.rb
```
# Be sure to restart your server when you modify this file.

# Add new inflection rules using the following format. Inflections
# are locale specific, and you may define rules for as many different
# locales as you wish. All of these examples are active by default:
# ActiveSupport::Inflector.inflections(:en) do |inflect|
#   inflect.plural /^(ox)$/i, "\\1en"
#   inflect.singular /^(ox)en/i, "\\1"
#   inflect.irregular "person", "people"
#   inflect.uncountable %w( fish sheep )
# end

# These inflection rules are supported but not enabled by default:
# ActiveSupport::Inflector.inflections(:en) do |inflect|
#   inflect.acronym "RESTful"
# end

ActiveSupport::Inflector.inflections do |inflect|
  inflect.irregular 'tax', 'taxes'
end
```

If you have legacy tables you have to deal with or don't like this behavior, you can control the table name associated with a given model by setting the table_name for a given class:

```
class Sheep < ApplicationRecord
  self.table_name = "sheep"
end
```

> **David says:**
> ## Where Are Our Attributes?
>
> The notion of a database administrator (DBA) as a separate role from programmer has led some developers to see strict boundaries between code and schema. Active Record blurs that distinction, and no other place is that more apparent than in the lack of explicit attribute definitions in the model.
>
> But fear not. Practice has shown that it makes little difference whether we're looking at a database schema, a separate XML mapping file, or inline attributes in the model. The composite view is similar to the separations already happening in the model-view-controller pattern—just on a smaller scale.
>
> Once the discomfort of treating the table schema as part of the model definition has dissipated, you'll start to realize the benefits of keeping DRY. When you need to add an attribute to the model, you simply have to create a new migration and reload the application.
>
> Taking the "build" step out of schema evolution makes it just as agile as the rest of the code. It becomes much easier to start with a small schema and extend and change it as needed.

Instances of Active Record classes correspond to rows in a database table. These objects have attributes corresponding to the columns in the table. You probably noticed that our definition of class Order didn't mention any of the columns in the orders table. That's because Active Record determines them dynamically at runtime. Active Record reflects on the schema inside the database to configure the classes that wrap tables.

In the Depot application, our orders table is defined by the following migration:

rails80/depot_r/db/migrate/20250420000008_create_orders.rb
```ruby
class CreateOrders < ActiveRecord::Migration[8.0]
  def change
    create_table :orders do |t|
      t.string :name
      t.text :address
      t.string :email
      t.integer :pay_type

      t.timestamps
    end
  end
end
```

Let's use the handy-dandy bin/rails console command to play with this model. First, we'll ask for a list of column names:

```
depot> bin/rails console
Loading development environment (Rails 8.0.2)
3.1.3 :001 > Order.column_names
 => ["id", "name", "address", "email", "pay_type", "created_at", "updated_at"]
```

Then we'll ask for the details of the pay_type column:

```
>> Order.columns_hash["pay_type"]
 =>
#<ActiveRecord::ConnectionAdapters::Column:0x00000001094cc200
 @collation=nil,
 @comment=nil,
 @default=nil,
 @default_function=nil,
 @name="pay_type",
 @null=true,
 @sql_type_metadata=
  #<ActiveRecord::ConnectionAdapters::SqlTypeMetadata:0x00000001094dc178
   @limit=nil,
   @precision=nil,
   @scale=nil,
   @sql_type="integer",
   @type=:integer>>
```

Notice that Active Record has gleaned a fair amount of information about the pay_type column. It knows that it's an integer, it has no default value, it isn't the primary key, and it may contain a null value. Rails obtained this information by asking the underlying database the first time we tried to use the Order class.

The attributes of an Active Record instance generally correspond to the data in the corresponding row of the database table. For example, our orders table might contain the following data:

```
depot> sqlite3 -line storage/development.sqlite3 "select * from orders limit 1"
         id = 1
       name = Dave Thomas
    address = 123 Main St
      email = customer@example.com
   pay_type = 0
 created_at = 2022-02-14 14:39:12.375458
 updated_at = 2022-02-14 14:39:12.375458
```

If we fetched this row into an Active Record object, that object would have seven attributes. The id attribute would be 1 (an Integer), the name attribute would be the string "Dave Thomas", and so on.

We access these attributes using accessor methods. Rails automatically constructs both attribute readers and attribute writers when it reflects on the schema:

```
o = Order.find(1)
puts o.name              #=> "Dave Thomas"
o.name = "Fred Smith"    # set the name
```

Setting the value of an attribute doesn't change anything in the database—we must save the object for this change to become permanent.

The value returned by the attribute readers is cast by Active Record to an appropriate Ruby type if possible (so, for example, if the database column is a timestamp, a Time object will be returned). If we want to get the raw value of an attribute, we append _before_type_cast to its name, as shown in the following code:

```
Order.first.pay_type                    #=> "Check", a string
Order.first.pay_type_before_type_cast   #=> 0, an integer
```

Inside the code of the model, we can use the read_attribute() and write_attribute() private methods. These take the attribute name as a string parameter.

We can see the mapping between SQL types and their Ruby representation in the following table. Decimal and Boolean columns are slightly tricky.

SQL Type	Ruby Class
int, integer	Integer
float, double	Float
decimal, numeric	BigDecimal
char, varchar, string	String
interval, date	Date
datetime, time	Time
clob, blob, text	String
boolean	See text

Rails maps columns with Decimals with no decimal places to Integer objects; otherwise, it maps them to BigDecimal objects, ensuring that no precision is lost.

In the case of Boolean, a convenience method is provided with a question mark appended to the column name:

```
user = User.find_by(name: "Dave")
if user.superuser?
  grant_privileges
end
```

In addition to the attributes we define, there are a number of attributes that either Rails provides automatically or have special meaning.

Additional Columns Provided by Active Record

A number of column names have special significance to Active Record. Here's a summary:

created_at, created_on, updated_at, updated_on
> These are automatically updated with the timestamp of a row's creation or last update. Make sure the underlying database column is capable of receiving a date, datetime, or string. Rails applications conventionally use the _on suffix for date columns and the _at suffix for columns that include a time.

id
> This is the default name of a table's primary key column (in Identifying Individual Rows, on page 320).

xxx_id
> This is the default name of a foreign key reference to a table named with the plural form of xxx.

xxx_count
> This maintains a counter cache for the child table xxx.

Additional plugins, such as acts_as_list,[1] may define additional columns.

Both primary keys and foreign keys play a vital role in database operations and merit additional discussion.

Locating and Traversing Records

In the Depot application, LineItems have direct relationships to three other models: Cart, Order, and Product. Additionally, models can have indirect relationships mediated by resource objects. The relationship between Orders and Products through LineItems is an example of such a relationship.

All of this is made possible through IDs.

Identifying Individual Rows

Active Record classes correspond to tables in a database. Instances of a class correspond to the individual rows in a database table. Calling Order.find(1), for

---

1. https://github.com/rails/acts_as_list

instance, returns an instance of an Order class containing the data in the row with the primary key of 1.

If you're creating a new schema for a Rails application, you'll probably want to go with the flow and let it add the id primary key column to all your tables. But if you need to work with an existing schema, Active Record gives you a way of overriding the default name of the primary key for a table.

For example, we may be working with an existing legacy schema that uses the ISBN as the primary key for the books table.

We specify this in our Active Record model using something like the following:

```
class LegacyBook < ApplicationRecord
  self.primary_key = "isbn"
end
```

Normally, Active Record takes care of creating new primary key values for records that we create and add to the database—they'll be ascending integers (possibly with some gaps in the sequence). However, if we override the primary key column's name, we also take on the responsibility of setting the primary key to a unique value before we save a new row. Perhaps surprisingly, we still set an attribute called id to do this. As far as Active Record is concerned, the primary key attribute is always set using an attribute called id. The primary_key= declaration sets the name of the column to use in the table. In the following code, we use an attribute called id even though the primary key in the database is isbn:

```
book = LegacyBook.new
book.id = "0-12345-6789"
book.title = "My Great American Novel"
book.save
# ...
book = LegacyBook.find("0-12345-6789")
puts book.title      # => "My Great American Novel"
p book.attributes    #=> {"isbn" =>"0-12345-6789",
                     #    "title"=>"My Great American Novel"}
```

Just to make life more confusing, the attributes of the model object have the column names isbn and title—id doesn't appear. When you need to set the primary key, use id. At all other times, use the actual column name.

Model objects also redefine the Ruby id() and hash() methods to reference the model's primary key. This means that model objects with valid IDs may be used as hash keys. It also means that unsaved model objects can't reliably be used as hash keys (because they won't yet have a valid ID).

One final note: Rails considers two model objects as equal (using ==) if they are instances of the same class and have the same primary key. This means that unsaved model objects may compare as equal even if they have different attribute data. If you find yourself comparing unsaved model objects (which isn't a particularly frequent operation), you might need to override the == method.

As we'll see, IDs also play an important role in relationships.

Specifying Relationships in Models

Active Record supports three types of relationship between tables: one-to-one, one-to-many, and many-to-many. You indicate these relationships by adding declarations to your models: has_one, has_many, belongs_to, and the wonderfully named has_and_belongs_to_many.

One-to-One Relationships

A one-to-one association (or, more accurately, a one-to-zero-or-one relationship) is implemented using a foreign key in one row in one table to reference at most a single row in another table. A *one-to-one* relationship might exist between orders and invoices: for each order there's at most one invoice.

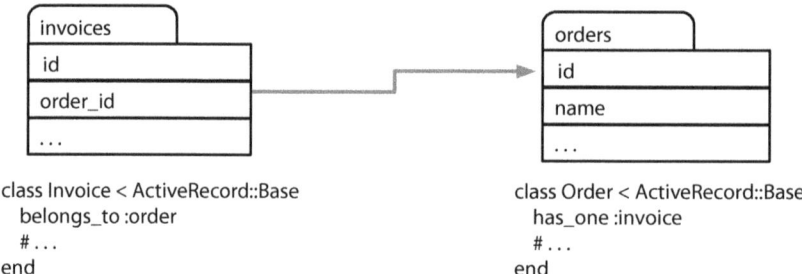

As the example shows, we declare this in Rails by adding a has_one declaration to the Order model and by adding a belongs_to declaration to the Invoice model.

An important rule is illustrated here: the model for the table that contains the foreign key *always* has the belongs_to declaration.

One-to-Many Relationships

A one-to-many association allows you to represent a collection of objects. For example, an order might have any number of associated line items. In the database, all the line item rows for a particular order contain a foreign key column referring to that order, as shown in the figure on page 323.

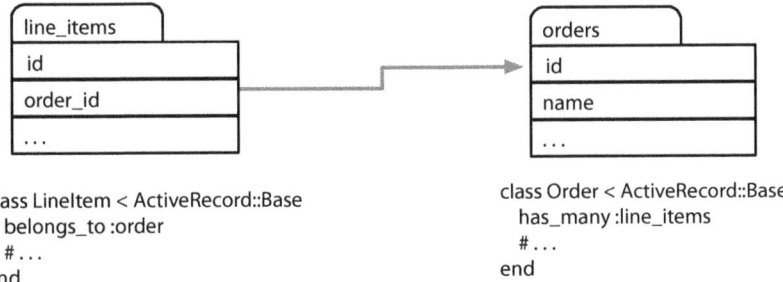

In Active Record, the parent object (the one that logically contains a collection of child objects) uses has_many to declare its relationship to the child table, and the child table uses belongs_to to indicate its parent. In our example, class LineItem belongs_to :order, and the orders table has_many :line_items.

Note that, again, because the line item contains the foreign key, it has the belongs_to declaration.

Many-to-Many Relationships

Finally, we might categorize our products. A product can belong to many categories, and each category may contain multiple products. This is an example of a *many-to-many* relationship. It's as if each side of the relationship contains a collection of items on the other side.

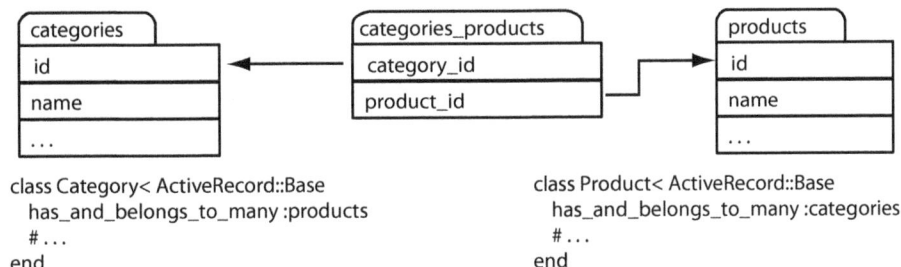

In Rails we can express this by adding the has_and_belongs_to_many declaration to both models.

Many-to-many associations are symmetrical—both of the joined tables declare their association with each other using "habtm."

Rails implements many-to-many associations using an intermediate join table. This contains foreign key pairs linking the two target tables. Active Record assumes that this join table's name is the concatenation of the two target table names in alphabetical order. In our example, we joined the table categories to the table products, so Active Record will look for a join table named categories_products.

We can also define join tables directly. In the Depot application, we defined a LineItems join, which joined Products to either Carts or Orders. Defining it ourselves also gave us a place to store an additional attribute, namely, a quantity.

Now that we've covered data definitions, the next thing you would naturally want to do is access the data contained within the database, so let's do that.

Creating, Reading, Updating, and Deleting (CRUD)

Names such as SQLite and MySQL emphasize that all access to a database is via the Structured Query Language (SQL). In most cases, Rails will take care of this for you, but that's completely up to you. As you'll see, you can provide clauses or even entire SQL statements for the database to execute.

If you're familiar with SQL already, as you read this section take note of how Rails provides places for familiar clauses such as select, from, where, group by, and so on. If you're not already familiar with SQL, one of the strengths of Rails is that you can defer knowing more about such things until you actually need to access the database at this level.

In this section, we'll continue to work with the Order model from the Depot application for an example. We'll be using Active Record methods to apply the four basic database operations: create, read, update, and delete.

Creating New Rows

Given that Rails represents tables as classes and rows as objects, it follows that we create rows in a table by creating new objects of the appropriate class. We can create new objects representing rows in our orders table by calling Order.new(). We can then fill in the values of the attributes (corresponding to columns in the database). Finally, we call the object's save() method to store the order back into the database. Without this call, the order would exist only in our local memory.

```
rails80/e1/ar/new_examples.rb
an_order = Order.new
an_order.name     = "Dave Thomas"
an_order.email    = "dave@example.com"
an_order.address  = "123 Main St"
an_order.pay_type = "check"
an_order.save
```

Active Record constructors take an optional block. If present, the block is invoked with the newly created order as a parameter. This might be useful if you wanted to create and save an order without creating a new local variable.

```
rails80/e1/ar/new_examples.rb
Order.new do |o|
  o.name    = "Dave Thomas"
  # . . .
  o.save
end
```

Finally, Active Record constructors accept a hash of attribute values as an optional parameter. Each entry in this hash corresponds to the name and value of an attribute to be set. This is useful for doing things like storing values from HTML forms into database rows.

```
rails80/e1/ar/new_examples.rb
an_order = Order.new(
  name:     "Dave Thomas",
  email:    "dave@example.com",
  address:  "123 Main St",
  pay_type: "check")
an_order.save
```

Note that in all of these examples we didn't set the id attribute of the new row. Because we used the Active Record default of an integer column for the primary key, Active Record automatically creates a unique value and sets the id attribute as the row is saved. We can subsequently find this value by querying the attribute:

```
rails80/e1/ar/new_examples.rb
an_order = Order.new
an_order.name = "Dave Thomas"
# ...
an_order.save
puts "The ID of this order is #{an_order.id}"
```

The new() constructor creates a new Order object in memory; we have to remember to save it to the database at some point. Active Record has a convenience method, create(), that both instantiates the model object and stores it into the database:

```
rails80/e1/ar/new_examples.rb
an_order = Order.create(
  name:     "Dave Thomas",
  email:    "dave@example.com",
  address:  "123 Main St",
  pay_type: "check")
```

You can pass create() an array of attribute hashes; it'll create multiple rows in the database and return an array of the corresponding model objects:

```
rails80/e1/ar/new_examples.rb
orders = Order.create(
  [ { name:     "Dave Thomas",
      email:    "dave@example.com",
      address:  "123 Main St",
      pay_type: "check"
    },
    { name:     "Andy Hunt",
      email:    "andy@example.com",
      address:  "456 Gentle Drive",
      pay_type: "po"
    } ] )
```

The *real* reason that new() and create() take a hash of values is that you can construct model objects directly from form parameters:

```
@order = Order.new(order_params)
```

If you think this line looks familiar, it's because you've seen it before. It appears in orders_controller.rb in the Depot application.

Reading Existing Rows

Reading from a database involves first specifying which particular rows of data you're interested in—you'll give Active Record some kind of criteria, and it will return objects containing data from the row(s) matching the criteria.

The most direct way of finding a row in a table is by specifying its primary key. Every model class supports the find() method, which takes one or more primary key values. If given just one primary key, it returns an object containing data for the corresponding row (or throws an ActiveRecord::RecordNotFound exception). If given multiple primary key values, find() returns an array of the corresponding objects. Note that in this case a RecordNotFound exception is raised if *any* of the IDs can't be found (so if the method returns without raising an error, the length of the resulting array will be equal to the number of IDs passed as parameters).

```
an_order = Order.find(27)   # find the order with id == 27

# Get a list of product ids from a form, then
# find the associated Products
product_list = Product.find(params[:product_ids])
```

Often, though, you need to read in rows based on criteria other than their primary key value. Active Record provides additional methods enabling you to express more complex queries.

> **David says:**
> ## To Raise or Not to Raise?
>
> When you use a finder driven by primary keys, you're looking for a particular record. You expect it to exist. A call to Person.find(5) is based on our knowledge of the people table. We want the row with an ID of 5. If this call is unsuccessful—if the record with the ID of 5 has been destroyed—we're in an exceptional situation. This mandates the raising of an exception, so Rails raises RecordNotFound.
>
> On the other hand, finders that use criteria to search are looking for a *match*. So, Person.where(name: 'Dave').first is the equivalent of telling the database (as a black box) "Give me the first person row that has the name Dave." This exhibits a distinctly different approach to retrieval; we're not certain up front that we'll get a result. It's entirely possible the result set may be empty. Thus, returning nil in the case of finders that search for one row and an empty array for finders that search for many rows is the natural, nonexceptional response.

SQL and Active Record

To illustrate how Active Record works with SQL, pass a string to the where() method call corresponding to a SQL where clause. For example, to return a list of all orders for Dave with a payment type of "po," we could use this:

```
pos = Order.where("name = 'Dave' and pay_type = 'po'")
```

The result will be an ActiveRecord::Relation object containing all the matching rows, each neatly wrapped in an Order object.

That's fine if our condition is predefined, but how do we handle it when the name of the customer is set externally (perhaps coming from a web form)? One way is to substitute the value of that variable into the condition string:

```
# get the name from the form
name = params[:name]
# DON'T DO THIS!!!
pos = Order.where("name = '#{name}' and pay_type = 'po'")
```

As the comment suggests, this isn't a good idea. Why? It leaves the database wide open to something called a *SQL injection* attack, which the Ruby on Rails Guides[2] describe in more detail. For now, take it as a given that substituting a string from an external source into a SQL statement is effectively the same as publishing your entire database to the whole online world.

---

2. http://guides.rubyonrails.org/security.html#sql-injection

Instead, the safe way to generate dynamic SQL is to let Active Record handle it. Doing this allows Active Record to create properly escaped SQL, which is immune from SQL injection attacks. Let's see how this works.

If we pass multiple parameters to a where() call, Rails treats the first parameter as a template for the SQL to generate. Within this SQL, we can embed placeholders, which will be replaced at runtime by the values in the rest of the array.

One way of specifying placeholders is to insert one or more question marks in the SQL. The first question mark is replaced by the second element of the array, the next question mark by the third, and so on. For example, we could rewrite the previous query as this:

```
name = params[:name]
pos = Order.where(["name = ? and pay_type = 'po'", name])
```

We can also use named placeholders. We do that by placing placeholders of the form :name into the string and by providing corresponding values in a hash, where the keys correspond to the names in the query:

```
name     = params[:name]
pay_type = params[:pay_type]
pos = Order.where("name = :name and pay_type = :pay_type",
                  pay_type: pay_type, name: name)
```

We can take this a step further. Because params is effectively a hash, we can simply pass it all to the condition. If we have a form that can be used to enter search criteria, we can use the hash of values returned from that form directly:

```
pos = Order.where("name = :name and pay_type = :pay_type",
                  params[:order])
```

We can take this even further. If we pass just a hash as the condition, Rails generates a where clause using the hash keys as column names and the hash values as the values to match. Thus, we could have written the previous code even more succinctly:

```
pos = Order.where(params[:order])
```

Be careful with this latter form of condition: it takes *all* the key-value pairs in the hash you pass in when constructing the condition. An alternative would be to specify which parameters to use explicitly:

```
pos = Order.where(name: params[:name],
                  pay_type: params[:pay_type])
```

Regardless of which form of placeholder you use, Active Record takes great care to quote and escape the values being substituted into the SQL. Use these forms of dynamic SQL, and Active Record will keep you safe from injection attacks.

Using Like Clauses

We might be tempted to use parameterized like clauses in conditions:

```
# Doesn't work
User.where("name like '?%'", params[:name])
```

Rails doesn't parse the SQL inside a condition and so doesn't know that the name is being substituted into a string. As a result, it will go ahead and add extra quotes around the value of the name parameter. The correct way to do this is to construct the full parameter to the like clause and pass that parameter into the condition:

```
# Works
User.where("name like ?", params[:name]+"%")
```

Of course, if we do this, we need to consider that characters such as percent signs, should they happen to appear in the value of the name parameter, will be treated as wildcards.

Subsetting the Records Returned

Now that we know how to specify conditions, let's turn our attention to the various methods supported by ActiveRecord::Relation, starting with first() and all().

As you may have guessed, first() returns the first row in the relation. It returns nil if the relation is empty. Similarly, all() returns all the rows as an array. ActiveRecord::Relation also supports many of the methods of Array objects, such as each() and map(). It does so by implicitly calling the all() first.

It's important to understand that the query isn't evaluated until one of these methods is used. This enables us to modify the query in a number of ways, namely, by calling additional methods, prior to making this call. Let's look at these methods now.

order

SQL doesn't require rows to be returned in any particular order unless we explicitly add an order by clause to the query. The order() method lets us specify the criteria we'd normally add after the order by keywords. For example, the following query would return all of Dave's orders, sorted first by payment type and then by shipping date (the latter in descending order):

```
orders = Order.where(name: 'Dave').
  order("pay_type, shipped_at DESC")
```

limit

We can limit the number of rows returned by calling the limit() method. Generally when we use the limit method, we'll probably also want to specify the sort order to ensure consistent results. For example, the following returns the first ten matching orders:

```
orders = Order.where(name: 'Dave').
  order("pay_type, shipped_at DESC").
  limit(10)
```

offset

The offset() method goes hand in hand with the limit() method. It allows us to specify the offset of the first row in the result set that will be returned:

```
# The view wants to display orders grouped into pages,
# where each page shows page_size orders at a time.
# This method returns the orders on page page_num (starting
# at zero).
def Order.find_on_page(page_num, page_size)
  order(:id).limit(page_size).offset(page_num*page_size)
end
```

We can use offset in conjunction with limit to step through the results of a query *n* rows at a time.

select

By default, ActiveRecord::Relation fetches all the columns from the underlying database table—it issues a select * from... to the database. Override this with the select() method, which takes a string that will appear in place of the * in the select statement.

This method allows us to limit the values returned in cases where we need only a subset of the data in a table. For example, our table of podcasts might contain information on the title, speaker, and date and might also contain a large BLOB containing the MP3 of the talk. If you just wanted to create a list of talks, it would be inefficient to also load the sound data for each row. The select() method lets us choose which columns to load:

```
list = Talk.select("title, speaker, recorded_on")
```

joins

The joins() method lets us specify a list of additional tables to be joined to the default table. This parameter is inserted into the SQL immediately after the name of the model's table and before any conditions specified by the first parameter. The join syntax is database-specific. The following code returns a list of all line items for the book called *Programming Ruby*:

```
LineItem.select('li.quantity').
  where("pr.title = 'The Pragmatic Programmer'").
  joins("as li inner join products as pr on li.product_id = pr.id")
```

readonly

The readonly() method causes ActiveRecord::Resource to return Active Record objects that cannot be stored back into the database.

If we use the joins() or select() method, objects will automatically be marked readonly.

group

The group() method adds a group by clause to the SQL:

```
summary = LineItem.select("sku, sum(amount) as amount").
                  group("sku")
```

lock

The lock() method takes an optional string as a parameter. If we pass it a string, it should be a SQL fragment in our database's syntax that specifies a kind of lock. With MySQL, for example, a *share mode* lock gives us the latest data in a row and guarantees that no one else can alter that row while we hold the lock. We could write code that debits an account only if there are sufficient funds using something like the following:

```
Account.transaction do
  ac = Account.where(id: id).lock("LOCK IN SHARE MODE").first
  ac.balance -= amount if ac.balance > amount
  ac.save
end
```

If we don't specify a string value or we give lock() a value of true, the database's default exclusive lock is obtained (normally this will be "for update"). We can often eliminate the need for this kind of locking using transactions (discussed starting in Transactions, on page 344).

Databases do more than simply find and reliably retrieve data; they also do a bit of data reduction analysis. Rails provides access to these methods too.

Getting Column Statistics

Rails has the ability to perform statistics on the values in a column. For example, given a table of products, we can calculate the following:

```
average = Product.average(:price)   # average product price
max     = Product.maximum(:price)
min     = Product.minimum(:price)
total   = Product.sum(:price)
number  = Product.count
```

These all correspond to aggregate functions in the underlying database, but they work in a database-independent manner.

As before, methods can be combined:

```
Order.where("amount > 20").minimum(:amount)
```

These functions aggregate values. By default, they return a single result, producing, for example, the minimum order amount for orders meeting some condition. However, if you include the group method, the functions instead produce a series of results, one result for each set of records where the grouping expression has the same value. For example, the following calculates the maximum sale amount for each state:

```
result = Order.group(:state).maximum(:amount)
puts result   #=> {"TX"=>12345, "NC"=>3456, ...}
```

This code returns an ordered hash. You index it using the grouping element ("TX", "NC", ... in our example). You can also iterate over the entries in order using each(). The value of each entry is the value of the aggregation function.

The order and limit methods come into their own when using groups.

For example, the following returns the three states with the highest orders, sorted by the order amount:

```
result = Order.group(:state).
              order("max(amount) desc").
              limit(3)
```

This code is no longer database independent—to sort on the aggregated column, we had to use the SQLite syntax for the aggregation function (max, in this case).

Scopes

As these chains of method calls grow longer, making the chains themselves available for reuse becomes a concern. Once again, Rails delivers. An Active Record *scope* can be associated with a Proc and therefore may have arguments:

```
class Order < ActiveRecord::Base
  scope :last_n_days, ->(days) { where('updated < ?' , days) }
end
```

Such a named scope would make finding the worth of last week's orders a snap.

```
orders = Order.last_n_days(7)
```

Simpler scopes may have no parameters at all:

```
class Order < ActiveRecord::Base
  scope :checks, -> { where(pay_type: :check) }
end
```

Scopes can also be combined. Finding the last week's worth of orders that were paid by check is just as straightforward:

```
orders = Order.checks.last_n_days(7)
```

In addition to making your application code easier to write and easier to read, scopes can make your code more efficient. The previous statement, for example, is implemented as a single SQL query.

ActiveRecord::Relation objects are equivalent to an anonymous scope:

```
in_house = Order.where('email LIKE "%@pragprog.com"')
```

Of course, relations can also be combined:

```
in_house.checks.last_n_days(7)
```

Scopes aren't limited to where conditions; we can do pretty much anything we can do in a method call: limit, order, join, and so on. Just be aware that Rails doesn't know how to handle multiple order or limit clauses, so be sure to use these only once per call chain.

In nearly every case, the methods we've been describing are sufficient. But Rails isn't satisfied with only being able to handle nearly every case, so for cases that require a human-crafted query, there's an API for that too.

Writing Our Own SQL

Each of the methods we've been looking at contributes to the construction of a full SQL query string. The method find_by_sql() lets our application take full control. It accepts a single parameter containing a SQL select statement (or an array containing SQL and placeholder values, as for find()) and returns an array of model objects (that's potentially empty) from the result set. The attributes in these models will be set from the columns returned by the query. We'd normally use the select * form to return all columns for a table, but this isn't required:

```
rails80/e1/ar/find_examples.rb
orders = LineItem.find_by_sql("select line_items.* from line_items, orders " +
                              " where order_id = orders.id                 " +
                              "   and orders.name = 'Dave Thomas'          ")
```

Only those attributes returned by a query will be available in the resulting model objects. We can determine the attributes available in a model object using the attributes(), attribute_names(), and attribute_present?() methods. The first returns a hash of attribute name-value pairs, the second returns an array of names, and the third returns true if a named attribute is available in this model object:

```
rails80/e1/ar/find_examples.rb
orders = Order.find_by_sql("select name, pay_type from orders")
first = orders[0]
p first.attributes
p first.attribute_names
p first.attribute_present?("address")
```

This code produces the following:

```
{"name"=>"Dave Thomas", "pay_type"=>"check"}
["name", "pay_type"]
false
```

find_by_sql() can also be used to create model objects containing derived column data. If we use the as xxx SQL syntax to give derived columns a name in the result set, this name will be used as the name of the attribute:

```
rails80/e1/ar/find_examples.rb
items = LineItem.find_by_sql("select *,                                    " +
                             "   products.price as unit_price,             " +
                             "   quantity*products.price as total_price,   " +
                             "   products.title as title                   " +
                             " from line_items, products                   " +
                             " where line_items.product_id = products.id ")
li = items[0]
puts "#{li.title}: #{li.quantity}x#{li.unit_price} => #{li.total_price}"
```

As with conditions, we can also pass an array to find_by_sql(), where the first element is a string containing placeholders. The rest of the array can be either a hash or a list of values to be substituted.

```
Order.find_by_sql(["select * from orders where amount > ?",
                   params[:amount]])
```

In the old days of Rails, people frequently resorted to using find_by_sql(). Since then, all the options added to the basic find() method mean you can avoid resorting to this low-level method.

> **David says:**
> # But Isn't SQL Dirty?
>
> Ever since developers first wrapped relational databases with an object-oriented layer, they've debated the question of how deep to run the abstraction. Some object-relational mappers seek to eliminate the use of SQL entirely, hoping for object-oriented purity by forcing all queries through an OO layer.
>
> Active Record does not. It was built on the notion that SQL is neither dirty nor bad, just verbose in the trivial cases. The focus is on removing the need to deal with the verbosity in those trivial cases (writing a ten-attribute insert by hand will leave any programmer tired) but keeping the expressiveness around for the hard queries—the type SQL was created to deal with elegantly.
>
> Therefore, you shouldn't feel guilty when you use find_by_sql() to handle either performance bottlenecks or hard queries. Start out using the object-oriented interface for productivity and pleasure and then dip beneath the surface for a close-to-the-metal experience when you need to do so.

Reloading Data

In an application where the database is potentially being accessed by multiple processes (or by multiple applications), there's always the possibility that a fetched model object has become stale—someone may have written a more recent copy to the database.

To some extent, this issue is addressed by transactional support (which we describe in Transactions, on page 344). However, there will still be times where you need to refresh a model object manually. Active Record makes this possible with one line of code—call its reload() method, and the object's attributes will be refreshed from the database:

```
stock = Market.find_by(ticker: "RUBY")
loop do
  puts "Price = #{stock.price}"
  sleep 60
  stock.reload
end
```

In practice, reload() is rarely used outside the context of unit tests.

Updating Existing Rows

After such a long discussion of finder methods, you'll be pleased to know that there's not much to say about updating records with Active Record.

If you have an Active Record object (perhaps representing a row from our orders table), you can write it to the database by calling its save() method. If this object had previously been read from the database, this save will update the existing row; otherwise, the save will insert a new row.

If an existing row is updated, Active Record will use its primary key column to match it with the in-memory object. The attributes contained in the Active Record object determine the columns that will be updated—a column will be updated in the database only if its value has been changed. In the following example, all the values in the row for order 123 can be updated in the database table:

```
order = Order.find(123)
order.name = "Fred"
order.save
```

However, in the following example, the Active Record object contains just the attributes id, name, and paytype—only these columns can be updated when the object is saved. (Note that you have to include the id column if you intend to save a row fetched using find_by_sql().)

```
orders = Order.find_by_sql("select id, name, pay_type from orders where id=123")
first = orders[0]
first.name = "Wilma"
first.save
```

In addition to the save() method, Active Record lets us change the values of attributes and save a model object in a single call to update():

```
order = Order.find(321)
order.update(name: "Barney", email: "barney@bedrock.com")
```

The update() method is most commonly used in controller actions where it merges data from a form into an existing database row:

```
def save_after_edit
  order = Order.find(params[:id])
  if order.update(order_params)
    redirect_to action: :index
  else
    render action: :edit
  end
end
```

We can combine the functions of reading a row and updating it using the class methods update() and update_all(). The update() method takes an id parameter and a set of attributes. It fetches the corresponding row, updates

the given attributes, saves the result to the database, and returns the
model object.

```
order = Order.update(12, name: "Barney", email: "barney@bedrock.com")
```

We can pass update() an array of IDs and an array of attribute value hashes,
and it will update all the corresponding rows in the database, returning an
array of model objects.

Finally, the update_all() class method allows us to specify the set and where
clauses of the SQL update statement. For example, the following increases the
prices of all products with *Java* in their title by 10 percent:

```
result = Product.update_all("price = 1.1*price", "title like '%Java%'")
```

The return value of update_all() depends on the database adapter; most (but
not Oracle) return the number of rows that were changed in the database.

save, save!, create, and create!

It turns out that there are two versions of the save and create methods. The
variants differ in the way they report errors.

  - save returns true if the record was saved; it returns nil otherwise.
  - save! returns true if the save succeeded; it raises an exception otherwise.
  - create returns the Active Record object regardless of whether it was successfully saved. You'll need to check the object for validation errors if you want to determine whether the data was written.
  - create! returns the Active Record object on success; it raises an exception otherwise.

Let's look at this in a bit more detail.

Plain old save() returns true if the model object is valid and can be saved:

```
if order.save
  # all OK
else
  # validation failed
end
```

It's up to us to check on each call to save() to see that it did what we expected.
The reason Active Record is so lenient is that it assumes save() is called in the
context of a controller's action method and the view code will be presenting
any errors back to the end user. And for many applications, that's the case.

But if we need to save a model object in a context where we want to make sure to handle all errors programmatically, we should use save!(). This method raises a RecordInvalid exception if the object couldn't be saved:

```
begin
  order.save!
rescue RecordInvalid => error
  # validation failed
end
```

Deleting Rows

Active Record supports two styles of row deletion. First, it has two class-level methods, delete() and delete_all(), that operate at the database level. The delete() method takes a single ID or an array of IDs and deletes the corresponding row(s) in the underlying table. delete_all() deletes rows matching a given condition (or all rows if no condition is specified). The return values from both calls depend on the adapter but are typically the number of rows affected. An exception isn't thrown if the row doesn't exist prior to the call.

```
Order.delete(123)
User.delete([2,3,4,5])
Product.delete_all(["price > ?", @expensive_price])
```

The various destroy methods are the second form of row deletion provided by Active Record. These methods all work via Active Record model objects.

The destroy() instance method deletes from the database the row corresponding to a particular model object. It then freezes the contents of that object, preventing future changes to the attributes.

```
order = Order.find_by(name: "Dave")
order.destroy
# ... order is now frozen
```

There are two class-level destruction methods: destroy() (which takes an ID or an array of IDs) and destroy_all() (which takes a condition). Both methods read the corresponding rows in the database table into model objects and call the instance-level destroy() method of those objects. Neither method returns anything meaningful.

```
Order.destroy_all(["shipped_at < ?", 30.days.ago])
```

Why do we need both the delete and destroy class methods? The delete methods bypass the various Active Record callback and validation functions, while the destroy methods ensure that they're all invoked. In general, it's better to use the destroy methods if you want to ensure that your database is consistent according to the business rules defined in your model classes.

We covered validation in Chapter 7, Task B: Validation and Unit Testing, on page 85. We cover callbacks next.

Participating in the Monitoring Process

Active Record controls the life cycle of model objects—it creates them, monitors them as they're modified, saves and updates them, and watches sadly as they're destroyed. Using callbacks, Active Record lets our code participate in this monitoring process. We can write code that gets invoked at any significant event in the life of an object. With these callbacks we can perform complex validation, map column values as they pass in and out of the database, and even prevent certain operations from completing.

Active Record defines sixteen callbacks. Fourteen of these form before-after pairs and bracket some operation on an Active Record object. For example, the before_destroy callback will be invoked just before the destroy() method is called, and after_destroy will be invoked after. The two exceptions are after_find and after_initialize, which have no corresponding before_*xxx* callback. (These two callbacks are different in other ways too, as we'll see later.)

In the following figure we can see how Rails wraps the fourteen paired callbacks around the basic create, update, and destroy operations on model objects. Perhaps surprisingly, the before and after validation calls aren't strictly nested.

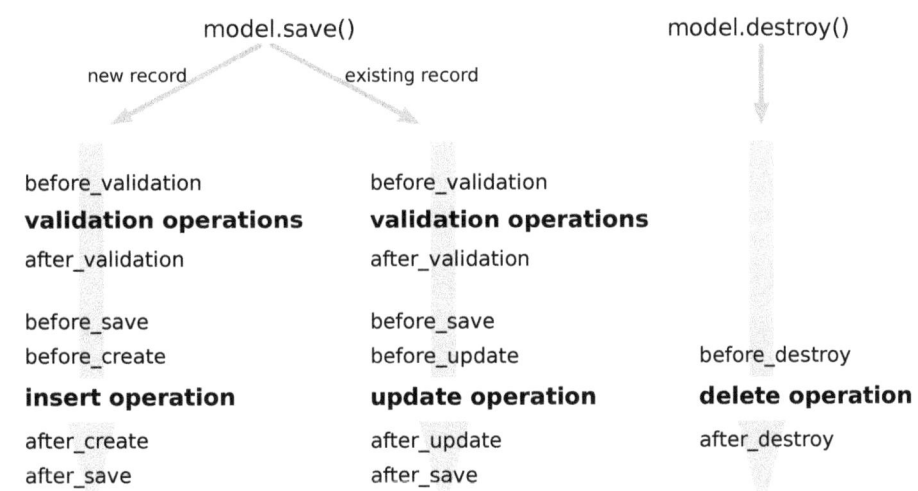

The before_validation and after_validation calls also accept the on: :create or on: :update parameter, which will cause the callback to be called only on the selected operation.

In addition to these sixteen calls, the after_find callback is invoked after any find operation, and after_initialize is invoked after an Active Record model object is created.

To have your code execute during a callback, you need to write a handler and associate it with the appropriate callback.

We have two basic ways of implementing callbacks.

The preferred way to define a callback is to declare handlers. A handler can be either a method or a block. You associate a handler with a particular event using class methods named after the event. To associate a method, declare it as private or protected, and specify its name as a symbol to the handler declaration. To specify a block, simply add it after the declaration. This block receives the model object as a parameter:

```ruby
class Order < ActiveRecord::Base
  before_validation :normalize_credit_card_number
  after_create do |order|
    logger.info "Order #{order.id} created"
  end
  protected
  def normalize_credit_card_number
    self.cc_number.gsub!(/[-\s]/, '')
  end
end
```

You can specify multiple handlers for the same callback. They will generally be invoked in the order they're specified unless a handler throws :abort, in which case the callback chain is broken early.

Alternatively, you can define the callback instance methods using callback objects, inline methods (using a proc), or inline eval methods (using a string). See the online documentation for more details.[3]

Grouping Related Callbacks Together

If you have a group of related callbacks, it may be convenient to group them into a separate handler class. These handlers can be shared between multiple models. A handler class is simply a class that defines callback methods (before_save(), after_create(), and so on). Create the source files for these handler classes in app/models.

---

3. http://api.rubyonrails.org/classes/ActiveRecord/Callbacks.html#label-Types+of+callbacks

In the model object that uses the handler, you create an instance of this handler class and pass that instance to the various callback declarations. A couple of examples will make this clearer.

If our application uses credit cards in multiple places, we might want to share our normalize_credit_card_number() method across multiple models. To do that, we'd extract the method into its own class and name it after the event we want it to handle. This method will receive a single parameter, the model object that generated the callback:

```ruby
class CreditCardCallbacks

  # Normalize the credit card number
  def before_validation(model)
    model.cc_number.gsub!(/[-\s]/, '')
  end
end
```

Now, in our model classes, we can arrange for this shared callback to be invoked:

```ruby
class Order < ActiveRecord::Base
  before_validation CreditCardCallbacks.new
  # ...
end
class Subscription < ApplicationRecord
  before_validation CreditCardCallbacks.new
  # ...
end
```

In this example, the handler class assumes that the credit card number is held in a model attribute named cc_number; both Order and Subscription would have an attribute with that name. But we can generalize the idea, making the handler class less dependent on the implementation details of the classes that use it.

For example, we could create a generalized encryption and decryption handler. This could be used to encrypt named fields before they're stored in the database and to decrypt them when the row is read back. You could include it as a callback handler in any model that needed the facility.

The handler needs to encrypt a given set of attributes in a model just before that model's data is written to the database. Because our application needs to deal with the plain-text versions of these attributes, it arranges to decrypt them again after the save is complete. It also needs to decrypt the data when a row is read from the database into a model object. These requirements mean we have to handle the before_save, after_save, and after_find events. Because we need to decrypt the database row both after saving and when we find a new row, we can save code by aliasing the after_find() method to after_save()—the same method will have two names:

rails80/e1/ar/encrypter.rb
```ruby
class Encrypter
  # We're passed a list of attributes that should
  # be stored encrypted in the database
  def initialize(attrs_to_manage)
    @attrs_to_manage = attrs_to_manage
  end

  # Before saving or updating, encrypt the fields using the NSA and
  # DHS approved Shift Cipher
  def before_save(model)
    @attrs_to_manage.each do |field|
      model[field].tr!("a-z", "b-za")
    end
  end

  # After saving, decrypt them back
  def after_save(model)
    @attrs_to_manage.each do |field|
      model[field].tr!("b-za", "a-z")
    end
  end

  # Do the same after finding an existing record
  alias_method :after_find, :after_save
end
```

This example uses trivial encryption—you might want to beef it up before using this class for real.

We can now arrange for the Encrypter class to be invoked from inside our orders model:

```ruby
require "encrypter"
class Order < ActiveRecord::Base
  encrypter = Encrypter.new([:name, :email])
  before_save encrypter
  after_save  encrypter
  after_find  encrypter
protected
  def after_find
  end
end
```

We create a new Encrypter object and hook it up to the events before_save, after_save, and after_find. This way, just before an order is saved, the method before_save() in the encrypter will be invoked, and so on.

So why do we define an empty after_find() method? Remember that we said that for performance reasons after_find and after_initialize are treated specially. One of the consequences of this special treatment is that Active Record won't know to call an after_find handler unless it sees an actual after_find() method in the model class. We have to define an empty placeholder to get after_find processing to take place.

This is all very well, but every model class that wants to use our encryption handler would need to include some eight lines of code, just as we did with our Order class. We can do better than that. We'll define a helper method that does all the work and make that helper available to all Active Record models. To do that, we'll add it to the ApplicationRecord class:

rails80/e1/ar/encrypter.rb
```ruby
class ApplicationRecord < ActiveRecord::Base
  self.abstract_class = true

  def self.encrypt(*attr_names)
    encrypter = Encrypter.new(attr_names)

    before_save encrypter
    after_save  encrypter
    after_find  encrypter

    define_method(:after_find) { }
  end
end
```

Given this, we can now add encryption to any model class's attributes using a single call:

```ruby
class Order < ApplicationRecord
  encrypt(:name, :email)
end
```

A small driver program lets us experiment with this:

```ruby
o = Order.new
o.name    = "Dave Thomas"
o.address = "123 The Street"
o.email   = "dave@example.com"
o.save
puts o.name

o = Order.find(o.id)
puts o.name
```

On the console, we see our customer's name (in plain text) in the model object:

```
ar> ruby encrypter.rb
Dave Thomas
Dave Thomas
```

In the database, however, the name and email address are obscured by our industrial-strength encryption:

```
depot> sqlite3 -line storage/development.sqlite3 "select * from orders"
     id = 1
user_id =
   name = Dbwf Tipnbt
address = 123 The Street
  email = ebwf@fybnqmf.dpn
```

Callbacks are a fine technique, but they can sometimes result in a model class taking on responsibilities that aren't really related to the nature of the model. For example, in Participating in the Monitoring Process, on page 339, we created a callback that generated a log message when an order was created. That functionality isn't really part of the basic Order class—we put it there because that's where the callback executed.

When used in moderation, such an approach doesn't lead to significant problems. If, however, you find yourself repeating code, consider using concerns[4] instead.

Transactions

A database transaction groups a series of changes in such a way that either the database applies all of the changes or it applies none of the changes. The classic example of the need for transactions (and one used in Active Record's own documentation) is transferring money between two bank accounts. The basic logic is straightforward:

```
account1.deposit(100)
account2.withdraw(100)
```

But we have to be careful. What happens if the deposit succeeds but for some reason the withdrawal fails (perhaps the customer is overdrawn)? We'll have added $100 to the balance in account1 without a corresponding deduction from account2. In effect, we'll have created $100 out of thin air.

Transactions to the rescue. A transaction is something like the Three Musketeers with their motto "All for one and one for all." Within the scope of a transaction, either every SQL statement succeeds or they all have no effect. Putting that another way, if any statement fails, the entire transaction has no effect on the database.

---

4. https://api.rubyonrails.org/classes/ActiveSupport/Concern.html

In Active Record we use the transaction() method to execute a block in the context of a particular database transaction. At the end of the block, the transaction is committed, updating the database, *unless* an exception is raised within the block, in which case the database rolls back all of the changes. Because transactions exist in the context of a database connection, we have to invoke them with an Active Record class as a receiver.

Thus, we could write this:

```
Account.transaction do
  account1.deposit(100)
  account2.withdraw(100)
end
```

Let's experiment with transactions. We'll start by creating a new database table. (Make sure your database supports transactions, or this code won't work for you.)

rails80/e1/ar/transactions.rb
```
create_table :accounts, force: true do |t|
  t.string  :number
  t.decimal :balance, precision: 10, scale: 2, default: 0
end
```

Next, we'll define a rudimentary bank account class. This class defines instance methods to deposit money to and withdraw money from the account. It also provides some basic validation—for this particular type of account, the balance can never be negative.

rails80/e1/ar/transactions.rb
```
class Account < ActiveRecord::Base
  validates :balance, numericality: {greater_than_or_equal_to: 0}
  def withdraw(amount)
    adjust_balance_and_save!(-amount)
  end
  def deposit(amount)
    adjust_balance_and_save!(amount)
  end
  private
  def adjust_balance_and_save!(amount)
    self.balance += amount
    save!
  end
end
```

Let's look at the helper method, adjust_balance_and_save!(). The first line simply updates the balance field. The method then calls save! to save the model data. (Remember that save!() raises an exception if the object cannot be saved—we use the exception to signal to the transaction that something has gone wrong.)

So now let's write the code to transfer money between two accounts. It's pretty straightforward:

rails80/e1/ar/transactions.rb
```
peter = Account.create(balance: 100, number: "12345")
paul  = Account.create(balance: 200, number: "54321")

Account.transaction do
  paul.deposit(10)
  peter.withdraw(10)
end
```

We check the database, and, sure enough, the money got transferred:

```
depot> sqlite3 -line storage/development.sqlite3 "select * from accounts"
     id = 1
 number = 12345
balance = 90

     id = 2
 number = 54321
balance = 210
```

Now let's get radical. If we start again but this time try to transfer $350, we'll run Peter into the red, which isn't allowed by the validation rule. Let's try it:

rails80/e1/ar/transactions.rb
```
peter = Account.create(balance: 100, number: "12345")
paul  = Account.create(balance: 200, number: "54321")
```

rails80/e1/ar/transactions.rb
```
Account.transaction do
  paul.deposit(350)
  peter.withdraw(350)
end
```

When we run this, we get an exception reported on the console:

```
.../validations.rb:736:in `save!': Validation failed: Balance is negative
from transactions.rb:46:in `adjust_balance_and_save!'
     :          :          :
from transactions.rb:80
```

Looking in the database, we can see that the data remains unchanged:

```
depot> sqlite3 -line storage/development.sqlite3 "select * from accounts"
     id = 1
 number = 12345
balance = 100
```

```
      id = 2
  number = 54321
 balance = 200
```

However, there's a trap waiting for you here. The transaction protected the database from becoming inconsistent, but what about our model objects? To see what happened to them, we have to arrange to intercept the exception to allow the program to continue running:

rails80/e1/ar/transactions.rb
```
peter = Account.create(balance: 100, number: "12345")
paul  = Account.create(balance: 200, number: "54321")
```

rails80/e1/ar/transactions.rb
```
begin
  Account.transaction do
    paul.deposit(350)
    peter.withdraw(350)
  end
rescue
  puts "Transfer aborted"
end

puts "Paul has #{paul.balance}"
puts "Peter has #{peter.balance}"
```

What we see is a little surprising:

```
Transfer aborted
Paul has 550.0
Peter has -250.0
```

Although the database was left unscathed, our model objects were updated anyway. This is because Active Record wasn't keeping track of the before and after states of the various objects—in fact, it couldn't, because it had no easy way of knowing just which models were involved in the transactions.

Built-In Transactions

When we discussed parent and child tables in Specifying Relationships in Models, on page 322, we said that Active Record takes care of saving all the dependent child rows when you save a parent row. This takes multiple SQL statement executions (one for the parent and one each for any changed or new children).

Clearly, this change should be atomic, but until now we haven't been using transactions when saving these interrelated objects. Have we been negligent?

Fortunately, no. Active Record is smart enough to wrap all the updates and inserts related to a particular save() (and also the deletes related to a destroy())

in a transaction; either they all succeed or no data is written permanently to the database. You need explicit transactions only when you manage multiple SQL statements yourself.

While we've covered the basics, transactions are actually very subtle. They exhibit the so-called ACID properties: they're Atomic, they ensure Consistency, they work in Isolation, and their effects are Durable (they're made permanent when the transaction is committed). It's worth finding a good database book and reading up on transactions if you plan to take a database application live.

What We Just Did

We learned the relevant data structures and naming conventions for tables, classes, columns, attributes, IDs, and relationships. We saw how to create, read, update, and delete this data. Finally, we now understand how transactions and callbacks can be used to prevent inconsistent changes.

This, coupled with validation as described in Chapter 7, Task B: Validation and Unit Testing, on page 85, covers all the essentials of Active Record that every Rails programmer needs to know. If you have specific needs beyond what is covered here, look to the Rails Guides[5] for more information.

The next major subsystem to cover is Action Pack, which covers both the view and controller portions of Rails.

---

5. http://guides.rubyonrails.org/

In this chapter, you'll see:
- Representational State Transfer (REST)
- Defining how requests are routed to controllers
- Selecting a data representation
- Testing routes
- The controller environment
- Rendering and redirecting
- Sessions, flash, and callbacks

CHAPTER 21

Action Dispatch and Action Controller

Action Pack lies at the heart of Rails applications. It consists of three Ruby modules: ActionDispatch, ActionController, and ActionView. Action Dispatch routes requests to controllers. Action Controller converts requests into responses. Action View is used by Action Controller to format those responses.

As a concrete example, in the Depot application, we routed the root of the site (/) to the index() method of the StoreController. At the completion of that method, the template in app/views/store/index.html.erb was rendered. Each of these activities was orchestrated by modules in the Action Pack component.

Working together, these three submodules provide support for processing incoming requests and generating outgoing responses. In this chapter, we'll look at both Action Dispatch and Action Controller. In the next chapter, we'll cover Action View.

When we looked at Active Record, we saw it could be used as a freestanding library; we can use Active Record as part of a nonweb Ruby application. Action Pack is different. Although it's possible to use it directly as a framework, you probably won't. Instead, you'll take advantage of the tight integration offered by Rails. Components such as Action Controller, Action View, and Active Record handle the processing of requests, and the Rails environment knits them together into a coherent (and easy-to-use) whole. For that reason, we'll describe Action Controller in the context of Rails. Let's start by looking at how Rails applications handle requests. We'll then dive down into the details of routing and URL handling. We'll continue by looking at how you write code in a controller. Finally, we'll cover sessions, flash, and callbacks.

Dispatching Requests to Controllers

At its most basic, a web application accepts an incoming request from a browser, processes it, and sends a response.

A question immediately springs to mind: how does the application know what to do with the incoming request? A shopping cart application will receive requests to display a catalog, add items to a cart, create an order, and so on. How does it route these requests to the appropriate code?

It turns out that Rails provides two ways to define how to route a request: a comprehensive way that you'll use when you need to and a convenient way that you'll generally use whenever you can.

The comprehensive way lets you define a direct mapping of URLs to actions based on pattern matching, requirements, and conditions. The convenient way lets you define routes based on resources, such as the models that you define. And because the convenient way is built on the comprehensive way, you can freely mix and match the two approaches.

In both cases, Rails encodes information in the request URL and uses a subsystem called Action Dispatch to determine what should be done with that request. The actual process is flexible, but at the end of it Rails has determined the name of the *controller* that handles this particular request along with a list of any other request parameters. In the process, either one of these additional parameters or the HTTP method itself is used to identify the *action* to be invoked in the target controller.

Rails routes support the mapping between URLs and actions based on the contents of the URL and on the HTTP method used to invoke the request. We've seen how to do this on a URL-by-URL basis using anonymous or named routes. Rails also supports a higher-level way of creating groups of related routes. To understand the motivation for this, we need to take a little diversion into the world of representational state transfer (REST).

REST: Representational State Transfer

The ideas behind REST were formalized in Chapter 5 of Roy Fielding's 2000 PhD dissertation.[1] In a REST approach, servers communicate with clients using stateless connections. All the information about the state of the interaction between the two is encoded into the requests and responses between them. Long-term state is kept on the server as a set of identifiable *resources*.

---

1. http://www.ics.uci.edu/~fielding/pubs/dissertation/rest_arch_style.htm

Clients access these resources using a well-defined (and severely constrained) set of resource identifiers (URLs in our context). REST distinguishes the content of resources from the presentation of that content. REST is designed to support highly scalable computing while constraining application architectures to be decoupled by nature.

This description contains a lot of abstract stuff. What does REST mean in practice?

First, the formalities of a RESTful approach mean that network designers know when and where they can cache responses to requests. This enables load to be pushed out through the network, increasing performance and resilience while reducing latency.

Second, the constraints imposed by REST can lead to easier-to-write (and maintain) applications. RESTful applications don't worry about implementing remotely accessible services. Instead, they provide a regular (and straightforward) interface to a set of resources. Your application implements a way of listing, creating, editing, and deleting each resource, and your clients do the rest.

Let's make this more concrete. In REST, we use a basic set of verbs to operate on a rich set of nouns. If we're using HTTP, the verbs correspond to HTTP methods (GET, PUT, PATCH, POST, and DELETE, typically). The nouns are the resources in our application. We name those resources using URLs.

The Depot application that we produced contained a set of products. There are implicitly two resources here: first, the individual products, each of which constitutes a resource, and second, the collection of products.

To fetch a list of all the products, we could issue an HTTP GET request against this collection, say on the path /products. To fetch the contents of an individual resource, we have to identify it. The Rails way would be to give its primary key value (that is, its ID). Again we'd issue a GET request, this time against the URL /products/1.

To create a new product in our collection, we use an HTTP POST request directed at the /products path, with the post data containing the product to add. Yes, that's the same path we used to get a list of products. If you issue a GET to it, it responds with a list, and if you do a POST to it, it adds a new product to the collection.

Take this a step further. We've already seen you can retrieve the content of a product—you just issue a GET request against the path /products/1. To update that product, you'd issue an HTTP PUT request against the same URL. And, to delete it, you could issue an HTTP DELETE request, using the same URL.

Take this further. Maybe our system also tracks users. Again, we have a set of resources to deal with. REST tells us to use the same set of verbs (GET, POST, PATCH, PUT, and DELETE) against a similar-looking set of URLs (/users, /users/1, and so on).

Now we see some of the power of the constraints imposed by REST. We're already familiar with the way Rails constrains us to structure our applications a certain way. Now the REST philosophy tells us to structure the interface to our applications too. Suddenly our world gets a lot simpler.

Rails has direct support for this type of interface; it adds a kind of macro route facility, called *resources*. Let's take a look at how the config/routes.rb file might have looked back in Creating a Rails Application, on page 65:

```
Depot::Application.routes.draw do
  resources :products
end
```

The resources line caused seven new routes to be added to our application. Along the way, it assumed that the application will have a controller named ProductsController, containing seven actions with given names.

You can take a look at the routes that were generated for us. We do this by making use of the handy rails routes command.

```
      Prefix Verb    URI Pattern
                     Controller#Action
    products GET     /products(.:format)
                     {:action=>"index", :controller=>"products"}
             POST    /products(.:format)
                     {:action=>"create", :controller=>"products"}
 new_product GET     /products/new(.:format)
                     {:action=>"new", :controller=>"products"}
edit_product GET     /products/:id/edit(.:format)
                     {:action=>"edit", :controller=>"products"}
     product GET     /products/:id(.:format)
                     {:action=>"show", :controller=>"products"}
             PATCH   /products/:id(.:format)
                     {:action=>"update", :controller=>"products"}
             DELETE  /products/:id(.:format)
                     {:action=>"destroy", :controller=>"products"}
```

All the routes defined are spelled out in a columnar format. The lines will generally wrap on your screen; in fact, they had to be broken into two lines per route to fit on this page. The columns are (optional) route name, HTTP method, route path, and (on a separate line on this page) route requirements.

Fields in parentheses are optional parts of the path. Field names preceded by a colon are for variables into which the matching part of the path is placed for later processing by the controller.

Now let's look at the seven controller actions that these routes reference. Although we created our routes to manage the products in our application, let's broaden this to talk about resources—after all, the same seven methods will be required for all resource-based routes:

index
> Returns a list of the resources.

create
> Creates a new resource from the data in the POST request, adding it to the collection.

new
> Constructs a new resource and passes it to the client. This resource won't have been saved on the server. You can think of the new action as creating an empty form for the client to fill in.

show
> Returns the contents of the resource identified by params[:id].

update
> Updates the contents of the resource identified by params[:id] with the data associated with the request.

edit
> Returns the contents of the resource identified by params[:id] in a form suitable for editing.

destroy
> Destroys the resource identified by params[:id].

You can see that these seven actions contain the four basic CRUD operations (create, read, update, and delete). They also contain an action to list resources and two auxiliary actions that return new and existing resources in a form suitable for editing on the client.

If for some reason you don't need or want all seven actions, you can limit the actions produced using :only or :except options on your resources:

```
resources :comments, except: [:update, :destroy]
```

Several of the routes are named routes enabling you to use helper functions such as products_url and edit_product_url(id:1).

Note that each route is defined with an optional format specifier. We'll cover formats in more detail in Selecting a Data Representation, on page 359.

Let's take a look at the controller code:

rails80/depot_a/app/controllers/products_controller.rb
```ruby
class ProductsController < ApplicationController
  before_action :set_product, only: %i[ show edit update destroy ]

  # GET /products or /products.json
  def index
    @products = Product.all
  end

  # GET /products/1 or /products/1.json
  def show
  end

  # GET /products/new
  def new
    @product = Product.new
  end

  # GET /products/1/edit
  def edit
  end

  # POST /products or /products.json
  def create
    @product = Product.new(product_params)

    respond_to do |format|
      if @product.save
        format.html { redirect_to @product,
          notice: "Product was successfully created." }
        format.json { render :show, status: :created,
          location: @product }
      else
        format.html { render :new,
          status: :unprocessable_entity }
        format.json { render json: @product.errors, status: :unprocessable_entity }
      end
    end
  end

  # PATCH/PUT /products/1 or /products/1.json
  def update
    respond_to do |format|
      if @product.update(product_params)
        format.html { redirect_to @product,
          notice: "Product was successfully updated." }
        format.json { render :show, status: :ok, location: @product }
```

```ruby
    else
      format.html { render :edit,
        status: :unprocessable_entity }
      format.json { render json: @product.errors, status: :unprocessable_entity }
    end
  end
end

# DELETE /products/1 or /products/1.json
def destroy
  @product.destroy!

  respond_to do |format|
    format.html { redirect_to products_path, status: :see_other,
      notice: "Product was successfully destroyed." }
    format.json { head :no_content }
  end
end

private
  # Use callbacks to share common setup or constraints between actions.
  def set_product
    @product = Product.find(params.expect(:id))
  end

  # Only allow a list of trusted parameters through.
  def product_params
    params.expect(product: [ :title, :description, :image, :price ])
  end
end
```

Notice how we have one action for each of the RESTful actions. The comment before each shows the format of the URL that invokes it.

Notice also that many of the actions contain a respond_to() block. As we saw in Chapter 11, Task F: Hotwiring the Storefront, on page 143, Rails uses this to determine the type of content to send in a response. The scaffold generator automatically creates code that will respond appropriately to requests for HTML or JSON content. We'll play with that in a little while.

The views created by the generator are fairly straightforward. The only tricky thing is the need to use the correct HTTP method to send requests to the server.

For example, the view for the index action looks like this:

rails80/depot_a/app/views/products/index.html.erb
```erb
<div class="w-full">
  <% if notice.present? %>
    <p class="py-2 px-3 bg-green-50 mb-5 text-green-500 font-medium
              rounded-lg inline-block" id="notice">
      <%= notice %>
    </p>
  <% end %>

  <div class="flex justify-between items-center pb-8">
    <h1 class="mx-auto font-bold text-4xl">Products</h1>
  </div>

  <table id="products" class="mx-auto">
    <tfoot>
      <tr>
        <td colspan="3">
          <div class="mt-8">
            <%= link_to 'New product',
                        new_product_path,
                        class: "inline rounded-lg py-3 px-5 bg-green-600
                                text-white block font-medium" %>
          </div>
        </td>
      </tr>
    </tfoot>

    <tbody>
      <% @products.each do |product| %>
        <tr class="<%= cycle('bg-green-50', 'bg-white') %>">

          <td class="px-2 py-3">
            <%= image_tag(product.image, class: 'w-40') %>
          </td>

          <td>
            <h1 class="text-xl font-bold"><%= product.title %></h1>
            <p class="my-3">
              <%= truncate(strip_tags(product.description),
                          length: 80) %>
            </p>
            <p>
              <%= number_to_currency(product.price) %>
            </p>
          </td>

          <td class="px-3">
            <ul>
              <li>
                <%= link_to 'Show',
                            product,
                            class: 'hover:underline' %>
              </li>
```

```erb
          <li>
            <%= link_to 'Edit',
                        edit_product_path(product),
                        class: 'hover:underline' %>
          </li>
          <li>
            <%= button_to 'Destroy',
                          product,
                          method: :delete,
                          class: 'hover:underline',
                          data: { turbo_confirm: "Are you sure?" } %>
          </li>
        </ul>
      </td>
    </tr>
  <% end %>
  </tbody>
  </table>
</div>
```

The links to the actions that edit a product and add a new product should both use regular GET methods, so a standard link_to works fine. However, the request to destroy a product must issue an HTTP DELETE, so the call includes the method: :delete option to button_to.

Adding Additional Actions

Rails resources provide you with an initial set of actions, but you don't need to stop there. For example, if you want to add an interface to allow people to fetch a list of people who bought any given product, you can add an extension to the resources call:

```ruby
Depot::Application.routes.draw do
  resources :products do
    get :who_bought, on: :member
  end
end
```

That syntax is straightforward. It says "We want to add a new action named who_bought, invoked via an HTTP GET. It applies to each member of the collection of products."

Instead of specifying :member, if we instead specified :collection, then the route would apply to the collection as a whole. This is often used for scoping; for example, you may have collections of products on clearance or products that have been discontinued.

Nested Resources

Often our resources themselves contain additional collections of resources. For example, we may want to allow folks to review our products. Each review would be a resource, and collections of reviews would be associated with each product resource. Rails provides a convenient and intuitive way of declaring the routes for this type of situation:

```
resources :products do
  resources :reviews
end
```

This defines the top-level set of product routes and additionally creates a set of subroutes for reviews. Because the review resources appear inside the products block, a review resource *must* be qualified by a product resource. This means that the path to a review must always be prefixed by the path to a particular product. To fetch the review with ID 4 for the product with an ID of 99, you'd use a path of /products/99/reviews/4.

The named route for /products/:product_id/reviews/:id is product_review, not simply review. This naming simply reflects the nesting of these resources.

As always, you can see the full set of routes generated by our configuration by using the rails routes command.

Routing Concerns

So far, we've been dealing with a fairly small set of resources. On a larger system there may be types of objects for which a review may be appropriate or to which a who_bought action might reasonably be applied. Instead of repeating these instructions for each resource, consider refactoring your routes using concerns to capture the common behavior.

```
concern :reviewable do
  resources :reviews
end
resources :products, concern: :reviewable
resources :users, concern: :reviewable
```

The preceding definition of the products resource is equivalent to the one in the previous section.

Shallow Route Nesting

At times, nested resources can produce cumbersome URLs. A solution to this is to use shallow route nesting:

```
resources :products, shallow: true do
  resources :reviews
end
```

This will enable the recognition of the following routes:

```
/products/1         => product_path(1)
/products/1/reviews => product_reviews_index_path(1)
/reviews/2          => reviews_path(2)
```

Try the rails routes command to see the full mapping.

Selecting a Data Representation

One of the goals of a REST architecture is to decouple data from its representation. If a human uses the URL path /products to fetch products, they should see nicely formatted HTML. If an application asks for the same URL, it could elect to receive the results in a code-friendly format (YAML, JSON, or XML, perhaps).

We've already seen how Rails can use the HTTP Accept header in a respond_to block in the controller. However, it isn't always easy (and sometimes it's plain impossible) to set the Accept header. To deal with this, Rails allows you to pass the format of response you'd like as part of the URL. As you've seen, Rails accomplishes this by including a field called :format in your route definitions. To do this, set a :format parameter in your routes to the file extension of the MIME type you'd like returned:

```
GET    /products(.:format)
       {:action=>"index", :controller=>"products"}
```

Because a full stop (period) is a separator character in route definitions, :format is treated as just another field. Because we give it a nil default value, it's an optional field.

Having done this, we can use a respond_to() block in our controllers to select our response type depending on the requested format:

```
def show
  respond_to do |format|
    format.html
    format.json { render json: @product.to_json }
  end
end
```

Given this, a request to /store/show/1 or /store/show/1.html will return HTML content, while /store/show/1.xml will return XML, and /store/show/1.json will return JSON. You can also pass the format in as an HTTP request parameter:

```
GET HTTP://pragprog.com/store/show/123?format=xml
```

Although the idea of having a single controller that responds with different content types seems appealing, the reality is tricky. In particular, it turns out that error handling can be tough. Although it's acceptable on error to redirect a user to a form, showing them a nice flash message, you have to adopt a different strategy when you serve XML. Consider your application architecture carefully before deciding to bundle all your processing into single controllers.

Rails makes it straightforward to develop an application that's based on resource-based routing. Many claim it greatly simplifies the coding of their applications. However, it isn't always appropriate. Don't feel compelled to use it if you can't find a way of making it work. And you can always mix and match. Some controllers can be resource based, and others can be based on actions. Some controllers can even be resource based with a few extra actions.

Processing of Requests

In the previous section, we worked out how Action Dispatch routes an incoming request to the appropriate code in your application. Now let's see what happens inside that code.

Action Methods

When a controller object processes a request, it looks for a public instance method with the same name as the incoming action. If it finds one, that method is invoked. If it doesn't find one and the controller implements method_missing(), that method is called, passing in the action name as the first parameter and an empty argument list as the second. If no method can be called, the controller looks for a template named after the current controller and action. If found, this template is rendered directly. If none of these things happens, an AbstractController::ActionNotFound error is generated.

Controller Environment

The controller sets up the environment for actions (and, by extension, for the views that they invoke). Many of these methods provide direct access to information contained in the URL or request:

action_name
> The name of the action currently being processed.

cookies
> The cookies associated with the request. Setting values into this object stores cookies on the browser when the response is sent. Rails support for sessions is based on cookies. We discuss sessions in Rails Sessions, on page 372.

headers
> A hash of HTTP headers that will be used in the response. By default, Cache-Control is set to no-cache. You might want to set Content-Type headers for special-purpose applications. Note that you shouldn't set cookie values in the header directly—use the cookie API to do this.

params
> A hash-like object containing request parameters (along with pseudoparameters generated during routing). It's hash-like because you can index entries using either a symbol or a string—params[:id] and params['id'] return the same value. Idiomatic Rails applications use the symbol form.

request
> The incoming request object. It includes these attributes:
>
> - request_method returns the request method, one of :delete, :get, :head, :post, or :put.
>
> - method returns the same value as request_method except for :head, which it returns as :get because these two are functionally equivalent from an application point of view.
>
> - delete?, get?, head?, post?, and put? return true or false based on the request method.
>
> - xml_http_request? and xhr? return true if this request was issued by one of the Ajax helpers. Note that this parameter is independent of the method parameter.
>
> - url(), which returns the full URL used for the request.
>
> - protocol(), host(), port(), path(), and query_string(), which return components of the URL used for the request, based on the following pattern: protocol://host:port/path?query_string.
>
> - domain(), which returns the last two components of the domain name of the request.
>
> - host_with_port(), which is a host:port string for the request.
>
> - port_string(), which is a :port string for the request if the port isn't the default port (80 for HTTP, 443 for HTTPS).
>
> - ssl?(), which is true if this is an SSL request; in other words, the request was made with the HTTPS protocol.
>
> - remote_ip(), which returns the remote IP address as a string. The string may have more than one address in it if the client is behind a proxy.

- env(), the environment of the request. You can use this to access values set by the browser, such as this:

  request.**env**['HTTP_ACCEPT_LANGUAGE']

- accepts(), which is an array with Mime::Type objects that represent the MIME types in the Accept header.
- format(), which is computed based on the value of the Accept header, with Mime[:HTML] as a fallback.
- content_type(), which is the MIME type for the request. This is useful for put and post requests.
- headers(), which is the complete set of HTTP headers.
- body(), which is the request body as an I/O stream.
- content_length(), which is the number of bytes purported to be in the body.

Rails leverages a gem named Rack to provide much of this functionality. See the documentation of Rack::Request for full details.

response
> The response object, filled in during the handling of the request. Normally, this object is managed for you by Rails. As we'll see when we look at callbacks in Callbacks, on page 378, we sometimes access the internals for specialized processing.

session
> A hash-like object representing the current session data. We describe this in Rails Sessions, on page 372.

In addition, a logger is available throughout Action Pack.

Responding to the User

Part of the controller's job is to respond to the user, which is done in four ways:

- The most common way is to render a template. In terms of the MVC paradigm, the template is the view, taking information provided by the controller and using it to generate a response to the browser.
- The controller can return a string directly to the browser without invoking a view. This is fairly rare but can be used to send error notifications.
- The controller can return nothing to the browser. This is sometimes used when responding to an Ajax request. In all cases, however, the controller returns a set of HTTP headers because some kind of response is expected.

- The controller can send other data to the client (something other than HTML). This is typically a download of some kind (perhaps a PDF document or a file's contents).

A controller always responds to the user exactly one time per request. This means you should have just one call to a render(), redirect_to(), or send_*xxx*() method in the processing of any request. (A DoubleRenderError exception is thrown on the second render.)

Because the controller must respond exactly once, it checks to see whether a response has been generated just before it finishes handling a request. If not, the controller looks for a template named after the controller and action and automatically renders it. This is the most common way that rendering takes place. You may have noticed that in most of the actions in our shopping cart tutorial we never explicitly rendered anything. Instead, our action methods set up the context for the view and return. The controller notices that no rendering has taken place and automatically invokes the appropriate template.

You can have multiple templates with the same name but with different extensions (for example, .html.erb, .xml.builder, and .js.erb). If you don't specify an extension in a render request, Rails assumes html.erb.

Rendering Templates

A *template* is a file that defines the content of a response for our application. Rails supports three template formats out of the box: *erb*, which is embedded Ruby code (typically with HTML); *builder*, a more programmatic way of constructing XML content; and *RJS*, which generates JavaScript. We'll talk about the contents of these files starting in Using Templates, on page 381.

By convention, the template for *action* of *controller* will be in the file app/views/controller/action.type.xxx (where *type* is the file type, such as html, atom, or js; and *xxx* is one of erb, builder, or scss). The app/views part of the name is the default. You can override this for an entire application by setting this:

ActionController.prepend_view_path dir_path

The render() method is the heart of all rendering in Rails. It takes a hash of options that tell it what to render and how to render it.

It's tempting to write code in our controllers that looks like this:

```
# DO NOT DO THIS
def update
  @user = User.find(params[:id])
  if @user.update(user_params)
```

```
    render action: show
  end
  render template: "fix_user_errors"
end
```

It seems somehow natural that the act of calling render (and redirect_to) should somehow terminate the processing of an action. This isn't the case. The previous code will generate an error (because render is called twice) in the case where update succeeds.

Let's look at the render options used in the controller here (we'll look separately at rendering in the view starting in Partial-Page Templates, on page 402):

render()
> With no overriding parameter, the render() method renders the default template for the current controller and action. The following code will render the template app/views/blog/index.html.erb:
> ```
> class BlogController < ApplicationController
>   def index
>     render
>   end
> end
> ```
> So will the following (as the default behavior of a controller is to call render() if the action doesn't):
> ```
> class BlogController < ApplicationController
>   def index
>   end
> end
> ```
> And so will this (because the controller will call a template directly if no action method is defined):
> ```
> class BlogController < ApplicationController
> end
> ```

render(text: string)
> Sends the given string to the client. No template interpretation or HTML escaping is performed.
> ```
> class HappyController < ApplicationController
>   def index
>     render(text: "Hello there!")
>   end
> end
> ```

render(inline: string, [type: "erb"|"builder"|"scss"], [locals: hash])

Interprets *string* as the source to a template of the given type, rendering the results back to the client. You can use the :locals hash to set the values of local variables in the template.

The following code adds method_missing() to a controller if the application is running in development mode. If the controller is called with an invalid action, this renders an inline template to display the action's name and a formatted version of the request parameters:

```
class SomeController < ApplicationController
  if RAILS_ENV == "development"
    def method_missing(name, *args)
      render(inline: %{
        <h2>Unknown action: #{name}</h2>
        Here are the request parameters:<br/>
        <%= debug(params) %> })
    end
  end
end
```

render(action: action_name)

Renders the template for a given action in this controller. Sometimes folks use the :action form of render() when they should use redirects. See the discussion starting in Redirects, on page 368, for why this is a bad idea.

```
def display_cart
  if @cart.empty?
    render(action: :index)
  else
    # ...
  end
end
```

Note that calling render(:action...) doesn't call the action method; it simply displays the template. If the template needs instance variables, these must be set up by the method that calls the render() method.

Let's repeat this, because this is a mistake that beginners often make: calling render(:action...) doesn't invoke the action method. It simply renders that action's default template.

render(template: name, [locals: hash])

Renders a template and arranges for the resulting text to be sent back to the client. The :template value must contain both the controller and action parts of the new name, separated by a forward slash. The following code will render the template app/views/blog/short_list:

```
class BlogController < ApplicationController
  def index
    render(template: "blog/short_list")
  end
end
```

render(file: path)
> Renders a view that may be entirely outside of your application (perhaps one shared with another Rails application). By default, the file is rendered without using the current layout. This can be overridden with layout: true.

render(partial: name, ...)
> Renders a partial template. We talk about partial templates in depth in Partial-Page Templates, on page 402.

render(nothing: true)
> Returns nothing—sends an empty body to the browser.

render(xml: stuff)
> Renders *stuff* as text, forcing the content type to be application/xml.

render(json: stuff, [callback: hash])
> Renders *stuff* as JSON, forcing the content type to be application/json. Specifying :callback will cause the result to be wrapped in a call to the named callback function.

render(:update) do |page| ... end
> Renders the block as an RJS template, passing in the page object.
> ```
> render(:update) do |page|
>   page[:cart].replace_html partial: 'cart', object: @cart
>   page[:cart].visual_effect :blind_down if @cart.total_items == 1
> end
> ```

All forms of render() take optional :status, :layout, and :content_type parameters. The :status parameter provides the value used in the status header in the HTTP response. It defaults to "200 OK". Do not use render() with a 3xx status to do redirects; Rails has a redirect() method for this purpose.

The :layout parameter determines whether the result of the rendering will be wrapped by a layout. (We first came across layouts in Iteration C2: Adding a Page Layout, on page 105. We'll look at them in depth starting in Reducing Maintenance with Layouts and Partials, on page 398.) If the parameter is false, no layout will be applied. If set to nil or true, a layout will be applied only if there's one associated with the current action. If the :layout parameter has a string as a value, it'll be taken as the name of the layout to use when rendering. A layout is never applied when the :nothing option is in effect.

The :content_type parameter lets you specify a value that will be passed to the browser in the Content-Type HTTP header.

Sometimes it's useful to be able to capture what would otherwise be sent to the browser in a string. The render_to_string() method takes the same parameters as render() but returns the result of rendering as a string—the rendering isn't stored in the response object and so won't be sent to the user unless you take some additional steps.

Calling render_to_string doesn't count as a real render. You can invoke the real render method later without getting a DoubleRender error.

Sending Files and Other Data

We've looked at rendering templates and sending strings in the controller. The third type of response is to send data (typically, but not necessarily, file contents) to the client.

send_data(data, options...)

This sends a data stream to the client. Typically the browser will use a combination of the content type and the disposition, both set in the options, to determine what to do with this data.

```
def sales_graph
  png_data = Sales.plot_for(Date.today.month)
  send_data(png_data, type: "image/png", disposition: "inline")
end
```

The options are as follows:

:disposition *(string)*
> Suggests to the browser that the file should be displayed inline (option inline) or downloaded and saved (option attachment, the default).

:filename *string*
> A suggestion to the browser of the default filename to use when saving this data.

:status *(string)*
> The status code (defaults to "200 OK").

:type *(string)*
> The content type, defaulting to application/octet-stream.

:url_based_filename *boolean*
> If true and :filename isn't set, this option prevents Rails from providing the basename of the file in the Content-Disposition header. Specifying

the basename of the file is necessary to make some browsers handle i18n filenames correctly.

A related method is send_file, which sends the contents of a file to the client.

send_file(path, options...)

This sends the given file to the client. The method sets the Content-Length, Content-Type, Content-Disposition, and Content-Transfer-Encoding headers.

:buffer_size (number)
: The amount sent to the browser in each write if streaming is enabled (:stream is true).

:disposition (string)
: Suggests to the browser that the file should be displayed inline (option inline) or downloaded and saved (option attachment, the default).

:filename (string)
: A suggestion to the browser of the default filename to use when saving the file. If not set, defaults to the filename part of *path*.

:status string
: The status code (defaults to "200 OK").

:stream (true or false)
: If false, the entire file is read into server memory and sent to the client. Otherwise, the file is read and written to the client in :buffer_size chunks.

:type (string)
: The content type, defaulting to application/octet-stream.

You can set additional headers for either send_ method by using the headers attribute in the controller:

```
def send_secret_file
  send_file("/files/secret_list")
  headers["Content-Description"] = "Top secret"
end
```

We show how to upload files starting in Uploading Files to Rails Applications, on page 387.

Redirects

An HTTP redirect is sent from a server to a client in response to a request. In effect, it says, "I'm done processing this request, and you should go here to see the results." The redirect response includes a URL that the client should try next along with some status information saying whether this redirection is permanent (status code 301) or temporary (307). Redirects are sometimes used when web pages are reorganized; clients accessing pages in the old locations will get referred to the page's new home. More commonly, Rails applications use redirects to pass the processing of a request off to some other action.

Redirects are handled behind the scenes by web browsers. Normally, the only way you'll know that you've been redirected is a slight delay and the fact that the URL of the page you're viewing will have changed from the one you requested. This last point is important—as far as the browser is concerned, a redirect from a server acts pretty much the same as having an end user enter the new destination URL manually.

Redirects turn out to be important when writing well-behaved web applications. Let's look at a basic blogging application that supports comment posting. After a user has posted a comment, our application should redisplay the article, presumably with the new comment at the end.

It's tempting to code this using logic such as the following:

```
class BlogController
  def display
    @article = Article.find(params[:id])
  end

  def add_comment
    @article = Article.find(params[:id])
    comment  = Comment.new(params[:comment])
    @article.comments << comment
    if @article.save
      flash[:note] = "Thank you for your valuable comment"
    else
      flash[:note] = "We threw your worthless comment away"
    end
    # DON'T DO THIS
    render(action: 'display')
  end
end
```

The intent here was clearly to display the article after a comment has been posted. To do this, the developer ended the add_comment() method with a call to render(action:'display'). This renders the display view, showing the updated article to the end user. But think of this from the browser's point of view. It sends a URL ending in blog/add_comment and gets back an index listing. As far as the browser is concerned, the current URL is still the one that ends in blog/add_comment. This means that if the user hits Refresh or Reload (perhaps to see whether anyone else has posted a comment), the add_comment URL will be sent again to the application. The user intended to refresh the display, but the application sees a request to add another comment. In a blog application, this kind of unintentional double entry is inconvenient. In an online store, it can get expensive.

In these circumstances, the correct way to show the added comment in the index listing is to redirect the browser to the display action. We do this using the Rails redirect_to() method. If the user subsequently hits Refresh, it will simply reinvoke the display action and not add another comment.

```
def add_comment
  @article = Article.find(params[:id])
  comment = Comment.new(params[:comment])
  @article.comments << comment
  if @article.save
    flash[:note] = "Thank you for your valuable comment"
  else
    flash[:note] = "We threw your worthless comment away"
  end
➤ redirect_to(action: 'display')
end
```

Rails has a lightweight yet powerful redirection mechanism. It can redirect to an action in a given controller (passing parameters), to a URL (on or off the current server), or to the previous page.

Let's look at these three forms in turn:

redirect_to(action: ..., options...) Sends a temporary redirection to the browser based on the values in the options hash. The target URL is generated using url_for(), so this form of redirect_to() has all the smarts of Rails routing code behind it.

redirect_to(path) Redirects to the given path. If the path doesn't start with a protocol (such as http://), the protocol and port of the current request will be prepended. This method doesn't perform any rewriting on the URL, so it shouldn't be used to create paths that are intended to link to actions in the application (unless you generate the path using url_for or a named route URL generator).

```
def save
  order = Order.new(params[:order])
  if order.save
    redirect_to action: "display"
  else
    session[:error_count] ||= 0
    session[:error_count] += 1
    if session[:error_count] < 4
      self.notice = "Please try again"
```

```
    else
      # Give up -- user is clearly struggling
      redirect_to("/help/order_entry.html")
    end
  end
end
```

redirect_to(:back)   Redirects to the URL given by the HTTP_REFERER header in the current request.

```
def save_details
  unless params[:are_you_sure] == 'Y'
    redirect_to(:back)
  else
    # ...
  end
end
```

By default all redirections are flagged as temporary (they'll affect only the current request). When redirecting to a URL, it's possible you might want to make the redirection permanent. In that case, set the status in the response header accordingly:

```
headers["Status"] = "301 Moved Permanently"
redirect_to("http://my.new.home")
```

Because redirect methods send responses to the browser, the same rules apply as for the rendering methods—you can issue only one per request.

So far, we've been looking at requests and responses in isolation. Rails also provides a number of mechanisms that span requests.

Objects and Operations That Span Requests

While the bulk of the state that persists across requests belongs in the database and is accessed via Active Record, some other bits of state have different life spans and need to be managed differently. In the Depot application, while the Cart itself was stored in the database, knowledge of which cart is the current cart was managed by sessions. Flash notices were used to communicate messages such as "Can't delete the last user" to the next request after a redirect. And callbacks were used to extract locale data from the URLs themselves.

In this section, we'll explore each of these mechanisms in turn.

Rails Sessions

A Rails session is a hash-like structure that persists across requests. Unlike raw cookies, sessions can hold any objects (as long as those objects can be marshaled), which makes them ideal for holding state information in web applications. For example, in our store application, we used a session to hold the shopping cart object between requests. The Cart object could be used in our application just like any other object. But Rails arranged things such that the cart was saved at the end of handling each request and, more important, that the correct cart for an incoming request was restored when Rails started to handle that request. Using sessions, we can pretend that our application stays around between requests.

And that leads to an interesting question: exactly where does this data stay around between requests? One choice is for the server to send it down to the client as a cookie. This is the default for Rails. It places limitations on the size and increases the bandwidth but means that there's less for the server to manage and clean up. Note that the contents are (by default) encrypted, which means that users can neither see nor tamper with the contents.

The other option is to store the data on the server. It requires more work to set up and is rarely necessary. First, Rails has to keep track of sessions. It does this by creating (by default) a 32-hex character key (which means there are 16^{32} possible combinations). This key is called the *session ID*, and it's effectively random. Rails arranges to store this session ID as a cookie (with the key _session_id) on the user's browser. Because subsequent requests come into the application from this browser, Rails can recover the session ID.

Second, Rails keeps a persistent store of session data on the server, indexed by the session ID. When a request comes in, Rails looks up the data store using the session ID. The data that it finds there is a serialized Ruby object. It deserializes this and stores the result in the controller's session attribute, where the data is available to our application code. The application can add to and modify this data to its heart's content. When it finishes processing each request, Rails writes the session data back into the data store. There it sits until the next request from this browser comes along.

What should you store in a session? You can store anything you want, subject to a few restrictions and caveats:

- Some restrictions apply on what kinds of object you can store in a session. The details depend on the storage mechanism you choose (which we'll look at shortly). In the general case, objects in a session must be serializable (using Ruby's `Marshal` functions). This means, for example, that you can't store an I/O object in a session.

- If you store any Rails model objects in a session, you'll have to add `model` declarations for them. This causes Rails to preload the model class so that its definition is available when Ruby comes to deserialize it from the session store. If the use of the session is restricted to just one controller, this declaration can go at the top of that controller.

```
class BlogController < ApplicationController
  model :user_preferences
  # . . .
```

However, if the session might get read by another controller (which is likely in any application with multiple controllers), you'll probably want to add the declaration to application_controller.rb in app/controllers.

- You probably don't want to store massive objects in session data—put them in the database and reference them from the session. This is particularly true for cookie-based sessions, where the overall limit is 4 KB.

- You probably don't want to store volatile objects in session data. For example, you might want to keep a tally of the number of articles in a blog and store that in the session for performance reasons. But if you do that, the count won't get updated if some other user adds an article.

  It's tempting to store objects representing the currently logged-in user in session data. This might not be wise if your application needs to be able to invalidate users. Even if a user is disabled in the database, their session data will still reflect a valid status.

  Store volatile data in the database, and reference it from the session instead.

- You probably don't want to store critical information solely in session data. For example, if your application generates an order confirmation number in one request and stores it in session data so that it can be saved to the database when the next request is handled, you risk losing that number if the user deletes the cookie from their browser. Critical information needs to be in the database.

One more caveat—and it's a big one. If you store an object in session data, then the next time you come back to that browser, your application will end up retrieving that object. However, if in the meantime you've updated your application, the object in session data may not agree with the definition of that object's class in your application, and the application will fail while processing the request. You have three options here. One is to store the object in the database using conventional models and keep just the ID of the row in the session. Model objects are far more forgiving of schema changes than the Ruby marshaling library. The second option is to manually delete all the session data stored on your server whenever you change the definition of a class stored in that data.

The third option is slightly more complex. If you add a version number to your session keys and change that number whenever you update the stored data, you'll only ever load data that corresponds with the current version of the application. You can potentially version the classes whose objects are stored in the session and use the appropriate classes depending on the session keys associated with each request. This last idea can be a lot of work, so you'll need to decide whether it's worth the effort.

Because the session store is hash-like, you can save multiple objects in it, each with its own key.

There's no need to also disable sessions for particular actions. Because sessions are lazily loaded, simply don't reference a session in any action in which you don't need a session.

Session Storage

Rails has a number of options when it comes to storing your session data. Each has good and bad points. We'll start by listing the options and then compare them at the end.

The session_store attribute of ActionController::Base determines the session storage mechanism—set this attribute to a class that implements the storage strategy. This class must be defined in the ActiveSupport::Cache::Store module. You use symbols to name the session storage strategy; the symbol is converted into a CamelCase class name.

session_store = :cookie_store
> This is the default session storage mechanism used by Rails, starting with version 2.0. This format represents objects in their marshaled form, which allows any serializable data to be stored in sessions but is limited to 4 KB total. This is the option we used in the Depot application.

session_store = :active_record_store

> You can use the activerecord-session_store gem[2] to store your session data in your application's database using ActiveRecordStore.

session_store = :drb_store

> DRb is a protocol that allows Ruby processes to share objects over a network connection. Using the DRbStore database manager, Rails stores session data on a DRb server (which you manage outside the web application). Multiple instances of your application, potentially running on distributed servers, can access the same DRb store. DRb uses Marshal to serialize objects.

session_store = :mem_cache_store

> memcached is a freely available, distributed object caching system maintained by Dormando.[3] memcached is more complex to use than the other alternatives and is probably interesting only if you're already using it for other reasons at your site.

session_store = :memory_store

> This option stores the session data locally in the application's memory. Because no serialization is involved, any object can be stored in an in-memory session. As we'll see in a minute, this generally isn't a good idea for Rails applications.

session_store = :file_store

> Session data is stored in flat files. It's pretty much useless for Rails applications because the contents must be strings. This mechanism supports the additional configuration options :prefix, :suffix, and :tmpdir.

Comparing Session Storage Options

With all these session options to choose from, which should you use in your application? As always, the answer is "it depends."

When it comes to performance, there are few absolutes, and everyone's context is different. Your hardware, network latencies, database choices, and possibly even the weather will impact how all the components of session storage interact. Our best advice is to start with the simplest workable solution and then monitor it. If it starts to slow you down, find out why before jumping out of the frying pan.

---

2. https://github.com/rails/activerecord-session_store#installation
3. http://memcached.org/

If you have a high-volume site, keeping the size of the session data small and going with cookie_store is the way to go.

If we rule out memory store as being too simplistic, file store as too restrictive, and memcached as overkill, the server-side choices boil down to CookieStore, Active Record store, and DRb-based storage. Should you need to store more in a session than you can with cookies, we recommend you start with an Active Record solution. If, as your application grows, you find this becoming a bottleneck, you can migrate to a DRb-based solution.

Session Expiry and Cleanup

One problem with all the server-side session storage solutions is that each new session adds something to the session store. This means you'll eventually need to do some housekeeping or you'll run out of server resources.

Another reason to tidy up sessions is that many applications don't want a session to last forever. Once a user has logged in from a particular browser, the application might want to enforce a rule that the user stays logged in only as long as they're active; when they log out or some fixed time after they last use the application, their session should be terminated.

You can sometimes achieve this effect by expiring the cookie holding the session ID. But this is open to end-user abuse. Worse, it's hard to synchronize the expiry of a cookie on the browser with the tidying up of the session data on the server.

We therefore suggest you expire sessions by simply removing their server-side session data. Should a browser request subsequently arrive containing a session ID for data that's been deleted, the application will receive no session data; the session will effectively not be there.

Implementing this expiration depends on the storage mechanism being used.

For Active Record–based session storage, use the updated_at columns in the sessions table. You can delete all sessions that haven't been modified in the last hour (ignoring daylight saving time changes) by having your sweeper task issue SQL such as this:

```
delete from sessions
 where now() - updated_at > 3600;
```

For DRb-based solutions, expiry takes place within the DRb server process. You'll probably want to record timestamps alongside the entries in the session data hash. You can run a separate thread (or even a separate process) that periodically deletes the entries in this hash.

In all cases, your application can help this process by calling reset_session() to delete sessions when they're no longer needed (for example, when a user logs out).

Flash: Communicating Between Actions

When we use redirect_to() to transfer control to another action, the browser generates a separate request to invoke that action. That request will be handled by our application in a fresh instance of a controller object—instance variables that were set in the original action aren't available to the code handling the redirected action. But sometimes we need to communicate between these two instances. We can do this using a facility called the *flash*.

The flash is a temporary scratchpad for values. It's organized like a hash and stored in the session data, so you can store values associated with keys and later retrieve them. It has one special property. By default, values stored into the flash during the processing of a request will be available during the processing of the immediately following request. Once that second request has been processed, those values are removed from the flash.

Probably the most common use of the flash is to pass error and informational strings from one action to the next. The intent here is that the first action notices some condition, creates a message describing that condition, and redirects to a separate action. By storing the message in the flash, the second action is able to access the message text and use it in a view. An example of such usage can be found in Iteration E1 on page 134.

It's sometimes convenient to use the flash as a way of passing messages into a template in the current action. For example, our display() method might want to output a cheery banner if there isn't another, more pressing note. It doesn't need that message to be passed to the next action—it's for use in the current request only. To do this, it could use flash.now, which updates the flash but doesn't add to the session data.

While flash.now creates a transient flash entry, flash.keep does the opposite, making entries that are currently in the flash stick around for another request cycle. If you pass no parameters to flash.keep, then all the flash contents are preserved.

Flashes can store more than just text messages—you can use them to pass all kinds of information between actions. Obviously, for longer-term information you'd want to use the session (probably in conjunction with your database) to store the data, but the flash is great if you want to pass parameters from one request to the next.

Because the flash data is stored in the session, all the usual rules apply. In particular, every object must be serializable. We strongly recommend passing only basic objects like Strings or Hashes in the flash.

Callbacks

Callbacks enable you to write code in your controllers that wrap the processing performed by actions—you can write a chunk of code once and have it be called before or after any number of actions in your controller (or your controller's subclasses). This turns out to be a powerful facility. Using callbacks, we can implement authentication schemes, logging, response compression, and even response customization.

Rails supports three types of callbacks: before, after, and around. Such callbacks are called just prior to and/or just after the execution of actions. Depending on how you define them, they either run as methods inside the controller or are passed to the controller object when they are run. Either way, they get access to details of the request and response objects, along with the other controller attributes.

Before and After Callbacks

As their names suggest, before and after callbacks are invoked before or after an action. Rails maintains two chains of callbacks for each controller. When a controller is about to run an action, it executes all the callbacks on the before chain. It executes the action before running the callbacks on the after chain.

Callbacks can be passive, monitoring activity performed by a controller. They can also take a more active part in request handling. If a before action callback returns false, then processing of the callback chain terminates and the action isn't run. A callback may also render output or redirect requests, in which case the original action never gets invoked.

Callback declarations also accept blocks and the names of classes. If a block is specified, it'll be called with the current controller as a parameter. If a class is given, its filter() class method will be called with the controller as a parameter.

By default, callbacks apply to all actions in a controller (and any subclasses of that controller). You can modify this with the :only option, which takes one or more actions on which the callback is invoked, and the :except option, which lists actions to be excluded from callback.

The before_action and after_action declarations append to the controller's chain of callbacks. Use the variants prepend_before_action() and prepend_after_action() to put callbacks at the front of the chain.

After callbacks can be used to modify the outbound response, changing the headers and content if required. Some applications use this technique to perform global replacements in the content generated by the controller's templates (for example, by substituting a customer's name for the string <customer/> in the response body). Another use might be compressing the response if the user's browser supports it.

Around callbacks wrap the execution of actions. You can write an around callback in two different styles. In the first, the callback is a single chunk of code. That code is called before the action is executed. If the callback code invokes yield, the action is executed. When the action completes, the callback code continues executing.

Thus, the code before the yield is like a before action callback, and the code after is the after action callback. If the callback code never invokes yield, the action isn't run—this way you can achieve the same result as a before action callback returning false.

The benefit of around callbacks is that they can retain context across the invocation of the action.

As well as passing around_action the name of a method, you can pass it a block or a filter class.

If you use a block as a callback, it'll be passed two parameters: the controller object and a proxy for the action. Use call() on this second parameter to invoke the original action.

A second form allows you to pass an object as a callback. This object should implement a method called filter(). This method will be passed the controller object. It yields to invoke the action.

Like before and after callbacks, around callbacks take :only and :except parameters.

Around callbacks are (by default) added to the callback chain differently: the first around action callback added executes first. Subsequently added around callbacks will be nested within existing around callbacks.

Callback Inheritance

If you subclass a controller containing callbacks, the callbacks will be run on the child objects as well as in the parent. But callbacks defined in the children won't run in the parent.

If you don't want a particular callback to run in a child controller, you can override the default processing with the skip_before_action and skip_after_action declarations. These accept the :only and :except parameters.

You can use skip_action to skip any action callback (before, after, and around). However, it works only for callbacks that were specified as the (symbol) name of a method.

What We Just Did

We learned how Action Dispatch and Action Controller cooperate to enable our server to respond to requests. The importance of this can't be emphasized enough. In nearly every application, this is the primary place where the creativity of your application is expressed. While Active Record and Action View are hardly passive, our routes and our controllers are where the action is.

We started this chapter by covering the concept of REST, which was the inspiration for the way in which Rails approaches the routing of requests. We saw how this provided seven basic actions as a starting point and how to add more actions. We also saw how to select a data representation (for example, JSON or XML). And we covered how to test routes.

We then covered the environment that Action Controller provides for your actions as well as the methods it provides for rendering and redirecting. Finally, we covered sessions, flash, and callbacks, each of which is available for use in your application's controllers.

Along the way, we showed how these concepts were used in the Depot application. Now that you've seen each in use and have been exposed to the theory behind each, how you combine and use these concepts is limited only by your own creativity.

In the next chapter, we'll cover the remaining component of Action Pack, namely, Action View, which handles the rendering of results.

In this chapter, you'll see:
- Templates
- Forms including fields and uploading files
- Helpers
- Layouts and partials

CHAPTER 22

Action View

We've seen how the routing component determines which controller to use and how the controller chooses an action. We've seen how the controller and action between them decide what to render to the user. Normally, rendering takes place at the end of the action and involves a template. That's what this chapter is all about. Action View encapsulates all the functionality needed to render templates, most commonly generating HTML, XML, or JavaScript back to the user. As its name suggests, Action View is the view part of our MVC trilogy.

In this chapter, we'll start with templates, for which Rails provides a range of options. We'll then cover a number of ways in which users provide input: forms, file uploads, and links. We'll complete this chapter by looking at a number of ways to reduce maintenance using helpers, layouts, and partials.

Using Templates

When you write a view, you're writing a template: something that will get expanded to generate the final result. To understand how these templates work, we need to look at three areas:

- Where the templates go
- The environment they run in
- What goes inside them

Where Templates Go

The render() method expects to find templates in the app/views directory of the current application. Within this directory, the convention is to have a separate subdirectory for the views of each controller. Our Depot application, for instance, includes products and store controllers. As a result, our application has templates in app/views/products and app/views/store. Each directory typically contains templates named after the actions in the corresponding controller.

You can also have templates that aren't named after actions. You render such
templates from the controller using calls such as these:

```
render(action:    'fake_action_name')
render(template:  'controller/name')
render(file:      'dir/template')
```

The last of these allows you to store templates anywhere on your filesystem.
This is useful if you want to share templates across applications.

The Template Environment

Templates contain a mixture of fixed text and code. The code in the template
adds dynamic content to the response. That code runs in an environment
that gives it access to the information set up by the controller:

- All instance variables of the controller are also available in the template.
  This is how actions communicate data to the templates.

- The controller object's flash, headers, logger, params, request, response, and session
  are available as accessor methods in the view. Apart from the flash, view
  code probably shouldn't use these directly, because the responsibility for
  handling them should rest with the controller. However, we do find this
  useful when debugging. For example, the following html.erb template uses
  the debug() method to display the contents of the session, the details of
  the parameters, and the current response:

  ```
  <h4>Session</h4>   <%= debug(session) %>
  <h4>Params</h4>    <%= debug(params) %>
  <h4>Response</h4>  <%= debug(response) %>
  ```

- The current controller object is accessible using the attribute named controller. This allows the template to call any public method in the controller
  (including the methods in ActionController::Base).

- The path to the base directory of the templates is stored in the attribute
  base_path.

What Goes in a Template

Out of the box, Rails supports two types of templates:

- ERB templates are a mixture of content and embedded Ruby. They're
  typically used to generate HTML pages.

- Jbuilder[1] templates generate JSON responses.

---

1. https://github.com/rails/jbuilder

By far, the one that you'll be using the most will be ERB. In fact, you made extensive use of ERB templates in developing the Depot application.

So far in this chapter, we've focused on producing output. In Chapter 21, Action Dispatch and Action Controller, on page 349, we focused on processing input. In a well-designed application, these two aren't unrelated: the output we produce contains forms, links, and buttons that guide the end user to producing the next set of inputs. As you might expect by now, Rails provides a considerable amount of help in this area too.

Generating Forms

HTML provides a number of elements, attributes, and attribute values that control how input is gathered. You certainly could hand-code your form directly into the template, but there's no need to.

In this section, we'll cover a number of *helpers* that Rails provides that assist with this process. In Using Helpers, on page 391, we'll show you how you can create your own helpers.

HTML provides a number of ways to collect data in forms. A few of the more common means are shown in the following screenshot. Note that the form itself isn't representative of any sort of typical use; in general, you'll use only a subset of these methods to collect data.

Let's look at the template that was used to produce that form:

rails80/views/app/views/form/input.html.erb
```erb
<%= form_for(:model) do |form| %>
  <p>
    <%= form.label :input %>
    <%= form.text_field :input, :placeholder => 'Enter text here...' %>
  </p>
```

```erb
     <p>
       <%= form.label :address, :style => 'float: left' %>
       <%= form.text_area :address, :rows => 3, :cols => 40 %>
10   </p>

     <p>
       <%= form.label :color %>:
       <%= form.radio_button :color, 'red' %>
15     <%= form.label :red %>
       <%= form.radio_button :color, 'yellow' %>
       <%= form.label :yellow %>
       <%= form.radio_button :color, 'green' %>
       <%= form.label :green %>
20   </p>

     <p>
       <%= form.label 'condiment' %>:
       <%= form.check_box :ketchup %>
25     <%= form.label :ketchup %>
       <%= form.check_box :mustard %>
       <%= form.label :mustard %>
       <%= form.check_box :mayonnaise %>
       <%= form.label :mayonnaise %>
30   </p>

     <p>
       <%= form.label :priority %>:
       <%= form.select :priority, (1..10) %>
35   </p>

     <p>
       <%= form.label :start %>:
       <%= form.date_select :start %>
40   </p>

     <p>
       <%= form.label :alarm %>:
       <%= form.time_select :alarm %>
45   </p>
     <% end %>
```

In that template, you'll see a number of labels, such as the one on line 3. You use labels to associate text with an input field for a specified attribute. The text of the label will default to the attribute name unless you specify it explicitly.

You use the text_field() and text_area() helpers (on lines 4 and 9, respectively) to gather single-line and multiline input fields. You may specify a placeholder, which will be displayed inside the field until the user provides a value. Not every browser supports this function, but those that don't simply will display an empty box. Since this will degrade gracefully, there's no need for you to design to the least common denominator—make use of this feature, because those who can see it will benefit from it immediately.

Placeholders are one of the many small "fit and finish" features provided with HTML5, and once again, Rails is ready even if the browser your users have installed is not. You can use the search_field(), telephone_field(), url_field(), email_field(), number_field(), and range_field() helpers to prompt for a specific type of input. How the browser will make use of this information varies. Some may display the field slightly differently to more clearly identify its function. Safari on Mac, for example, will display search fields with rounded corners and will insert a little x for clearing the field once data entry begins. Some may provide added validation. For example, Opera will validate URL fields prior to submission. The iPad will even adjust the virtual onscreen keyboard to provide ready access to characters such as the @ sign when entering an email address.

Although the support for these functions varies by browser, those that don't provide extra support for these functions simply display a plain, unadorned input box. Once again, nothing is gained by waiting. If you have an input field that's expected to contain an email address, don't simply use text_field()—go ahead and start using email_field() now.

Lines 14, 24, and 34 demonstrate three different ways to provide a constrained set of options. Although the display may vary a bit from browser to browser, these approaches are all well supported across all browsers. The select() method is particularly flexible—it can be passed an Enumeration as shown here, an array of pairs of name-value pairs, or a Hash. A number of form options helpers[2] are available to produce such lists from various sources, including the database.

Finally, lines 39 and 44 show prompts for a date and time, respectively. As you might expect by now, Rails provides plenty of options here too.[3]

Not shown in this example are hidden_field() and password_field(). A hidden field isn't displayed at all, but the value is passed back to the server. This may be useful as an alternative to storing transient data in sessions, enabling data from one request to be passed onto the next. Password fields are displayed, but the text entered in them is obscured.

---

2. http://api.rubyonrails.org/classes/ActionView/Helpers/FormOptionsHelper.html
3. http://api.rubyonrails.org/classes/ActionView/Helpers/DateHelper.html

This is more than an adequate starter set for most needs. Should you find that you have additional needs, you're likely to find a helper or gem is already available for you. A good place to start is with the Rails Guides.[4]

Meanwhile, let's explore how the data form's submit is processed.

Processing Forms

In the figure on page 387 we can see how the various attributes in the model pass through the controller to the view, on to the HTML page, and back again into the model. The model object has attributes such as name, country, and password. The template uses helper methods to construct an HTML form to let the user edit the data in the model. Note how the form fields are named. The country attribute, for example, maps to an HTML input field with the name user[country].

When the user submits the form, the raw POST data is sent back to our application. Rails extracts the fields from the form and constructs the params hash. Simple values (such as the id field, extracted by routing from the form action) are stored directly in the hash. But if a parameter name has brackets in it, Rails assumes that it is part of more structured data and constructs a hash to hold the values. Inside this hash, the string inside the brackets acts as the key. This process can repeat if a parameter name has multiple sets of brackets in it.

Form Parameters	Params
id=123	{ id: "123" }
user[name]=Dave	{ user: { name: "Dave" } }
user[address][city]=Wien	{ user: { address: { city: "Wien" } } }

In the final part of the integrated whole, model objects can accept new attribute values from hashes, which allows us to say this:

```
user.update(user_params)
```

Rails integration goes deeper than this. Looking at the .html.erb file in the preceding figure, we can see that the template uses a set of helper methods to create the form's HTML; these are methods such as form_with() and text_field().

Before moving on, it's worth noting that params may be used for more than text. Entire files can be uploaded. We'll cover that next.

---

4. http://guides.rubyonrails.org/form_helpers.html

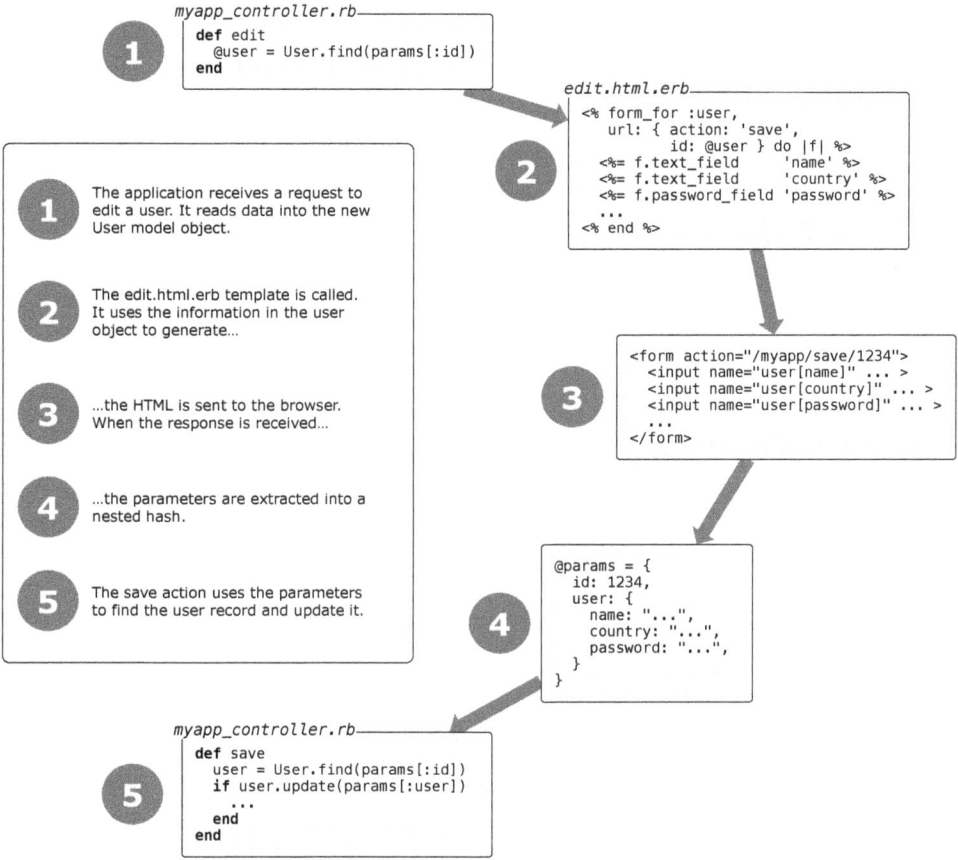

Uploading Files to Rails Applications

Your application may allow users to upload files. For example, a bug-reporting system might let users attach log files and code samples to a problem ticket, or a blogging application could let its users upload a small image to appear next to their articles.

In HTTP, files are uploaded as a *multipart/form-data* POST message. As the name suggests, forms are used to generate this type of message. Within that form, you'll use <input> tags with type="file". When rendered by a browser, this allows the user to select a file by name. When the form is subsequently submitted, the file or files will be sent back along with the rest of the form data.

To illustrate the file upload process, we'll show some code that allows a user to upload an image and display that image alongside a comment. To do this, we first need a pictures table to store the data:

```ruby
# rails80/e1/views/db/migrate/20170425000004_create_pictures.rb
class CreatePictures < ActiveRecord::Migration
  def change
    create_table :pictures do |t|
      t.string :comment
      t.string :name
      t.string :content_type
      # If using MySQL, blobs default to 64k, so we have to give
      # an explicit size to extend them
      t.binary :data, :limit => 1.megabyte
    end
  end
end
```

We'll create a somewhat artificial upload controller just to demonstrate the process. The get action is pretty conventional; it simply creates a new picture object and renders a form:

```ruby
# rails80/e1/views/app/controllers/upload_controller.rb
class UploadController < ApplicationController
  def get
    @picture = Picture.new
  end
  # . . .
  private
    # Never trust parameters from the scary internet, only allow the white
    # list through.
    def picture_params
      params.require(:picture).permit(:comment, :uploaded_picture)
    end
end
```

The get template contains the form that uploads the picture (along with a comment). Note how we override the encoding type to allow data to be sent back with the response:

```erb
<%# rails80/e1/views/app/views/upload/get.html.erb %>
<%= form_for(:picture,
            url: {action: 'save'},
            html: {multipart: true}) do |form| %>

  Comment:           <%= form.text_field("comment") %><br/>
  Upload your picture: <%= form.file_field("uploaded_picture") %><br/>

  <%= submit_tag("Upload file") %>
<% end %>
```

The form has one other subtlety. The picture uploads into an attribute called uploaded_picture. However, the database table doesn't contain a column of that name. That means that there must be some magic happening in the model:

```
rails80/e1/views/app/models/picture.rb
class Picture < ActiveRecord::Base
  validates_format_of :content_type,
                      with: /\Aimage/,
                      message: "must be a picture"

  def uploaded_picture=(picture_field)
    self.name         = base_part_of(picture_field.original_filename)
    self.content_type = picture_field.content_type.chomp
    self.data         = picture_field.read
  end

  def base_part_of(file_name)
    File.basename(file_name).gsub(/[^\w._-]/, '')
  end
end
```

We define an accessor called uploaded_picture=() to receive the file uploaded by the form. The object returned by the form is an interesting hybrid. It's file-like, so we can read its contents with the read() method; that's how we get the image data into the data column. It also has the attributes content_type and original_filename, which let us get at the uploaded file's metadata. Accessor methods pick all this apart, resulting in a single object stored as separate attributes in the database.

Note that we also add a validation to check that the content type is of the form image/*xxx*. We don't want someone uploading JavaScript.

The save action in the controller is totally conventional:

```
rails80/e1/views/app/controllers/upload_controller.rb
def save
  @picture = Picture.new(picture_params)
  if @picture.save
    redirect_to(action: 'show', id: @picture.id)
  else
    render(action: :get)
  end
end
```

Now that we have an image in the database, how do we display it? One way is to give it its own URL and link to that URL from an image tag. For example, we could use a URL such as upload/picture/123 to return the image for picture 123. This would use send_data() to return the image to the browser. Note how we set the content type and filename—this lets browsers interpret the data and supplies a default name should the user choose to save the image:

rails80/e1/views/app/controllers/upload_controller.rb
```ruby
def picture
  @picture = Picture.find(params[:id])
  send_data(@picture.data,
            filename: @picture.name,
            type: @picture.content_type,
            disposition: "inline")
end
```

Finally, we can implement the show action, which displays the comment and the image. The action simply loads the picture model object:

rails80/e1/views/app/controllers/upload_controller.rb
```ruby
def show
  @picture = Picture.find(params[:id])
end
```

In the template, the image tag links back to the action that returns the picture content. In the following screenshot, we can see the get and show actions.

rails80/e1/views/app/views/upload/show.html.erb
```erb
<h3><%= @picture.comment %></h3>

<img src="<%= url_for(:action => 'picture', :id => @picture.id) %>"/>
```

If you'd like an easier way of dealing with uploading and storing images, take a look at Active Storage,[5] which we used in Chapter 16, Task K: Receive Emails and Respond with Rich Text, on page 247.

Forms and uploads are just two examples of helpers that Rails provides. Next we'll show you how you can provide your own helpers and introduce you to a number of other helpers that come with Rails.

---

5. https://edgeguides.rubyonrails.org/active_storage_overview.html

Using Helpers

Earlier we said it's OK to put code in templates. Now we're going to modify that statement. It's perfectly acceptable to put *some* code in templates—that's what makes them dynamic. However, it's poor style to put too much code in templates.

Three main reasons for this stand out. First, the more code you put in the view side of your application, the easier it is to let discipline slip and start adding application-level functionality to the template code. This is definitely poor form; you want to put application stuff in the controller and model layers so that it's available everywhere. This will pay off when you add new ways of viewing the application.

The second reason is that html.erb is basically HTML. When you edit it, you're editing an HTML file. If you have the luxury of having professional designers create your layouts, they'll want to work with HTML. Putting a bunch of Ruby code in there just makes it hard to work with.

The final reason is that code embedded in views is hard to test, whereas code split out into helper modules can be isolated and tested as individual units.

Rails provides a nice compromise in the form of helpers. A *helper* is simply a module containing methods that assist a view. Helper methods are output-centric. They exist to generate HTML (or XML, or JavaScript)—a helper extends the behavior of a template.

Your Own Helpers

By default, each controller gets its own helper module. Additionally, there's an application-wide helper named application_helper.rb. It won't be surprising to learn that Rails makes certain assumptions to help link the helpers into the controller and its views. While all view helpers are available to all controllers, it's often good practice to organize helpers. Helpers that are unique to the views associated with the ProductController tend to be placed in a helper module called ProductHelper in the file product_helper.rb in the app/helpers directory. You don't have to remember all these details—the rails generate controller script creates a stub helper module automatically.

We can use helpers to clean up the application layout a bit. Currently we have the following:

```
<h3><%= @page_title || "Pragmatic Store" %></h3>
```

Let's move the code that works out the page title into a helper method. Because we're in the store controller, we edit the store_helper.rb file in app/helpers:

```
module StoreHelper
  def page_title
    @page_title || "Pragmatic Store"
  end
end
```

Now the view code simply calls the helper method:

```
<h3><%= page_title %></h3>
```

(We might want to eliminate even more duplication by moving the rendering of the entire title into a separate partial template, shared by all the controller's views, but we don't talk about partial templates until Partial-Page Templates, on page 402.)

Helpers for Formatting and Linking

Rails comes with a bunch of built-in helper methods, available to all views. Here, we'll touch on the highlights, but you'll probably want to look at the Action View RDoc for the specifics—there's a lot of functionality in there.

Aside from the general convenience these helpers provide, many of them also handle internationalization and localization. In Chapter 15, Task J: Internationalization, on page 225, we translated much of the application. Many of the helpers we used handled that for us, such as number_to_currency(). It's always a good practice to use Rails helpers where they're appropriate, even if it seems just as easy to hard-code the output you want.

Formatting Helpers

One set of helper methods deals with dates, numbers, and text:

```
<%= distance_of_time_in_words(Time.now, Time.local(2016, 12, 25)) %>
    4 months

<%= distance_of_time_in_words(Time.now, Time.now + 33, include_seconds: false) %>
    1 minute

<%= distance_of_time_in_words(Time.now, Time.now + 33, include_seconds: true) %>
    Half a minute

<%= time_ago_in_words(Time.local(2012, 12, 25)) %>
    7 months

<%= number_to_currency(123.45) %>
    $123.45
```

```erb
<%= number_to_currency(234.56, unit: "CAN$", precision: 0) %>
```
    CAN$235

```erb
<%= number_to_human_size(123_456) %>
```
    120.6 KB

```erb
<%= number_to_percentage(66.66666) %>
```
    66.667%

```erb
<%= number_to_percentage(66.66666, precision: 1) %>
```
    66.7%

```erb
<%= number_to_phone(2125551212) %>
```
    212-555-1212

```erb
<%= number_to_phone(2125551212, area_code: true, delimiter: " ") %>
```
    (212) 555 1212

```erb
<%= number_with_delimiter(12345678) %>
```
    12,345,678

```erb
<%= number_with_delimiter(12345678, delimiter: "_") %>
```
    12_345_678

```erb
<%= number_with_precision(50.0/3, precision: 2) %>
```
    16.67

The debug() method dumps out its parameter using YAML and escapes the result so it can be displayed in an HTML page. This can help when trying to look at the values in model objects or request parameters:

```erb
<%= debug(params) %>
```

```
--- !ruby/hash:HashWithIndifferentAccess
name: Dave
language: Ruby
action: objects
controller: test
```

Yet another set of helpers deals with text, using methods to truncate strings and highlight words in a string:

```erb
<%= simple_format(@trees) %>
```

Formats a string, honoring line and paragraph breaks. You could give it the plain text of the Joyce Kilmer poem *Trees*,[6] and it would add the HTML to format it as follows.

---

6. https://www.poetryfoundation.org/poetrymagazine/poems/12744/trees

```
<p> I think that I shall never see <br />A poem lovely as a tree.</p> <p>A
tree whose hungry mouth is prest <br />Against the sweet earth's flowing
breast; </p>
```

`<%= excerpt(@trees, "lovely", 8) %>`

...A poem lovely as a tre...

`<%= highlight(@trees, "tree") %>`

I think that I shall never see A poem lovely as a `<strong class="high‐light">tree</strong>`. A `<strong class="highlight">tree</strong>` whose hungry mouth is prest Against the sweet earth's flowing breast;

`<%= truncate(@trees, length: 20) %>`

I think that I sh...

There's a method to pluralize nouns:

`<%= pluralize(1, "person") %>` but `<%= pluralize(2, "person") %>`

1 person but 2 people

If you'd like to do what the fancy websites do and automatically hyperlink URLs and email addresses, there are helpers to do that. Another one strips hyperlinks from text.

Back in Iteration A2 on page 77, we saw how the cycle() helper can be used to return the successive values from a sequence each time it's called, repeating the sequence as necessary. This is often used to create alternating styles for the rows in a table or list. The current_cycle() and reset_cycle() methods are also available.

Finally, if you're writing something like a blog site or you're allowing users to add comments to your store, you could offer them the ability to create their text in Markdown (BlueCloth)[7] or Textile (RedCloth)[8] format. These are formatters that take text written in human-friendly markup and convert it into HTML.

Linking to Other Pages and Resources

The ActionView::Helpers::AssetTagHelper and ActionView::Helpers::UrlHelper modules contain a number of methods that let you reference resources external to the current template. Of these, the most commonly used is link_to(), which creates a hyperlink to another action in your application:

`<%= link_to "Add Comment", new_comments_path %>`

---

7. https://github.com/rtomayko/rdiscount
8. http://redcloth.org/

The first parameter to link_to() is the text displayed for the link. The next is a string or hash specifying the link's target.

An optional third parameter provides HTML attributes for the generated link:

```
<%= link_to "Delete", product_path(@product),
    { class: "dangerous", method: 'delete' }
%>
```

This third parameter also supports two additional options that modify the behavior of the link. Each requires JavaScript to be enabled in the browser.

The :method option is a hack—it allows you to make the link look to the application as if the request were created by a POST, PUT, PATCH, or DELETE, rather than the normal GET method. This is done by creating a chunk of JavaScript that submits the request when the link is clicked—if JavaScript is disabled in the browser, a GET will be generated.

The :data parameter allows you to set custom data attributes. The most commonly used one is the :confirm option, which takes a short message. If present, an unobtrusive JavaScript driver will display the message and get the user's confirmation before the link is followed:

```
<%= link_to "Delete", product_path(@product),
                method: :delete,
                data: { confirm: 'Are you sure?' }
%>
```

The button_to() method works the same as link_to() but generates a button in a self-contained form rather than a straight hyperlink. This is the preferred method of linking to actions that have side effects. However, these buttons live in their own forms, which imposes a couple of restrictions: they cannot appear inline, and they cannot appear inside other forms.

Rails has conditional linking methods that generate hyperlinks if some condition is met or just return the link text otherwise. link_to_if() and link_to_unless() take a condition parameter, followed by the regular parameters to link_to. If the condition is true (for link_to_if) or false (for link_to_unless), a regular link will be created using the remaining parameters. If not, the name will be added as plain text (with no hyperlink).

The link_to_unless_current() helper creates menus in sidebars where the current page name is shown as plain text and the other entries are hyperlinks:

```erb
<ul>
<% %w{ create list edit save logout }.each do |action| %>
  <li>
    <%= link_to_unless_current(action.capitalize, action: action) %>
  </li>
<% end %>
</ul>
```

The link_to_unless_current() helper may also be passed a block that's evaluated only if the current action is the action given, effectively providing an alternative to the link. There's also a current_page() helper method that simply tests whether the current page was generated by the given options.

As with url_for(), link_to() and friends also support absolute URLs:

```erb
<%= link_to("Help", "http://my.site/help/index.html") %>
```

The image_tag() helper creates <img> tags. Optional :size parameters (of the form *widthxheight*) or separate width and height parameters define the size of the image:

```erb
<%= image_tag("/assets/dave.png", class: "bevel", size: "80x120") %>
<%= image_tag("/assets/andy.png", class: "bevel",
              width: "80", height: "120") %>
```

If you don't give an :alt option, Rails synthesizes one for you using the image's filename. If the image path doesn't start with a / character, Rails assumes that it lives under the app/assets/images directory.

You can make images into links by combining link_to() and image_tag():

```erb
<%= link_to(image_tag("delete.png", size: "50x22"),
            product_path(@product),
            data: { confirm: "Are you sure?" },
            method: :delete)
%>
```

The mail_to() helper creates a mailto: hyperlink that, when clicked, normally loads the client's email application. It takes an email address, the name of the link, and a set of HTML options. Within these options, you can also use :bcc, :cc, :body, and :subject to initialize the corresponding email fields. Finally, the magic option encode: "javascript" uses client-side JavaScript to obscure the generated link, making it harder for spiders to harvest email addresses from your site. Unfortunately, it also means your users won't see the email link if they have JavaScript disabled in their browsers.

```erb
<%= mail_to("support@pragprog.com", "Contact Support",
            subject: "Support question from #{@user.name}",
            encode:  "javascript") %>
```

As a weaker form of obfuscation, you can use the :replace_at and :replace_dot options to replace the at sign and dots in the displayed name with other strings. This is unlikely to fool harvesters.

The AssetTagHelper module also includes helpers that make it easy to link to style sheets and JavaScript code from your pages and to create autodiscovery Atom feed links. We created links in the layouts for the Depot application using the stylesheet_link_tag() and javascript_importmap_tags() methods in the head:

```erb
rails80/depot_r/app/views/layouts/application.html.erb
<!DOCTYPE html>
<html>
  <head>
  <title><%= content_for(:title) || "Pragprog Books Online Store" %></title>
    <meta name="viewport" content="width=device-width,initial-scale=1">
    <meta name="apple-mobile-web-app-capable" content="yes">
    <meta name="mobile-web-app-capable" content="yes">
    <%= csrf_meta_tags %>
    <%= csp_meta_tag %>

    <%= yield :head %>

    <%# Enable PWA manifest for installable apps (make sure to enable in
        config/routes.rb too!) %>
    <%#= tag.link rel: "manifest", href: pwa_manifest_path(format: :json) %>

    <link rel="icon" href="/icon.png" type="image/png">
    <link rel="icon" href="/icon.svg" type="image/svg+xml">
    <link rel="apple-touch-icon" href="/icon.png">

    <%# Includes all stylesheet files in app/assets/stylesheets %>
    <%= stylesheet_link_tag :app, "data-turbo-track": "reload" %>
    <%= javascript_importmap_tags %>
  </head>
```

The javascript_importmap_tags() method produces a list JavaScript filenames (assumed to live in app/javascript) which enables these resources to be imported by your application.

By default, image and style sheet assets are assumed to live in the images and stylesheets directories relative to the application's assets directory. If the path given to an asset tag method starts with a forward slash, then the path is assumed to be absolute and no prefix is applied. Sometimes it makes sense to move this static content onto a separate box or to different locations on the current box. Do this by setting the configuration variable asset_host:

```
config.action_controller.asset_host = "http://media.my.url/assets"
```

Although this list of helpers may seem to be comprehensive, Rails provides many more; new helpers are introduced with each release, and a select few are retired or moved off into a plugin where they can be evolved at a different pace than Rails.

Reducing Maintenance with Layouts and Partials

So far in this chapter we've looked at templates as isolated chunks of code and HTML. But one of the driving ideas behind Rails is honoring the DRY principle and eliminating the need for duplication. The average website, though, has lots of duplication:

- Many pages share the same tops, tails, and sidebars.
- Multiple pages may contain the same snippets of rendered HTML (a blog site, for example, may display an article in multiple places).
- The same functionality may appear in multiple places. Many sites have a standard search component or a polling component that appears in most of the sites' sidebars.

Rails provides both layouts and partials that reduce the need for duplication in these three situations.

Layouts

Rails allows you to render pages that are nested inside other rendered pages. Typically this feature is used to put the content from an action within a standard site-wide page frame (title, footer, and sidebar). In fact, if you've been using the generate script to create scaffold-based applications, then you've been using these layouts all along.

When Rails honors a request to render a template from within a controller, it actually renders two templates. Obviously, it renders the one you ask for (or the default template named after the action if you don't explicitly render anything). But Rails also tries to find and render a layout template (we'll talk about how it finds the layout in a second). If it finds the layout, it inserts the action-specific output into the HTML produced by the layout.

Let's look at a layout template:

```
<html>
  <head>
    <title>Form: <%= controller.action_name %></title>
    <%= stylesheet_link_tag 'scaffold' %>
  </head>
```

```
    <body>
      <%= yield :layout %>
    </body>
</html>
```

The layout sets out a standard HTML page, with the head and body sections. It uses the current action name as the page title and includes a CSS file. In the body is a call to yield. This is where the magic takes place. When the template for the action was rendered, Rails stored its content, labeling it :layout. Inside the layout template, calling yield retrieves this text. In fact, :layout is the default content returned when rendering, so you can write yield instead of yield :layout. We personally prefer the slightly more explicit version.

Suppose the my_action.html.erb template contained this:

```
<h1><%= @msg %></h1>
```

And also suppose the controller set @msg to Hello, World!. Then the browser would see the following HTML:

```
<html>
  <head>
    <title>Form: my_action</title>
    <link href="/stylesheets/scaffold.css" media="screen"
          rel="Stylesheet" type="text/css" />
  </head>
  <body>
    <h1>Hello, World!</h1>
  </body>
</html>
```

Locating Layout Files

As you've probably come to expect, Rails does a good job of providing defaults for layout file locations, but you can override the defaults if you need something different.

Layouts are controller-specific. If the current request is being handled by a controller called *store*, Rails will by default look for a layout called store (with the usual .html.erb or .xml.builder extension) in the app/views/layouts directory. If you create a layout called application in the layouts directory, it will be applied to all controllers that don't otherwise have a layout defined for them.

You can override this using the layout declaration inside a controller. The most basic invocation is to pass it the name of a layout as a string. The following declaration will make the template in the file standard.html.erb or standard.xml.builder the layout for all actions in the store controller.

The layout file will be looked for in the app/views/layouts directory:

```
class StoreController < ApplicationController
  layout "standard"
  # ...
end
```

You can qualify which actions will have the layout applied to them using the :only and :except qualifiers:

```
class StoreController < ApplicationController
  layout "standard", except: [ :rss, :atom ]
  # ...
end
```

Specifying a layout of nil turns off layouts for a controller.

Sometimes you need to change the appearance of a set of pages at runtime. For example, a blogging site might offer a different-looking side menu if the user is logged in, or a store site might have different-looking pages if the site is down for maintenance. Rails supports this need with dynamic layouts. If the parameter to the layout declaration is a symbol, it's taken to be the name of a controller instance method that returns the name of the layout to be used:

```
class StoreController < ApplicationController
  layout :determine_layout
  # ...
  private

  def determine_layout
    if Store.is_closed?
      "store_down"
    else
      "standard"
    end
  end
end
```

Subclasses of a controller use the parent's layout unless they override it using the layout directive. Finally, individual actions can choose to render using a specific layout (or with no layout at all) by passing render() the :layout option:

```
def rss
  render(layout: false)   # never use a layout
end
```

```
def checkout
  render(layout: "layouts/simple")
end
```

Passing Data to Layouts

Layouts have access to all the same data that's available to conventional templates. In addition, any instance variables set in the normal template will be available in the layout (because the regular template is rendered before the layout is invoked). This might be used to parameterize headings or menus in the layout. For example, the layout might contain this:

```
<html>
  <head>
    <title><%= @title %></title>
    <%= stylesheet_link_tag 'scaffold' %>
  </head>
  <body>
    <h1><%= @title %></h1>
    <%= yield :layout %>
  </body>
</html>
```

An individual template could set the title by assigning to the @title variable:

```
<% @title = "My Wonderful Life" %>
<p>
  Dear Diary:
</p>
<p>
  Yesterday I had pizza for dinner. It was nice.
</p>
```

We can take this further. The same mechanism that lets us use yield :layout to embed the rendering of a template into the layout also lets you generate arbitrary content in a template, which can then be embedded into any template.

For example, different templates may need to add their own template-specific items to the standard page sidebar. We'll use the content_for mechanism in those templates to define content and then use yield in the layout to embed this content into the sidebar.

In each regular template, use a content_for to give a name to the content rendered inside a block. This content will be stored inside Rails and won't contribute to the output generated by the template:

```
<h1>Regular Template</h1>

<% content_for(:sidebar) do %>
  <ul>
```

```
      <li>this text will be rendered</li>
      <li>and saved for later</li>
      <li>it may contain <%= "dynamic" %> stuff</li>
  </ul>
<% end %>
<p>
  Here's the regular stuff that will appear on
  the page rendered by this template.
</p>
```

Then, in the layout, use yield :sidebar to include this block in the page's sidebar:

```
<!DOCTYPE .... >
<html>
  <body>
    <div class="sidebar">
      <p>
        Regular sidebar stuff
      </p>
      <div class="page-specific-sidebar">
        <%= yield :sidebar %>
      </div>
    </div>
  </body>
</html>
```

This same technique can be used to add page-specific JavaScript functions into the <head> section of a layout, create specialized menu bars, and so on.

Partial-Page Templates

Web applications commonly display information about the same application object or objects on multiple pages. A shopping cart might display an order line item on the shopping cart page and again on the order summary page. A blog application might display the contents of an article on the main index page and again at the top of a page soliciting comments. Typically this would involve copying snippets of code between the different template pages.

Rails, however, eliminates this duplication with the *partial-page templates* (more frequently called *partials*). You can think of a partial as a kind of subroutine. You invoke it one or more times from within another template, potentially passing it objects to render as parameters. When the partial template finishes rendering, it returns control to the calling template.

Internally, a partial template looks like any other template. Externally, there's a slight difference. The name of the file containing the template code must start with an underscore character, differentiating the source of partial templates from their more complete brothers and sisters.

For example, the partial to render a blog entry might be stored in the file _article.html.erb in the normal views directory, app/views/blog:

```
<div class="article">
  <div class="articleheader">
    <h3><%= article.title %></h3>
  </div>
  <div class="articlebody">
    <%= article.body %>
  </div>
</div>
```

Other templates use the render(partial:) method to invoke this:

```
<%= render(partial: "article", object: @an_article) %>
<h3>Add Comment</h3>
. . .
```

The :partial parameter to render() is the name of the template to render (but without the leading underscore). This name must be both a valid filename and a valid Ruby identifier (so a-b and 20042501 aren't valid names for partials). The :object parameter identifies an object to be passed into the partial. This object will be available within the template via a local variable with the same name as the template. In this example, the @an_article object will be passed to the template, and the template can access it using the local variable article. That's why we could write things such as article.title in the partial.

You can set additional local variables in the template by passing render() a :locals parameter. This takes a hash where the entries represent the names and values of the local variables to set:

```
render(partial: 'article',
       object:  @an_article,
       locals:  { authorized_by: session[:user_name],
                  from_ip:       request.remote_ip })
```

Partials and Collections

Applications commonly need to display collections of formatted entries. A blog might show a series of articles, each with text, author, date, and so on. A store might display entries in a catalog, where each has an image, a description, and a price.

The :collection parameter to render() works in conjunction with the :partial parameter. The :partial parameter lets us use a partial to define the format of an individual entry, and the :collection parameter applies this template to each member of the collection.

To display a list of article model objects using our previously defined _article.html.erb partial, we could write this:

```
<%= render(partial: "article", collection: @article_list) %>
```

Inside the partial, the local variable article will be set to the current article from the collection—the variable is named after the template. In addition, the variable article_counter will have its value set to the index of the current article in the collection.

The optional :spacer_template parameter lets you specify a template that will be rendered between each of the elements in the collection. For example, a view might contain the following:

rails80/e1/views/app/views/partial/_list.html.erb
```
<%= render(partial:         "animal",
           collection:      %w{ ant bee cat dog elk },
           spacer_template: "spacer")
%>
```

This uses _animal.html.erb to render each animal in the given list, rendering the partial _spacer.html.erb between each. Say _animal.html.erb contains this:

rails80/e1/views/app/views/partial/_animal.html.erb
```
<p>The animal is <%= animal %></p>
```

And _spacer.html.erb contains this:

rails80/e1/views/app/views/partial/_spacer.html.erb
```
<hr />
```

Your users would see a list of animal names with a line between each.

Shared Templates

If the first option or :partial parameter to a render call is a String with no slashes, Rails assumes that the target template is in the current controller's view directory. However, if the name contains one or more / characters, Rails assumes that the part up to the last slash is a directory name and the rest is the template name. The directory is assumed to be under app/views. This makes it easy to share partials and subtemplates across controllers.

The convention among Rails applications is to store these shared partials in a subdirectory of app/views called shared. Render shared partials using statements such as these:

```
<%= render("shared/header", locals: {title: @article.title}) %>
<%= render(partial: "shared/post", object: @article) %>
...
```

In this previous example, the @article object will be assigned to the local variable post within the template.

Partials with Layouts

Partials can be rendered with a layout, and you can apply a layout to a block within any template:

```
<%= render partial: "user", layout: "administrator" %>
<%= render layout: "administrator" do %>
  # ...
<% end %>
```

Partial layouts are to be found directly in the app/views directory associated with the controller along with the customary underbar prefix, such as app/views/users/_administrator.html.erb.

Partials and Controllers

It isn't just view templates that use partials. Controllers also get in on the act. Partials give controllers the ability to generate fragments from a page using the same partial template as the view. This is particularly important when you're using Ajax support to update just part of a page from the controller—use partials, and you know your formatting for the table row or line item that you're updating will be compatible with that used to generate its brethren initially.

Taken together, partials and layouts provide an effective way to make sure that the user interface portion of your application is maintainable. But being maintainable is only part of the story; doing so in a way that also performs well is also crucial.

What We Just Did

Views are the public face of Rails applications, and we've seen that Rails delivers extensive support for what you need to build robust and maintainable user and application programming interfaces.

We started with templates, of which Rails provides built-in support for three types: ERB, Builder, and SCSS. Templates make it easy for us to provide HTML, JSON, XML, CSS, and JavaScript responses to any request. We'll discuss adding another option in Creating HTML Templates with Slim, on page 430.

We dove into forms, which are the primary means by which users will interact with your application. Along the way, we covered uploading files.

We continued with helpers, which enable us to factor out complex application logic to allow our views to focus on presentation aspects. We explored a number of helpers that Rails provides, ranging from basic formatting to hypertext links, which are the final way in which users interact with HTML pages.

We completed our tour of Action View by covering two related ways of factoring out large chunks of content for reuse. We use layouts to factor out the outermost layers of a view and provide a common look and feel. We use partials to factor out common inner components, such as a single form or table.

That covers how a user with a browser will access our Rails application. Next up: covering how we define and maintain the schema of the database our application will use to store data.

In this chapter, you'll see:
- Naming migration files
- Renaming and columns
- Creating and renaming tables
- Defining indices and keys
- Using native SQL

CHAPTER 23

Migrations

Rails encourages an agile, iterative style of development. We don't expect to get everything right the first time. Instead, we write tests and interact with our customers to refine our understanding as we go.

For that to work, we need a supporting set of practices. We write tests to help us design our interfaces and to act as a safety net when we change things, and we use version control to store our application's source files, allowing us to undo mistakes and to monitor what changes day to day.

But there's another area of the application that changes, an area that we can't directly manage using version control. The database schema in a Rails application constantly evolves as we progress through the development: we add a table here, rename a column there, and so on. The database changes in step with the application's code.

With Rails, each of those steps is made possible through the use of a *migration*. You saw this in use throughout the development of the Depot application, starting when we created the first products table in Generating the Scaffold, on page 66, and when we performed such tasks as adding a quantity to the line_items table in Iteration E1: Creating a Smarter Cart, on page 127. Now it's time to dig deeper into how migrations work and what else you can do with them.

Creating and Running Migrations

A migration is simply a Ruby source file in your application's db/migrate directory. Each migration file's name starts with a number of digits (typically fourteen) and an underscore. Those digits are the key to migrations, because they define the sequence in which the migrations are applied—they're the individual migration's version number.

The version number is the Coordinated Universal Time (UTC) timestamp at the time the migration was created. These numbers contain the four-digit year, followed by two digits each for the month, day, hour, minute, and second, all based on the mean solar time at the Royal Observatory in Greenwich, London. Because migrations tend to be created relatively infrequently and the accuracy is recorded down to the second, the chances of any two people getting the same timestamp is vanishingly small. And the benefit of having timestamps that can be deterministically ordered far outweighs the miniscule risk of this occurring.

Here's what the db/migrate directory of our Depot application looks like:

```
depot> ls db/migrate
20250420000001_create_products.rb
20250420000002_create_carts.rb
20250420000003_create_line_items.rb
20250420000004_add_quantity_to_line_items.rb
20250420000005_combine_items_in_cart.rb
20250420000006_create_orders.rb
20250420000007_add_order_id_to_line_item.rb
20250420000008_create_users.rb
```

Although you could create these migration files by hand, it's easier (and less error prone) to use a generator. As we saw when we created the Depot application, two generators create migration files:

- The *model* generator creates a migration to in turn create the table associated with the model (unless you specify the --skip-migration option). As the example that follows shows, creating a model called discount also creates a migration called *yyyyMMddhhmmss*_create_discounts.rb:

  ```
  depot> bin/rails generate model discount
        invoke  active_record
  ➤     create    db/migrate/20250420133549_create_discounts.rb
        create    app/models/discount.rb
        invoke    test_unit
        create      test/models/discount_test.rb
        create      test/fixtures/discounts.yml
  ```

- You can also generate a migration on its own.

  ```
  depot> bin/rails generate migration add_price_column
        invoke  active_record
  ➤     create    db/migrate/20250420133814_add_price_column.rb
  ```

Later, starting in Anatomy of a Migration, on page 410, we'll see what goes in the migration files. But for now, let's jump ahead a little in the workflow and see how to run migrations.

Running Migrations

Migrations are run using the db:migrate Rake task:

depot> `bin/rails db:migrate`

To see what happens next, let's dive down into the internals of Rails.

The migration code maintains a table called schema_migrations inside every Rails database. This table has just one column, called version, and it will have one row per successfully applied migration.

When you run bin/rails db:migrate, the task first looks for the schema_migrations table. If it doesn't yet exist, it'll be created.

The migration code then looks at the migration files in db/migrate and skips from consideration any that have a version number (the leading digits in the filename) that's already in the database. It then proceeds to apply the remainder of the migrations, creating a row in the schema_migrations table for each.

If we were to run migrations again at this point, nothing much would happen. Each of the version numbers of the migration files would match with a row in the database, so there'd be no migrations to apply.

But if we subsequently create a new migration file, it will have a version number not in the database. This is true even if the version number was *before* one or more of the already applied migrations. This can happen when multiple users are using a version control system to store the migration files. If we then run migrations, this new migration file—and only this migration file—will be executed. This may mean that migrations are run out of order, so you might want to take care and ensure that these migrations are independent. Or you might want to revert your database to a previous state and then apply the migrations in order.

You can force the database to a specific version by supplying the VERSION= parameter to the rake db:migrate command:

depot> `bin/rails db:migrate VERSION=20250420000009`

If the version you give is greater than any of the migrations that have yet to be applied, these migrations will be applied.

If, however, the version number on the command line is less than one or more versions listed in the schema_migrations table, something different happens. In these circumstances, Rails looks for the migration file whose number matches the database version and *undoes* it. It repeats this process until there are no more versions listed in the schema_migrations table that exceed the number you specified on the command line. That is, the migrations are unapplied in reverse order to take the schema back to the version that you specify.

You can also redo one or more migrations:

depot> `bin/rails db:migrate:redo STEP=3`

By default, redo will roll back one migration and rerun it. To roll back multiple migrations, pass the STEP= parameter.

Anatomy of a Migration

Migrations are subclasses of the Rails class ActiveRecord::Migration. When necessary, migrations can contain up() and down() methods:

```
class SomeMeaningfulName < ActiveRecord::Migration
  def up
    # ...
  end
  def down
    # ...
  end
end
```

The name of the class, after all uppercase letters are downcased and preceded by an underscore, must match the portion of the filename after the version number. For example, the previous class could be found in a file named 20250420000017_some_meaningful_name.rb. No two migrations can contain classes with the same name.

The up() method is responsible for applying the schema changes for this migration, while the down() method undoes those changes. Let's make this more concrete. Here's a migration that adds an e_mail column to the orders table:

```
class AddEmailToOrders < ActiveRecord::Migration
  def up
    add_column :orders, :e_mail, :string
  end
  def down
    remove_column :orders, :e_mail
  end
end
```

See how the down() method undoes the effect of the up() method? You can also see a bit of duplication here. In many cases, Rails can detect how to automatically undo a given operation. For example, the opposite of add_column() is clearly remove_column(). In such cases, by simply renaming up() to change(), you can eliminate the need for a down():

```
class AddEmailToOrders < ActiveRecord::Migration
  def change
    add_column :orders, :e_mail, :string
  end
end
```

Now isn't that much cleaner?

Column Types

The third parameter to add_column specifies the type of the database column. In the prior example, we specified that the e_mail column has a type of :string. But what does this mean? Databases typically don't have column types of :string.

Remember that Rails tries to make your application independent of the underlying database; you could develop using SQLite 3 and deploy to Postgres if you wanted, for example. But different databases use different names for the types of columns. If you used a SQLite 3 column type in a migration, that migration might not work if applied to a Postgres database. So, Rails migrations insulate you from the underlying database type systems by using logical types. If we're migrating a SQLite 3 database, the :string type will create a column of type varchar(255). On Postgres, the same migration adds a column with the type char varying(255).

The types supported by migrations are :binary, :boolean, :date, :datetime, :decimal, :float, :integer, :string, :text, :time, and :timestamp. The default mappings of these types for the database adapters in Rails are shown in the following tables:

	db2	mysql	openbase	oracle
:binary	blob(32768)	blob	object	blob
:boolean	decimal(1)	tinyint(1)	boolean	number(1)
:date	date	date	date	date
:datetime	timestamp	datetime	datetime	date
:decimal	decimal	decimal	decimal	decimal
:float	float	float	float	number
:integer	int	int(11)	integer	number(38)
:string	varchar(255)	varchar(255)	char(4096)	varchar2(255)
:text	clob(32768)	text	text	clob
:time	time	time	time	date
:timestamp	timestamp	datetime	timestamp	date

	postgresql	sqlite	sqlserver	sybase
:binary	bytea	blob	image	image
:boolean	boolean	boolean	bit	bit
:date	date	date	date	datetime
:datetime	timestamp	datetime	datetime	datetime
:decimal	decimal	decimal	decimal	decimal
:float	float	float	float(8)	float(8)
:integer	integer	integer	int	int
:string	(note 1)	varchar(255)	varchar(255)	varchar(255)
:text	text	text	text	text
:time	time	datetime	time	time
:timestamp	timestamp	datetime	datetime	timestamp

Using these tables, you could work out that a column declared to be :integer in a migration would have the underlying type integer in SQLite 3 and number(38) in Oracle.

You can use three options when defining most columns in a migration; decimal columns take an additional two options. Each of these options is given as a key: value pair. The common options are as follows:

null: true or false If false, the underlying column has a not null constraint added (if the database supports it). Note that this is independent of any presence: true validation, which may be performed at the model layer.

limit: size This sets a limit on the size of the field. It appends the string (*size*) to the database column type definition.

default: value This sets the default value for the column. Since it's performed by the database, you don't see this in a new model object when you initialize it or even when you save it. You have to reload the object from the database to see this value. Note that the default is calculated once, at the point the migration is run, so the following code will set the default column value to the date and time when the migration was run:

```
add_column :orders, :placed_at, :datetime, default: Time.now
```

In addition, decimal columns take the options :precision and :scale. The :precision option specifies the number of significant digits that will be stored, and the :scale option determines where the decimal point will be located in these digits (think of the scale as the number of digits after the decimal point). A decimal number with a precision of 5 and a scale of 0 can store numbers from -99,999 to +99,999. A decimal number with a precision of 5 and a scale of 2 can store the range -999.99 to +999.99.

The :precision and :scale parameters are optional for decimal columns. However, incompatibilities between different databases lead us to strongly recommend that you include the options for each decimal column.

Here are some column definitions using the migration types and options:

```
add_column :orders, :attn, :string, limit: 100
add_column :orders, :order_type, :integer
add_column :orders, :ship_class, :string, null: false, default: 'priority'
add_column :orders, :amount, :decimal, precision: 8, scale: 2
```

Renaming Columns

When we refactor our code, we often change our variable names to make them more meaningful. Rails migrations allow us to do this to database column names too. For example, a week after we first added it, we might decide that e_mail isn't the best name for the new column. We can create a migration to rename it using the rename_column() method:

```
class RenameEmailColumn < ActiveRecord::Migration
  def change
    rename_column :orders, :e_mail, :customer_email
  end
end
```

As rename_column() is reversible, separate up() and down() methods aren't required in order to use it.

Note that the rename doesn't destroy any existing data associated with the column. Also be aware that renaming isn't supported by all the adapters.

Changing Columns

change_column() Use the change_column() method to change the type of a column or to alter the options associated with a column. Use it the same way you'd use add_column, but specify the name of an existing column. Let's say that the order type column is currently an integer, but we need to change it to be a string. We want to keep the existing data, so an order type of 123 will become the string "123". Later, we'll use noninteger values such as "new" and "existing".

Changing from an integer column to a string is one line of code:

```
def up
  change_column :orders, :order_type, :string
end
```

However, the opposite transformation is problematic. We might be tempted to write the obvious down() migration:

```
def down
  change_column :orders, :order_type, :integer
end
```

But if our application has taken to storing data like "new" in this column, the down() method will lose it—"new" can't be converted to an integer. If that's acceptable, then the migration is acceptable as it stands. If, however, we want to create a one-way migration—one that can't be reversed—we'll want to stop the down migration from being applied. In this case, Rails provides a special exception that we can throw:

```
class ChangeOrderTypeToString < ActiveRecord::Migration
  def up
    change_column :orders, :order_type, :string, null: false
  end

  def down
    raise ActiveRecord::IrreversibleMigration
  end
end
```

ActiveRecord::IrreversibleMigration is also the name of the exception that Rails will raise if you attempt to call a method that can't be automatically reversed from within a change() method.

Managing Tables

So far we've been using migrations to manipulate the columns in existing tables. Now let's look at creating and dropping tables:

```
class CreateOrderHistories < ActiveRecord::Migration
  def change
    create_table :order_histories do |t|
      t.integer :order_id, null: false
      t.text :notes

      t.timestamps
    end
  end
end
```

create_table() takes the name of a table (remember, table names are plural) and a block. (It also takes some optional parameters that we'll look at in a minute.) The block is passed a table definition object, which we use to define the columns in the table.

Generally the call to drop_table() isn't needed, as create_table() is reversible. drop_table() accepts a single parameter, which is the name of the table to drop.

The calls to the various table definition methods should look familiar—they're similar to the add_column method we used previously, except these methods don't take the name of the table as the first parameter and the name of the method itself is the data type desired. This reduces repetition.

Note that we don't define the id column for our new table. Unless we say otherwise, Rails migrations automatically add a primary key called id to all tables they create. For a deeper discussion of this, see Primary Keys, on page 418.

The timestamps method creates both the created_at and updated_at columns, with the correct timestamp data type. Although there's no requirement to add these columns to any particular table, this is yet another example of Rails making it easy for a common convention to be implemented easily and consistently.

Options for Creating Tables

You can pass a hash of options as a second parameter to create_table. If you specify force: true, the migration will drop an existing table of the same name before creating the new one. This is a useful option if you want to create a migration that forces a database into a known state, but there's clearly a potential for data loss.

The temporary: true option creates a temporary table—one that goes away when the application disconnects from the database. This is clearly pointless in the context of a migration, but as we'll see later, it does have its uses elsewhere.

The options: "xxxx" parameter lets you specify options to your underlying database. They're added to the end of the CREATE TABLE statement, right after the closing parenthesis. Although this is rarely necessary with SQLite 3, it may at times be useful with other database servers. For example, some versions of MySQL allow you to specify the initial value of the autoincrementing id column. We can pass this in through a migration as follows:

```
create_table :tickets, options: "auto_increment = 10000" do |t|
  t.text :description
  t.timestamps
end
```

Behind the scenes, migrations will generate the following DDL from this table description when configured for MySQL:

```
CREATE TABLE "tickets" (
  "id" int(11) default null auto_increment primary key,
  "description" text,
  "created_at" datetime,
  "updated_at" datetime
) auto_increment = 10000;
```

Be careful when using the :options parameter with MySQL. The Rails MySQL database adapter sets a default option of ENGINE=InnoDB. This overrides any local defaults you have and forces migrations to use the InnoDB storage engine for new tables. Yet, if you override :options, you'll lose this setting; new tables will be created using whatever database engine is configured as the default for your site. You may want to add an explicit ENGINE=InnoDB to the options string to force the standard behavior in this case. You probably want to keep using InnoDB if you're using MySQL because this engine gives you transaction support. You might need this support in your application, and you'll definitely need it in your tests if you're using the default of transactional test fixtures.

Renaming Tables

If refactoring leads us to rename variables and columns, then it's probably not a surprise that we sometimes find ourselves renaming tables too. Migrations support the rename_table() method:

```
class RenameOrderHistories < ActiveRecord::Migration
  def change
    rename_table :order_histories, :order_notes
  end
end
```

Rolling back this migration undoes the change by renaming the table back.

Problems with rename_table

When we rename tables in migrations, a subtle problem arises.

For example, let's assume that in migration 4 we create the order_histories table and populate it with some data:

```
def up
  create_table :order_histories do |t|
    t.integer :order_id, null: false
    t.text :notes

    t.timestamps
  end

  order = Order.find :first
  OrderHistory.create(order_id: order, notes: "test")
end
```

Later, in migration 7, we rename the table order_histories to order_notes. At this point we'll also have renamed the model OrderHistory to OrderNote.

Now we decide to drop our development database and reapply all migrations. When we do so, the migrations throw an exception in migration 4: our application no longer contains a class called OrderHistory, so the migration fails.

One solution, proposed by Tim Lucas, is to create local dummy versions of the model classes needed by a migration within the migration. For example, the following version of the fourth migration will work even if the application no longer has an OrderHistory class:

```
class CreateOrderHistories < ActiveRecord::Migration
➤   class Order < ApplicationRecord::Base; end
➤   class OrderHistory < ApplicationRecord::Base; end
    def change
      create_table :order_histories do |t|
        t.integer :order_id, null: false
        t.text :notes

        t.timestamps
      end

      order = Order.find :first
      OrderHistory.create(order: order_id, notes: "test")
    end
end
```

This works as long as our model classes don't contain any additional functionality that would have been used in the migration—all we're creating here is a bare-bones version.

Defining Indices

Migrations can (and probably should) define indices for tables. For example, we might notice that once our application has a large number of orders in the database, searching based on the customer's name takes longer than we'd like. It's time to add an index using the appropriately named add_index() method:

```
class AddCustomerNameIndexToOrders < ActiveRecord::Migration
  def change
    add_index :orders, :name
  end
end
```

If we give add_index the optional parameter unique: true, a unique index will be created, forcing values in the indexed column to be unique.

By default the index will be given the name *index_table_on_column*. We can override this using the name: "somename" option. If we use the :name option when adding an index, we'll also need to specify it when removing the index.

We can create a *composite index*—an index on multiple columns—by passing an array of column names to add_index.

Indices are removed using the remove_index() method.

Primary Keys

Rails assumes every table has a numeric primary key (normally called id) and ensures the value of this column is unique for each new row added to a table. We'll rephrase that.

Rails doesn't work too well unless each table has a primary key that Rails can manage. By default, Rails will create numeric primary keys, but you can also use other types such as UUIDs, depending on what your actual database provides. Rails is less fussy about the name of the column. So for your average Rails application, our strong advice is to go with the flow and let Rails have its id column.

If you decide to be adventurous, you can start by using a different name for the primary key column (but keeping it as an incrementing integer). Do this by specifying a :primary_key option on the create_table call:

```
create_table :tickets, primary_key: :number do |t|
  t.text :description

  t.timestamps
end
```

This adds the number column to the table and sets it up as the primary key:

```
$ sqlite3 storage/development.sqlite3 ".schema tickets"
CREATE TABLE tickets ("number" INTEGER PRIMARY KEY AUTOINCREMENT
NOT NULL, "description" text DEFAULT NULL, "created_at" datetime
DEFAULT NULL, "updated_at" datetime DEFAULT NULL);
```

The next step in the adventure might be to create a primary key that isn't an integer. Here's a clue that the Rails developers don't think this is a good idea: migrations don't let you do this (at least not directly).

Tables with No Primary Key

Sometimes we may need to define a table that has no primary key. The most common case in Rails is for *join tables*—tables with just two columns where each column is a foreign key to another table. To create a join table using migrations, we have to tell Rails not to automatically add an id column:

```
create_table :authors_books, id: false do |t|
  t.integer :author_id, null: false
  t.integer :book_id,   null: false
end
```

In this case, you might want to investigate creating one or more indices on this table to speed navigation between books and authors.

Advanced Migrations

Most Rails developers use the basic facilities of migrations to create and maintain their database schemas. But every now and then it's useful to push migrations just a bit further. This section covers some more advanced migration usage.

Using Native SQL

Migrations give you a database-independent way of maintaining your application's schema. However, if migrations don't contain the methods you need to be able to do what you need to do, you'll need to drop down to database-specific code. Rails provides two ways to do this. One is with options arguments to methods like add_column(). The second is the execute() method.

When you use options or execute(), you might well be tying your migration to a specific database engine, because any SQL you provide in these two locations uses your database's native syntax.

An example of where you might need to use raw SQL is if you're creating a custom data type inside your database. Postgres, for example, allows you to specify *enumerated types*. Enumerated types work just fine with Rails; but to create them in a migration, you have to use SQL and thus execute(). Suppose we wanted to create an enumerated type for the various pay types we supported in our checkout form (which we created in Chapter 12, Task G: Check Out!, on page 165):

```
class AddPayTypes < ActiveRecord::Migrations[6.0]
  def up
    execute %{
      CREATE TYPE
        pay_type
      AS ENUM (
        'check',
        'credit card',
        'purchase order'
      )
    }
  end
```

```
  def down
    execute "DROP TYPE pay_type"
  end
end
```

Note that if you need to model your database using execute(), you should consider changing your schema dump format from "ruby" to "SQL," as outlined in the Rails Guide.[1] The schema dump is used during tests to create an empty database with the same schema you're using in production.

Custom Messages and Benchmarks

Although not exactly an advanced migration, something that's useful to do within advanced migrations is to output our own messages and benchmarks. We can do this with the say_with_time() method:

```
def up
  say_with_time "Updating prices..." do
    Person.all.each do |p|
      p.update_attribute :price, p.lookup_master_price
    end
  end
end
```

say_with_time() prints the string passed before the block is executed and prints the benchmark after the block completes.

When Migrations Go Bad

Migrations suffer from one serious problem. The underlying DDL statements that update the database schema aren't transactional. This isn't a failing in Rails—most databases don't support the rolling back of create table, alter table, and other DDL statements.

Let's look at a migration that tries to add two tables to a database:

```
class ExampleMigration < ActiveRecord::Migration
  def change
    create_table :one do ...
    end
    create_table :two do ...
    end
  end
end
```

---

1. http://guides.rubyonrails.org/active_record_migrations.html#schema-dumping-and-you

In the normal course of events, the up() method adds tables, one and two, and the down() method removes them.

But what happens if there's a problem creating the second table? We'll end up with a database containing table one but not table two. We can fix whatever the problem is in the migration, but now we can't apply it—if we try, it will fail because table one already exists.

We could try to roll the migration back, but that won't work. Because the original migration failed, the schema version in the database wasn't updated, so Rails won't try to roll it back.

At this point, you could mess around and manually change the schema information and drop table one. But it probably isn't worth it. Our recommendation in these circumstances is simply to drop the entire database, re-create it, and apply migrations to bring it back up-to-date. You'll have lost nothing, and you'll know you have a consistent schema.

All this discussion suggests that migrations are dangerous to use on production databases. Should you run them? We really can't say. If you have database administrators in your organization, it'll be their call. If it's up to you, you'll have to weigh the risks. But if you decide to go for it, you really must back up your database first. Then you can apply the migrations by going to your application's directory on the machine with the database role on your production servers and executing this command:

depot> `RAILS_ENV=production bin/rails db:migrate`

This is one of those times where the legal notice at the start of this book kicks in. We're not liable if this deletes your data.

Schema Manipulation Outside Migrations

All the migration methods described so far in this chapter are also available as methods on Active Record connection objects and so are accessible within the models, views, and controllers of a Rails application.

For example, you might have discovered that a particular long-running report runs a lot faster if the orders table has an index on the city column. But that index isn't needed during the day-to-day running of the application, and tests have shown that maintaining it slows the application appreciably.

Let's write a method that creates the index, runs a block of code, and then drops the index. This could be a private method in the model or could be implemented in a library:

```
def run_with_index(*columns)
  connection.add_index(:orders, *columns)
  begin
    yield
  ensure
    connection.remove_index(:orders, *columns)
  end
end
```

The statistics-gathering method in the model can use this as follows:

```
def get_city_statistics
  run_with_index(:city) do
    # .. calculate stats
  end
end
```

What We Just Did

While we had been informally using migrations throughout the development of the Depot application and even into deployment, in this chapter we saw how migrations are the basis for a principled and disciplined approach to configuration management of the schema for your database.

You learned how to create, rename, and delete columns and tables, to manage indices and keys, to apply and back out entire sets of changes, and even to add your own custom SQL into the mix, all in a completely reproducible manner.

At this point we've covered the externals of Rails. The next chapter is going to show a few more involved ways of customizing Rails to demonstrate just how flexible Rails can be when you need it. We'll see how to use RSpec for testing, use Slim instead of ERB for templating, and use Webpack to manage your CSS.

In this chapter, you'll see:
- Replacing Rails' testing framework with RSpec
- Using Slim for HTML templates instead of ERB

CHAPTER 24

Customizing and Extending Rails

As you've come to learn, Rails provides an answer for almost every question you have about building a modern web application. It provides the basics for handling requests, accessing a database, writing user interfaces, and running tests. It does this by having a tightly integrated design, which is often referred to as Rails being "opinionated software."

This tight coupling comes at a price. If, for example, the way Rails manages CSS doesn't meet the needs of your project, you could be in trouble. Or if you prefer to write your tests in a different way, Rails doesn't give you a lot of options. Or does it? In the early days of Rails, customizing it was difficult or impossible. Starting with Rails 3, much effort was expended to make Rails more customizable. With Rails 8, developers have the flexibility to use the tools they prefer or that work the way they want them to work. That's what we'll explore in this chapter.

We'll replace four parts of Rails in this chapter. First, we'll write a Web Component instead of using Stimulus. Then we'll see how to use RSpec instead of Rails' default testing library to write our tests. Next, we'll replace ERB for the alternative templating language Slim. Finally, we'll see how to manage CSS using Webpack instead of putting it in app/assets/stylesheets. This chapter will demonstrate another benefit to Rails, which is that you don't have to throw out the parts that work for you to use alternatives that work better. Let's get started.

Creating a Reusable Web Component

Web Components[1] are an industry standard way of extending HTML itself to implement custom behaviors and presentation.

---

1. https://developer.mozilla.org/en-US/docs/Web/Web_Components

You don't need to start from scratch when building a web component. You can build upon a rich ecosystem of npm[2] packages. We'll make use of lit.[3] We start by "pinning" it to our application so that it can be imported:

```
> bin/importmap pin lit
Pinning "lit" to https://.../index.js
Pinning "@lit/reactive-element" to https://.../reactive-element.js
Pinning "lit-element/lit-element.js" to https://.../lit-element.js
Pinning "lit-html" to https://.../lit-html.js
Pinning "lit-html/is-server.js" to https://.../is-server.js
```

Next, we'll write a web component. The following example renders the current time in blue. Create a directory named app/javascript/elements and create a file named current-time.js in that directory with the following contents:

```
import {html, css, LitElement} from 'lit';

class CurrentTime extends LitElement {
  static styles = css`span { color: blue }`;

  render() {
    return html`<span>${new Date().toLocaleTimeString()}</span>`;
  }
}
customElements.define('current-time', CurrentTime);
```

This code imports three properties from the lit package and defines a class that extends LitElement by defining a style that's scoped to this single element function that returns an HTML fragment. Finally, a new custom element is defined and associated with this class.

Next, we import this file into our application by adding a single line to app/javascript/application.js:

```
// Configure your import map in config/importmap.rb.
// Read more: https://github.com/rails/importmap-rails
import "@hotwired/turbo-rails"
import "controllers"
➤ import "./elements/current-time.js"
```

With this in place, the current time can be added to any HTML template by adding the following HTML:

```
<current-time>
```

---

2. https://www.npmjs.com/
3. https://lit.dev/

This just scratches the surface of what can be done with Web Components. On the lit site you can find plenty of examples. A good place to start is on the page for Reactive Controllers,[4] which shows how you can add state and reactivity to a clock element.

Testing with RSpec

RSpec is an alternative to MiniTest, which Rails uses. It's different in almost every way, and many developers prefer it. Here's what one of our existing tests might look like written in RSpec:

```
RSpec.describe Cart do

  let(:cart)     { Cart.create }
  let(:book_one) { products(:pragprog) }
  let(:book_two) { products(:two) }

  before do
    cart.add_product(book_one).save!
    cart.add_product(book_two).save!
  end

  it "can have multiple products added" do
    expect(cart.line_items.size).to eq(2)
  end

  it "calculates the total price of all products" do
    expect(cart.total_price).to eq(book_one.price + book_two.price)
  end
end
```

It almost looks like a different programming language! Developers who prefer RSpec like that the test reads like English: "Describe Cart, it can have multiple products added, expect cart.line_items.size to eq 2."

We're going to quickly go through how to write tests in RSpec without too much explanation. A great book for that is already available—*Effective Testing with RSpec 3 [MD17]*—so we'll learn just enough RSpec to see it working with Rails, which demonstrates Rails' configurability. Although many developers who use RSpec set it up from the start of a project, you don't have to. RSpec can be added at any time, and that's what we'll do here.

Add rspec-rails to your Gemfile, putting it in the development and test groups:

```
group :development, :test do
  gem 'rspec-rails'
end
```

---

4. https://lit.dev/docs/composition/controllers/

After you bundle install, a new generator will set up RSpec for you:

```
> bin/rails generate rspec:install
    create  .rspec
    create  spec
    create  spec/spec_helper.rb
    create  spec/rails_helper.rb
```

Verify the configuration is working by running the new task Rspec installed, spec:

```
> bin/rails spec
No examples found.

Finished in 0.00058 seconds (files took 0.11481 seconds to load)
0 examples, 0 failures
```

Let's reimplement the test for Cart as an RSpec test or *spec*. RSpec includes generators to create starter specs for us, similar to what Rails does with scaffolding. To create a model spec, use the spec:model generator:

```
> bin/rails generate spec:model Cart
      create  spec/models/cart_spec.rb
```

Now rerun spec, and we can see RSpec's generator has created a pending spec:

```
> bin/rails spec
Pending: (Failures listed here are expected and do not affect
         your suite's status)

  1) Cart add some examples to (or delete) spec/models/cart_spec.rb
     # Not yet implemented
     # ./spec/models/cart_spec.rb:4

Finished in 0.00284 seconds (files took 1.73 seconds to load)
1 example, 0 failures, 1 pending
```

To reimplement the test for Cart as a spec, let's first review the existing test:

rails80/depot_u/test/models/cart_test.rb
```ruby
require "test_helper"

class CartTest < ActiveSupport::TestCase
  def setup
    @cart     = Cart.create
    @book_one = products(:pragprog)
    @book_two = products(:two)
  end

  test "add unique products" do
    @cart.add_product(@book_one).save!
    @cart.add_product(@book_two).save!
    assert_equal 2, @cart.line_items.size
    assert_equal @book_one.price + @book_two.price, @cart.total_price
  end
```

```
    test "add duplicate product" do
      @cart.add_product(@book_one).save!
      @cart.add_product(@book_one).save!
      assert_equal 2*@book_one.price, @cart.total_price
      assert_equal 1, @cart.line_items.size
      assert_equal 2, @cart.line_items[0].quantity
    end
end
```

The setup creates a cart and fetches two products from the fixtures. It then tests the add_product() in two ways: by adding two distinct products and by adding the same product twice.

Let's start with the setup. By default, RSpec is configured to look in spec/fixtures for fixtures. This is correct for a project using RSpec from the start, but for us, the fixtures are in test/fixtures. Change this by editing spec/rails_helper.rb:

rails80/depot_xa/spec/rails_helper.rb
```
RSpec.configure do |config|
  # Remove this line if you're not using ActiveRecord or ActiveRecord fixtures
  config.fixture_paths = [
➤   Rails.root.join('test/fixtures')
  ]
```

Back to the spec—its setup will need to create a Cart to use in our tests as well as fetch two products from fixtures. By default, fixtures aren't available in specs, but you can call fixtures() to make them available. Here's what the setup looks like:

rails80/depot_xa/spec/models/cart_spec.rb
```
require 'rails_helper'

RSpec.describe Cart, type: :model do
➤   fixtures :products
➤   subject(:cart) { Cart.new }
➤
➤   let(:book_one) { products(:pragprog) }
➤   let(:book_two) { products(:two) }
```

This definitely doesn't look like our original test! The call to subject() declares the variable cart, which you'll use in the tests later. The calls to let() declare other variables that can be used in the tests. The reason for two methods that seemingly do the same thing is an RSpec convention. The object that's the focus of the test is declared with subject(). Ancillary data needed for the test is declared with let().

The tests themselves will also look different from their equivalents in a standard Rails test. For one thing, they aren't called tests but rather *examples*. Also, it's customary for each example to make only one assertion. The existing test of adding different products makes two assertions, so in the spec, that means two examples.

Assertions look different in RSpec as well:

```
expect(actual_value).to eq(expected_value)
```

Applying this to the two assertions around adding distinct items, we have two examples (we'll show you where this code goes in a moment):

```
it "has two line items" do
  expect(cart.line_items.size).to eq(2)
end
it "has a total price of the two items' price" do
  expect(cart.total_price).to eq(book_one.price + book_two.price)
end
```

These assertions won't succeed unless items are added to the cart first. That code *could* go inside each example, but RSpec allows you to extract duplicate setup code into a block using before():

```
before do
  cart.add_product(book_one).save!
  cart.add_product(book_two).save!
end
it "has two line items" do
  expect(cart.line_items.size).to eq(2)
end
it "has a total price of the two items' price" do
  expect(cart.total_price).to eq(book_one.price + book_two.price)
end
```

This setup is only relevant to some of the tests of the add_product() method, specifically the tests around adding different items. To test adding the same item twice, you'll need different setups. To make this happen, wrap the above code in a block using context(). context() takes a string that describes the context we're creating and acts as a scope for before() blocks. It's also customary to wrap all examples of the behavior of a method inside a block given to describe(). Given all that, here's what the first half of your spec should look like:

rails80/depot_xa/spec/models/cart_spec.rb
```
describe "#add_product" do
  context "adding unique products" do
    before do
      cart.add_product(book_one).save!
      cart.add_product(book_two).save!
    end

    it "has two line items" do
      expect(cart.line_items.size).to eq(2)
    end
```

```
➤     it "has a total price of the two items' price" do
➤       expect(cart.total_price).to eq(book_one.price + book_two.price)
➤     end
➤ end
```

Here's the second half of the spec, which tests the behavior of add_product() when adding the same item twice:

rails80/depot_xa/spec/models/cart_spec.rb
```
  require 'rails_helper'

  RSpec.describe Cart, type: :model do
➤   fixtures :products
➤   subject(:cart) { Cart.new }
➤
➤   let(:book_one) { products(:pragprog) }
➤   let(:book_two) { products(:two) }
➤
➤   describe "#add_product" do
➤     context "adding unique products" do
➤       before do
➤         cart.add_product(book_one).save!
➤         cart.add_product(book_two).save!
➤       end
➤
➤       it "has two line items" do
➤         expect(cart.line_items.size).to eq(2)
➤       end
➤       it "has a total price of the two items' price" do
➤         expect(cart.total_price).to eq(book_one.price + book_two.price)
➤       end
➤     end
➤
➤     context "adding duplicate products" do
➤       before do
➤         cart.add_product(book_one).save!
➤         cart.add_product(book_one).save!
➤       end
➤
➤       it "has one line item" do
➤         expect(cart.line_items.size).to eq(1)
➤       end
➤       it "has a line item with a quantity of 2" do
➤         expect(cart.line_items.first.quantity).to eq(2)
➤       end
➤       it "has a total price of twice the product's price" do
➤         expect(cart.total_price).to eq(book_one.price * 2)
➤       end
➤     end
    end

  end
```

Running `bin/rails spec`, it should pass:

```
> bin/rails spec
.....
Finished in 0.11007 seconds (files took 1.72 seconds to load)
5 examples, 0 failures
```

A lot of code in this file isn't executing a test, but all the calls to `describe()`, `context()`, and `it()` aren't for naught. Passing `SPEC_OPTS="--format=doc"` to the spec task, the test output is formatted like the documentation of the Cart class:

```
> bin/rails spec SPEC_OPTS="--format=doc"

Cart
  #add_product
    adding unique products
      has two line items
      has a total price of the two items' price
    adding duplicate products
      has one line item
      has a line item with a quantity of 2
      has a total price of twice the product's price

Finished in 0.14865 seconds (files took 1.76 seconds to load)
5 examples, 0 failures
```

Also note that rspec-rails changes the Rails generators to create empty spec files in spec/ instead of test files in test/. This means that you use all the generators and scaffolding you're used to in your normal workflow without having to worry about the wrong type of test file being created.

If all of this seems strange to you, you're not alone. It *is* strange, and the reasons RSpec is designed this way, as well as why you might want to use it, are nuanced and beyond the scope of this book. The main point all this proves is that you can replace a major part of Rails with an alternative and still get all the benefits of the rest of Rails. It's also worth noting that RSpec is popular, and you're very likely to see it in the wild.

Let's learn more about Rails' configurability by replacing another major piece of Rails—ERB templates.

Creating HTML Templates with Slim

Slim is a templating language that can replace ERB.[5] It's designed to require much less code to achieve the same results, and it does this by using a nested structure instead of HTML tags. Consider this ERB:

---

5. http://slim-lang.com

```erb
<h2><%= t('.title') %></h2>
<table>
  <%= render(cart.line_items) %>

  <tr class="total_line">
    <td colspan="2">Total</td>
    <td class="total_cell"><%= number_to_currency(cart.total_price) %></td>
  </tr>
</table>
```

In Slim, it would look like so:

```slim
h2
  = t('.title')
table
  = render(cart.line_items)

  tr.total_line
    td.colspan=2
      Total
    td.total_cell
      = number_to_currency(cart.total_price)
```

Slim treats each line as an opening HTML tag, and anything indented under that line will be rendered inside that tag. Helper methods and instance variables can be accessed using =, like so:

```slim
ul
  li = link_to @product.name, product_path(@product)
```

To execute logic, such as looping over a collection, use -, like so:

```slim
ul
  - @products.each do |product|
    li
      - if product.available?
        = link_to product.name, product_path(product)
      - else
        = "#{product.name} out of stock"
```

The code after - is executed as Ruby, but note that no end keyword is needed—Slim inserts that for you.

Slim allows you to specify HTML classes by following a tag with a . and the class name:

```slim
h1.title This title has the "title" class!
```

And, in a final bit of ultracompactness, if you want to create a div with an HTML class on it, you can omit div entirely. This creates a div with the class login-form that contains two text inputs:

```
.login-form
  input type=text name=username
  input type=password name=password
```

Putting all this together, let's install Slim and reimplement the home page in app/views/store/index.html.erb using it. This will demonstrate how Rails allows us to completely replace its templating engine.

First, install slim-rails:

```
bundle add slim-rails
```

Once this command completes, your Rails app will now render files ending in .slim as a Slim template. We can see this by removing app/views/store/index.html.erb and creating app/views/stores/index.slim like so:

rails80/depot_xb/app/views/store/index.slim
```
- if notice
  aside#notice = notice

h1 = t('.title_html')

ul.catalog
  - cache @products do
    - @products.each do |product|
      - cache product do
        li
          = image_tag(product.image)
          h2 = product.title
          p = sanitize(product.description)
          .price
            = number_to_currency(product.price)
            = button_to t('.add_html'),
              line_items_path(product_id: product, locale: I18n.locale),
                remote: true
```

Restart your server if you have it running, and you should see the home page render the same as before.

In addition to being able to render Slim, installing slim-rails changes Rails generators to create Slim files instead of ERB, so all of the scaffolding and other generators you're used to will now produce Slim templates automatically. You can even convert your existing ERB templates to Slim by using the erb2slim command, available by installing the html2slim RubyGem.[6]

---

6. https://github.com/slim-template/html2slim

Customizing Rails in Other Ways

Customizing the edges of Rails, like you did in the preceding section with CSS, HTML templates, and tests, tends to be more straightforward, and more options are out there for you. Customizing Rails' internals is more difficult. If you want, you can remove Active Record entirely and use libraries like Sequel or ROM,[7,8] but you'd be giving up a lot—Active Record is tightly coupled with many parts of Rails.

Tight coupling is usually viewed as a problem, but it's this coupling that allows you to be so productive using Rails. The more you change your Rails app into a loosely coupled assembly of unrelated libraries, the more work you have to do getting the pieces to talk to each other. Finding the right balance is up to you, your team, or your project.

The Rails ecosystem is also filled with plugins and enhancements to address common needs that aren't common enough to be added to Rails itself. For example, Kaminari provides pagination for when you need to let a user browse hundreds or thousands of records.[9] Ransack and Searchkick provide advanced ways of searching your database with Active Record.[10,11] CarrierWave makes uploading files to your Rails app much more straightforward than hand-rolling it yourself.[12]

And if you want to analyze and improve the code inside your Rails app, RuboCop can check that you're using a consistent style,[13] while Brakeman can check for common security vulnerabilities.[14]

These extras are the tip of the iceberg. The community of extensions and plugins for Rails is yet another benefit to building your next web application with Rails.

Where to Go from Here

Congratulations! We've covered a lot of ground together.

---

7. http://sequel.jeremyevans.net/
8. http://rom-rb.org/
9. https://github.com/kaminari/kaminari
10. https://github.com/activerecord-hackery/ransack
11. https://github.com/ankane/searchkick
12. https://github.com/carrierwaveuploader/carrierwave
13. https://github.com/bbatsov/rubocop
14. https://github.com/presidentbeef/brakeman

In Part I, you installed Rails, verified the installation using a basic application, got exposed to the architecture of Rails, and got acquainted (or maybe reacquainted) with the Ruby language.

In Part II, you iteratively built an application and built up test cases along the way. We designed this application to touch on all aspects of Rails that every developer needs to be aware of.

Whereas Parts I and II of this book each served a single purpose, Part III served a dual role.

For some of you, Part III methodically filled in the gaps and covered enough for you to get real work done. For others, these will be the first steps of a much longer journey.

For most of you, the real value is a bit of both. A firm foundation is required for you to be able to explore further. And that's why we started this part with a chapter that not only covered the convention and configuration of Rails but also covered the generation of documentation.

Then we proceeded to devote a chapter each to the model, view, and controller, which are the backbone of the Rails architecture. We covered topics ranging from database relationships to the REST architecture to HTML forms and helpers.

We covered migration as an essential maintenance tool for the deployed application's database.

Finally, we split Rails apart and explored the concept of gems from a number of perspectives, from making use of individual Rails components separately to making full use of the foundation upon which Rails is built and, finally, to building and extending the framework to suit your needs.

At this point, you have the necessary context and background to more deeply explore whatever areas suit your fancy or are needed to solve that vexing problem you face. We recommend you start by visiting the Ruby on Rails site and exploring each of the links across the top of that page.[15] Some of this will be quick refreshers of materials presented in this book, but you'll also find plenty of links to current information on how to report problems, learn more, and keep up-to-date.

Additionally, please continue to contribute to the forums mentioned in the book's introduction.

---

15. http://rubyonrails.org/

Pragmatic Bookshelf has more books on Ruby and Rails subjects as well as plenty of related categories that go beyond Ruby and Rails, such as technical practices; testing, design, and cloud computing; and tools, frameworks, and languages.

You can find these and many other categories at http://www.pragprog.com/.

We hope you've enjoyed learning about Ruby on Rails as much as we've enjoyed writing this book!

Bibliography

[Atk24] Andrew Atkinson. *High Performance PostgreSQL for Rails*. The Pragmatic Bookshelf, Dallas, TX, 2024.

[Ise19] Rob Isenberg. *Docker for Rails Developers*. The Pragmatic Bookshelf, Dallas, TX, 2019.

[MD17] Myron Marston and Erin Dees (formerly Ian Dees). *Effective Testing with RSpec 3*. The Pragmatic Bookshelf, Dallas, TX, 2017.

[TH19] David Thomas and Andrew Hunt. *The Pragmatic Programmer, 20th Anniversary Edition*. The Pragmatic Bookshelf, Dallas, TX, 2019.

[Tho24] Noel Rappin, with Dave Thomas. *Programming Ruby 3.3 (5th Edition)*. The Pragmatic Bookshelf, Dallas, TX, 2024.

Index

SYMBOLS

& (ampersand), prefix operator, 49
<<() append method, 45
=> arrow syntax, 45
@ (at sign), prefixing instance variables, 42, 50
\ (backslash)
    multiple-line commands, 67
    regular expressions, 47
    string substitutions, 44
{} (braces)
    array of words, 45
    blocks, 48
    hashes, 45–46
[] (brackets)
    array indices, 44
    array of words, 45
    hash indices, 46
^ (caret), multiple-line commands, 67
: (colon), prefixing symbols, 42
|| conditional evaluation, 55
. (dot)
    CSS selectors, 109
    filenames, 83
    prefixing translation function, 230
    specifying HTML classes in Slim, 431
" (double quotes), strings, 43, 75
<%=...%> embedded Ruby code, 23
== equality operator, 322
! (exclamation point), bang methods, 55
#{...} expression interpolation, 44
/ (forward slash), regular expressions, 46
(hash mark)
    comments, 43
    CSS selectors, 109
-> lambda syntax, 56
=~ match operator, 46
() (parentheses)
    method calls, 42
    regular expressions, 46
    in REST routes, 353
? (question mark)
    predicate methods, 55
    SQL placeholders, 328
%r{...} regular expressions, 46
; (semicolon), ending statements, 43
' (single quotes), strings, 43
%(...) string literals, 75
_ (underscore)
    in names, 42, 311, 315
    partial templates, 145
    prefixing partial templates, 402
| (vertical bar)
    arguments in blocks, 48
    regular expressions, 46

DIGITS

1Password, 281

A

-a option for committing, 100
\A sequence, 47
:abort symbol, 118
Accept header, 359
accepts() method, 362
accessors, 51, 102, 319, 389
ACID properties, 348
Action Cable, broadcasting updates, 158–162
Action Controller
    about, 349
    action methods, 360–371
    callbacks and controllers, 378–380
    dispatching requests, 350–360
    flash and, 377
    objects and operations that span requests, 371–380
    processing requests, 360–371
    redirects, 368–371
    rendering templates, 363–367
    sending files and data, 367–368
    sending strings, 364, 367
    sessions and controllers, 372–377
Action Dispatch
    about, 349
    concerns, 358
    dispatching requests, 350–360
    REST and, 350–360

Action Mailbox
    about, 247
    conductors, 251–253
    creating mailboxes, 250
    receiving email, 247–253
    responding with rich text, 259–267
    setup, 248
    storing email, 253–259
    testing, 256–259
Action Mailer
    checking sent mail, 204
    configuring email, 190–191
    sending email, 189–195, 264
    testing email, 195
action methods
    about, 360
    environment, 360–362
    user response, 362–371
Action Pack, 39, 349, *see also* Action Controller; Action Dispatch; Action View
Action Text, 247, 259–267
Action View
    about, 349, 381–406
    files, uploading, 387–390
    forms, generating, 383–386
    forms, processing, 386
    helpers, using, 391–398
    layouts, 398–402
    partial templates, 402–405
    templates, using, 381–383
action_name parameter, 360
ActionMailer::Base.deliveries() method, 204
ActionNotFound error, 360
actions, *see also* Action Cable; Action Controller; Action Dispatch; Action Mailer; Action View; REST
    about, 34
    adding, 357
    callbacks and controllers, 378–380
    flash and controllers, 377
    limiting, 353
    link_to_unless_current(), 396
    list of, 353
    mapping URLs to, 216, 350
    qualifying layouts, 400

redirecting to, 370
selecting in callbacks, 378
Active Job
    about, 189, 197
    background processing, 197–205
    creating classes, 200
    real time page updates with Hotwire, 80
    resources, 205
Active Record, *see also* migrations
    about, 37, 315
    callbacks for monitoring of objects, 339–344
    column statistics, 331
    CRUD, 324–339
    custom SQL queries, 333–334
    data, defining, 315–320
    encryption, 341–344
    hook methods, 221
    plugins, 433
    relationships, specifying, 322–324
    reloading data, 335
    rows returned, ordering, 329, 333
    rows returned, subsetting, 329–331
    rows, creating, 324–326
    rows, deleting, 338
    rows, finding, 326–331
    rows, finding by ID, 320–322
    rows, updating, 335–338
    scopes, 332
    session data, storing, 375–376
    SQL and, 335
    tables associated with classes, 315–320
    transactions, 331, 344–348
Active Storage
    about, 38, 247
    configuration, 249–250
    connecting views to, 78
    deploying to cloud with Kamal, 286
    uploading and storing images, 390
ActiveJob::TestHelper module, 203
activerecord-session_store gem, 375
ActiveSupport::TestCase class, 89

acts_as_list plugin, 320
add_column() method, 410–411
add_index() method, 417
add_product() method, 140
AddXXXToTABLE pattern, 127
after callbacks, 378
after_action callback, 378
after_commit() callback, 80
after_create callback, 339
after_destroy callback, 221, 339
after_find callback, 339–341, 343
after_initialize callback, 339–340, 343
after_save callback, 339, 341
after_update callback, 339
after_validation callback, 339
Agile Manifesto, xix
agile practices, xix–xx
Ajax, partial templates, 405
all() method, 329
allow_unauthenticated_access(), 217
allowlisting, 217
AlmaLinux, 10
ampersand (&), prefix operator, 49
animation attribute, 156
animations, CSS, 156–158
any?() method, 90
APIs, documentation, xxiii
app directory, 18, 305
application.html.erb file, 105
application.rb file, 310
application_helper.rb file, 391
ApplicationController class, 227
applications
    accessible by other machines, 20
    architecture, 33–40
    creating, 17–19, 65
    dependencies, 305
    directories, 17, 22, 305
    helpers, 391
    layouts, 105–107
    quitting, 19, 31
    reloading automatically, 24
    running, 19–20, 70
    starting when deploying, 277
    URL of, 21, 25, 70, 102
@apply directive, 170

AppSignal, 292
apt-get, 271
ARG instruction, 270
around callbacks, 379
around_action callback, 379
array literals, 44
arrays
    about, 44
    SQL queries, 329
    of words, 45
arrow syntax (=>), 45
as: option, 102
asdf, 8
assert() method, 89–92, 185–186
assert_match() method, 196
assert_redirected_to() method, 137
assert_select() method, 109–110, 113
assertions, 90–92, 109–110, 185–186, 196, 427, see also testing
asset_host variable, 397
assets, precompiling, 273
assets directory, 397
AssetTagHelper class, 394–398
assignment shortcut, 55
_at suffix, 320
at sign (@), prefixing instance variables, 42, 50
Atom feeds, 397
attr_accessor method, 51
attr_reader method, 51
attr_writer method, 51
attribute_names() method, 334
attribute_present?() method, 334
attributes
    accessor methods, 319
    custom SQL queries, 334
    custom data, 395
    labels, 384
    lack of explicit definitions, 317
    raw values, 319
    reloading, 335
    setting, 324
attributes() method, 334
authenticating
    authentication generator, xiii, 207
    exercises, 223
    permitting access, 217–218
    users, 207–215
autoload paths, 306
average() method, 331
AWS Secrets Manager, 281

B

back end, 205
:back parameter, 371
background colors, cycling, 77
background processing, 197–205
backing up databases, 289
backslash (\)
    multiple-line commands, 67
    regular expressions, 47
    string substitutions, 44
bang methods, 55
banners, adding, 105
base_path attribute, 382
:bcc parameter, 396
bcrypt-ruby gem, 305
before callbacks, 378
before() method, 428
before_action callback, 121, 167, 227, 378
before_create callback, 339
before_destroy callback, 339
before_save callback, 339, 341
_before_type_cast suffix, 319
before_update callback, 339
before_validation callback, 339
belongs_to() method, 117, 174, 176, 322–323
benchmarks, 420
bin directory, 18, 308
bin/dev command, 69
:binary column type, 411
binstubs, 18
Bitwarden, 281
blocks
    about, 48
    callbacks, 340, 378–379
    converting into a Proc class, 56
    passing, 48
blogging application, 369
BlueCloth, 394
body() method, 362
:body parameter, 396
:boolean column type, 411
Booleans, 319, 411
braces ({})
    array of words, 45
    blocks, 48
    hashes, 45–46
brackets ([])
    array indices, 44
    array of words, 45
    hash indices, 46
Brakeman, 433
brew install command, 8
broadcast_replace_later_to() method, 162
broadcasting updates, 158–163
browsers
    JavaScript debugging facilities, 163
    system tests using, 184–187
build method, 122
build-essential package, 272
bundle exec command, 19
bundle install command, 11
Bundler, 305
button_to() method, 81, 119, 136, 395
buttons
    adding, 119–124, 136, 166, 395
    decrementing, 163
    deleting items, 141
    disabling, 183
    styling, 120
    translating, 234

C

Cache-Control parameter, 361
caching
    controller role, 40
    counter, 320
    headers, 361
    partial results, 110–112
    resources, 112
    REST, 351
    Russian doll, 112
    toggling, 110
call() method, 379
callbacks
    Active Record, 339–344
    after, 378
    around, 379
    before, 378

cart example, 121
controllers and, 378–380
grouping, 340–344
handlers, 340–344
inheritance, 379
limiting access, 378
locale, setting, 227
nesting, 379
ordering, 340
passing objects as, 379
permitting access, 217–218
rendering JSON, 366
selecting actions, 378
skipping, 217, 380
types, 378
capitalize() method, 44
Capybara, 184–187
caret (^), multiple-line commands, 67
CarrierWave, 433
cart for Depot, *see also* checkout for Depot; orders for Depot
broadcasting updates, 158–162
buttons, 119–124, 136, 148
capturing cart items into order, 174–178
Checkout button, 166
connecting to products, 116–119
counter, 125
creating, 115–116
deleting, 175
emptying, 136–140
error handling, 132–136
hiding, 391
highlighting changes, 155–158
identifier, 115
item count, adding, 127–132
orders, capturing, 165–178
partial templates, 144–147
price totals, 139
retrieving, 115
security, 132, 136
in sidebar, 144–155
styling, 138
testing, 118, 124, 132, 137, 140, 148–150, 158, 168, 173, 426–430

translations, 234
Turbo-based, 150–155
case, of names, 42, 311
catalog for Depot, *see also* products for Depot
broadcasting updates, 158–162
caching partial results, 110–112
cart in sidebar, 144–155
creating listing, 101–104
displaying, 101–113
testing, 108–110
:cc parameter, 192, 396
cd command, 66
certificate management, Thruster, 274
change() method, 410, 414
change, agile practices for, xx
change_column() method, 413
channels, 160
checkout. command, 100
checkout for Depot, *see also* cart for Depot; orders for Depot
Checkout button in cart, 166
checkout form, 168–174
confirmation emails, 189–196
dynamic fields for payment, 178–182
errors, 167, 176
order form, 166–174
orders, capturing, 165–178
payment processing, running in background, 196–205
system testing, 203–205
testing, 168, 173, 184–187
translations, 237–243
validations, 173, 184
Chrome browser, system tests using, 184–187
chruby, 8
CI (continuous integration), 12
class attribute, 244
class keyword, 50
class methods, 37, 50, 55, 340
classes
about, 41, 50–51

Active Job, 200
attributes of, associated with columns, 317–322
automatic loading, 312
callbacks, 378–379
combining utility classes in Tailwind, 170
defining, 50
instances of, associated with rows, 317–320
loading, for marshaled objects, 53
migrations and names, 410
names, 42, 50, 311–314, 410
specifying HTML classes in Slim, 431
tables associated with, 315–320
versioning and storing session data, 374
cleanup, session, 376
click_on() method, 186
CloudFlare, 280
CMD instruction, 274
CNCF's Distribution Registry, 280
code
limiting in templates, 391
shared, 116, 306
statistics, 298
third-party, 309
for this book, xxii
:collection parameter, 403
collections
partial templates, 403
scoping, 357
colon (:), prefixing symbols, 42
colors, highlighting changes, 155–158
columns
adding, 127–132, 410
changing column type, 413
class attributes associated with, 317–322
column types and migrations, 411–413
default data type, 165
default value, 127
fixtures, 93
listing, 317
mapped to attributes, 37
null value, allowing, 166
removing, 127, 410

renaming, 413
special, provided by Active Record, 320
statistics, 331
timestamps, 320, 411
updating records, 336
command line
about, 12
adding users, 209
multiple-line commands, 67
tab completion, 12
comments
formatting helpers, 394
Ruby, 43
uploading images, 390
committing, Git, 100
composite index, 418
concern statement, 358
concerns, 116, 121, 344, 358
concerns, separation of, 25, 34, 39, 359
conditional evaluation, 55
conductors, 251–253
config directory, 309–310
config.routes file, 227
config.ru file, 304
configuration
Bundler, 305
databases, 95
in Depot application, 297
directories, 309–310
documentation, 310
email, 190–191
environments, 310
Git, 7, 82
Rack, 304
routes, 216
selecting locale, 226
:confirm parameter, 395
confirmation boxes, 77
console
dbconsole, 177, 308
rails console, 209, 223, 255, 277, 308, 317
server console, 19, 70, 309
web console, 28–30, 149
console.log file, 182
constants, 42
constraints, REST, 350
constructors, 42

content types
forcing when rendering, 366
multiple, delivering, 194, 360
sending files and data, 367–368
Content-Disposition header, 368
Content-Length header, 368
Content-Transfer-Encoding header, 368
Content-Type header, 367–368
content_for mechanism, 401
content_length() method, 362
content_type() method, 362, 389
:content_type parameter, 367
context, forms, 169
context() method, 428
continuous integration (CI), 12
control structures, 47
controller attribute, 382
controllers, *see also* Action Controller; Action Dispatch; MVC architecture
about, 20, 34
action methods, 360–371
Action Pack support, 39
callbacks and, 378–380
creating, 20, 66, 101
default behavior, 21
in Depot application, 296
directory location, 22
dispatching requests, 350–360
environment, 360–362
error logging, 135
flash and, 377
form details, capturing, 174–178
grouping into modules, 312
mapping URLs to, 350
marshaled objects, 53
modifying, 128–132, 137–140
names, 70, 311–314
objects and operations that span requests, 371–380
overriding layouts, 399
partial templates and, 405

processing requests, 360–371
redirects, 368–371
rendering template actions, 362–367
sending files and data, 367–368
separating logic from data, 25
sessions and, 372–377
slow processing of, 196–205
Stimulus, 178–182
switching locales, 245
testing, 108–110, 118, 124, 137, 140, 148–150, 158, 168, 214–215, 217
user response, 362–371
writing helper methods, 391
convention over configuration, xviii, 26, 34, 66, 95
conventions, for this book, xxii
cookies
associated with request, 360
expiring, 376
storing session data, 372–374, 376
cookies object, 360
COPY instruction, 272
count() method, 331
counters, 125, 320
coupling, 34
create action, 150, 176, 353
create() method
about, 35
buttons, 119–124
error reports, 337
model objects, 325
order details for cart, 174–178
validation errors and, 97
create!() method, 74, 337
create_table() method, 414–415, 418
created_at column, 320, 415
created_on column, 320, 415
credentials (secrets), 275–276
cross-site request forgery attacks, 106

CRUD (create, read, update, delete) operations, 324–339, 353
csp_meta_tag() method, 106
csrf_meta_tags() method, 106
CSS, *see also* styling and style sheets
   animations, 156–158
   class attribute and, 244
   selector notation, 109
   Tailwind, 65–66, 75–80, 106, 170
curl, 271
currency
   converting numbers to, 107, 113
   formatting, 107, 113, 392
   internationalization, 107, 235–236, 246
current time, 24
current_cycle() method, 394
current_page() method, 396
cycle() method, 77, 394

D

-d option, containers, 277
\d sequence, 47
data, *see also* databases; models
   custom attributes, 395
   defining, 315–320
   fixture data, 92–95
   passing to layouts, 401
   reloading, 335
   seed data, 74–75
   sending, 367–368
:data parameter, 395
data types
   column types and migrations, 411–413
   default, for columns, 165
   Ruby, 43–47
   SQL to Ruby mappings, 319
data-controller field, 182
database drivers, 416
databases, *see also* Active Record; columns; migrations; models; rows; tables
   adapters, 16
   backing up, 289
   column statistics, 331
   column type mapping table, 411
   configuration files, 95
   connecting tables in, 116–119
   creating, 66–69
   deleting rows, 118, 338
   development database, 95
   drivers, 15, 416
   encryption, 341–344
   locale exercise, 246
   mapping types, 319
   in MVC diagram, 34
   production database, 95
   Rails support, 36
   saving form fields to, 174–178
   searching, 326–331
   seed data, 74–75
   SQL access to, 324–339
   supported by Rails, 15
   test database, 95
   transactions, 344–348
   updating rows, 335–338
   validating data, 85–88
DataDog, 290
:date column type, 411
dates
   column type, 411
   exercises, 113, 206
   form helpers, 385
   formatting helpers, 392
   mapping, 319
   _on suffix, 320
:datetime column type, 411
DB2, 411
Debian Bookworm, 271
Debian-based Linuxes, 9
debug() method, 382, 393
debugging
   Hotwire, 163
   JavaScript, 163
   templates, 382, 393
   viewing errors in web console, 28–30
:decimal column type, 411
decimals, 319, 411–412
declarations, 50, 117, 176, 322–324
decryption, *see* encryption
default values, 55
default: value option, 412
delete() method, 338
DELETE request
   linking helpers, 395
   links, 81
   POST substituted for, 81
   in REST, 351, 357
delete? attribute, 361
delete_all() method, 338
deleting
   cart items, 117
   columns, 127
   exercises, 141
   linking helpers, 395
   migrations, 131
   products, 77
   REST, 353
   rows, 118, 174, 338
   sessions, 373, 376–377
   tables, 414–419
   users, 219–222
deliver_later() method, 193, 197
deliver_now() method, 193
denylisting, 217
dependencies, directory, 305
dependent: parameter, 117
deploy command (Kamal), 288
deployment
   about, 269
   backing up databases, 289
   building images, 271–273
   changes with Rails 8, xiii
   converting SQLite database to PostgreSQL, 292
   Docker containers, starting, 277
   Docker images, 277
   Docker, installing, 277
   exercises, 293
   local deployment with Docker, 269–278
   logs, making searchable, 290–292
   monitoring tools, 292
   requirements, 3
   review of, 298
   running in production, 288–293
   scaling, 292
   secrets (credentials), managing, 275–276
   starting application, 277
   to cloud, 274, 278–288
Depot application, *see also* cart for Depot; catalog for Depot; checkout for Depot; orders for Depot; products for Depot
   about, 59–64, 295–299

Index • 445

administration in sidebar, 218–222
administrative users, adding, 209
administrative users, permitting access for, 217–218
controllers, 296
creating application, 65–74
CRUD operations, 324–339
data requirements, 62–64
database, creating, 66–69
database, migrating, 68–69
deployment, 269–293, 298
development approach, 59
directories, 66
email, receiving, 247–253
email, responding with rich text, 259–267
email, sending, 189–196, 264
email, storing, 253–259
email, testing, 256–259
migrations, 408
models, 295–296
page flow, 61
REST, 351–360
running, 70
scaffold, 66–68
Slim templates, 432
specification, 60–64
statistics, 298
testing, 297, 426–430
translations, 230–243
use cases, 60
views, 296
describe() method, 428
deserialization, *see* encryption
desktop organization, 15
destroy action, 353
destroy() method, 136–138, 338–339, 347
destroy: parameter, 117, 174
destroy_all() method, 338
--detach option, containers, 277
development, incremental, 59
development environment
Active Storage setup, 249
automatic reloading, 24
setup, 3, 12–15
development.log, 308

Devkit, 4
dialog boxes, confirmation, 77
digest password type, 208, 215
Digital Ocean, 279
digits, regular expressions, 47
dir command, 18, 66
directories
applications, 305
assets, 397
fixtures, 92
images, 397
layouts, 399, 405
library, 305–307
listing contents, 18, 66
structure, 17, 22, 303–310
tasks, 307
templates, 363, 381, 404
tests, 89, 305
views, 381
distance_of_time_in_words() method, 392
div in Slim, 431
do/end blocks, 48
Docker
base images, 270
cloud deployment with Kamal, 278–288
container registries, 280
containers, starting, 277
development setup, 3–4
images, about, 269
images, building, 271–273, 277, 281
installing, 277
instructions, 270
local deployment with, 269–278
docker compose build command, 277
docker compose up command, 277
docker-compose.yml file, 274
DockerHub, 280
documentation, Rails, xxiii, 15, *see also* resources
DOM (Document Object Model), 151, 156–157, 163
domain() method, 361
domain names, deploying to cloud with Kamal, 280, 284
Don't Repeat Yourself principle, *see* DRY principle
Doppler, 281

Dormando, 375
dot (.)
CSS selectors, 109
filenames, 83
prefixing translation function, 230
specifying HTML classes in Slim, 431
DoubleRenderError exception, 363
down() method, 129, 410, 414
downloads, 363
DRb, 375–376
DRbStore, 375–376
drivers, database, 416
drop_table() method, 415
DRY (Don't Repeat Yourself) principle, xviii, xx, 317, 398–405
duplication, avoiding, *see* DRY principle
dynamic content, *see* ERB templates

E

each() method, 329, 332
eager-loads, 293
edit action, 353
editors, selecting, 13–14
Effective Testing with RSpec 3, 425
Elastic Search, 290
Emacs, 13
email
auto-deletion of, 255
configuring, 190–191
delivery method, 190
exercises, 206, 267
form helpers, 385
internationalization, 192
linking helpers, 394, 396
multiple content types, 194
plain-text, 265
processing in background, 197
receiving, 247–253
responding with rich text, 259–267
sending, 189–195, 264–265
storing, 253–259
templates, 192, 195
testing, 190, 195, 256–259
email_field() method, 172, 385

Embedded Ruby, *see* ERB templates
:encode parameter, 396
encryption
    DRbStore, 375
    flash data, 378
    session data, 372
    using callback handler, 341–344
end keyword, 43, 47
ENGINE=InnoDB option, 416
entity names, 233, 241
ENTRYPOINT, deploying with Docker, 273
enum declaration, 165, 172
enumerated types
    Postgres, 419
    Ruby, 165, 172
ENV instruction, 271
env() method, 362
environment.rb file, 310
environments
    configuring, 310
    roles, 310
    staging, 310
    switching, 310
environments directory, 310
ERB templates
    about, 23, 39, 363, 382
    catalog display, 103–104
    compared to Slim, 430
    converting to Slim, 432
    names, 26
    testing Action Mailbox, 258
    for views, 22–23
erb2slim command, 432
errors, *see also* exceptions
    empty form fields, 176
    exercises, 140, 206
    form fields, 170
    handling different content types, 360
    handling in before_action, 167
    handling with flashes, 132–136, 377
    handling with rollback, 221, 344
    installation, 18
    logging, 134–136
    marshaling, 53
    messages, adding to, 92
    messages, built-in, 96

messages, returning as string without a view, 362
messages, translating, 240–241, 243
missing methods, 360
partials, 148–150
readability, xxiii
redirecting after, 135
rendering, 363
start-up, 70
validation, 86–87, 90–92, 100
viewing in web console, 28–30
errors() method, 90
errors object, 118
escape sequence, \u00D7, 132
escaping, SQL, 327
European General Data Protection Regulation (GDPR), 255
:except option
    actions, 353
    qualifying layouts, 400
exceptions, *see also* errors
    create! and save! raising, 337, 345
    DoubleRenderError exception, 363
    handling with rollback, 221
    intercepted by rescue clauses, 49, 134, 221
    IrreversibleMigration exception, 414
    RecordInvalid exception, 338
    RecordNotFound exception, 132, 326–327
    save!() method, 337
excerpt() method, 394
exchange rates, 246
exclamation point (!), bang methods, 55
execute() method, 419–420
exercises, *see* Playtime exercises
expand_path() method, 56
expiry, session, 376
EXPOSE 80, 273
expression interpolation, 44
extensions, templates, 363

F
field_with_errors, 170
Fielding, Roy, 350
fields
    dynamic, 178–182
    form helpers, 385
    hiding, 385
    limiting size, 412
    validating, 86
:file_store option, 375
files
    directory structure, 303–310
    fixtures, 92
    ignoring in Git, 82
    layouts, 399
    listing, 18, 66, 83
    metadata, 389
    names, 83, 311–314, 367
    navigation, editor support for, 13
    rendering to, 366
    requiring full path for, 56
    RSpec, 430
    sending, 367–368
    storing session data, 375
    uploading, 387–390
filter() method, 378–379
find() method, 326–327, 334
find_by() method, 128
find_by_sql() method, 333–335
Firebird, 16
first() method, 329
fixtures, 92–99, 257, 427
fixtures() directive, 95, 427
flash
    about, 134–136
    controllers and, 377
    error messages, 377
    removing messages, 138
    translating messages, 243
flash attribute, 382
flash.keep option, 377
flash.now option, 377
floating numbers, 319, 411
force: option, 415
foreign keys
    about, 117
    custom migrations example, 419–420
    relationships, 322
    set automatically, 176
    xxx_id column, 320

form helpers, 168–174
form.select element, 182
form_with helper, 244
form_with() method, 169
format() method, 362
:format parameter, 359
formats
    data representation, REST, 359
    helper methods, 392–398
    request actions, 362
    route specifier, 354, 359
    templates, 363
forms
    capturing information from, 174–178
    constrained options, fields for, 385
    context, 169
    creating, 168–174
    dynamic, 178–182
    generating, 383–386
    helpers, 383–386
    labels, 384
    modifying, 71–72
    names, 169
    new user, 212
    order form, 166–174
    processing, 386
    relationships to tables, 174
    switching locale, 244–245
    text areas, 384
    text fields, 384
    validations, 173
forward slash (/), regular expressions, 46
fragment caching, 110–112
FROM instruction, 270, 272
:from mail parameter, 192
functional testing, 108–110, 124, 305

G

gcr.io, 280
GDPR (European General Data Protection Regulation), 255
gem install command, 7, 9, 11
gem list command, 11
gem server command, xxiii
Gemfile file, 305
Gemfile.lock file, 305
generators, *see* rails generate command

get action, 388, 390
GET request
    linking helpers, 395
    in REST, 351
    side effects, 81
get? attribute, 361
ghcr.io, 280
Git
    about, 12
    checking status, 100
    committing work, 100
    configuring, 7, 82
    exercises, 82
    ignoring files, 82
    resources, 12
git config command, 7
git package, deploying with Docker, 272
.gitignore file, 82
Gitlab, 280
global replacements with callbacks, 379
:greater_than_or_equal_to option, 87, 91
group() method, 331–332

H

handler class, 340–344
handlers, callbacks, 340–344
has_and_belongs_to_many declaration, 323
has_many() method, 117, 174, 176, 323
has_no_field?(), 186
has_one() method, 322
has_rich_text() method, 261
has_secure_password() method, 208
hash keys, 45
hash literals, 45
hash mark (#)
    comments, 43
    CSS selectors, 109
hash() method, 321
hashes
    about, 44–46
    hash keys, 45, 321
    passing as parameters, 46
    placeholders, 328
head? attribute, 361
headers
    caching, 361
    cookies, 361

    request actions, 362
    sending files, 368
headers attribute, 382
headers() method, 362
headers parameter, 361, 368
Heinemeier Hansson, David, xxiii
Hello, World! app, 20–30, 399
helper methods
    directory, 391
    for formatting and linking, 392–398
    forms, 168–174, 383–386
    named routes, 353
    organizing, 391
    uploading files, 387–390
    using, 391–398
    for view templates, 27–28
    writing, 391
helper modules
    about, 52, 391
    controller role, 40
    default, 391
Hetzner, 279
Hetzner Cloud, 279
Hetzner Robot, 279
hidden_div_if() method, 391
hidden_field() method, 385
hiding
    cart, 391
    form fields, 385
High Performance PostgreSQL for Rails, 293
highlight() method, 394
highlighting
    changes, 155–158, 163
    formatting helpers, 394
    syntax, in editor, 13
    testing, 158
Homebrew, 7
Honeybadger, 292
hook methods, 118, 221
host() method, 361
host_with_port() method, 361
hosts
    binding to, 20
    request actions, 361
Hotwire
    about, 143
    incremental style, 163
    real time page updates, 78, 81
    troubleshooting, 163

HTML, *see also* ERB templates
   entity names, 233, 241
   mailers, 194
   Slim templates, 430–432
   stripping tags from, 77
.html.erb files, *see* ERB templates
html2slim gem, 432
html_safe method, 226
HTTP requests, *see* redirects; requests
HTTP/2 proxies, 273
HTTP_REFERER header, 371
HTTPS, 361

I
-i email option, 190
I18n module
   selecting locale, 226–229
   switching locale, 244–245
   translations, 230–243
id column
   about, 320
   automatically set, 325, 415
   default primary key, 321
   importance of, 120
   records, finding by ID, 320–322
   renaming, 321, 418
   storing in session, 115
id() method, 321
IDEs, 14
IDs
   migration version/ID, 131, 408–409
   session ID, 372, 376
IETF (Internet Engineering Task Force), 159
if statements, 47
image field, deploying to cloud with Kamal, 284
image_tag() method, 77, 104, 396
images
   Depot product listing, 74–80
   directory, 397
   displaying, 389
   exercises, 163
   linking helpers, 396
   making into links, 396
   tags, 104, 396

uploading files, 387–390
validating URLS for, 88, 91
images directory, 397
import maps
   importmap pin command, 424
   javascript_importmap_tags() method, 397
import statement, 424
importmap pin command, 424
include statement, 121, 293
incremental development, 59
indentation
   automatic, in editor, 13
   fixtures, 93
   Ruby, 43
   YAML, 52, 232
index action, 353, 355
index() method, 102–103, 215
indices
   arrays, 44
   composite, 418
   defining, 417
   functional testing, 109
   hashes, 46
   manipulating outside migrations, 421
inflections, 316
inheritance, callbacks, 379
InnoDB storage, 416
installing
   development environment, 12–15
   errors, 18
   examining results, 18
   on Linux, 9–11
   on macOS, 7–9
   packages on Debian, 271
   Rails, 3–16
   RSpec, 425
   Ruby, 4, 7, 10
   Slim, 432
   on Windows, 4–7
instance methods
   for actions, 360
   defining, 50–51
   for layouts, 400
   in ORM, 37
instance variables
   about, 50
   accessing, 51
   available in templates, 382
   lost after redirect, 134
   names, 42, 50

:integer column type, 411, 413
internationalization
   about, 225
   characters, 226, 233
   currency, 107, 235–236, 246
   exercises, 246
   locale, selecting, 226–229
   locale, switching, 244–245
   mailers, 192
   routes, 226–227
   scope, 227
   sending files and data, 367
   translations, 230–243
Internet Engineering Task Force (IETF), 159
invalid?() method, 90
IP address
   deploying to cloud with Kamal, 284
   request actions, 361
IrreversibleMigration exception, 414
iterators, 48

J
JavaScript, *see also* React; Webpack
   Action Cable, 159–162
   debugging, 163
   email helpers, 396
   linking helpers, 395, 397
   RJS templates, 363, 366
   testing, 184–187
javascript_importmap_tags() method, 397
Jbuilder templates, 382
JDBC, 16
join tables, 323, 330, 418
joins() method, 330
JSON
   exercises, 183
   Jbuilder templates generating, 382
   rendering templates, 366
   specifying data format, 359
   templates, 39

K
Kamal
   building images locally, 281
   deploy command, 288

deployment to cloud with, 274, 278–288
logs, watching in real time, 290
resources on, 278
setup command, 288
Kamal Handbook, 278
Kaminari, 433
keyframes, 156
@keyframes directive, 156
keys, *see also* primary keys
foreign, 117, 176, 320, 322, 419–420
hash keys, 45, 321

L

label() method, 169
labels, forms, 384
lambda expressions, 56
lambda operator, 56
LANGUAGES array, 244
LastPass, 281
layout directive, 399–400
:layout parameter, 399–402
layouts, *see also* styling and style sheets; templates
about, 398
for application, 105–107
avoiding duplication with, 398–402
directories, 399
dynamic, 400
files, 399
functional testing, 109
internationalization, 230–245
overriding for controllers, 399
partial templates and, 405
passing data to, 401
switching locale, 244–245
wrapping renderings, 366
layouts directory, 399
:length option, 100
less command, 15, 135
let() method, 427
lib directory, 305–307
libjemalloc2, 271, 273
libraries
directory, 305–307
Linux installation and, 9
loading, 306
requiring, 307

libvips, 271
like clauses, 329
limit() method, 330, 332–333
limit: size option, 412
line breaks, 393
line_items_path() method, 119
link_to() method, 27, 77, 394–398
link_to_if() method, 395
link_to_unless() method, 395
link_to_unless_current() method, 395
links
between pages, 26–28
generating conditionally, 395
helper methods, 394–398
images as, 396
tags for, generating, 106
to REST actions, 357
Linux
database drivers, 16
installing Rails, 9–11
scrolling log files, 135
lit package, 424–425
Litestream, 289
load balancers, 293
load path
about, 310
enabling autoloading, 306
requiring files not in, 56
loading, automatic, 312
local variables
names, 42
partial templates, 403
locale
selecting, 226–229
switching, 244–245
translations, 239
:locals parameter, 403
lock() method, 331
log directory, 275, 308
log files
deploying to cloud with Kamal, 285, 290–292
directory, 308
errors, 134–136
scrolling, 15, 135
searchable, 290–292
viewing, 135
logger, 134–135, 362
logger object, 362, 382
logging out, 376

logic, Ruby, 47–50, *see also* separation of concerns
login
authenticating users, 207–215
deleting users, 219–222
exercises, 222
log out, 376
permitting access, 217–218
plugins, 222
styling, 218–222
testing, 217
Loki, 290
looping, *see* blocks; iterators
ls -a command, 83
ls command, 18, 66, 83
Lucas, Tim, 417

M

macOS
database drivers, 16
installing Rails, 7–9
tracking log files, 135
machines, deploying with Kamal, 279
mail() method, 192
mail_to() method, 396
mailboxes, *see* Action Mailbox
mailers, 191–195, *see also* email
many-to-many relationships, 323
map() method, 329
mapping, *see also* ORM libraries
arrays, 329
column types, 411
models to tables, 66
objects to forms, 168
SQL to Ruby types, 319
URLs to actions, 350
Markdown (BlueCloth), 394
marshaling, 53, 375
master key, 276, 286
maximum() method, 331
memcached system, 375
:memory_store option, 375
messages, *see* email; errors; exceptions
method attribute, 361
:method parameter, 395
method: :delete method, 81
method_missing() method, 360

methods, *see also* helper methods; instance methods
  about, 50–51, 144
  accessors, 51, 102, 319, 389
  action methods, 360–371
  bang methods, 55
  callback handlers, 340
  class methods, 37, 50, 55, 340
  defining, 43
  hook methods, 118, 221
  invoking, 42
  missing methods, 360
  names, 42
  passing blocks, 48
  predicate methods, 55
  private methods, 51, 116
  protected methods, 51
  public methods, 51
Migration class, 410
migrations
  about, 68, 407–408, 410–414
  advanced, 419–420
  applying, 68
  checking status, 131
  column types, 411–413
  columns, adding or removing, 127–132
  columns, changing, 413
  columns, renaming, 413
  creating, 129, 407–408
  custom benchmarks, 420
  custom messages, 420
  deleting, 131
  directory, 407
  down, 129, 410, 414
  exercises, 81, 140
  filenames, 408
  indices, defining, 417
  irreversible, 414
  join tables, 418
  listing, 307
  multiple, 166
  names, 127
  naming convention, 407
  one-way, 414
  order, 409
  redoing, 410
  rolling back, 131, 221, 409, 420
  running, 128, 409–410
  schema manipulation outside of, 421
  tables defined by, 317–320
  tables, creating, 414–419
  tables, dropping, 415
  tables, force dropping, 415
  tables, renaming, 416
  timestamps, 68, 408
  troubleshooting, 420
  undoing and reapplying, 63
  up, 129, 410
  using native SQL, 419–420
  version number, 131, 408–409
  version, forcing, 409
MIME types
  request actions, 362
  specifying, 359
minimum() method, 331
MiniTest, 89
MiniTest::Test class, 89
mise-en-place, installing with, 7, 10
Model-View-Controller (MVC) architecture, *see* MVC architecture
models, *see also* Active Record; databases; MVC architecture; unit testing
  about, 20, 33, 176, 295
  creating, 66, 253
  in Depot application, 295–296
  equality, 322
  foreign keys, 117, 322
  generator, 408
  mapping to forms, 168
  mapping to tables, 66
  marshaled objects, 53
  moving logic from controller, 198
  names, 66, 311–314
  object life cycle, 339–344
  objects and storing session data, 373
  Rails support, 36–38
  records, finding by ID, 320–322
  relationships, specifying, 322–324
  reloading, 335
  testing, 89–99
  translating names, 242
  validating, 85–88
modules
  about, 52
  automatic loading, 312
  grouping controllers into, 312
  names, 42, 52, 311–314
monitoring tools, 292
MSYS2, 4–5
MVC (Model-View-Controller) architecture
  about, xvii, 20, 33–36
  diagram, 34
mx-auto class, 77
MySQL
  column type table, 411
  database adapter, 16
  database driver, 416
  options: parameter, 415
  share mode, 331

N

%n placeholder, 236
\n, forcing newlines with, 44
name completion, 13
:name option, 418
named routes, 353, 358
names
  channels, 160
  classes, 42, 50, 410
  columns, renaming, 413
  constants, 42
  controller, 70
  controllers, 311–314
  email templates, 195
  files, 83, 367
  fixtures, 92–93
  form fields, 169
  instance variables, 42, 50
  internationalization, 230, 233
  local variables, 42
  methods, 42
  migrations, 127, 408
  models, 66
  modifying the inflection file, 316
  modules, 42, 52
  naming conventions, 311–314
  parameters, 42
  partial templates, 145, 402
  primary keys, 418
  routes, 352
  Ruby, 42
  tables, 66, 315–320, 414
  tables, renaming, 416
  templates, 195, 363, 381
  uploading images, 389

users, 211
variables, 42
naming conventions, 311–314
  for nonbreaking space, 236
NeoVim, 14
nested resources, 358
nesting, callbacks, 379
new action, 166, 168–169, 176, 353
new() method, 42, 324
New Relic, 292
newline character, replacing string with, 44
nil, 44, 46
no-cache parameter, 361
nonbreaking space character, 236
NoScript plugin, 163
:notice parameter, 135
notices
    error redirects, 135
    flash and controller, 377
npm packages, 424
null value, allowing for columns, 166
null: option, 412
number.currency.format configuration, 235
number_field() method, 385
number_to_currency() method, 77, 107, 113, 392
number_to_human_size() method, 392–393
number_to_percentage() method, 392–393
number_to_phone() method, 392–393
number_with_delimiter() method, 392–393
number_with_precision() method, 392–393
numbers
    column types, 411–412
    converting to currency, 107, 113
    formatting, 107, 109, 392
    functional testing, 109
    internationalization, 235–236, 246
    mapping, 319

precision, 393, 412
validating, 87, 91
numericality() option, 87

O

:object parameter, 403
Object Storage, deploying to cloud with Kamal, 280
object-oriented programming, see OO programming
object-relational mapping (ORM) libraries, xxiv, 36–38, see also Active Record
objects
    associating errors with, 118
    creating, 42
    equality, 322
    life cycle, 339–344
    mapping to forms, 168
    marshaling, 53
    passing as callback, 379
    passing into partial templates, 403
    saving, 176
    storing session data, 372
offset() method, 330
onchange event handler, 244
one-to-many relationships, 322
one-to-one relationships, 322
:only option
    limiting actions, 353
    qualifying layouts, 400
_on suffix, 320
OO (object-oriented) programming
    relational databases and, 36
    Ruby used for, 41–43
op= assignment shortcut, 55
Openbase, column type table, 411
OpenStruct class, 198
options: parameter, 415
Oracle, 16, 411
order() method, 103, 329, 332–333
ordering
    callback handlers, 340
    of items, 103
    migrations, 409
    SQL queries, 329, 332–333
    users, 212

orders for Depot, see also cart for Depot; checkout for Depot
    capturing, 165–178
    confirmation emails, 189–196
    connecting to slow payment processor, 197–205
    deleting, 174
    exercises, 206
    order form, 166–174
    support emails, 254
    translations, 237–243
ORM (object-relational mapping) libraries, xxiv, 36–38, see also Active Record

P

page flow, 61
Pago (fictional payment processor), 197–205
paragraph breaks, 393
parameters
    names, 42
    passing with flash, 377
    passing hashes as, 46
    passing to partials, 144
    processing forms, 386
params object
    about, 122, 361
    forms, 386
    placeholders, 328
    views, 382
parentheses (())
    method calls, 42
    regular expressions, 46
    in REST routes, 353
:partial parameter, 403
partial templates
    about, 144, 402
    avoiding duplication with, 402–405
    collections, 403
    controllers, 405
    for dynamic fields, 180
    mailers, 193, 195
    names, 145, 402
    passing parameters to, 144
    rendering, 144–147, 366, 403–405
    shared, 404
    with Turbo, 151–155
partials, see partial templates
password managers, 281, 286
password_field() method, 385

passwords
  exercises, 223
  form helpers, 385
  hashing, 207, 215
  obscuring, 385
  password managers, 281, 286
  validating, 208
PATCH request
  linking helpers, 395
  POST substituted for, 81
_path, appending to controller name, 119
path() method, 361
paths, *see also* load path
  base_path attribute, 382
  expanding, 56
  pathnames to views, 103
  redirecting to, 370
  request actions, 361
  requiring full path for, 56
  REST requests, 352
payment
  processing in background, 196–205
  types, 184
  validations, 184
percentages, formatting helpers, 392
perform_enqueued_jobs() method, 203
perform_later() method, 202
performance, REST, 351
pessimistic version operator, 11
pgloader, 292
phone numbers, formatting helpers, 392
pkg-config package, 272
placeholders, 328, 384
Playtime exercises
  administration, 222
  authentication, 223
  broadcasting, 163
  buttons, 163
  counters, 125
  date, 113, 206
  deployment, 293
  email, 206, 267
  error messages, 140
  errors, 206
  expressions, 31
  images, 163
  internationalization, 246
  iteration, 31
  JSON, 183

layouts, 113
migration, 187
migrations, 81, 140
order checkout, 206
passwords, 223
rollbacks, 81
sessions, 125
tests, 113, 140, 187, 223
time, 113
validations, 100, 184, 223
version control, 82
XML, 183
plugins
  customizing with, 433
  login, 222
pluralize() method, 125, 215, 394
plurals
  naming conventions, 311, 313, 316
  translations, 241
port_string() method, 361
ports
  deploying locally with Docker, 275
  request actions, 361
POST request
  about, 35
  for buttons, 119
  linking helpers, 395
  locale switchers and forms, 245
  processing forms, 386
  in REST, 351
  substitution for other HTTP methods, 81
  uploading files, 387
post? attribute, 361
PostgreSQL
  about, 3
  column type table, 411
  converting SQLite to, 292
  database adapter, 16
  Queue Classic, 205
:precision option, 412
precompile, 273
predicate methods, 55
preloads, 293
prepend_after_action() method, 378
prepend_before_action() method, 378
presence: true parameter, 86
prices
  exercises, 140

formatting, 107, 109
internationalization, 107, 235–236, 246
validating, 87, 91
primary database, backing up, 289
primary keys
  about, 315, 418
  automatic creation, 415
  default, 321
  finding rows, 320, 326
  id column, 320
  names, 418
  overriding, 321
  tables without, 418
primary_key attribute, 321
:primary_key option, 418
private directive, 51, 116
private methods, 51, 116
Proc
  converting blocks to, 56
  scopes, 332
process() method, 250
Procfile.dev file, 70
Product Maintenance application, *see* Depot application
production, database for, 95
production.log, 308
products for Depot
  adding, 71–72
  catalog display, 101–113
  connecting to cart, 116–119
  count, adding, 127–132
  database, creating, 66–69
  database, migrating, 68–69
  form for, modifying, 71–72
  formatting prices, 107
  list of, styling, 75–80
  list of, viewing, 69–80
  locale exercise, 246
  ordering, 103
  seed data, 74–75
  testing validations, 89–99
  validating, 85–88
products() method, 96
Programming Ruby 3.3, 41
:prompt parameter, 172
Propshaft Digest stamping, xxi
protected methods, 51
protocol() method, 361
public directory, 308

public methods, 51
public.ecr.aws, 280
PUT request
    linking helpers, 395
    POST substituted for, 81
    in REST, 351
put? attribute, 361
puts() method, 43, 97
px-2 class, 78
py-3 class, 78

Q

quay.io, 280
query_string() method, 361
question mark (?)
    predicate methods, 55
    SQL placeholders, 328
Queue Classic, 205
queuing, background jobs, 201, 205
quotation marks, strings, 43, 75

R

Rack, 304, 362
Rack Middlewares, 304
Rails
    advantages, xvii–xx
    customizing and extending, 423–433
    directory structure, 303–310
    documentation, xxiii, 15
    installing, 3–16
    requirements, 3
    resources, 434
    standards, xix
    upgrading version used, 11
    versions, 3, 11, 17–18
rails about command, 18
rails command, 17–19, 308
Rails component, 304
rails console command, 209, 223, 255, 277, 308, 317
rails db:migrate command, 68, 116, 128, 166, 254, 409
rails db:migrate redo command, 410
rails db:migrate:status command, 131
rails db:rollback command, 131
rails db:seed command, 75
rails dbconsole command, 177, 308
rails destroy command, 309
rails dev:cache command, 110
Rails Doctrine, xviii
rails generate authentication command, 207
rails generate command, 200, 309
rails generate controller command, 20, 101, 314
rails generate mailbox command, 250
rails generate mailer command, 191, 264
rails generate migration command, 127, 129, 408
rails generate model command, 253, 408
rails generate rspec:install command, 426
rails generate scaffold command, 66–68, 115–116
Rails Metal, 304
rails new command, 17, 65, 303, 309
rails routes command, 352
rails runner command, 309
rails server -e command, 310
rails server command, 19, 70, 309
rails spec command, 426
rails stats command, 298
rails test command, 97
rails test:all command, 182
rails test:system command, 184
rails.vim plugin, 14
RAILS_ENV=production command, 421
RAILS_MASTER_KEY, 277
raise method, 49
Rake
    resources, 308
    tasks, 131, 248, 262, 305, 307, 409
rake -D command, 305
rake -T command, 305
Rakefile file, 305
Ransack, 433
rbenv, 8
Reactive Controllers, 425
read() method, 389
read_attribute() method, 319
readability
    errors, xxiii
    fixture names, 93
    Rails, xviii
    Ruby structures, 54
README file, 305
readonly() method, 331
receive_inbound_email_from_mail() method, 256
received() method, 193
RecordInvalid exception, 338
RecordNotFound exception, 132, 326
records, *see* Active Record; databases; rows
recovery, 63
RedCloth, 394
RedHat-based Linuxes, 10
redirect_to() method, 135, 175, 363, 370–371
redirects
    back to previous page, 371
    controllers and, 368–371
    errors, 135
    exactly one call, 363
    permanent, 371
    switching locales, 245
    testing, 215
    to display, 175, 370–371
redis, background jobs requiring, 205
redo command, 63
Reenskaug, Trygve, 33
regular expressions
    about, 46
    in assert_select(), 110
Relation class, 329, 333
relational databases, 36, *see also* databases
relationships
    creating, 122
    forms, 169
    between forms and tables, 174
    locating and traversing records, 320–322
    order checkout, 169
    specifying, 322–324
    between tables, 117–119
    types, 322–324
reload() method, 335

reloading
  apps, 24
  data, 335
remote_ip() method, 361
remove_column() method, 410
remove_index() method, 418
RemoveXXXFromTABLE pattern, 127
rename_column() method, 413
rename_table() method, 416
renaming
  columns, 413
  primary key, 418
  tables, 416
render() method
  about, 363–367
  exactly one call, 363
  layouts, specifying, 400
  partial templates, 145, 403–405
  template location, 381
render_to_string() method, 162, 367
rendering, *see also* Action View
  about, 363–367
  actions, 362–367
  caching and, 110
  errors, 363
  to files, 366
  layouts, specifying, 400
  partial templates, 144–147, 366, 403–405
  redirects and, 366
  rerendering, 110
  to strings, 162, 364, 367
repetition, regular expressions, 47
:replace_at option, 397
:replace_dot option, 397
Representational State Transfer (REST), 350–360
request URLs, 21
request object, 361, 382
request_method attribute, 361
requests
  about, 34, 81
  actions for, specifying, 216
  callbacks and, 378–380
  dispatching, 350–360
  flash and controllers, 377
  objects and operations that span requests, 371–380

  passing parameters with flash, 377
  processing , 360–371
  redirects, 368–371
  REST and, 350–360
  sessions and, 372–377
  status response, 366–368, 371
require method, 56
require statement, 307, 312
rescue clauses, 49, 134, 221
rescue_from clause, 134, 221
reset_cycle() method, 394
reset_session() method, 377
Resource class, 331
resources
  Action Mailbox, 248
  Active Job, 205
  Active Storage, 249, 390
  assert_select() method, 110
  for this book, xxiv
  caching, 112
  callbacks, 340
  Capybara, 186
  configuration, 310
  creating, 353
  form options helpers, 385
  Git, 12
  Kamal, 278
  Rack, 304, 362
  Rails, xxiii, 15, 434
  Rake, 308
  RSpec, 425
  Ruby, 56
  translations of common strings, 241
resources (REST), 350–360
resources statement, 352, 358
respond_to() method, 150, 355, 359
response object, 362, 382
REST (Representational State Transfer), 350–360
return keyword, 43
rich_textarea() method, 262
RJS templates, 363, 366
rollbacks
  automatic, 221
  exercises, 81
  of migrations, 131, 409, 420
Rollbar, 292
ROM, 433
root statement, 216

routes, *see also* Action Controller; Action Dispatch; Action View
  concerns, 358
  dispatching requests, 350–360
  editing config/routes.rb file, 216
  format specifiers, 354
  generating, 352
  internationalization, 226–227
  listing, 227, 352, 358
  named, 353, 358
  naming, 352
  nesting resources, 358
  processing requests, 360–371
  REST, 350–360
  selecting data representation, 359
  setting root URL, 102
  shallow route nesting, 358
  specifying actions for requests, 216
  specifying format, 359
  URL parsing, 25
  ways to define, 350
routes command, 358
routing, 34, 40
routing() method, 250
rows
  class instances associated with, 317–320
  creating, 324–326
  deleting, 118, 174, 338
  encryption, 341–344
  finding, 326–331
  fixtures, 93
  locking, 331
  mapped to objects, 37
  specifying, 320
  timestamps, 320
  updating, 335–338
RSpec, testing with, 425–430
rspec-rails gem, 425, 430
RuboCop, 433
Ruby
  about, 41–43
  advantages, xviii
  blocks, 48
  control structures, 47
  data types, 43–47
  example, 53
  exceptions, 49
  idioms, 54–56

installing, 4, 7, 10
iterators, 48
logic, 47–50
marshaling, 53
names, 42, 311
as object-oriented language, 41–43
organizing structures, 50–52
resources, 56
versions, 3–4, 7–8, 10, 16
versions, installing multiple, 10
RubyGems, xxiii, 11
RubyInstaller, 4
RubyMine, 14
RUN instruction, 271
Russian doll caching, 112
RVM, 8

S

\s sequence, 47
sanitize() method, 104
save action, 389
save() method, 324, 336–337, 339, 347
save!() method, 75, 337, 345
saving
    exceptions, 337, 345
    rows, 324, 336
    transactions, 347
    uploading files, 389
say_with_time() method, 420
scaffolding
    about, 34
    actions, 119
    directory structure created by, 303–305
    fixtures defaults, 95
    generating authentication, 207
    generating scaffold, 66–68, 115–116
    REST actions, 355
:scale option, 412
scaling, deployment, 292
schema_migrations table, 409
schemas, see databases; migrations
scopes, Active Record, 332
scoping routes for REST actions, 357
Scout, 292
script wrappers, 308

scripts, see generators
search_field() method, 385
searching, databases, 326–331
Searchkick, 433
SECRET_KEY_BASE, 273
secrets, deploying to cloud with Kamal, 285
secrets (credentials), 275–276
security
    channels, 160
    cross-site forgery request attacks, 106
    email helpers, 396
    forms, 173
    passwords, 207
    permitted parameters, removing, 136
    permitting access, 217–218
    personal data protections, 255
    plugins, 433
    RecordNotFound exception, 132
    sanitize() method, 104
    SQL injection attack, 327
seed data, importing, 74–75
seeds.rb file, 74
select() method, 186, 330, 333–334, 385
select_tag helper, 244
selectors, CSS, 109
self. prefix, 50
self.new method, 55
semicolon (;), ending statements, 43
send_data() method, 367–368, 389
send_file() method, 368
send_xxx() method, 363
:sendmail symbol, 190
Sentry, 292
separation of concerns, 25, 34, 39, 255, 359
Sequel, 433
serialization, see encryption
servers, see also Apache
    quitting, 19, 70
    restarting for recovery, 63
    starting, 69, 309
    storing session data, 372
service field, deploying to cloud with Kamal, 284

session ID, 372, 376
session object, 362, 382
session_store attribute, 374
sessions
    controller role, 40, 372–377
    deleting, 376–377
    exercises, 125
    expiry and cleanup, 376
    storing and retrieving items with, 115
    storing session data, 372–376
set_cart() method, 121
set_i18n_locale_from_params method, 228
:set_locale helper, 245
setup command (Kamal), 288
setup() method, 98
shallow route nesting, 358
share mode lock, 331
shared directory, 404
shipped() method, 194
Shopify, 280
show action, 353, 390
sidebars
    adding, 105
    creating, 146
    exercises, 113
    linking helpers, 395
    login, 218–222
    moving cart to, 144–155
    passing data to layouts, 401
Sidekiq, 205
simple_format() method, 393
size, limiting field, 412
skip_action callback, 380
skip_after_action declaration, 380
skip_before_action declaration, 380
skip_before_action() method, 217
Slim templates, 430–432
slim-rails gem, 432
:smtp symbol, 190
:spacer_template parameter, 404
spaces
    fixtures, 93
    nonbreaking space character, 236
    whitespaces in regular expressions, 47
specs, see RSpec

sprintf() method, 107
SQL
    Active Record and, 324–339
    custom migrations, 419–420
    database adapter, 16
    escaping, 327
    injection attacks, 327
    mapping to Ruby types, 319
    verbosity, 335
    writing custom queries, 333–334
SQLite 3
    advantages, 66
    column type table, 411
    command-line interface package, 271
    configuration files, 95
    converting to PostgreSQL, 292
    database adapter, 16
    examples for this book and, 15
    versions, 3
sqlite3 package, 271
SSH keys, 279
SSL
    configuring, 276
    disabling, 276
    load balancers, 293
    request process, 361
ssl?() method, 361
staging environment, 310
state, REST, *see* REST
state, maintaining, *see* models
statement modifiers, 48
static web pages, 308
statistics
    of code, 298
    column, 331
status, of migration, 131
Stimulus framework, 178–182, 238
store_index_path method, 102
store_index_url method, 102
streams, 160, 368
:string column type, 411, 413
string literals, 43, 75
strings
    column type, 411, 413
    creating, 43

formatting helpers, 393–394
interpolation, 44
quotes, 43, 75
regular expressions, 46
rendering to, 162, 364, 367
returning without a view, 362
sending files and data, 367
strip_tags() method, 77
stylesheet_link_tag() method, 106, 397
stylesheets directory, 397
styling and style sheets, *see also* CSS; layouts; templates
    buttons, 120
    cycling, 394
    directory, 397
    helpers, 397
    highlighting changes, 155–158
    locale switcher, 244
    login, 218–222
    new user form, 212
    product list, 75–80
    sanitize() method, 104
    table-based, 138
:subject mail parameter, 192, 396
subject() method, 427
substitutions, 44
sudo apt-get install command, 9
sudo apt-get update command, 9
sudo dnf install command, 10
sum() method, 139, 331
support emails, *see* Action Mailbox
Sybase, column type table, 411
symbols
    hash keys, 45
    in Ruby, 42
syntax highlighting, 13
system testing, 184–187, 203–205

T

t (translate method), 230
-t email option, 190
tab completion, 12
table_name attribute, 316

tables
    associated with classes, 315–320
    columns, adding, 127–132
    columns, removing, 127, 338
    columns, statistics, 331
    creating, 66, 320, 414–419
    foreign keys, 176
    indices, defining, 417
    join tables, 323, 330, 418
    mapped to classes, 37
    mapping to models, 66
    migrations defining, 317–320
    names, 66, 311–320, 414
    without primary key, 418
    records, finding by ID, 320–322
    relationship to forms, 174
    renaming, 416
    rows, creating, 324–326
    rows, removing, 118, 338
    searching, 326–331
    setting table name, 316
    temporary, 415
    updating, 335–338
tail command, 15, 135
Tailwind CSS framework
    about, 65–66
    combining utility classes, 170
    page layouts, 106
    table templates, using, 75–80
tasks directory, 307
tasks, Rake, 131, 248, 262, 305, 307, 409
telephone_field() method, 385
templates, *see also* Action View; ERB templates; layouts; partial templates; rendering; styling and style sheets
    about, 382
    caching partial results, 111
    catalog display, 103–104
    code in, limiting, 391
    controller object accessible in, 382
    creating, 215
    debugging, 382
    defined, 363
    directory, 381–382, 404
    email, 191–195

extensions, 363
form helpers, 168–174, 383–386
forms, 168–174
instance variables accessible in, 382
Jbuilder, 382
modifying, 128
names, 195, 363, 381
passing messages with flash, 377
rendering, 363–367
rendering actions, 362–367
RJS, 363, 366
shared, 382, 404
Slim, 430–432
for tables, 75
translating, 230–235
types, 39, 363, 382
uploading files, 387–390
XML, 363

temporary files, 309
temporary tables, 415
temporary: option, 415
Terminal, 7
terminals, Windows, 6
test directory, 305
:test symbol, 190
test...do syntax, 89
test.log, 308
testing, *see also* functional testing
about, 149, 297
agile principles, xx
cart for Depot, 118, 124, 132, 137, 140, 148–150, 158, 168, 173, 426–430
catalog for Depot, 108–110
checkout for Depot, 168, 173, 184–187
connecting to slow payment processor, 197
controllers, 215, 217
directories, 89, 305
email, 190, 195, 256–259
exercises, 113, 140, 187, 223
fixtures, 92–99, 257
functional testing, 108–110, 124
JavaScript, 184–187
logs, 308
MiniTest framework, 89

products for Depot, 89–99
Rails support for, xvii
redirects, 215
with RSpec, 425–430
running all tests, 182
running tests, 97
seed data for, 74–75
syntax, 89
system testing, 184–187, 203–205
test data, 74–75
test database, 95
unit testing, 89–99
user administration, 214, 217

:text column type, 411
text_area() method, 172, 262, 384
text_field() method, 169, 172, 384
Textile (RedCloth), 394
third-party code, 309
Thruster, 273
tight coupling, 423, 433
time
  _at suffix, 320
  column type, 411
  exercises, 113
  form helpers, 385
  formatting helpers, 392
  Hello, World! app, 23–25
  mapping, 319
:time column type, 411
Time.now() method, 24
time_ago_in_words() method, 392
timeouts, 197
:timestamp column type, 411
timestamps
  column type, 411
  columns and rows, 320
  DRbStore, 376
  migrations, 68, 408
  tables, 415
  updating, xxii
timestamps method, 415
titles
  translating, 232
  validating, 87, 92
  writing with helper, 391
tmp directory, 309
:to mail parameter, 192
to_a() method, 329
to_plain_text() method, 265

touch command, xxii
transaction() method, 345–348
transactions, 220, 331, 344–348, 416
translate method, 230–236
translations
  common strings, resources, 241
  error messages, 240–241, 243
  pluralization, 241
  supplying, 230–243
troubleshooting, *see also* testing
  Hotwire, 163
  migrations, 420
  recovery, 63
truncate() method, 77, 193, 394
trust command (mise), 8
Turbo framework, xxi, 80, 106, 150–155
turbo streams, 150–155
turbo_frame_tag() method, 161
turbo_stream_from() method, 161
twiddle-wakka, 11
types, enumerated, 419

U

%u placeholder, 236
\u00D7 escape sequence, 132
Ubuntu Linux, installing Rails, 9–11
underscore (_)
  in names, 42, 311, 315
  partial templates, 145
  prefixing partial templates, 402
Unicode, 132
unique: option, 417
:uniqueness parameter, 87
unit testing, 89–99, 305
unless statement, 48
until statement, 48
up() method, 129, 410
update action, 353
update() method, 215, 336
update_all() method, 336
updated_at column, 320
updated_on column, 320
updates to user, broadcasting, 158–163

updating, *see also* migrations
    conflicts between application and session data, 373
    Rails version, 11
    REST, 353
    RJS templates, 366
    tracking, 320
uploading, files, 387–390
url() attribute, 361
url_field() method, 385
url_for() method, 370
UrlHelper class, 394–398
URLs
    of applications, 21, 25, 70
    broken, 30
    displaying images, 389
    form helpers, 385
    internationalization, 226–227
    linking helpers, 394–398
    mapping to actions, 216, 350
    redirects, 135, 368–371
    request actions, 361
    root URL of applications, 102
    shallow route nesting, 358
    validating, 88, 91
use cases, 60
use command (mise), 8
:user_id, login, 218
users
    adding from command line, 209
    allowlisting, 217
    authenticating, 207–215
    deleting, 219–222
    permitting access, 217–218
    storing current user in session data, 373
    styling login, 218–222
    testing user administration, 214, 217
UTF-8, 226

V

validate() method, 88
validates() method, 86–88
validations
    callbacks diagram, 339
    checkout, 184
    Depot, 184

email, 195
errors, 86–87, 90–92, 100
exercises, 100, 184, 223
forms, 173
implementing, 85–88
passwords, 208
testing, 89–99
uploading files, 389
uploading images, 88
values
    aggregating, 332
    default value for columns, 412
    form fields, 169
    limiting in SQL queries, 330
    statistics, 331
variables, names, 42, 311–314
Vector, 291
vendor directory, 309
version control, *see also* Git
    about, 12
    credentials and, 276
    exercises, 82
    ignoring files, 82
    migrations and, 409
version number
    migrations, 408–409
    session data, 374
versions
    Rails, 3, 11, 17–18
    Ruby, 3–4, 7–8, 10, 16
    Ruby, installing multiple, 10
    SQLite, 3
vertical bar (|)
    arguments in blocks, 48
    regular expressions, 46
views, *see also* Action View; MVC architecture; templates
    about, 20, 33, 296
    Action Pack support, 39
    buttons, 136
    catalog display, 101–104
    connecting Active Storage to, 78
    creating, 22, 66
    in Depot application, 296
    directory, 22, 381
    ERB templates for, 22–23
    linking pages, 26–28
    names, 311–314
    partial templates, 144–147
    pathnames to, 103

rendering to strings, 162
REST actions, 355
returning a string without, 362
separating logic from data, 25
views directory, 381
Vim, 13
virtual machine, running Rails, 19
Virtual Private Server (VPS), 279
visit() method, 186
Visual Studio Code, 4, 14
volumes, deploying to cloud with Kamal, 285
volumes directory, 289
VPS Virtual Private Server, 279

W

%w sequence, 45
\w sequence, 47
Web Components, 423–425
web console, 28–30, 149
WebSockets, 158–162
where() method, 327
which ruby command, 16
while statement, 47
whitespaces, regular expressions, 47
wildcards
    regular expressions, 47
    SQL, 329
Windows
    database drivers, 16
    development environment for, 4
    installing Rails, 4–7
    launching terminal, 6
    listing directory contents, 66
    log file viewing, 135
    multiple-line commands, 67
    quitting applications, 31
    scrolling log files, 135
Windows Defender, 4
Windows Subsystem for Linux, 4
Windows Terminal, 4, 15
WORKDIR instruction, 270
wrappers, script, 308

write_attribute() method, 319
WSL (Windows Subsystem for Linux), 4

X

xhr? attribute, 361
XML
    exercises, 183
    rendering templates, 366
    requests, 361
    specifying data format, 359
    templates, 39, 363
xml_http_request? attribute, 361
xxx_count column, 320
xxx_id column, 320

Y

YAML
    about, 52
    format for fixtures, 92
    internationalization, 232, 242
Yellow Fade Technique, 155
yield method
    about, 48
    around callbacks, 379
    layouts, 106, 399, 401

Z

\z sequence, 47
Zed, 14

Thank you!

We hope you enjoyed this book and that you're already thinking about what you want to learn next. To help make that decision easier, we're offering you this gift.

Head on over to https://pragprog.com right now, and use the coupon code BUYANOTHER2025 to save 30% on your next ebook. Offer is void where prohibited or restricted. This offer does not apply to any edition of *The Pragmatic Programmer* ebook.

And if you'd like to share your own expertise with the world, why not propose a writing idea to us? After all, many of our best authors started off as our readers, just like you. With up to a 50% royalty, world-class editorial services, and a name you trust, there's nothing to lose. Visit https://pragprog.com/become-an-author/ today to learn more and to get started.

Thank you for your continued support. We hope to hear from you again soon!

The Pragmatic Bookshelf

Rails Scales!

Rails doesn't scale. So say the naysayers. They're wrong. Ruby on Rails runs some of the biggest sites in the world, impacting the lives of millions of users while efficiently crunching petabytes of data. This book reveals how they do it, and how you can apply the same techniques to your applications. Optimize everything necessary to make an application function at scale: monitoring, product design, Ruby code, software architecture, database access, caching, and more. Even if your app may never have millions of users, you reduce the costs of hosting and maintaining it.

Cristian Planas
(270 pages) ISBN: 9798888651025. $52.95
https://pragprog.com/book/cprpo

Agile Web Development with Rails 7.2

Rails 7.2 completely redefined what it means to produce fantastic user experiences and provides a way to achieve all the benefits of single-page applications—at a fraction of the complexity. Rails 7.2 integrated the Hotwire frameworks of Stimulus and Turbo directly as the new defaults, together with that hot newness of import maps. The result is a toolkit so powerful that it allows a single individual to create modern applications upon which they can build a competitive business. The way it used to be.

Sam Ruby
(472 pages) ISBN: 9798888651049. $67.95
https://pragprog.com/book/rails72

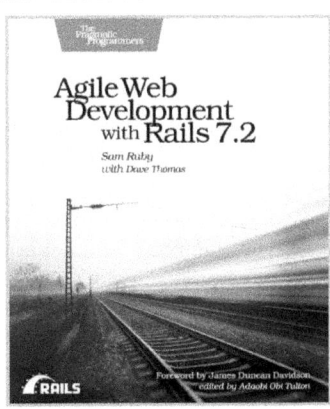

Programming Ruby 3.3 (5th Edition)

Ruby is one of the most important programming languages in use for web development. It powers the Rails framework, which is the backing of some of the most important sites on the web. The Pickaxe Book, named for the tool on the cover, is the definitive reference on Ruby, a highly-regarded, fully object-oriented programming language. This updated edition is a comprehensive reference on the language itself, with a tutorial on the most important features of Ruby—including pattern matching and Ractors—and describes the language through Ruby 3.3.

Noel Rappin, with Dave Thomas
(716 pages) ISBN: 9781680509823. $65.95
https://pragprog.com/book/ruby5

High Performance PostgreSQL for Rails

Build faster, more reliable Rails apps by taking the best advanced PostgreSQL and Active Record capabilities, and using them to solve your application scale and growth challenges. Gain the skills needed to comfortably work with multi-terabyte databases, and with complex Active Record, SQL, and specialized Indexes. Develop your skills with PostgreSQL on your laptop, then take them into production, while keeping everything in sync. Make slow queries fast, perform any schema or data migration without errors, use scaling techniques like read/write splitting, partitioning, and sharding, to meet demanding workload requirements from Internet scale consumer apps to enterprise SaaS.

Andrew Atkinson
(454 pages) ISBN: 9798888650387. $64.95
https://pragprog.com/book/aapsql

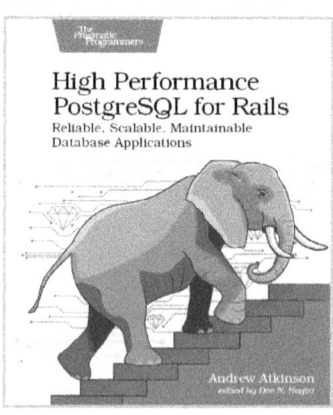

Learn to Program, Third Edition

It's easier to learn how to program a computer than it has ever been before. Now everyone can learn to write programs for themselves—no previous experience is necessary. Chris Pine takes a thorough, but lighthearted approach that teaches you the fundamentals of computer programming, with a minimum of fuss or bother. Whether you are interested in a new hobby or a new career, this book is your doorway into the world of programming.

Chris Pine
(230 pages) ISBN: 9781680508178. $45.95
https://pragprog.com/book/ltp3

Modern Front-End Development for Rails, Second Edition

Improve the user experience for your Rails app with rich, engaging client-side interactions. Learn to use the Rails 7 tools and simplify the complex JavaScript ecosystem. It's easier than ever to build user interactions with Hotwire, Turbo, and Stimulus. You can add great front-end flair without much extra complication. Use React to build a more complex set of client-side features. Structure your code for different levels of client-side needs with these powerful options. Add to your toolkit today!

Noel Rappin
(408 pages) ISBN: 9781680509618. $55.95
https://pragprog.com/book/nrclient2

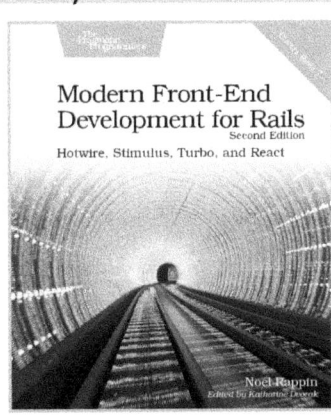

The Pragmatic Bookshelf

The Pragmatic Bookshelf features books written by professional developers for professional developers. The titles continue the well-known Pragmatic Programmer style and continue to garner awards and rave reviews. As development gets more and more difficult, the Pragmatic Programmers will be there with more titles and products to help you stay on top of your game.

Visit Us Online

This Book's Home Page
https://pragprog.com/book/rails8
Source code from this book, errata, and other resources. Come give us feedback, too!

Keep Up-to-Date
https://pragprog.com
Join our announcement mailing list (low volume) or follow us on Twitter @pragprog for new titles, sales, coupons, hot tips, and more.

New and Noteworthy
https://pragprog.com/news
Check out the latest Pragmatic developments, new titles, and other offerings.

Save on the ebook

Save on the ebook versions of this title. Owning the paper version of this book entitles you to purchase the electronic versions at a terrific discount.

PDFs are great for carrying around on your laptop—they are hyperlinked, have color, and are fully searchable. Most titles are also available for the iPhone and iPod touch, Amazon Kindle, and other popular e-book readers.

Send a copy of your receipt to support@pragprog.com and we'll provide you with a discount coupon.

Contact Us

Online Orders:	*https://pragprog.com/catalog*
Customer Service:	*support@pragprog.com*
International Rights:	*translations@pragprog.com*
Academic Use:	*academic@pragprog.com*
Write for Us:	*http://write-for-us.pragprog.com*